WAGES AND REGULARITY OF EMPLOYMENT

IN THE

DRESS AND WAIST INDUSTRY OF NEW YORK CITY

BY

NAHUM I. STONE, M. A.

SUBMITTED IN PARTIAL FULFILLMENT OF THE REQUIREMENTS FOR THE DEGREE OF DOCTOR OF PHILOSOPHY.

IN THE

FACULTY OF POLITICAL SCIENCE
COLUMBIA UNIVERSITY

New York
1915

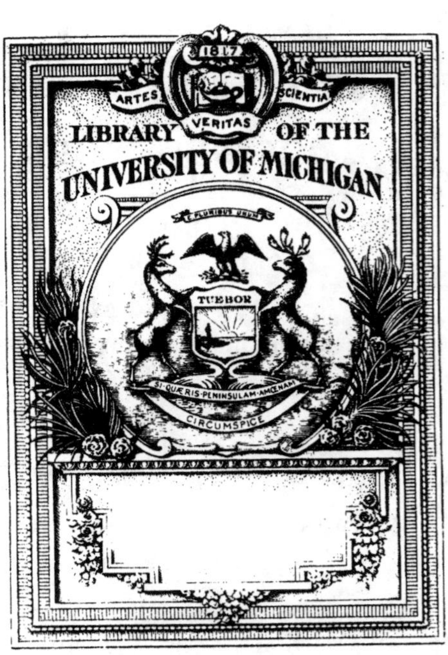
1817
ARTES
SCIENTIA
VERITAS
LIBRARY OF THE
UNIVERSITY OF MICHIGAN
TUEBOR
SI·QUÆRIS·PENINSULAM·AMŒNAM
CIRCUMSPICE

WAGES AND REGULARITY OF EMPLOYMENT

IN THE

DRESS AND WAIST INDUSTRY OF NEW YORK CITY

BY

NAHUM I. STONE, M. A.

SUBMITTED IN PARTIAL FULFILLMENT OF THE REQUIREMENTS FOR THE DEGREE OF DOCTOR OF PHILOSOPHY.

IN THE

FACULTY OF POLITICAL SCIENCE
COLUMBIA UNIVERSITY

New York
1915

CONTENTS.

LIST OF CHARTS.

[This report was prepared for and under the direction of the Wage-Scale Board of the Dress and Waist Industry, by N. I. Stone, Chief Statistician.]

BULLETIN OF THE

U. S. BUREAU OF LABOR STATISTICS.

WHOLE NO. 146. WASHINGTON. APRIL 28, 1914.

WAGES AND REGULARITY OF EMPLOYMENT AND STANDARDIZATION OF PIECE RATES IN THE DRESS AND WAIST INDUSTRY OF NEW YORK CITY.[1]

BY N. I. STONE.

PART I.—WAGES AND REGULARITY OF EMPLOYMENT.

INTRODUCTION AND SUMMARY.

The investigation covered by the present report was made under the direction of the wage-scale board in compliance with the provisions of article 8 of the protocol of peace entered into on January 18, 1913, between the International Ladies' Garment Workers' Union and the Dress and Waist Manufacturers' Association. Article 8 calls for "a complete and exhaustive examination into the existing rates paid for labor, the earnings of the operatives, and the classification of garments in the industry."

The investigation was started at the end of March and completed in August, but the presentation of the report and of the summary of the findings has been delayed until the present time, owing to the necessity of taking up the second investigation ordered by the wage-scale board under the provision of article 7 of the protocol, "with a view to establishing as nearly practicably as possible a scientific basis for the fixing of piece and week-work prices throughout the industry."

As this new investigation, requiring the timing of various operations in the manufacture of dresses and waists, could be carried on only while the factories were busy and as the fall season is very short, it was necessary to concentrate all efforts on that work and to postpone the writing of the report as to the first investigation

[1] The author is under obligations to the officers of the wage-scale board, particularly Mr. I. B. Hyman, chairman of the board, and Mr. S. Polakoff, chief clerk of the board for the union, for assistance rendered; also to Mr. A. H. G. Baron, Mr. Sigmund Haiman, and Miss Eva Joffe of the staff of the board.

until after the closing of the fall season. The results of the second investigation, dealing with the standardization of piece rates, will be reported separately.

The investigation constituting the subject of this report covered 520 shops employing about 31,500 people (not counting designers, foremen, forewomen, packers, and office force) who constituted nearly nine-tenths of all the workers known to be employed in the dress and waist industry in Greater New York. Of the 520 shops, 289 were association shops and 231 nonassociation shops having individual agreements with the union identical with the protocol in so far as wages and hours were concerned.

Although the number of the nonassociation union shops was not much less than that of association shops, they employed only 6,690 people as against 24,795 in the association shops. This is due to the fact that most of the association shops are large, while most of the nonassociation shops are small. With few exceptions, it may be said that all the large and important shops of the industry are affiliated with the association and subject to the conditions of work prescribed in the protocol. The two groups combined employ about nine-tenths of all the workers engaged in the dress and waist industry of Greater New York, leaving only about one-tenth of the workers to the 200-odd nonassociation nonunion shops.

The investigation disclosed the fact that more than $9,300,000 was paid out in wages in 1912 in shops employing 20,524 workers in the busiest week of that year, the busiest week as used here and elsewhere throughout the text of this report, unless otherwise noted, meaning the week in which the maximum number of persons were employed. From this it is estimated that the total wages paid to nearly 37,000 workers in the dress and waist industry of Greater New York in 1913 exceeded $17,000,000 and represented an output of dresses and waists of a wholesale market value of close to $100,000,000.[1]

Of the 29,439 persons found working in the dress and waist shops in 1913 whose sex and occupation were ascertained, 24,728 were women and 4,711 were men, making the proportion of women to men over 5 to 1, or, putting it in a percentage form, 84 per cent of all the employees were women and 16 per cent were men. Of the 16,418 operators, 13,993 were women and 2,425 were men, making the proportion of men and women practically the same as above. Some of the occupations outside of operating are almost entirely monopolized by women, while others are filled exclusively by men. Among those in which women are exclusively or almost exclusively employed are assorters, cleaners, embroiderers, examiners, finishers, drapers, and

[1] For an explanation of this estimate see pages 20, 21.

joiners. Among the ironers—i. e., those working with a light iron—the number of women is about twice as large as that of men. Pressers, meaning those who work with a heavy iron, are exclusively men; so also are the cutters.

The following statement gives a summary of the employees covered by the investigation according to sex and showing the number employed in association or nonassociation shops. It also shows the number of operators of each sex employed as week workers and as pieceworkers. These figures include only employees for whom sex and occupation were ascertained:

Shops	520
Association	289
Nonassociation	231
Persons employed	29, 439
In association shops	23, 304
Females	19, 773
Males	3, 531
In nonassociation shops	6, 135
Females	4, 955
Males	1, 180
Total females	24, 728
Total males	4, 711
Operators employed	16, 418
Females	13, 993
Week workers	6, 936
Pieceworkers	7, 057
Males	2, 425
Week workers	917
Pieceworkers	1, 508
Total week workers	7, 853
Total pieceworkers	8, 565

The accompanying chart (No. 1) shows in graphic form the figures just presented, together with corresponding percentages.

EFFECT OF THE PROTOCOL ON WAGES.

WAGES IN ASSOCIATION AND NONASSOCIATION UNION SHOPS.

In summing up the results of the investigation, the most salient as well as the most important fact alike to the employers and the employees in the dress and waist industry is the general increase in wages in practically every branch of the industry and every occupation in which its workers are engaged. The increase took place in association as well as in nonassociation union shops. In some cases the increase is more pronounced in association shops, in others in the nonassociation shops. As a rule, the difference in wages as between these two classes of shops has been found to be determined not by the affiliation or nonaffiliation of the shops with the association, but

CHART 1. PROPORTION OF ASSOCIATION AND NONASSOCIATION SHOPS IN THE INDUSTRY, OF EMPLOYEES IN EACH CLASS OF SHOPS, BY SEX, AND OF WEEK WORKERS AND PIECEWORKERS AMONG OPERATORS, 1913.

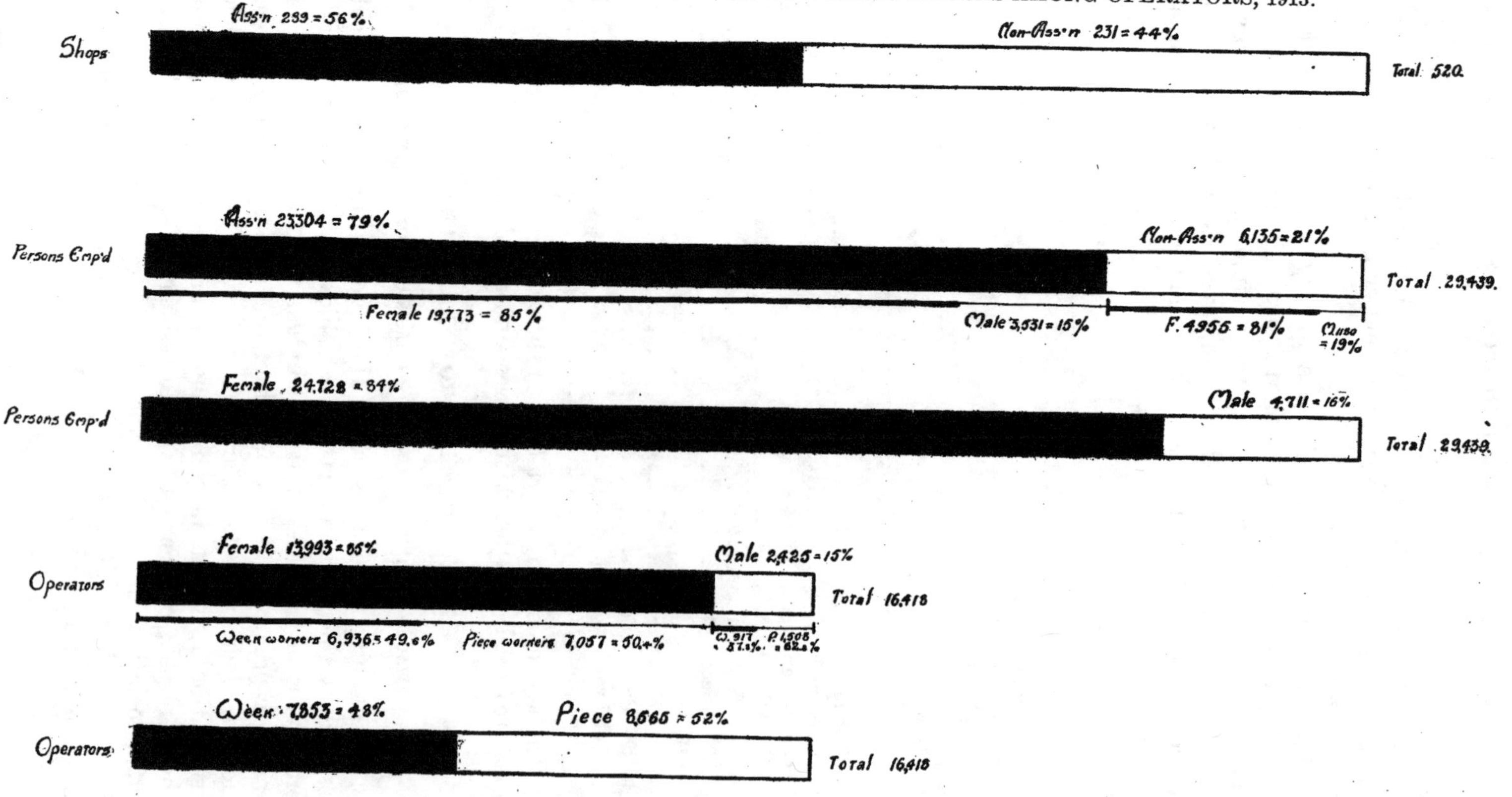

Shops
Ass'n 289 = 56%
Non-Ass'n 231 = 44%
Total 520

Persons Emp'd
Ass'n 23304 = 79%
Non-Ass'n 6,135 = 21%
Total 29,439.
Female 19,773 = 85%
Male 3,531 = 15%
F. 4956 = 81%
M. 1180 = 19%

Persons Emp'd
Female 24,728 = 84%
Male 4,711 = 16%
Total 29,439.

Operators
Female 13,993 = 85%
Male 2,425 = 15%
Total 16,418
Week workers 6,936 = 49.6%
Piece workers 7,057 = 50.4%
W. 917 = 37.8%
P. 1,508 = 62.2%

Operators
Week 7,853 = 48%
Piece 8,565 = 52%
Total 16,418

by the character of the goods manufactured. Shops making the better grade of garments require workers of higher skill, who naturally command higher rates of wages than the less skilled workers employed in the shops making cheap garments. The group of shops making cheaper garments is designated in this report by the letter A and those making the higher-grade garments by the letter B. The general rule found to prevail with regard to wages is that the association and nonassociation union shops in the B groups pay higher wages than the association and nonassociation A shops. Unless this fact is borne in mind, one can just as easily prove that the association shops pay higher wages than the nonassociation by comparing association B with nonassociation A shops, as the contrary fact, namely, that the nonassociation union shops pay higher wages than the association shops by comparing the nonassociation union B with the association A shops. In other words, association B shops pay higher wages than association A or nonassociation A shops; nonassociation B shops pay generally higher wages than association A or nonassociation A shops. When, however, we compare association B with nonassociation B, or association A with nonassociation A shops, there is no general rule, sometimes one, sometimes the other paying higher wages, the difference between the two being comparatively small. Thus the wages of cleaners have been found to be higher in the nonassociation A than in the association A shops, and in turn higher in association A than in association B shops. This is due, as explained elsewhere in the report, to the fact that the large shops employ a considerable number of errand girls who carry work from one part of the shop to another and do other errands, and work on cleaning when they have nothing else to do. These girls are naturally paid lower wages than girls who do cleaning exclusively, which is the case in smaller shops where there is no call for errand girls. Because the nonassociation shops are mostly small and the association shops are mostly large, the former make a better showing in the case of the wages of cleaners than the latter.

On the other hand, in the case of women operators, whether working by the piece (Table 23) or by the week (Table 21), no uniform tendency can be discovered in comparing association A shops with nonassociation A shops or association B shops with nonassociation B shops, the proportion of workers in different wage groups being sometimes greater in the association shops and sometimes in the nonassociation shops.

In the case of finishers working by the week, the association B shops had a higher proportion of girls getting from $9 a week down and from $12 a week up than the nonassociation B shops and a smaller proportion of those getting from $9 to $12, while in the A shops the nonassociation group was above the association in the proportion of girls receiving the minimum rate of $8 a week and up, except those earning $16 a week or more of whom there were a few in the association B shops.

The earnings of the finishers working by the piece were, on the whole, higher in the association A shops than in the nonassociation A shops and in the association B shops than in the nonassociation B shops.

These instances are sufficient to indicate that neither the association nor the nonassociation shops as such can be said to be paying uniformly higher rates than the other, the difference being principally between shops making higher and lower grade garments, respectively, regardless of their affiliation or nonaffiliation with the association.

WAGES OF WEEK WORKERS PROVIDED FOR IN THE PROTOCOL.

As stated above, there has been a general increase in wages in the industry since the protocol went into effect. This is especially true and lends itself to clear demonstration in the case of all occupations for which a minimum rate is provided in the protocol. Table 1, which follows, presents a summary of the wages for such occupations:

TABLE 1.—SUMMARY OF WAGES IN OCCUPATIONS FOR WHICH MINIMUM RATES ARE FIXED BY THE PROTOCOL, SHOWING PERCENTAGE OF WORKERS RECEIVING LESS THAN THE PROTOCOL MINIMUM, AND IN THE GROUPS RECEIVING THE MINIMUM AND OVER, 1912 AND 1913.

Occupation and classification of weekly wages.	Association A.		Nonassociation A.		Association B.		Nonassociation B.		Total.		Increase (+) or decrease (−) per cent.
	1912	1913	1912	1913	1912	1913	1912	1913	1912	1913	
Cleaners:											
Under $6 [1]	59.1	35.4	47.3	25.9	67.6	48.9	......	......	60.3	37.3	−38.1
$6 to $6.99	20.3	29.3	20.9	38.0	15.3	25.8	......	......	18.9	29.9	+58.2
$7 and over	20.6	35.3	31.8	36.1	17.1	25.3	......	......	20.8	32.7	+57.2
Total	100.0	100.0	100.0	100.0	100.0	100.0	......	......	100.0	100.0	......
Drapers:											
Under $12	30.1	15.6	28.8	21.7	24.5	8.3	......	......	27.5	13.0	−40.3
$12 to $13.99	33.8	25.5	45.5	18.4	29.2	20.4	......	......	32.6	22.9	
$14 [2] to $15.99	31.0	48.8	22.7	47.4	37.2	56.6	......	......	32.8	51.5	+57.0
$16 and over	5.1	10.1	3.0	12.5	9.1	14.7	......	......	7.1	12.6	+77.1
Total	100.0	100.0	100.0	100.0	100.0	100.0	......	......	100.0	100.0	......
Examiners:											
Under $10 [2]	46.7	38.4	......	......	36.1	19.8	......	......	42.2	29.7	−29.6
$10 to $11.99	31.4	39.5	......	......	27.5	34.1	......	......	29.9	37.7	+26.1
$12 and over	21.9	22.1	......	......	36.4	46.1	......	......	28.0	32.5	+16.1
Total	100.0	100.0	......	......	100.0	100.0	......	......	100.0	100.0	......

[1] No minimum wage for cleaners is provided for in the protocol, but an understanding was reached between the conferees who signed the protocol that no cleaner be paid less than $6 per week. This understanding was later confirmed in a formal decision at one of the early meetings of the board of grievances.

[2] Minimum protocol rate.

TABLE 1.—SUMMARY OF WAGES IN OCCUPATIONS FOR WHICH MINIMUM RATES ARE FIXED BY THE PROTOCOL, SHOWING PERCENTAGE OF WORKERS RECEIVING LESS THAN THE PROTOCOL MINIMUM, AND IN THE GROUPS RECEIVING THE MINIMUM AND OVER, 1912 AND 1913—Concluded.

Occupation and classification of weekly wages.	Association A.		Nonassociation A.		Association B.		Nonassociation B.		Total.		Increase (+) or decrease (−) per cent.
	1912	1913	1912	1913	1912	1913	1912	1913	1912	1913	
Finishers:											
Under $8 [1]	54.0	28.8	51.4	25.3	47.1	18.6	36.5	21.4	49.3	23.6	−52.1
$8 to $8.99	21.3	34.1	19.7	34.9	20.3	38.2	27.0	26.1	21.2	35.3	+66.5
$9 and over	24.7	37.1	28.9	39.8	32.6	43.2	36.5	52.5	29.5	41.1	+39.3
Total	100.0	100.0	100.0	100.0	100.0	100.0	100.0	100.0	100.0	100.0	......
Ironers:											
Under $12 [1]	75.7	52.5	......	......	61.0	49.6	......	......	69.8	51.2	−26.6
$12 to $13.99	14.5	32.4	......	......	27.1	23.3	......	......	19.6	29.7	+52.0
$14 and over	9.9	15.1	......	......	11.9	27.1	......	......	10.5	19.1	+81.9
Total	100.0	100.0	......	......	100.0	100.0	......	......	100.0	100.0	......
Sample makers:											
Under $14 [1]	41.0	20.7	......	......	44.3	34.0	......	......	43.0	26.4	−38.6
$14 to $15.99	36.4	50.3	......	......	27.9	38.9	......	......	30.0	42.6	+42.0
$16 and over	22.6	29.0	......	......	27.8	27.1	......	......	27.0	31.2	+15.6
Total	100.0	100.0	......	......	100.0	100.0	......	......	100.0	100.0	......
Joiners:											
Under $12 [1]	......	......	......	......	......	......	......	......	55.7	47.0	−15.6
$12 to $13.99	......	......	......	......	......	......	......	......	39.4	44.6	+13.2
$14 and over	......	......	......	......	......	......	......	......	4.9	8.4	+71.4
Total	......	......	......	......	......	......	......	......	100.0	100.0	......

[1] Minimum protocol rate.

According to this table there has been in every case a decided reduction in the percentage of persons receiving less than the minimum protocol rate, and in every instance there has been a very marked increase in the proportion of those in the group receiving the minimum protocol rate and a similar, though smaller increase in the proportion of those in the group receiving the higher rates. Thus, the proportion of cleaners receiving less than the minimum of $6 a week [1] has been reduced from 60.3 per cent of the total in 1912 to 37.3 per cent in 1913. The percentage of drapers receiving less than the minimum protocol rate of $14 a week has been reduced from 60.1 per cent in 1912 to 35.9 per cent in 1913. The percentage of joiners receiving less than the minimum protocol rate of $12 a week has been reduced from 55.7 per cent in 1912 to 47 per cent in 1913. The percentage of examiners receiving less than the minimum protocol rate of $10 a week has been reduced from 42.2 per cent in 1912 to 29.7 per cent in 1913. The percentage of finishers receiving less than the minimum protocol rate of $8 a week has gone down from 49.3 per cent in 1912 to 23.6 per cent in 1913. The percentage of women ironers receiving less than

[1] No minimum wage for cleaners is provided for in the protocol, but an understanding was reached between the conferees who signed the protocol that no cleaner be paid less than $6 per week. This understanding was later confirmed in a formal decision at one of the early meetings of the board of grievances.

the minimum protocol rate of $12 a week has gone down from 69.8 per cent in 1912 to 51.2 per cent in 1913. The percentage of sample makers receiving less than the minimum protocol rate of $14 a week has been reduced from 43.0 per cent in 1912 to 26.4 per cent in 1913. The proportion of cutters receiving less than the minimum protocol rate has been reduced from 81.3 per cent in 1912 to 56 per cent in 1913. These 56 per cent in 1913 include, to a large extent, cutters of various degrees of apprenticeship, for whom the protocol provides rates of $6, $12, and $18, according to the length of service. The proportion of cutters receiving these rates has increased in each case. Thus, those getting $6 to $6.99 a week increased from 2.7 per cent in 1912 to 3.8 per cent in 1913. Those getting $12 to $13.99 a week formed the same percentage both years, namely 8.5 per cent, and those getting $18 to $19.99 a week increased from 8.8 per cent in 1912 to 10.9 per cent in 1913. On the other hand, the percentage of those receiving odd rates, that is, rates below $25, other than the three mentioned, has been reduced from 61 per cent in 1912 to 32.8 per cent in 1913.[1]

Corresponding to this general reduction in the relative number of persons receiving less than the protocol rate, there has been an increase in the percentage of those receiving the minimum protocol rate and more than that rate. A good deal has been said in the trade about the tendency of the minimum to become the maximum. It is, therefore, interesting to compare the proportion of those receiving the minimum rate with those receiving more than the minimum in each occupation for which a minimum rate has been provided in the protocol. Thus, in the case of cleaners, the number of those in the group receiving the minimum of $6 a week constituted 29.9 per cent of all the cleaners, while those receiving $7 and over was 32.7 per cent, the number of those receiving more than the minimum thus exceeding the number of workers receiving the minimum. It should be noted that, in the case of cleaners here quoted, the table gives the number of those receiving $6 to $6.99. While the great bulk of workers in that group were getting the minimum of $6 a week, there were a number receiving $6.50 and a few receiving $6.75, which should have been added to the group of those receiving more than the minimum. This would involve, however, so much additional clerical labor that it could not be undertaken in the closing days of the completion of this report. This remark applies likewise to the percentages of the other occupations which follow: In the case of drapers, the proportion of those receiving from $14 (the minimum) to less than $16 was 51.5 per cent, while those receiving $16 or more constituted 12.6 per cent of the total. Of joiners the proportion receiving from the minimum rate of $12 to less than $14 a week was 44.6 per cent and the

[1] For rates paid cutters see Table 51, pages 114, 115.

proportion receiving $14 and over was 8.4 per cent. In the case of examiners, 37.7 per cent received from $10 (the minimum) to $11.99 a week and 32.5 per cent received $12 a week or more. If the number of those who received from $10.50 to $11.50 could be separated, it would in all probability show as large a number of examiners receiving more than the minimum rate of $10 a week as of those who received the exact minimum rate. In the case of finishers, the proportion of those receiving from $8 (the minimum) to $8.99 a week was 35.3 per cent, and of those receiving $9 or more the proportion was 41.1 per cent. In this case, the number of those receiving more than the minimum exceeded that of the workers receiving the minimum rate. In the case of ironers those receiving from the minimum of $12 to $13.99 a week made up 29.7 per cent and those receiving $14 or more a little over 19 per cent. If the proportion of those receiving $12.50, $13, and $13.50 were added to the group receiving more than the minimum rate of $12 a week, the percentages of those receiving the minimum and more than the minimum would probably be about equal. The percentage of sample makers receiving from the minimum rate of $14 to $15.99 a week was 42.6 and of those receiving $16 and over the percentage was 31.2. Here too, the proportion of those receiving the minimum or more than the minimum would probably be about equal if those receiving $14.50, $15, and $15.50 could be added to the proper group.

Summing up the effect of providing minimum rates in the protocol, it may be said that in all the occupations thus provided for the proportion of those receiving less than the minimum protocol rate was reduced one-fourth to one-half of what it had been before the signing of the protocol, but that about one-fourth of the workers for whom minimum rates were provided are still getting less than the minimum rate.

WAGES OF WEEK WORKERS NOT PROVIDED FOR IN THE PROTOCOL.

The increase in wages was not confined to the occupations for which minimum rates have been provided in the protocol. Practically every occupation shows the same tendency, though the increase, as a rule, is not so large and not always so uniform as in the case of the occupations with protocol rates. Thus, among the assorters, the per cent of those receiving less than $8 a week declined from 30.2 to 27.2 with a corresponding increase in the percentage of those receiving $8 a week or more. In the case of embroiderers there has been a decline in the proportion of those receiving less than $8 a week from nearly 25 per cent of the total in 1912 to less than 13 per cent, or about one-half, in 1913. In the case of male pressers and ironers there has been an increase in the percentage of those receiving $20 a week and over from 11.3 in 1912 to 28.1 in 1913. Taking the operators as a whole, we find that among the women working by the week, there has been an increase among those receiving $14 a week and more from 16.6 per cent of the total in 1912 to 23.5 per cent in 1913, among the men working by the week those receiving $16 a week and up increased from 26.8 per cent in 1912 to 38.2 per cent in 1913. The same is true of all the important branches of operating in which the work is done by the week. Thus, among the hemstitchers, the percentage of those receiving $12 a week and more increased from 30.1 in 1912 to 51.4 in 1913. The women lace runners earning $9 a week or more increased from 53.8 per cent in 1912 to 78.3 per cent in 1913. The women trimmers receiving $12 a week or more increased from 30.5 per cent in 1912 to 46.8 per cent in 1913. The women tuckers receiving $14 a week or more increased from 22.0 per cent in 1912 to 56.5 per cent in 1913, while the percentage of men tuckers receiving the same wage increased from 52.8 in 1912 to 75.6 in 1913.

EARNINGS OF PIECEWORKERS.

What has been said about the week workers is likewise true of the pieceworkers. Thus, among the women ironers working by the piece, the per cent of those earning $20 a week or more during the busiest week of the year increased from 13.4 in 1912 to 24.6 in 1913. While among the men there has been no such marked uniformity, some wage groups showing increases and other groups showing reductions, on the whole there has been an improvement, the percentage of those earning $16 and up having increased from 62.7 in 1912 to 65.9 in 1913. Among the operators the women pieceworkers earning $14 a week or more during the busiest week of the year increased from 33.7 per cent in 1912 to 49.9 per cent in 1913. Among the men, the per cent of those earning the same amounts increased from 69 to 77.1. Skirt operators working by the piece and earning $16 a week or more increased from 53.3 per cent in 1912 to 68.9 in 1913. Women trimmers working by the piece and earning $[illegible] a week or more increased from 18.9 per cent in 1912 to 49.8 per cent in 1913. Men tuckers earning $14 a week or more increased from [illegible] per cent to 75.6 per cent.

EFFECT OF THE PROTOCOL ON HOURS OF WORK.

ALL SHOPS COMBINED.

The figures given in Table 2, which follows, show that the protocol was no less effective in shortening the hours of work than it was in increasing the pay of the workers in the dress and waist industry. This table relates to week workers in the entire industry.

TABLE 2.—NUMBER AND PER CENT OF WEEK WORKERS EMPLOYED EACH CLASSIFIED NUMBER OF HOURS DURING THE BUSIEST WEEK OF THE YEAR, FOR THE ENTIRE INDUSTRY, 1912 AND 1913.

Hours employed	Number.				Per cent.			
	Cutters.		Other employees.		Cutters.		Other employees.	
	1912	1913	1912	1913	1912	1913	1912	1913
Under 10 hours	6	12	124	117				
10 and under 20 hours	3	9	151	205				
20 and under 30 hours	8	15	309	356	11.4	12.7	22.6	29.4
30 and under 40 hours	27	26	529	534				
40 and under 50 hours	106	155	1,778	2,980				
50 hours	205	969	1,352	5,352	15.6	56.7	10.6	37.5
51 and under 53 hours	299	178	2,428	1,677	38.6	20.1	34.0	23.3
53 and under 55 hours	207	165	1,923	1,646				
55 and under 60 hours	188	131	2,635	1,106				
60 and under 65 hours	146	34	1,135	248				
65 and under 70 hours	94	13	339	38	34.3	10.5	32.8	9.8
70 and under 73 hours	13	1	47	4				
73 and under 75 hours			6					
75 hours and over	[1] 9		[2] 29					
Total	1,311	1,708	12,785	14,263	100.0	100.0	100.0	100.0

[1] Highest, 78 hours. [2] Highest, 82½ hours.

The normal hours of work which varied from 52 to 54½ hours per week in 1912 have been reduced to 50 in 1913. Overtime has been limited to 4 hours per week and not more than 2 hours in one day. As shown in the above table, the report bears ample testimony to the enforcement of these provisions. Comparing the figures for 1912 with those for 1913 it was found that for the industry as a whole the number of persons working more than 50 hours a week has been greatly reduced, while the number working 50 hours or less has increased. Excluding cutters, all of whom are men, the proportion of week workers employed 51 hours or more has been reduced from 66.8 per cent in 1912 to 33.1 per cent in 1913. Of those working 50 hours a week the proportion has increased from 26 per cent in 1912 to 37.5 per cent in 1913. The proportion of those working less than 50 hours also has increased from 22.6 per cent in 1912 to 29.4 per cent in 1913.

The same tendencies are observed in the case of the cutters, the proportion of those working 51 hours and over decreasing from 72.9 per cent in 1912 to 30.6 per cent in 1913, while those working 50 hours increased from 15.6 to 56.7 per cent and those working under 50 hours increased from 11.4 to 12.7 per cent.

ASSOCIATION AND NONASSOCIATION SHOPS.

In both association and nonassociation shops the proportion of persons employed over 50 hours a week has been greatly reduced, as is shown in the section on "hours of labor."[1] In association shops the percentage of employees, excluding cutters, working 51 hours or over was reduced from 68 per cent in 1912 to only 33 per cent in 1913, while in nonassociation shops the reduction was from 61 to 34 per

[1] See Table 74, page 178.

cent. The proportion working 50 hours increased from 11 per cent in 1912 to 39 per cent in 1913 in association shops and from 10 to 30 per cent in nonassociation shops, while those working less than 50 hours increased from 22 to 28 per cent in association and from 28 to 37 per cent in nonassociation shops.

The proportion of cutters working 51 hours or over was reduced from 73 per cent in 1912 to 33 per cent in 1913 in association shops and from 72 to 20 per cent in nonassociation shops. Those working 50 hours increased from 16 to 55 per cent in association and from 15 to 65 per cent in nonassociation shops. In 1912 11 per cent and in 1913 12 per cent of the cutters worked less than 50 hours in association shops and in nonassociation shops the proportions were 12 and 15 per cent, respectively, for the two years.

REGULARITY OF EMPLOYMENT.

The dress and waist industry is no exception to the rest of the garment industries in being subject to extreme seasonal fluctuations. There are about six months of activity, four in the spring and two in the fall, half of them carried on under extreme, almost feverish, pressure, followed by an equal period of subnormal activity with almost complete stagnation for one month in the year.

The report shows that there are more extreme fluctuations in the wages from month to month than in the number employed. That is to say, there is a tendency to retain as many employees engaged during the busy season as possible and to keep all of them partly employed during the slow season. This is especially true of the pieceworkers, as it is to the interests of both the manufacturer and his employees—the manufacturer because it enables him to maintain his organization intact ready to respond to the demands of the market at a moment's notice; the workers, because it enables them to earn what little money they can during the dull season instead of remaining totally idle. In the case of week workers this is less true, the manufacturers preferring to keep busy all the time whatever workers they can retain. But here, too, there is a tendency to accede to the desires of the union and keep as many people on the pay roll as possible by dividing the force into two or more groups which report for duty at the factory by turns on alternate days or weeks, and at the same time are kept fully employed while at the factory.

It is significant to note that even during the busiest week of the year (which is the period covered by this report), 28 per cent of all the workers other than cutters in the association shops and 37 per cent of those in the nonassociation shops were employed less than 50 hours during that week.

Taking the wages paid out in the industry during the busiest week of the year and expressing this as 100, the investigation has shown that the average weekly wage earned by all the workers during 1912 was equal to 73 per cent of that of the busiest week of the year. That is to say, if a worker's wage during the busiest week of the year was equal to $15 a week, his weekly average throughout the year would amount to $10.94. This average is found to vary considerably in the four branches of the industry into which it has been divided, being 53 per cent in the nonassociation A shops, 44 per cent in the nonassociation B shops, 67 per cent in association A shops, and 71 per cent in association B shops.

Taking the association and the nonassociation union shops together, as shown in Table 2, it was found that, excluding cutters, 117 persons worked less than 10 hours during the busiest week of the year, 205 worked 10 and under 20 hours, 356 worked 20 and under 30 hours, 534 worked 30 and under 40 hours, and 2,980 worked 40 and under 50 hours a week. One cause for this idleness during part of the week is to be traced to the workers themselves who lose a part of their working hours through illness, tardiness in reporting for work, and other causes which may make it impossible for a worker to be at the shop. Another class among the part-time workers is made up of new employees who started to work during the week, or old employees who left before the end of the week. A third group consists of workers who are obliged to remain idle part of the time, owing to the inability of the manufacturer or the foreman to keep the working organization in smooth running order in all its parts. The failure of the cutting department to cut a certain lot of material on time or to cut up certain parts or trimmings may throw into temporary idleness one or more departments or some workers in one or more departments. The failure to provide a proper proportion of body makers, sleeve setters, tuckers, etc., may likewise cause a congestion at one stage of the work and idleness at another. Idleness due to these causes may be at a minimum during the height of the season and is much more frequent at other times in the year, when it is felt that it is not so important to maintain a strict balance between the different departments, since there are more workers at the factory than can be kept busy all the time. While this is true, it seriously interferes with the efficiency of the shop both among the workers and those responsible for its maintenance, as shown in Part II of this report, dealing with the standardization of piece rates.

EFFECT OF THE PROTOCOL ON SUBCONTRACTING.

The prohibition of subcontracting in the shops, called for in the protocol, has had a marked effect on that practice, causing a very decided falling off in the number of people working for subcontractors. Apprentices, however, are employed as assistants to skilled operators, only one apprentice being allowed to one operator, the practice having the sanction of both the union and the association.

SCOPE OF THE INVESTIGATION.

It was aimed to cover as far as possible every shop engaged in the manufacture of ladies' dresses or waists in Greater New York. The investigation covers all the available shops operating under the protocol or under individual agreements with the union which are identical with the protocol in all the essential provisions.

The investigation of the joint board of sanitary control carried out in March, 1913, revealed the existence of 707 shops, employing 36,858 persons. As there were at that time 310 shops affiliated with the association and 259 nonassociation union shops, this would leave 140 shops not subject to the jurisdiction either of the association or of the union. Of the 310 association shops, 6 refused to furnish information to the agents of the wage-scale board, and 15 shops were found to lack the necessary books or records to enable the agents to obtain the information required, leaving 289 association shops from which detailed information as to wages was obtained. In the investigation of the 259 nonassociation union shops 18 firms refused information, while in the case of 8 the books were found in such poor shape that they could not be utilized for the purpose of this study; 231 shops were found with available records. The total number of shops thus covered by the investigation was 520.

Information as to individual earnings was obtained for 29,439 employees working in the spring of 1913. In addition to these, wage data were obtained for people working in teams or "sets," as they are called in the trade, of two or more persons, of which at least 1,704 were known to be working in these 520 shops in the spring of 1913, although their number must have been larger, as explained more fully in the part of this report dealing with this subject. (See p. 148.) This makes the total number of employees for whom wages were obtained not less than 31,485, as compared with 36,858 persons found by the joint board of sanitary control. However, in this investigation, designers, foremen, foreladies (unless actually working at the machine), packers, and office force were not included, all of whom, except office force, were included in the figures of the joint board. It would be a conservative estimate to assume that the 520 shops investigated employ at least 1,500 people engaged as designers, foremen, forewomen, and packers, which, added to 31,485, would bring the total employed by the shops investigated to not less than 32,985, or nearly nine-tenths of the employees in the entire industry.

As will be seen from Table 68 (p. 159), more than $9,300,000 was paid out in wages during 1912 in the 260 shops which had records for that year. The number of people employed by the 260 shops during the busiest week was 20,524, as shown in Table 67 (p. 158). Since the number of people found employed during the busiest week in 1913 was 31,485 and the wages were, on the average, about 10 per cent higher than in 1912, the wages paid out in 1913 must have aggregated more than $15,700,000, in round numbers. Adding to that an additional one-tenth of the above amount for the nonunion shops, it is found that the total wages paid out in the dress and waist industry during the past year in Greater New York must have amounted to more than $17,000,000. As the wages constitute from 10 to 20 per cent of the selling price of the garments, the value of the output of the dress and waist industry in Greater New York is probably close to $100,000,000.

As will be shown further, the shops investigated cover a wide range—from the very smallest to the largest known to exist in the industry—and since they employ nine-tenths of all the people working in the industry in Greater New York, the data submitted in this report may be accepted as conclusive for the entire industry. This is especially true of the wages for 1912 presented in this report, which prevailed in the industry prior to the conclusion of the protocol, when wages were adjusted in all shops as a result of individual arrangements between the employers and their employees.

While it may be presumed that in 1913 wages in the shops free from protocol conditions did not follow the same course as in the remaining nine-tenths of the industry, it is very likely that they did not differ very materially in the two groups. For this there are two reasons: In the first place, the nonunion shops comprise not only the smallest shops, but also a number of high-grade shops in which wages are known to be just as high as in the protocol shops, if not higher; in the second place, as far as the shops manufacturing low-grade garments are concerned, it is reasonable to assume that a general increase of wages among nine-tenths of the people working in the industry would automatically compel an advance in wages of the remaining one-tenth, especially during the busy season of the year, when the demand for labor exceeds the supply and when the independent manufacturers would be obliged to raise the wages paid in their shops to the level of the other nine-tenths of the industry or be in danger of losing their help.

The number of people whose individual earnings were covered by the investigation is shown in the table following.

TABLE 3.—NUMBER AND PER CENT OF PERSONS EMPLOYED IN DIFFERENT OCCUPATIONS IN THE DRESS AND WAIST INDUSTRY, 1912 AND 1913.

Occupation.	Number.		Per cent.	
	1912	1913	1912	1913
Cleaners	1,637	2,086	6.8	7.1
Cutters	1,397	1,701	5.8	5.8
Drapers	979	1,321	4.1	4.5
Examiners	640	852	2.7	2.9
Finishers	4,352	5,363	18.1	18.2
Ironers and pressers	816	1,119	3.4	3.8
Joiners	69	207	.3	.7
All other	326	372	1.4	1.3
Total, nonoperators	10,216	13,021	42.6	44.2
Operators	13,771	16,418	57.4	55.8
Grand total	23,987	29,439	100.0	100.0

As seen from the table, the total number of workers as to whose individual earnings information was obtained was 23,987 in 1912 and 29,439 in 1913. The difference of 5,452 people does not represent an actual increase in the number of people employed in the industry; it is due largely to the absence of records of wages paid during the year 1912 in a number of shops for which information was obtained for 1913. The figures have been arranged in the above table to show what proportion of the total employees in the industry are engaged in each occupation. Thus it will be seen that the largest single group are the operators, who constituted in 1913 nearly 56 per cent of all the employees. In this group have been included all employees who operate sewing machines. All the other trades combined comprise less than one-half of the employees, namely, 44.2 per cent. The largest single group among these are the finishers, who form 18.2 per cent, or a little less than one-fifth of all the employees, followed by the cleaners, who constitute 7.1 per cent of the total.

COMPARISON OF ASSOCIATION AND NONASSOCIATION UNION SHOPS.

All the data collected indicate that most of the large shops are affiliated with the association and are thereby parties to the protocol, while the bulk of the nonassociation shops are of a comparatively small size. Table 4, which follows, has been prepared to facilitate ready comparison of the two groups. Both the nonassociation and the association shops are divided into nine groups, each according to the number of people they employ, as follows: (1) Shops employing less than 25 persons, (2) those employing from 25 to 49, (3) from 50 to 74, (4) from 75 to 99, (5) from 100 to 199, (6) from 200 to 299, (7) from 300 to 399, (8) from 400 to 499, (9) from 500 to 600.

TABLE 4.—NUMBER AND PER CENT OF ASSOCIATION AND NONASSOCIATION SHOPS EMPLOYING EACH CLASSIFIED NUMBER OF EMPLOYEES, AND NUMBER AND PER CENT OF EMPLOYEES IN SUCH SHOPS, 1913.

NUMBER.

Classified number of employees in each shop.	Association.		Nonassociation.		Total.	
	Shops.	Employees.	Shops.	Employees.	Shops.	Employees.
Under 25	17	337	119	1,905	136	2,242
25 to 49	85	3,352	86	2,975	171	6,327
50 to 74	67	4,217	19	1,169	86	5,386
75 to 99	47	4,199	6	500	53	4,699
100 to 199	59	8,425	1	141	60	8,566
200 to 299	6	1,427			6	1,427
300 to 399	4	1,338			4	1,338
400 to 499	2	972			2	972
500 to 600	1	528			1	528
Total	[1] 288	24,795	231	6,690	[1] 519	31,485

PER CENT.

Classified number of employees in each shop.	Association.		Nonassociation.		Total.	
	Shops.	Employees.	Shops.	Employees.	Shops.	Employees.
Under 25	5.9	1.4	51.5	28.5	26.2	7.1
25 to 49	29.5	13.5	37.2	44.5	32.9	20.1
50 to 74	23.3	17.0	8.2	17.5	16.6	17.1
75 to 99	16.3	16.9	2.6	7.5	10.2	14.9
100 to 199	20.5	34.0	.4	2.1	11.6	27.2
200 to 299	2.1	5.8			1.2	4.5
300 to 399	1.4	5.4			.8	4.2
400 to 499	.7	3.9			.4	3.1
500 to 600	.3	2.1			.2	1.7
Total	100.0	100.0	100.0	100.0	100.0	100.0

[1] In one case two shops have been tabulated as one.

As will be seen from Table 4, only 17 shops, or 5.9 per cent of all the association shops were found employing under 25 persons each, while in the nonassociation group 119 shops, constituting 51.5 per cent, or more than one-half of all the nonassociation shops, were found to be employing under 25 persons each. The most prevalent type in the association shops comprises the two groups employing 25 and under 75 people, the number of shops in these two groups constituting 52.8 per cent, or more than one-half of all the association shops. This type of shop is almost as prevalent among the nonassociation shops, constituting 45.4 per cent of the total. On the other hand, shops employing 100 people or more are found almost entirely in the association group, there being only 1 shop of that size in the nonassociation group, and 72 in the association group, constituting one-fourth of the entire group.

The contrast between association and nonassociation shops appears still more striking when we compare the total number of people employed by the respective groups. Of the 31,485 persons accounted for in Table 4, 24,795 were found employed in the 289 association shops, while only 6,690 were working in the 231 nonassociation shops. In other words, although the nonassociation shops constituted 44.4 per cent, or nearly one-half of all the shops, they employed only 21.2 per cent, or a little over one-fifth of all the people. This shows that the majority of the nonassociation shops are small shops. Looking at some of the separate groups, we find that more than half (51.2 per cent) of all the employees in association shops were working in shops of 100 or more employees, while in the nonassociation group only 2.1 per cent of all the employees fall in that class, which contains only 1 shop. The very opposite is true when the smallest shops are considered, namely, those employing under 25 persons each, which gave employment to 28.5 per cent of all the workers in the nonassociation shops and to 1.4 per cent in the association group. In the nonassociation group nearly three-fourths of all the employees (73.0 per cent) worked in shops having less than 50 employees, while in the association group shops of that size gave employment to only 14.9 per cent of all the workers.

Not only does the association contain the largest shops; it also embraces most of the shops manufacturing the higher grades of dresses and waists. Table 5, which follows, shows the proportion of high-grade and of low-grade garment shops in the nonassociation and the association groups. While there is a very wide range in the grade of goods manufactured in the dress and waist industry, varying from waists retailing for less than one dollar apiece to expensive gowns, the prices of which run into hundreds of dollars, it was found very difficult to arrange the shops in several groups, owing to the overlapping of the groups, very few shops confining themselves strictly to one grade of goods. It was therefore found necessary to divide the industry into two large classes as follows: (1) The class marked B, consisting of shops manufacturing cotton waists at not less than $16.50 per dozen, silk waists at not less than $27 per dozen, and dresses at not less than $5 apiece; (2) those marked A, manufacturing garments selling at prices below those mentioned above. Included in class A are the shops manufacturing exclusively $9-a-dozen waists which are indicated separately in a footnote in Table 5. The reasons for the adoption of the classification in Table 5 are given on page 41 in discussing the subject of wages.

TABLE 5.—SHOPS AND EMPLOYEES IN ASSOCIATION AND NONASSOCIATION GROUPS ACCORDING TO THE CLASS OF GOODS MANUFACTURED, 1913.

NUMBER.

Group.	Association.		Nonassociation.		Total.	
	Shops.	Employees.	Shops.	Employees.	Shops.	Employees.
A (low grade)[1]	184	14,821	196	5,479	380	20,300
B (high grade)	105	9,974	35	1,211	140	11,185
Total	289	24,795	231	6,690	520	31,485

[1] This group includes $9-a-dozen waist shops, as follows: Association, 21 shops, employing 1,935 persons; nonassociation, 38 shops, employing 1,125 persons; total, 59 shops, employing 3,060 persons.

TABLE 5.—SHOPS AND EMPLOYEES IN ASSOCIATION AND NONASSOCIATION GROUPS ACCORDING TO THE CLASS OF GOODS MANUFACTURED, 1913—Concluded.

PER CENT IN EACH GRADE.

Group.	Association.		Nonassociation.		Total.	
	Shops.	Employees.	Shops.	Employees.	Shops.	Employees.
A (low grade)[1]	64	60	85	82	73	64
B (high grade)	36	40	15	18	27	36
Total	100	100	100	100	100	100

PER CENT OF ASSOCIATION AND NONASSOCIATION SHOPS AND EMPLOYEES.

	Shops.			Employees.		
	Association.	Nonassociation.	Total.	Association.	Nonassociation.	Total.
A (low grade)	48	52	100	73	27	100
B (high grade)	75	25	100	89	11	100
Entire industry	56	44	100	79	21	100

[1] This group includes $9-a-dozen waist shops, which constituted 7 per cent of the association shops, employing 8 per cent of the association employees; 10 per cent of nonassociation shops, employing 17 per cent of nonassociation employees. Taking all the shops under investigation, they constituted 11 per cent of all the shops, employing 10 per cent of all the employees.

As will be seen from this table, of the 31,485 persons employed at the height of the season in the spring of 1913, 20,300, or 64 per cent, were employed by the A shops manufacturing the lower-grade garments, and 11,185 persons, or 36 per cent, worked in the B shops making the higher-priced garments. The 380 A shops included 59 shops manufacturing exclusively $9 a dozen waists and employing 3,060 persons, or less than 10 per cent, of the total employees in the shops under investigation. The table shows that a larger proportion of association shops consisted of the higher-grade shops than was the case in the nonassociation shops. In the former, 36 per cent of the shops, employing 40 per cent of the employees, were in class B, while in the nonassociation group, only 15 per cent of the shops, employing 18 per cent of the employees, were in that class. Taking all the A shops investigated, more than half, or 52 per cent, were in the nonassociation group and only 48 per cent in the association, while in the B group, 75 per cent, or three-fourths of all the shops, were in the association and only one-fourth in the nonassociation group. Taking into account the number of employees, we find that the association shops employed nearly three-fourths (73 per cent) of all the people working in A shops, and nearly nine-tenths (89 per cent) of all those working in B shops.

It is evident from Tables 3, 4, and 5 that the association shops occupy a commanding position in the dress and waist industry in the city of New York, including practically all of the shops employing more than 100 people, giving employment to four-fifths of the people working under union conditions of labor; between two-thirds and three-fourths of all the workers employed in the industry, and nearly nine-tenths of all the people employed in shops manufacturing the better-grade garments.

NUMBER OF WORKERS IN DIFFERENT OCCUPATIONS.

The number and per cent of people employed in each occupation in the association and the nonassociation shops is shown in Table 6, which follows. The group, operators, includes all those who work on sewing machines.

TABLE 6.—NUMBER AND PER CENT OF EMPLOYEES IN ASSOCIATION AND NONASSOCIATION SHOPS, BY OCCUPATIONS, 1913.

Occupation.	Number.			Per cent.		
	Association.	Nonassociation.	Total.	Association.	Nonassociation.	Total.
Cleaners	1,652	434	2,086	79	21	100
Cutters	1,422	279	1,701	84	16	100
Drapers	1,101	220	1,321	83	17	100
Examiners	750	102	852	88	12	100
Finishers	4,193	1,170	5,363	78	22	100
Ironers and pressers	946	173	1,119	85	15	100
Joiners	169	38	207	82	18	100
All others [1]	345	27	372	93	7	100
Total, nonoperators	10,578	2,443	13,021	81	19	100
Buttonhole makers	108	37	145	74	26	100
Button sewers	116	39	155	75	25	100
Closers and hemmers	104	30	134	78	22	100
Dressmakers	406	34	440	92	8	100
Hemstitchers	172	8	180	96	4	100
Lace runners	107	6	113	95	5	100
Sample makers	506	74	580	87	13	100
Skirt operators	340	59	399	85	15	100
Sleeve makers	239	105	344	69	31	100
Sleeve setters	97	42	139	70	30	100
Trimmers	587	47	634	93	7	100
Tuckers	588	287	875	67	33	100
Waist operators	4,671	1,154	5,825	80	20	100
Operators, not specified	4,685	1,770	6,455	73	27	100
Total, operators	12,726	3,692	16,418	78	22	100
Grand total	23,304	6,135	29,439	79	21	100

[1] Includes assorters, embroiderers, markers, and slopers.

A comparison of the proportion of association and nonassociation workers in each occupation, as shown in this table, will help to show the varying character of the association and the nonassociation shops. When the total number of employees is considered, 79 per cent of these work in association shops and 21 per cent in nonassociation shops. This percentage is not the same for the different occupations; thus, in the case of cutters, only 16 per cent were employed in nonassociation shops while 84 per cent worked in association shops. Similar percentages apply to drapers. This may be explained by the fact that the association group, having a greater proportion of large shops and shops making high-grade garments, requires more cutters, since in the case of high-grade garments only one garment or a few garments are cut at a time, while in cheap garments as many as 200 layers of cloth are cut at once, requiring naturally a smaller number of cutters in proportion to the rest of the operators. Furthermore, several of the larger shops included in the association have outside contractors working for them whom they supply in some cases with material already cut. These shops will, therefore, have a larger number of cutters in proportion to the operators employed on the premises than the small shops which are included in the nonassociation group. Another indication of the great proportion of high-grade shops in the association is the proportion of examiners, of whom there were 12 per cent employed in the nonassociation shops and 88 per cent in the association shops. The examining must naturally be done with greater care in the case of high-grade garments than it is in cheap garments, hence the large proportion of examiners, as compared with other employees, in the association shops.

Table 7, which follows, shows the number of men and women employed in the association and the nonassociation shops in the years 1912 and 1913, arranged according to their occupations, while Table 8 shows the percentage of men and women in each occupation for association and nonassociation shops combined:

TABLE 7.—NUMBER OF MALES AND FEMALES IN EACH OCCUPATION IN ASSOCIATION AND NONASSOCIATION SHOPS, 1912 AND 1913.

FEMALES.

Occupation.	1912			1913		
	Nonassociation.	Association.	Total.	Nonassociation.	Association.	Total.
Assorters	1	128	129	9	138	147
Cleaners	193	1,444	1,637	434	1,652	2,086
Cutters	....	....	....	....	....	....
Drapers	112	865	977	219	1,096	1,315
Embroiderers	19	148	167	15	168	183
Examiners	57	583	640	102	740	842
Finishers	628	3,724	4,352	1,170	4,193	5,363
Ironers and pressers	8	529	537	30	552	582
Joiners	1	63	64	33	163	196
Markers	....	7	7	2	13	15
Slopers	....	9	9	....	6	6
Total, nonoperators	1,019	7,500	8,519	2,014	8,721	10,735
Buttonhole makers	5	58	63	10	56	66
Button sewers	1	87	88	33	103	136
Closers and hemmers	7	77	84	17	87	104
Dressmakers	33	312	345	19	331	350
Hemstitchers	4	94	98	6	164	170
Lace runners	3	92	95	3	100	103
Sample makers	42	500	542	67	492	559
Skirt operators	1	231	232	22	206	228
Sleeve makers	49	160	209	95	205	300
Sleeve setters	22	44	66	25	61	86
Trimmers	22	524	546	43	569	612
Tuckers	105	411	516	211	416	627
Waist operators	607	3,982	4,589	958	4,103	5,061
Operators, not specified	688	3,967	4,655	1,432	4,159	5,591
Total, operators	1,589	10,539	12,128	2,941	11,052	13,993
Grand total	2,608	18,039	20,647	4,955	19,773	24,728

TABLE 7.—NUMBER OF MALES AND FEMALES IN EACH OCCUPATION IN ASSOCIATION AND NONASSOCIATION SHOPS, 1912 AND 1913—Concluded.

MALES.

Occupation.	1912			1913		
	Nonassociation.	Association.	Total.	Nonassociation.	Association.	Total.
Assorters		1	1		4	4
Cleaners						
Cutters	168	1,229	1,397	279	1,422	1,701
Drapers	1	1	2	1	5	6
Embroiderers		2	2		1	1
Examiners					10	10
Finishers						
Ironers and pressers	44	235	279	143	394	537
Joiners	3	2	5	5	6	11
Markers					3	3
Slopers	1	10	11	1	12	13
Total, nonoperators	217	1,480	1,697	429	1,857	2,286
Buttonhole makers	12	41	53	27	52	79
Button sewers		15	15	6	13	19
Closers and hemmers	5	15	20	13	17	30
Dressmakers	20	31	51	15	75	90
Hemstitchers		2	2	2	8	10
Lace runners	1	7	8	3	7	10
Sample makers	3	12	15	7	14	21
Skirt operators	5	76	81	37	134	171
Sleeve makers	4	25	29	10	34	44
Sleeve setters	9	27	36	17	36	53
Trimmers	4	8	12	4	18	22
Tuckers	40	115	155	76	172	248
Waist operators	67	495	562	196	568	764
Operators, not specified	164	440	604	338	526	864
Total, operators	334	1,309	1,643	751	1,674	2,425
Grand total	551	2,789	3,340	1,180	3,531	4,711

TOTAL MALES AND FEMALES.

Occupation.	1912			1913		
	Nonassociation.	Association.	Total.	Nonassociation.	Association.	Total.
Assorters	1	129	130	9	142	151
Cleaners	193	1,444	1,637	434	1,652	2,086
Cutters	168	1,229	1,397	279	1,422	1,701
Drapers	113	866	979	220	1,101	1,321
Embroiderers	19	150	169	15	169	184
Examiners	57	583	640	102	750	852
Finishers	628	3,724	4,352	1,170	4,193	5,363
Ironers and pressers	52	764	816	173	946	1,119
Joiners	4	65	69	38	169	207
Markers		7	7	2	16	18
Slopers	1	19	20	1	18	19
Total, nonoperators	1,236	8,980	10,216	2,443	10,578	13,021
Buttonhole makers	17	99	116	37	108	145
Button sewers	1	102	103	39	116	155
Closers and hemmers	12	92	104	30	104	134
Dressmakers	53	343	396	34	406	440
Hemstitchers	4	96	100	8	172	180
Lace runners	4	99	103	6	107	113
Sample makers	45	512	557	74	506	580
Skirt operators	6	307	313	59	340	399
Sleeve makers	53	185	238	105	239	344
Sleeve setters	31	71	102	42	97	139
Trimmers	26	532	558	47	587	634
Tuckers	145	526	671	287	588	875
Waist operators	674	4,477	5,151	1,154	4,671	5,825
Operators, not specified	852	4,407	5,259	1,770	4,685	6,455
Total, operators	1,923	11,848	13,771	3,692	12,726	16,418
Grand total	3,159	20,828	23,987	6,135	23,304	29,439

TABLE 8.—NUMBER AND PER CENT OF MALES AND FEMALES, BY OCCUPATIONS, 1912 AND 1913.

Occupation.	1912					1913				
	Number.			Per cent.		Number.			Per cent.	
	Females.	Males.	Total.	Females.	Males.	Females.	Males.	Total.	Females.	Males.
Assorters	129	1	130	99	1	147	4	151	97	3
Cleaners	1,637	......	1,637	100	......	2,086	......	2,086	100	......
Cutters	......	1,397	1,397	......	100	......	1,701	1,701	......	100
Drapers	977	2	979	100	(1)	1,315	6	1,321	100	(1)
Embroiderers	167	2	169	99	1	183	1	184	99	1
Examiners	640	......	640	100	......	842	10	852	99	1
Finishers	4,352	......	4,352	100	......	5,363	......	5,363	100	......
Ironers and pressers	537	279	816	66	34	582	537	1,119	52	48
Joiners	64	5	69	93	7	196	11	207	95	5
Markers	7	......	7	100	......	15	3	18	83	17
Slopers	9	11	20	45	55	6	13	19	32	68
Total, nonoperators	8,519	1,697	10,216	83	17	10,735	2,286	13,021	82	18
Buttonhole makers	63	53	116	54	46	66	79	145	46	54
Button sewers	88	15	103	85	15	136	19	155	88	12
Closers and hemmers	84	20	104	81	19	104	30	134	78	22
Dressmakers	345	51	396	87	13	350	90	440	80	20
Hemstitchers	98	2	100	98	2	170	10	180	94	6
Lace runners	95	8	103	92	8	103	10	113	91	9
Sample makers	542	15	557	97	3	559	21	580	96	4
Skirt operators	232	81	313	74	26	228	171	399	57	43
Sleeve makers	209	29	238	88	12	300	44	344	87	13
Sleeve setters	66	36	102	65	35	86	53	139	62	38
Trimmers	546	12	558	98	2	612	22	634	97	3
Tuckers	516	155	671	77	23	627	248	875	72	28
Waist operators	4,589	562	5,151	89	11	5,061	764	5,825	87	13
Operators not specified	4,655	604	5,259	89	11	5,591	864	6,455	87	13
Total, operators	12,128	1,643	13,771	88	12	13,993	2,425	16,418	85	15
Grand total	20,647	3,340	23,987	86	14	24,728	4,711	29,439	84	16

[1] Less than 0.5 of 1 per cent.

It will be seen from these two tables that of the total of 29,439 workers for whom individual earnings were ascertained, 24,728, or 84 per cent of the total, were women, while only 4,711, or 16 per cent, were men. That is to say, for every man there were more than five women employed in the industry. The proportion of men and women is not the same in each occupation. In some occupations, like cutters, men are the only workers. In others, like finishers, women are exclusively employed. Among drapers, embroiderers, and examiners, the number of men is so small as to be negligible. Of cleaners women constitute 100 per cent, and the majority of these are young girls who have just entered the trade.

Although ironing and pressing is work which calls for great physical endurance, as it must be done standing up all day and working with hot irons, the proportion of men and women is almost the same, the women slightly predominating, there being 52 per cent women and 48 per cent men.

Taking the operators as a whole, there were 13,993 women as against 2,425 men, there being thus 6 women operators for every man working at a machine. In some of the departments of operating, the women have the field entirely to themselves. In general, it may be said that where speed and quantity of output count for most, men, on account of their greater strength and endurance, are preferred. On the other hand, wherever the nature of the work calls for patience, delicate touch, and nimble fingers, women will be found holding the field. Thus trimming, which calls for deft and delicate handling of the lace and other trimming material, is almost exclusively done by women, the number of men being only 22, or 3 per cent, of a total of 634 trimmers. Sample making and hemstitching, also show a very small proportion of men, namely, 4 per cent in the case of sample makers and 6 per cent in the case of hemstitchers.

The largest proportion of men among operators is found in the case of buttonhole makers, where men outnumber women, 55 per cent being men, 45 per cent women. This is due to the fact that in many shops the value of a buttonhole maker who has the ability to take care of the machine in its frequent breakdowns is greatly appreciated, and in this respect men naturally have the advantage over women. Another group of operators in which men are present in large numbers is that of skirt operators, in which the women constitute 57 per cent and the men 43 per cent. In skirt operating long seams are the rule and speed is the chief requirement. Another group in which men are employed to a considerable extent is sleeve setting, in which their number exceeds one-third, there being 62 per cent women and 38 per cent men. In the group of tuckers 28 per cent are men and 72 per cent are women, and of the group of closers and hemmers men constitute less than one-fourth.

WEEK WORK AND PIECEWORK.

EXTENT IN DIFFERENT OCCUPATIONS.

The number of people working in the different occupations is given in detail in Table 9, and the extent to which week work and piecework prevailed among men and women in 1912 and 1913 is given for each occupation. In this table the number of operators working on different kinds of work is likewise given in detail, the operators being divided into 14 distinct occupations, as follows: Buttonhole makers, button sewers, closers and hemmers, dressmakers, hemstitchers, lace runners, sample makers, skirt operators, sleeve makers, sleeve setters, trimmers, tuckers, waist operators, and operators not specified.

In connection with Table 9, which gives figures for the industry as a whole, is presented Table 10, giving similar figures for shops making cheap waists sold to retail stores at $9 per dozen.

TABLE 9.—NUMBER OF WEEK WORKERS AND PIECEWORKERS, BY SEX, IN EACH OCCUPATION, 1912 AND 1913.

FEMALES.

Occupation.	1912			1913		
	Week workers.	Piece-workers.	Total.	Week workers.	Piece-workers.	Total.
Assorters	129	....	129	147	....	147
Cleaners	1,592	45	1,637	2,066	20	2,086
Drapers	952	25	977	1,268	47	1,315
Embroiderers	93	74	167	86	97	183
Examiners	640	....	640	842	....	842
Finishers	2,784	1,568	4,352	3,334	2,029	5,363
Ironers and pressers	305	232	537	407	175	582
Joiners	62	2	64	188	8	196
Markers	7	....	7	15	....	15
Slopers	9	....	9	6	....	6
Total, nonoperators	6,573	1,946	8,519	8,359	2,376	10,735
Buttonhole makers	46	17	63	45	21	66
Button sewers	69	19	88	113	23	136
Closers and hemmers	40	44	84	64	40	104
Dressmakers	68	277	345	56	294	350
Hemstitchers	93	5	98	148	22	170
Lace runners	78	17	95	83	20	103
Sample makers	540	2	542	551	8	559
Skirt operators	52	180	232	69	159	228
Sleeve makers	144	65	209	173	127	300
Sleeve setters	55	11	66	57	29	86
Trimmers	286	260	546	343	269	612
Tuckers	229	287	516	360	267	627
Waist operators	2,263	2,326	4,589	2,488	2,573	5,061
Operators, not specified	2,226	2,429	4,655	2,386	3,205	5,591
Total, operators	6,189	5,939	12,128	6,936	7,057	13,993
Grand total	12,762	7,885	20,647	15,295	9,433	24,728

MALES.

Occupation.	1912 Week workers.	1912 Piece-workers.	1912 Total.	1913 Week workers.	1913 Piece-workers.	1913 Total.
Assorters	1	....	1	4	....	4
Cutters	1,397	....	1,397	1,701	....	1,701
Drapers	1	1	2	5	1	6
Embroiderers	2	....	2	1	....	1
Examiners	....	....	....	10	....	10
Ironers and pressers	213	66	279	355	182	537
Joiners	2	3	5	7	4	11
Markers	....	....	....	3	....	3
Slopers	11	....	11	13	....	13
Total, nonoperators	1,627	70	1,697	2,099	187	2,286
Buttonhole makers	24	29	53	31	48	79
Button sewers	12	3	15	14	5	19
Closers and hemmers	11	9	20	14	16	30
Dressmakers	7	44	51	15	75	90
Hemstitchers	2	....	2	7	3	10
Lace runners	8	....	8	7	3	10
Sample makers	14	1	15	21	....	21
Skirt operators	37	44	81	64	107	171
Sleeve makers	11	18	29	12	32	44
Sleeve setters	16	20	36	25	28	53
Trimmers	8	4	12	9	13	22
Tuckers	83	72	155	109	139	248
Waist operators	277	285	562	332	432	764
Operators, not specified	245	359	604	257	607	864
Total, operators	755	888	1,643	917	1,508	2,425
Grand total	2,382	958	3,340	3,016	1,695	4,711

TABLE 9.—NUMBER OF WEEK WORKERS AND PIECEWORKERS, BY SEX, IN EACH OCCUPATION, 1912 AND 1913—Continued.

TOTAL MALES AND FEMALES.

Occupation.	1912			1913		
	Week workers.	Piece-workers.	Total.	Week workers.	Piece-workers.	Total.
Assorters	130		130	151		151
Cleaners	1,592	45	1,637	2,066	20	2,086
Cutters	1,397		1,397	1,701		1,701
Drapers	953	26	979	1,273	48	1,321
Embroiderers	95	74	169	87	97	184
Examiners	640		640	852		852
Finishers	2,784	1,568	4,352	3,334	2,029	5,363
Ironers and pressers	518	298	816	762	357	1,119
Joiners	64	5	69	195	12	207
Markers	7		7	18		18
Slopers	20		20	19		19
Total, nonoperators	8,200	2,016	10,216	10,458	2,563	13,021
Buttonhole makers	70	46	116	76	69	145
Button sewers	81	22	103	127	28	155
Closers and hemmers	51	53	104	78	56	134
Dressmakers	75	321	396	71	369	440
Hemstitchers	95	5	100	155	25	180
Lace runners	86	17	103	90	23	113
Sample makers	554	3	557	572	8	580
Skirt operators	89	224	313	133	266	399
Sleeve makers	155	83	238	185	159	344
Sleeve setters	71	31	102	82	57	139
Trimmers	294	264	558	352	282	634
Tuckers	312	359	671	469	406	875
Waist operators	2,540	2,611	5,151	2,820	3,005	5,825
Operators, not specified	2,471	2,788	5,259	2,643	3,812	6,455
Total, operators	6,944	6,827	13,771	7,853	8,565	16,418
Grand total	15,144	8,843	23,987	18,311	11,128	29,439

TABLE 10.—NUMBER OF WEEK WORKERS AND PIECEWORKERS, BY SEX, IN EACH OCCUPATION IN SHOPS MANUFACTURING WAISTS WHICH SELL AT $9 PER DOZEN TO RETAIL STORES, 1912 AND 1913.

FEMALES.

Occupation.	1912			1913		
	Week workers.	Piece-workers.	Total.	Week workers.	Piece-workers.	Total.
Assorters				1		1
Cleaners	316		316	319		319
Examiners	41		41	72	5	77
Finishers	22	30	52	51	39	90
Ironers	37	36	73	68	33	101
Markers	1		1	6		6
Total, nonoperators	417	66	483	517	77	594
Buttonhole makers	5	1	6	8		8
Button sewers	15		15	36	6	42
Closers and hemmers	8	3	11	19	5	24
Lace runners	3		3	5	2	7
Sample makers	10		10	17		17
Sleeve makers	52	12	64	68	13	81
Sleeve setters	14	3	17	23	6	29
Trimmers	21		21	25		25
Tuckers	27	1	28	35	12	47
Waist operators	782	165	947	986	234	1,220
Total, operators	937	185	1,122	1,222	278	1,500
Grand total	1,354	251	1,605	1,739	355	2,094

TABLE 10.—NUMBER OF WEEK WORKERS AND PIECEWORKERS, BY SEX, IN EACH OCCUPATION IN SHOPS MANUFACTURING WAISTS WHICH SELL AT $9 PER DOZEN TO RETAIL STORES, 1912 AND 1913—Concluded.

MALES.

Occupation.	1912			1913		
	Week workers.	Piece-workers.	Total.	Week workers.	Piece-workers.	Total.
Cutters	112	....	112	143	....	143
Ironers	42	17	59	69	26	95
Markers	....	....	....	3	....	3
Total, nonoperators	154	17	171	215	26	241
Buttonhole makers	4	11	15	10	16	26
Button sewers	6	....	6	6	2	8
Closers and hemmers	6	3	9	8	9	17
Lace runners	1	....	1	3	....	3
Sample makers	1	....	1	1	....	1
Sleeve makers	9	1	10	5	9	14
Sleeve setters	7	6	13	8	14	22
Trimmers	....	....	....	1	....	1
Tuckers	14	14	28	13	12	25
Waist operators	135	68	203	178	129	307
Total, operators	183	103	286	233	191	424
Grand total	337	120	457	448	217	665

TOTAL MALES AND FEMALES.

Occupation.	1912 Week workers.	1912 Piece-workers.	1912 Total.	1913 Week workers.	1913 Piece-workers.	1913 Total.
Assorters	....	....	....	1	....	1
Cleaners	316	....	316	319	....	319
Cutters	112	....	112	143	....	143
Examiners	41	....	41	72	5	77
Finishers	22	30	52	51	39	90
Ironers	79	53	132	137	59	196
Markers	1	....	1	9	....	9
Total, nonoperators	571	83	654	732	103	835
Buttonhole makers	9	12	21	18	16	34
Button sewers	21	....	21	42	8	50
Closers and hemmers	14	6	20	27	14	41
Lace runners	4	....	4	8	2	10
Sample makers	11	....	11	18	....	18
Sleeve makers	61	13	74	73	22	95
Sleeve setters	21	9	30	31	20	51
Trimmers	21	....	21	26	....	26
Tuckers	41	15	56	48	24	72
Waist operators	917	233	1,150	1,164	363	1,527
Total, operators	1,120	288	1,408	1,455	469	1,924
Grand total	1,691	371	2,062	2,187	572	2,759

It is unfortunate that the figures representing the numbers of employees for each of these occupations do not represent the actual number employed therein. The reason for this is that the pay rolls of the different concerns are not kept in a uniform manner; some concerns describe separately each class of operators, such as buttonhole makers, closers and hemmers, hemstitchers, etc.; other concerns designate every employee who works at a machine as an operator. The only way to overcome this difficulty would have been to interview personally each employee in the shop. Apart from the reluctance on the part of most employers to admit agents of the wage-scale board to the shops for that purpose, on the ground that it would interfere with the work of the employees, it would have greatly delayed the investigation and materially increased its cost. Even then a large number of cases could not have been investigated because a considerable number of the employees found on the books would not have been found working in the same shops at the time of the investigation.

The classification of the different kinds of operators is described in detail under the respective heads in the section devoted to wages of operators of different kinds.

The figures given in Table 9 for operators must, therefore, be considered correct only when taken for the operators as a whole, of whom 16,418 were found in 1913 as against 13,771 in 1912. For the separate subdivisions of operators, the figures are of value principally for comparative purposes, such as showing the proportion of week workers and pieceworkers in each group, relative numbers of men and women, comparative wages in 1912 and 1913, and as between one group of operators and another group.

RELATION OF SEX TO WEEK WORK AND PIECEWORK.

Table 9 throws an interesting light on the relation of sex to piecework and week work. On comparing the number of men and women engaged in piecework and week work in those branches of operating where the piecework system is employed to a considerable extent, it will be found that with the exception of dressmakers and skirt operators, men are engaged on piecework to a much greater extent than women. As there is particular interest in the conditions existing since the protocol went into effect, the 1913 figures will now be considered. Among buttonhole makers, the women had approximately one pieceworker to two week workers, while the men had three pieceworkers for every two week workers; in other words, the ratio of pieceworkers to week workers was three times as large among men as among women. Among closers and hemmers, the women had one and one-half week workers for every pieceworker, while the men had more pieceworkers than week workers; among sleeve makers, the women had one and one-third week workers to every pieceworker, while the men had nearly three pieceworkers to every week worker; among sleeve setters, the women had more than two week workers for every pieceworker, while the men had more pieceworkers than week workers; the same is true of the tuckers; among waist operators and operators not specified, the proportion of pieceworkers is much greater among the men than among the women. This is easily explained when what has been said on the preceding pages is borne in mind, namely, that men excel the women in speed and in endurance, while women show greater aptitude for work requiring patience and delicate handling. In the former case, piecework is more remunerative, while in the latter compensation by the week is frequently preferred both by the employer and by the worker.

RELATIVE ADVANTAGES OF WEEK WORK AND PIECEWORK.

Whether workers are to be compensated on a piece or a week basis depends to a large extent on the nature of the work. It is well known that, in adopting the protocol, the dress and waist industry upset a number of time-honored precedents and established new ones. One of these concerns the respective attitude of employers and employees to piecework and week work. The usual attitude of manufacturers in other industries is in favor of piecework, while the workers show a decided preference for week work. The manufacturer is guided in his attitude by the obvious desire of paying only for work done, since under the piecework system the pay of the worker is automatically cut off for every minute or second that he fails to turn out work. The workers object to the system on many grounds, chief of which are: (1) That the piecework system tends to speed up the worker to the limit of physical endurance, leading to a premature exhaustion of his strength and injuring his or her health generally; (2) that it deprives him of pay at more or less frequent intervals, due not only to lack of work but also frequently to lack of system in the distribution of work between the various departments, resulting in enforced idleness on his part, while he is obliged to remain at the factory waiting for work; (3) that it furnishes opportunities for foremen and subforemen to make favorites of some employees and to discriminate against others by keeping the favored workers as constantly at work as possible and giving them the best paying work, while the less favored are obliged to get along with what is left; (4) the fourth and chief objection of employees to the piecework system is based on what is a common practice in many industries, the tendency to reduce the piece rate as the workers gain in speed and find new "short cuts" in turning out the same work.

The idea on the part of the management is to keep the earnings of the employees within certain limits recognized as adequate under a standard set for different occupations or trades. The worker thus finds that, as soon as his earnings exceed the recognized limit, all additional exertion on his part not only will fail to bring him additional reward, but on the contrary will lead to a curtailment of the rate of pay for himself and his fellow workers. This feeling on the part of the worker, engendered by the attitude of his employers, leads frequently to an intentional limitation of output after it reaches the limit beyond which he has reason to expect a reduction in the rate of pay. This in turn engenders friction between the employers and employees and has, therefore, led to the general hostility to the piecework system on the part of workingmen and workingwomen. The workers' union in the dress and waist industry has upset this precedent along with many others. It was the workers who were insistent on the adoption of the piece-rate system for the industry at the time of concluding the protocol, while a large part of the manufacturers showed preference for the week-work system.

EXTENT OF WEEK WORK AND PIECEWORK PRIOR TO THE PROTOCOL.

The preference for week work among employers was confined chiefly to manufacturers of cheap garments, since the piece-rate system was already in vogue to a greater or less extent in shops manufacturing higher-grade garments before the protocol had gone into effect. This can be readily seen on comparing the figures in Tables 11 and 12, which follow:

TABLE 11.—NUMBER AND PER CENT OF WEEK WORKERS AND PIECEWORKERS, BY OCCUPATIONS, 1912 AND 1913.

Occupation.	1912					1913				
	Number.			Per cent.		Number.			Per cent.	
	Week workers.	Pieceworkers.	Total.	Week workers.	Pieceworkers.	Week workers.	Pieceworkers.	Total.	Week workers.	Pieceworkers.
Assorters	130	......	130	100	......	151	......	151	100	......
Cleaners	1,592	45	1,637	97	3	2,066	20	2,086	99	1
Cutters	1,397	......	1,397	100	......	1,701	......	1,701	100	......
Drapers	953	26	979	97	3	1,273	48	1,321	96	4
Embroiderers	95	74	169	56	44	87	97	184	47	53
Examiners	640	......	640	100	......	852	......	852	100	......
Finishers	2,784	1,568	4,352	64	36	3,334	2,029	5,363	62	38
Ironers and pressers	518	298	816	63	37	762	357	1,119	68	32
Joiners	64	5	69	93	7	195	12	207	94	6
Markers	7	......	7	100	......	18	......	18	100	......
Slopers	20	......	20	100	......	19	......	19	100	......
Total, nonoperators	8,200	2,016	10,216	80	20	10,458	2,563	13,021	80	20
Buttonhole makers	70	46	116	60	40	76	69	145	52	48
Button sewers	81	22	103	79	21	127	28	155	82	18
Closers and hemmers	51	53	104	49	51	78	56	134	58	42
Dressmakers	75	321	396	19	81	71	369	440	16	84
Hemstitchers	95	5	100	95	5	155	25	180	86	14
Lace runners	86	17	103	83	17	90	23	113	80	20
Sample makers	554	3	557	99	1	572	8	580	99	1
Skirt operators	89	224	313	28	72	133	266	399	33	67
Sleeve makers	155	83	238	65	35	185	159	344	54	46
Sleeve setters	71	31	102	70	30	82	57	139	59	41
Trimmers	294	264	558	53	47	352	282	634	56	44
Tuckers	312	359	671	46	54	469	406	875	54	46
Waist operators	2,540	2,611	5,151	49	51	2,820	3,005	5,825	48	52
Operators, not specified	2,471	2,788	5,259	47	53	2,643	3,812	6,455	41	59
Total, operators	6,944	6,827	13,771	50	50	7,853	8,565	16,418	48	52
Grand total	15,144	8,843	23,987	63	37	18,311	11,128	29,439	62	38

TABLE 12.—NUMBER AND PER CENT OF WEEK WORKERS AND PIECEWORKERS BY OCCUPATIONS, IN SHOPS MANUFACTURING WAISTS WHICH SELL AT $9 PER DOZEN, TO RETAIL STORES, 1912 AND 1913.

Occupation.	1912					1913				
	Number.			Per cent.		Number.			Per cent.	
	Week workers.	Pieceworkers.	Total.	Week workers.	Pieceworkers.	Week workers.	Pieceworkers.	Total.	Week workers.	Pieceworkers.
Assorters	......	......	......	......	......	1	......	1	100	......
Cleaners	316	......	316	100	......	319	......	319	100	......
Cutters	112	......	112	100	......	143	......	143	100	......
Examiners	41	......	41	100	......	72	5	77	94	6
Finishers	22	30	52	42	58	51	39	90	57	43
Ironers	79	53	132	60	40	137	59	196	70	30
Markers	1	......	1	100	......	9	......	9	100	......
Total, nonoperators	571	83	654	87	13	732	103	835	88	12
Buttonhole makers	9	12	21	43	57	18	16	34	53	47
Button sewers	21	......	21	100	......	42	8	50	84	16
Closers and hemmers	14	6	20	70	30	27	14	41	66	34
Lace runners	4	......	4	100	......	8	2	10	80	20
Sample makers	11	......	11	100	......	18	......	18	100	......
Sleeve makers	61	13	74	82	18	73	22	95	77	23
Sleeve setters	21	9	30	70	30	31	20	51	61	39
Trimmers	21	......	21	100	......	26	......	26	100	......
Tuckers	41	15	56	73	27	48	24	72	67	33
Waist operators	917	233	1,150	80	20	1,164	363	1,527	76	24
Total, operators	1,120	288	1,408	80	20	1,455	469	1,924	76	24
Grand total	1,691	371	2,062	82	18	2,187	572	2,759	79	21

Table 11 shows the extent of piecework and week work in each occupation for the industry as a whole, while Table 12 gives similar figures for the shops making cheap waists selling wholesale at $9 per dozen. Taking all employees, we find that while in the so-called $9 shops only 18 per cent of the employees worked by the piece in 1912, they constituted over one-third, or 37 per cent, of all the employees in the industry as a whole. In the case of operators, the difference was even more striking, the proportion of pieceworkers being 20 per cent in the $9 shops and as much as 50 per cent in the entire industry.

A clearer idea of the extent of piecework and week work in the different parts of the industry can be obtained by comparing shops which make cheap garments with those manufacturing high-grade garments.

Tables 13 and 14, which follow, contain the figures for six large shops in each class of the industry, respectively.

TABLE 13.—NUMBER AND PER CENT OF WEEK WORKERS AND PIECEWORKERS IN 6 SHOPS MANUFACTURING HIGH-GRADE GARMENTS, BY OCCUPATIONS, 1912 AND 1913.

Occupation.	1912					1913				
	Number.			Per cent.		Number.			Per cent.	
	Week workers.	Pieceworkers.	Total.	Week workers.	Pieceworkers.	Week workers.	Pieceworkers.	Total.	Week workers.	Pieceworkers.
Cleaners	9	.....	9	100	.....	8	.....	8	100	.....
Cutters	32	.....	32	100	.....	41	.....	41	100	.....
Embroiderers	14	.....	14	100	.....	15	.....	15	100	.....
Examiners	20	.....	20	100	.....	24	.....	24	100	.....
Finishers	50	43	93	54	46	60	50	110	55	45
Drapers	6	.....	6	100	.....	9	.....	9	100	.....
Ironers	17	22	39	44	56	16	.....	16	100	.....
Total, nonoperators	148	65	213	69	31	173	50	223	78	22
Buttonhole makers	1	1	2	50	50	1	4	5	20	80
Hemstitchers	3	.....	3	100	.....	4	.....	4	100	.....
Sample makers	82	.....	82	100	.....	80	.....	80	100	.....
Skirt operators	.....	34	34	.....	100	.....	.....	.....	.....	.....
Tuckers	2	11	13	15	85	2	1	3	67	33
Waist operators	.....	75	75	.....	100	.....	95	95	.....	100
Operators, not specified	25	208	233	11	89	56	254	310	18	82
Total, operators	113	329	442	26	74	143	354	497	29	71
Grand total	261	394	655	40	60	316	404	720	44	56

TABLE 14.—NUMBER AND PER CENT OF WEEK WORKERS AND PIECEWORKERS IN 6 SHOPS MANUFACTURING LOW-GRADE GARMENTS, BY OCCUPATIONS, 1912 AND 1913.

Occupation.	1912					1913				
	Number.			Per cent.		Number.			Per cent.	
	Week workers.	Pieceworkers.	Total.	Week workers.	Pieceworkers.	Week workers.	Pieceworkers.	Total.	Week workers.	Pieceworkers.
Cleaners	229	.....	229	100	.....	169	.....	169	100	.....
Cutters	45	.....	45	100	.....	42	.....	42	100	.....
Examiners	38	.....	38	100	.....	41	.....	41	100	.....
Finishers	4	5	9	44	56	28	22	50	56	44
Ironers	68	27	95	72	28	113	13	126	90	10
Markers	1	.....	1	100	.....	4	.....	4	100	.....
Total, nonoperators	385	32	417	92	8	397	35	432	92	8
Buttonhole makers	13	.....	13	100	.....	8	.....	8	100	.....
Button sewers	11	.....	11	100	.....	13	.....	13	100	.....
Closers and hemmers	12	.....	12	100	.....	20	2	22	91	9
Hemstitchers	3	.....	3	100	.....	5	.....	5	100	.....
Lace runners	16	.....	16	100	.....	17	.....	17	100	.....
Sample makers	5	.....	5	100	.....	7	.....	7	100	.....
Sleeve makers	18	.....	18	100	.....	20	.....	20	100	.....
Sleeve setters	7	.....	7	100	.....	14	.....	14	100	.....
Trimmers	46	.....	46	100	.....	51	.....	51	100	.....
Tuckers	50	.....	50	100	.....	39	1	40	98	2
Operators, not specified	644	124	768	84	16	566	137	703	81	19
Total, operators	825	124	949	87	13	760	140	900	84	16
Grand total	1,210	156	1,366	89	11	1,157	175	1,332	87	13

A comparison of the figures in the two tables is striking. It shows that in 1912, prior to the enactment of the protocol, 60 per cent, or not far from two-thirds, of all the employees in six large high-grade garment shops (Table 13) were paid by the piece, while in six large low-grade garment shops (Table 14) only 11 per cent, or about one-tenth, were pieceworkers. In the case of operators, the percentage of pieceworkers in the high-grade shops was still larger—namely, 74 per cent, or practically three-fourths of all the operators—while in the low-grade shops it was only 13 per cent.[1] When the special occupations of the operators are considered, it is found that there were no pieceworkers whatever among buttonhole makers, closers and hemmers, sleeve makers, sleeve setters, or tuckers in the six cheap-garment shops, while in the six high-grade shops, pieceworkers numbered as high as 85 per cent of the tuckers, 50 per cent of the buttonhole makers, 89 per cent of the operators not specified, and 100 per cent of the waist operators. Not all the shops, of course, manufacturing low-grade garments had such a percentage of pieceworkers, as has already been shown in commenting on the figures in Table 12, but the significance of the above figures lies in the tendency they disclose for the prevalence of week work in the shops manufacturing low-grade garments and the predominance of piecework at the other end of the industry.

In insisting, therefore, on the adoption of the piece-rate system throughout the industry, the union attempted to raise the conditions at the lower end of the industry to what they had already been at the higher end before the signing of the protocol.

WAGES.

METHOD OF OBTAINING WAGE DATA.

The ideal way of ascertaining the wages of workers in any industry is to find out their total earnings for an entire year. This is especially true of the garment industries which fluctuate with the seasons, alternating between periods of highest activity and weeks of absolute stagnation. The technical difficulties, however, in the way of obtaining the data as to the earnings of each of the 30,000 workers for an entire year proved no less serious in this case than in all wage investigations in which such an attempt has ever been made, and the investigation as to individual earnings had to be confined to those during the busiest week of the year, that is, the week showing the maximum number of employees. In order to obtain a comparison of the wages prevailing before and after the protocol, the figures were taken for the busiest week in 1912 and 1913, respectively. The investigation for 1913 was confined to the spring season, so that in every case the busiest week in 1913 means the busiest week in the

[1] The figure of 60 per cent for the six high-grade shops was obtained in spite of the fact that in the six shops was included one high-grade nonassociation shop, which is an exception to the rule, inasmuch as it employs week workers exclusively. If a typical high-grade association shop were substituted in its place, the proportion of pieceworkers would probably amount to at least 75 per cent of all the workers and to a still higher percentage of the operators.

spring of 1913,[1] while for 1912 the busiest week of the year was taken, whether spring or fall. In a great many cases there were no records of individual earnings for the spring of 1912 and those for the fall had to be taken.

The object of taking the busiest week was to secure information for the largest possible number of workers employed in the industry. It is well known, however, that earnings at the height of the season are much greater than at other times of the year. It would, therefore, be erroneous to draw the conclusion that the annual earnings of the workers are approximately equal to 50 times the earnings during the busiest week. Apart from the weeks when the workers are entirely idle, there are months when the weekly earnings are considerably less than during the busiest week of the year. In the case of week workers, an attempt has been made to overcome this difficulty by presenting in this report the weekly rates of wages rather than their earnings. But even these rates are in many instances higher at the height of the season than at other times of the year.

But in the case of pieceworkers, there being no regular weekly rates and no record being kept at the factories of the hours they are at work, total earnings during the week, including overtime, had necessarily to be taken.

There was but one means left to get at an approximate estimate of annual earnings and that was by ascertaining the regularity of employment in the industry. This was done and the results are discussed in detail on pages 160 and 161. As already pointed out the principal conclusion from the figures relating to regularity of employment, as shown by Table 68, is that the average weekly earnings of workers in the entire industry is 73 per cent of their earnings during the busiest week of the year and for the different branches of the industry is as follows: Association A, 67 per cent; association B, 71 per cent; nonassociation A, 53 per cent; nonassociation B, 44 per cent. This furnishes the key to an approximate estimate of the annual earnings of the various groups of workers from the earnings given in the following pages for the busiest week of the year.

METHOD OF PRESENTATION OF WAGE DATA.

As has already been pointed out in discussing Table 9, there are some occupations in the industry in which only women or only men are employed; cleaners or finishers furnish an illustration of the former, cutters of the latter. In most of the occupations, however, both men and women are employed. The same is true as to pieceworkers and week workers. As in the same occupation wages will differ according to sex and according to whether the workers are paid by the week or the piece, the wages are presented under each of these

[1] In a few cases there were no records for any week of 1913 and the manufacturers concerned were asked to keep a record for the ensuing week, which may not have been the busiest week. But the number of such cases did not exceed 10, all of them small shops.

four heads: (1) Pieceworkers, male; (2) Pieceworkers, female; (3) week workers, male; (4) week workers, female.

But few averages will be found in connection with the wage statistics in this report. This is due to the fact that averages are very misleading in cases where there is a wide range of figures. An illustration will make this clear. If wages in a certain occupation varied from, say, $10 to $15, an average of $12.50 would not be very far from either extreme; for the $12.50 worker, while better off than the $10 worker and not so well to do as the $15 worker, would be found maintaining a standard of life not differing very much from either of the other two. But where, as in the dress and waist industry, the range of wages takes in a great variety of standards varying all the way from $3 to $30 a week, an average of, say, $16 a week would be utterly misleading both as to the $3 as well as to the $30 a week workers. A better way, therefore, of summing up the wage data for the different occupations, it was thought, would be found by dividing the wage data for each occupation into a number of groups and by showing the number of people in each group and the percentage they form of the total. As it is important both to the employers and the employees to have the information in as much detail as practicable, the number of groups has been made quite large, namely, 18. The lowest group is that of workers getting under $3 a week; the next includes those earning from $3 to less than $4; the next from $4 to less than $5 and so on by $1 steps until $10 a week is reached, when each group is made to cover a range of $2. From $20 on, the groups advance by $2.50 each until $30 a week is reached, all workers earning $30 a week or over being put together.

These data are presented for the association and the nonassociation shops separately. Moreover, in view of the wide range of goods manufactured in the dress and waist industry, it was found necessary, as already stated, to divide the industry into at least two groups; one, called A, representing the shops manufacturing the cheaper garments; the other, called B, comprising the shops which turn out the higher grade of garments. While there are a great many more distinct kinds of shops, it was found impracticable to divide the industry into more than two groups, owing to the fact that but few shops confine themselves to the manufacture of one grade of garments, the number of grades being usually so large that any attempt to divide the industry into more than two groups would result in so much overlapping in individual shops as to make classification impossible. The line of demarcation adopted for the two groups is as follows: (1) Group B, which consists of shops manufacturing cotton waists selling at wholesale for not less than $16.50 per dozen, silk waists selling at not less than $27 per dozen, and dresses selling at not less than $5 apiece; (2) Group A, which includes shops manufacturing garments which sell at prices below those mentioned above. Even under this broad classification, a good deal of overlapping has proved unavoidable. Thus, if a shop devotes itself exclusively to $9-a-dozen waists, it clearly belongs in Group A, while one manufacturing waists selling from $16.50 to $24 a dozen would clearly belong to Group B. On the other hand, a shop manufacturing waists selling from $9 to $24, though it has a range which takes in both classes, has been classed with Group A. The reason for this classification is that the cheapest garment made usually determines the character of the work done in a shop. If a considerable quantity of cheap garments is made in the shop, the character of the help employed will be of a different kind from that employed in a shop in which no cheap garments, or very few of them, are being made. A shop making chiefly $9 and $16.50 waists has its help trained to pay more attention to quantity of output than to quality. If it adds a $24 line to its products, the character of the work on the $24 a dozen waists will not differ from that on the $16.50 or $9 waists, the difference between the two being solely that of material, a greater amount of lace, embroidery, and other trimmings, requiring in turn a greater amount of labor, though not a higher grade of workmanship. On the other hand, a shop which specializes on waists selling from $24 to $48 or $60 a dozen may manufacture also some of the cheaper kind to supply a limited demand from the stores which buy chiefly the high-grade garments. This shop will not employ special help for the cheaper garments, and, therefore, the workmanship on its $16.50 waists will be the same as on the higher-priced garments, the difference being in the quality of the material, in the elimination of most of the trimmings, saving cost of material and labor, etc.

From what has been said, it will be seen that the overlapping between the A and B shops, due to the fact that shops in either group are found to manufacture garments selling at the same price, is more apparent than real, the fundamental distinction being that of the character of the workmanship which is but roughly reflected in the selling price, the latter being unfortunately the only tangible criterion by which we can distinguish between the two.

The breaking up of the wage data first into 25 distinct groups according to occupation; then, into two groups according to sex, where more than one sex is employed; then again into piecework and week-work groups in occupations where both methods of compensation are in vogue; and then again into four groups, association A, association B, nonassociation A, and nonassociation B, while securing a very detailed presentation of the wage data, may be open to the criticism of failing to give a comprehensive and easily understood presentation of the wage situation in the industry. The need of such presentation has been recognized by providing general summaries both in the tables, where this was possible, and throughout the text in discussing the wages of each occupation and in the summary chapter of this report.

OPERATORS.

OCCUPATIONS OF OPERATORS.

By an operator in the dress and waist industry is meant any person working on a sewing machine. Operating work is not done with any uniformity in the industry. In the shops making cheap waists the work is divided to an extreme, each operator working on some small part of the garment and frequently specializing on only one particular seam in the garment, one closing the sides of the waist, another one doing the hemming, a third sewing lace (lace running), a fourth closing the shoulders, etc. Sometimes even this work is further subdivided. Thus, if a French seam is used in closing the sides of a waist, one operator will make the first seam, joining the front and back parts of the waist on the right side, while the other operator will trim off the raw edge and turn over the waist to put in the second seam on the wrong side. Sometimes a girl is employed especially to do the work of cutting off the raw edge. Subdivision of work in the other parts of the garment is also practiced to a great extent.

In shops making medium-priced garments or cheap garments on a piece-rate basis, it is customary to have "body makers." These are operators who make up the body of the waist (joining the shoulders, tacking the fronts and backs, making the centers, i. e., the buttonhole and button pieces, and sometimes sewing on the collar). In that case, there will still be considerable subdivision of labor, since the closer and hemmer will close the waist on the sides and hem the bottom; the sleeve maker will make the sleeves; the sleeve setter will set the sleeves into the waist; the tucker will make the tucks; the buttonhole maker will make the buttonholes; the button sewer will sew on the buttons; the hemstitcher will do the hemstitching; the skirt maker will make the skirt (if dresses are made in addition to waists), and the joiner will join the waist and skirt into a dress. Moreover, all the finer work which goes to set off the waist, the sewing on of the trimmings, laces, and embroideries will be done by "trimmers," so far as it is not simple enough to be done by lace runners.

In the high-grade shops where dresses and gowns are made, the subdivision of labor is still less, the operator or dressmaker making practically the entire garment in so far as sewing on the machine is concerned, and in addition to that in many cases doing her own draping instead of having that part of the work done by a draper. The hemming of the bottom of the skirt, the sewing on of the hooks and eyes, belts, and trimmings—in fact, all of the work that is to be done by hand—is done in these shops by finishers.

From what has just been said it will be clear why the designation of operators lacks uniformity on the pay rolls in the different shops.

In some shops everybody who works at a sewing machine is called an operator, and the term will include the entire range of workers from $4 or $5 a week beginners to the highest grade dressmakers. In other shops, usually those in which the subdivision of labor is greatest, the operators are designated separately according to the special work they do, but even in these shops it will frequently happen that in the case of some of the workers, say, lace runners, half will be designated as such and the other half as operators. In view of this fact, the numbers of the various classes of operators given in this report should not be taken as complete. But the combined number of operators of all kinds may be considered as fairly accurate. This makes it necessary to combine the earnings of all the operators into one group and discuss the changes which have occurred, considering in one group workers of such widely differing degrees of skill as distinguish a lace runner from a high-class dressmaker. At the same time, these figures will be helpful for comparative purposes both as between 1912 and 1913 and as between the different branches of the industry. Below is presented, therefore, an analysis of the wages of operators as a whole, followed by a separate presentation for the different divisions of operators mentioned above.

NUMBER AND CLASSES COVERED BY THE REPORT.

As shown by Table 8, records were found for 16,418 operators in 1913 and 13,771 in 1912. This does not mean that there were 2,647 more operators in 1913 than in 1912, but that information as to wages was available for so many more operators in 1913 than in 1912. Of those found in 1913, 2,425 were men and 13,993 were women, the number of men constituting 15 per cent and of women 85 per cent of all the operators. This shows that the overwhelming majority of the operators are women, who outnumber the men more than 5 to 1, the men specializing only in a few trades, such as buttonhole making, skirt operating, sleeve setting, and tucking. As regards pieceworkers and week workers, Table 9 shows that the division is about even among the women, there being 7,057 pieceworkers and 6,936 week workers, or practically the same number in each class. Among the men, however, the number of pieceworkers greatly exceeds that of week workers, being 1,508 for the pieceworkers as against 917 for the week workers.

WAGES OF OPERATORS.

In presenting the wages of operators the same general plan has been followed as for other workers employed in considerable numbers, the figures being shown separately for week workers and pieceworkers. Under each of these general classes tables are given showing for each sex the number and per cent of operators receiving each classified rate of wages, both in the industry as a whole and in shops making cheap garments. Similar tables are next presented for operators employed in association and nonassociation shops. A further subdivision shows the wages of female operators and of male operators in each of the four classes of shops—namely, shops designated as association A, association B, nonassociation A, and nonassociation B.

COMPARISON OF WAGES OF MEN AND WOMEN OPERATORS IN THE INDUSTRY AS A WHOLE.

Week workers.

As explained elsewhere in this report, the figures of the wages of week workers given in the tables which follow represent weekly rates. They take into account neither the time lost during the week nor the extra work done during overtime. In other words, when an operator is placed in the $9-a-week group it means that this is his or her regular weekly rate of pay, although during that particular week he may have worked only four days and earned $6 or have worked overtime and earned more than $10. On the other hand, the wages of pieceworkers reported are the actual earnings during the busiest week of the year.

The number and per cent of male and of female operators, week workers, receiving each classified rate of wages in 1912 and 1913 are shown for the industry as a whole in Table 15, which follows:

TABLE 15.—NUMBER AND PER CENT OF MALE AND FEMALE OPERATORS, WEEK WORKERS, IN THE INDUSTRY AS A WHOLE, RECEIVING EACH CLASSIFIED RATE OF WAGES PER WEEK, 1912 AND 1913.

Classified rates of wages per week.	Number.				Per cent receiving each classified rate.			
	Females.		Males.		Females.		Males.	
	1912	1913	1912	1913	1912	1913	1912	1913
Under $3	9				0.1			
$3 to $3.99	53	15	3	1	.9	0.2	0.4	0.1
$4 to $4.99	204	121	10	6	3.4	1.8	1.4	.7
$5 to $5.99	299	228	15	13	5.0	3.3	2.0	1.4
$6 to $6.99	432	457	12	32	7.2	6.7	1.6	3.5
$7 to $7.99	541	621	18	30	9.0	9.1	2.5	3.3
$8 to $8.99	564	633	33	36	9.4	9.3	4.5	3.9
$9 to $9.99	615	606	34	34	10.2	8.9	4.6	3.7
$10 to $11.99	1,160	1,284	84	74	19.3	18.8	11.5	8.1
$12 to $13.99	1,136	1,264	146	139	18.9	18.5	19.9	15.2
$14 to $15.99	672	1,056	181	199	11.2	15.4	24.7	21.8
$16 to $17.99	196	362	83	143	3.3	5.3	11.3	15.6
$18 to $19.99	93	136	61	111	1.5	2.0	8.3	12.1
$20 to $22.49	24	47	37	69	.4	.7	5.0	7.5
$22.50 to $24.99	6	4	9	17	.1	[1].1	1.2	1.9
$25 to $27.49	4	4	5	6	[2].1		.7	.7
$27.50 to $29.99	1			3				.3
$30 and over	1	2	2	1			.3	.1
Total	[3]6,010	[3]6,840	[3]733	[3]914	100.0	100.0	100.0	100.0

[1] Including $22.50 and over.
[2] Including $25 and over.
[3] Not including a number of week workers. These are indicated in Tables 26 to 48, showing the number of week workers and pieceworkers in different wage groups for each occupation.

Taking the figures in Table 15, the remarkable fact is noted that although the number of men operators was only 914 as against 6,840 women in 1913, making a ratio of more than 7 women to 1 man, yet there were a great many more men earning $20 a week and over than there were women, namely, 96 men as against only 57 women. The disparity in numbers is even more striking when expressed in percentages of each class of workers; the number of women receiving $20 and over constituted 0.8 per cent of all the women week workers, while the men in the corresponding groups formed 10.5 per cent of all the men week workers. If the line is drawn at $14 a week, it is found from the table that in the case of all the workers receiving less than $14 a week the percentage of women exceeds that of men, the lower the wages the greater being the excess of women over men. From $14 and up the relation between the two is reversed, the proportion of men exceeding that of women and increasing as the weekly rates advance. Thus the number of those receiving $12 to $13.99 constituted 18.5 per cent of the women and 15.2 per cent of the men. The next lower group, $10 to $11.99, included 18.8 per cent of the women and only 8.1 per cent of the men.

Starting with the group of $14 to $15.99 a week, it is found that in 1913 the women formed 15.4 per cent of all the women week workers, while the men comprised 21.8 per cent of male week workers. Employees getting $16 to $17.99 a week comprised 5.3 per cent of the women and 15.6 per cent of the men; those getting from $18 to $19.99 formed 2 per cent of the women and 12.1 per cent of the men; those getting from $20 to $22.49 a week comprised 0.7 per cent of the women and 7.5 per cent of the men.

The preceding figures may be summed up as follows: The proportion of workers in 1913 receiving wages of less than $6 a week formed over 5 per cent among the women and over 2 per cent among the men. Those earning $6 and less than $10 a week constituted nearly 34 per cent, or more than one-third of all the women, and over 14 per cent, or one-seventh, of all the men. Nearly 53 per cent, or more than half of all the women week workers, received wages of $10 and less than $16 a week, the proportion of men in the corresponding wage groups being a little over 45 per cent, or less than one-half, while 8 per cent of all the women and 38.2 per cent of the men received $16 and over per week.

Table 16, which follows, gives similar figures for operators working by the week in shops manufacturing garments of a cheap grade exclusively.

TABLE 16.—NUMBER AND PER CENT OF MALE AND FEMALE OPERATORS, WEEK WORKERS, RECEIVING EACH CLASSIFIED RATE OF WAGES PER WEEK, IN SHOPS MANUFACTURING GARMENTS SELLING TO RETAIL STORES AT $9 PER DOZEN EXCLUSIVELY, 1912 AND 1913.

Classified rates of wages per week.	Number.				Per cent receiving each classified rate.			
	Females.		Males.		Females.		Males.	
	1912	1913	1912	1913	1912	1913	1912	1913
Under $3	2				0.2			
$3 to $3.99	15	6	1	2	1.6	0.5	0.5	0.9
$4 to $4.99	70	24	8	3	7.5	2.0	4.4	1.3
$5 to $5.99	80	58	8	7	8.6	4.8	4.4	3.0
$6 to $6.99	142	156	6	13	15.2	12.8	3.3	5.6
$7 to $7.99	158	229	8	20	16.9	18.8	4.4	8.5
$8 to $8.99	121	187	12	16	13.0	15.4	6.5	6.8
$9 to $9.99	119	153	13	13	12.7	12.6	7.1	5.6
$10 to $11.99	145	252	28	18	15.5	20.7	15.3	7.7
$12 to $13.99	57	94	36	48	6.1	7.7	19.7	20.5
$14 to $15.99	23	50	43	37	2.5	4.1	23.5	15.8
$16 to $17.99	1	5	15	40	.1	.4	8.2	17.1
$18 to $19.99	1		2	8	.1		1.1	3.4
$20 to $22.49		1	3	8		.1	1.6	3.4
$22.50 to $24.99								
$25 to $27.49				1				.4
Total	934	1,215	183	234	100.0	100.0	100.0	100.0

Pieceworkers.

It is interesting to see how the difference in the earnings of men and women week workers compares with that of pieceworkers. Table 17 contains an answer to this question.

TABLE 17.—NUMBER AND PER CENT OF MALE AND FEMALE OPERATORS, PIECEWORKERS, IN THE INDUSTRY AS A WHOLE, EARNING EACH CLASSIFIED AMOUNT DURING THE BUSIEST WEEK OF THE YEAR, 1912 AND 1913.

Classified earnings per week.	Number.				Per cent.			
	Females.		Males.		Females.		Males.	
	1912	1913	1912	1913	1912	1913	1912	1913
Under $3	195	160	14	8	3.2	2.2	1.5	0.5
$3 to $3.99	105	83	8	14	1.7	1.2	.9	.9
$4 to $4.99	142	101	7	13	2.3	1.4	.8	.9
$5 to $5.99	181	136	11	6	3.0	1.9	1.2	.4
$6 to $6.99	242	166	10	17	4.0	2.3	1.1	1.1
$7 to $7.99	292	236	22	17	4.8	3.3	2.4	1.1
$8 to $8.99	384	310	32	32	6.3	4.3	3.5	2.1
$9 to $9.99	467	374	31	31	7.6	5.2	3.4	2.1
$10 to $11.99	912	974	76	97	14.9	13.6	8.4	6.4
$12 to $13.99	1,134	1,044	71	112	18.5	14.6	7.8	7.4
$14 to $15.99	684	968	90	157	11.2	13.5	9.9	10.4
$16 to $17.99	444	865	88	170	7.3	12.1	9.7	11.3
$18 to $19.99	362	590	86	167	5.9	8.2	9.5	11.1
$20 to $22.49	231	491	94	186	3.8	6.9	10.3	12.3
$22.50 to $24.99	178	321	65	170	2.9	4.5	7.1	11.3
$25 to $27.49	75	159	72	114	1.2	2.2	7.9	7.5
$27.50 to $29.99	45	96	51	65	.7	1.3	5.6	4.3
$30 and over	45	79	82	135	.7	1.1	9.0	8.9
Total	[1] 6,118	[1] 7,153	[1] 910	[1] 1,511	100.0	100.0	100.0	100.0

[1] Including a number of week workers for whom earnings but not rates of wages could he ascertained. These are indicated in Tables 26 to 48 showing the number of week workers and pieceworkers in the different wage groups for each occupation.

While the same general rule holds good of the pieceworkers as of the week workers, that a greater proportion of men than of women are employed in the higher-paid wage groups, and that a higher proportion of women than of men are employed in the lower wage groups, the line of demarcation among the pieceworkers begins at $18 a week instead of $14, as was found to be the case among the week workers. Thus the group of $18 to $19.99 a week contained 8.2 per cent of the total number of women in 1913 and only 11.1 per cent of the men, the difference between the proportion of men and women increasing as the wages increase. Below $18 the contrary was the case. The proportion of women employed in the $16 to $17.99 group was 12.1 per cent of all women as against 11.3 per cent for the men; in the $14 to 15.99 group, 13.6 per cent of all women and 10.4 per cent of all men, and so on down the scale of wages. The percentage of women earning $18 a week and over was 24.2 per cent, while for men the percentage was 55.4 per cent. That is to say, while more than half of all the men operators working by the piece earned $18 and over during the busiest week of 1913, the proportion of women earning the same wages was less than one-fourth. The number of women pieceworkers earning less than $6 a week formed 6.6 per cent of all the women pieceworkers, while among the men it amounted to 2.7 per cent; 15.1 per cent of the women pieceworkers earned $6 and less than $10 a week, while the number of men in the corresponding group constituted only 6.4 per cent; 53.8 per cent, or more than half of the women, earned $10 and less than $18 a week, while the number of men in the corresponding group was 35.5 per cent, or about one-third of all the men.

Table 18, which follows, gives similar figures showing number and per cent of pieceworkers earning each classified amount in shops manufacturing a cheap grade of garments:

TABLE 18.—NUMBER AND PER CENT OF MALE AND FEMALE OPERATORS, PIECE-WORKERS, EARNING EACH CLASSIFIED AMOUNT DURING THE BUSIEST WEEK OF THE YEAR, IN SHOPS MANUFACTURING GARMENTS SELLING WHOLESALE AT $9 PER DOZEN EXCLUSIVELY, 1912 AND 1913.

Classified earnings per week.	Number.				Per cent earning each classified rate.			
	Female.		Male.		Female.		Male.	
	1912	1913	1912	1913	1912	1913	1912	1913
Under $3	8	12	1	1	4.3	4.2	1.0	0.5
$3 to $3.99	1	4	2	4	.5	1.4	1.9	2.1
$4 to $4.99	8	4	5	2	4.3	1.4	4.9	1.0
$5 to $5.99	7	8	3	1	3.7	2.8	2.9	.5
$6 to $6.99	9	11	2	4	4.8	3.9	1.9	2.1
$7 to $7.99	17	10	2	7	9.0	3.5	1.9	3.7
$8 to $8.99	24	21	3	8	12.8	7.4	2.9	4.2
$9 to $9.99	26	22	4	....	13.8	7.7	3.9	....
$10 to $11.99	37	47	10	10	19.7	16.5	9.7	5.2
$12 to $13.99	27	42	9	15	14.4	14.8	8.7	7.9
$14 to $15.99	10	45	11	19	5.3	15.8	10.7	9.9
$16 to $17.99	7	21	10	18	3.7	7.4	9.7	9.4
$18 to $19.99	4	14	9	16	2.1	4.9	8.7	8.4
$20 to $22.49	1	10	13	20	.5	3.5	12.6	10.5
$22.50 to $24.99	1	5	4	32	.5	1.8	3.9	16.8
$25 to $27.49	1	4	3	9	.5	1.4	2.9	4.7
$27.50 to $29.99	....	2	5	11	....	.7	4.9	5.8
$30 and over	....	2	7	14	....	.7	6.8	7.3
Total	188	284	103	191	100.0	100.0	100.0	100.0

COMPARISON OF WAGES OF MEN AND WOMEN OPERATORS IN ASSOCIATION AND NONASSOCIATION SHOPS.

Week Workers.

What has been said of the comparative weekly rates of wages of men and women operators, week workers, in the industry as a whole is likewise true if the association and nonassociation shops are considered separately. The figures for these are given in Table 19, which follows:

TABLE 19.—NUMBER AND PER CENT OF MALE AND FEMALE OPERATORS, WEEK WORKERS, IN ASSOCIATION AND NONASSOCIATION SHOPS, RECEIVING EACH CLASSIFIED RATE OF WAGES PER WEEK, 1912 AND 1913.

NUMBER.

Classified rates of wages per week.	Association shops.				Nonassociation shops.			
	Females.		Males.		Females.		Males.	
	1912	1913	1912	1913	1912	1913	1912	1913
Under $3	9							
$3 to $3.99	46	11	3	1	7	4		
$4 to 4.99	186	93	8	4	18	28	2	2
$5 to $5.99	276	167	12	6	23	61	3	7
$6 to $6.99	354	328	8	22	78	129	4	10
$7 to $7.99	445	424	15	23	96	197	3	7
$8 to $8.99	456	443	29	20	108	190	4	16
$9 to $9.99	488	412	25	26	127	194	9	8
$10 to $11.99	939	888	63	48	222	396	21	26
$12 to $13.99	960	922	122	79	176	342	24	60
$14 to $15.99	588	840	141	142	84	216	40	57
$16 to $17.99	168	286	64	91	28	76	19	52
$18 to $19.99	78	114	53	66	14	22	8	45
$20 to $22.49	17	28	25	39	7	19	12	30
$22.50 to $24.99	4	2	9	7	2	2		10
$25 to $27.49	3	1	4	5	1	3	1	1
$27.50 to $29.99	1			3				
$30 and over	1	1	2			1		1
Total	5,019	4,960	583	582	991	1,880	150	332

PER CENT.

Classified rates of wages per week.	Association shops.				Nonassociation shops.			
	Females.		Males.		Females.		Males.	
	1912	1913	1912	1913	1912	1913	1912	1913
Under $3	0.2							
$3 to $3.99	.9	0.2	0.5	0.2	0.7	0.2		
$4 to $4.99	3.7	1.9	1.4	.7	1.8	1.5	1.3	0.6
$5 to $5.99	5.5	3.4	2.1	1.0	2.3	3.2	2.0	2.1
$6 to $6.99	7.1	6.6	1.4	3.8	7.9	6.9	2.7	3.0
$7 to $7.99	8.9	8.5	2.6	4.0	9.7	10.5	2.0	2.1
$8 to $8.99	9.1	8.9	5.0	3.4	10.9	10.1	2.7	4.8
$9 to $9.99	9.7	8.3	4.3	4.5	12.8	10.3	6.0	2.4
$10 to $11.99	18.7	17.9	10.8	8.2	22.4	21.1	14.0	7.8
$12 to $13.99	19.1	18.6	20.9	13.6	17.8	18.2	16.0	18.1
$14 to $15.99	11.7	16.9	24.2	24.4	8.5	11.5	26.7	17.2
$16 to $17.99	3.4	5.8	11.0	15.6	2.8	4.0	12.7	15.7
$18 to $19.99	1.5	2.3	9.1	11.3	1.4	1.2	5.3	13.6
$20 to $22.49	.3	.6	4.3	6.7	.7	1.0	8.0	9.0
$22.50 to $24.99	.1	[1] .1	1.5	1.2	.2	.1		3.0
$25 to $27.49	[2] .1		.7	.9	.1	.2	.6	.3
$27.50 to $29.99				.5				
$30 and over			.3					.3
Total	100.0	100.0	100.0	100.0	100.0	100.0	100.0	100.0

[1] Including $22.50 and over. [2] Including $25 and over.

Taking again as the dividing line those receiving $14 a week and over, Table 19 shows that in 1913 in the association shops the number of women receiving the above rates constituted 25.7 per cent of all the women, while the men in the corresponding wage groups formed 60.6 per cent of the total number of men. In the nonassociation shops the women receiving $14 a week or more comprised 18 per cent of all the women, and men 59.1 per cent of all the men, showing but a small difference in the proportion of men in the association and the nonassociation shops and a somewhat larger difference in the case of the women, the difference being in favor of the women in the association shops. The reason for this difference is that as already explained the association shops include a larger percentage of shops manufacturing higher-grade garments in which women operators must possess a greater skill than in the shops manufacturing the cheaper garments and therefore command higher rates of wages. In the case of men, however, the chief factor in determining their wages is their speed, which is equally valued wherever men operators are employed. This will be further confirmed by the figures and the charts referred to below.

Pieceworkers.

What has been said about the difference in the earnings of men and women pieceworkers in the industry as a whole is likewise true if they are compared in the association and the nonassociation shops separately. This is brought out in Table 20, which follows:

TABLE 20.—NUMBER AND PER CENT OF MALE AND FEMALE OPERATORS, PIECEWORKERS IN ASSOCIATION AND NONASSOCIATION SHOPS EARNING EACH CLASSIFIED AMOUNT DURING THE BUSIEST WEEK OF THE YEAR, 1912 AND 1913.

NUMBER.

Classified earnings per week.	Association shops.				Nonassociation shops.			
	Females.		Males.		Females.		Males.	
	1912	1913	1912	1913	1912	1913	1912	1913
Under $3	174	129	10	6	21	31	4	2
$3 to $3.99	93	67	5	3	12	16	3	11
$4 to $4.99	125	87	2	7	17	14	5	6
$5 to $5.99	149	116	5	3	32	20	6	3
$6 to $6.99	213	140	6	8	29	26	4	9
$7 to $7.99	255	192	17	11	37	44	5	6
$8 to $8.99	337	264	24	22	47	46	8	10
$9 to $9.99	422	311	23	24	45	63	8	7
$10 to $11.99	810	817	63	64	102	157	14	33
$12 to $13.99	1,054	856	55	73	80	188	14	39
$14 to $15.99	614	828	71	113	70	140	18	44
$16 to $17.99	399	756	70	122	45	10[illegible]	18	48
$18 to $19.99	328	503	70	128	34	87	17	39
$20 to $22.49	214	428	74	143	17	63	21	43
$22.50 to $24.99	173	291	53	119	5	30	12	51
$25 to $27.49	71	148	62	89	4	11	10	25
$27.50 to $29.99	44	85	41	47	1	11	10	18
$30 and over	45	74	75	110	....	5	7	25
Total	5,520	6,092	726	1,092	598	1,061	184	419

TABLE 20.—NUMBER AND PER CENT OF MALE AND FEMALE OPERATORS, PIECE-WORKERS, IN ASSOCIATION AND NONASSOCIATION SHOPS EARNING EACH CLASSIFIED AMOUNT DURING THE BUSIEST WEEK OF THE YEAR, 1912 AND 1913—Con.

PER CENT.

Classified earnings per week.	Association shops.				Nonassociation shops.			
	Females.		Males.		Females.		Males.	
	1912	1913	1912	1913	1912	1913	1912	1913
Under $3	3.2	2.1	1.4	0.5	3.5	2.9	2.2	0.5
$3 to $3.99	1.7	1.1	.7	.3	2.0	1.5	1.6	2.6
$4 to $4.99	2.3	1.4	.3	.6	2.8	1.3	2.7	1.4
$5 to $5.99	2.7	1.9	.7	.3	5.4	1.9	3.3	.7
$6 to $6.99	3.9	2.3	.8	.7	4.8	2.5	2.2	2.1
$7 to $7.99	4.6	3.2	2.3	1.0	6.2	4.1	2.7	1.4
$8 to $8.99	6.1	4.3	3.3	2.0	7.9	4.3	4.3	2.4
$9 to $9.99	7.6	5.1	3.2	2.2	7.5	5.9	4.3	1.7
$10 to $11.99	14.7	13.4	8.7	5.9	17.1	14.8	7.6	7.9
$12 to $13.99	19.1	14.1	7.6	6.7	13.4	17.8	7.6	9.3
$14 to $15.99	11.1	13.6	9.8	10.3	11.7	13.2	9.8	10.5
$16 to $17.99	7.2	12.4	9.7	11.2	7.5	10.3	9.8	11.5
$18 to $19.99	5.9	8.3	9.7	11.7	5.7	8.2	9.2	9.3
$20 to $22.49	3.9	7.0	10.2	13.1	2.8	6.0	11.4	10.3
$22.50 to $24.99	3.1	4.8	7.3	10.9	.8	2.8	6.5	12.1
$25 to $27.49	1.3	2.4	8.5	8.2	.7	1.0	5.4	6.0
$27.50 to $29.99	.8	1.4	5.6	4.3	.2	1.0	5.4	4.3
$30 and over	.8	1.2	10.3	10.1	....	.5	3.8	6.0
Total	100.0	100.0	100.0	100.0	100.0	100.0	100.0	100.0

This table shows that among the pieceworkers, as was found to be the case among the week workers, there is a larger percentage earning a high rate of wages in the association shops than there is in the nonassociation shops. Thus, the women pieceworkers earning $18 a week and over in 1913 constituted 25 per cent of all the women in the association shops and 19.5 per cent in the nonassociation shops. The percentage of men operators earning $18 a week and over was 58.3 in the association shops and 48 in the nonassociation shops. Among the week workers, as shown in Table 19, the women earning $14 a week or more constituted 25.8 per cent of all women week workers in the association shops and only 18 per cent in the nonassociation shops, while the percentage of men of the same groups was 60.7 in the association shops and 59 in the nonassociation shops. The reverse is evidently true of those earning the lower rates of wages who constituted a higher percentage in the nonassociation shops than they did in the association shops. These facts are brought out in Chart 2, the upper section of which shows the rates of wages of women operators, week workers, in nonassociation and association shops. As will be seen from that portion of the chart, the solid line representing the association shops is above the broken line representing the non-association shops in all wage groups of $12 a week and over except one, and is generally below that line for wages below $12 a week. The lower section of the chart shows a similar condition for women pieceworkers—the line representing the workers in the association shops being above the nonassociation-shop line in all wage groups above $14 a week, and below that line in nearly all wage groups below $14 a week.

The figures just stated as to the difference in wages for operators in association and nonassociation shops are of the highest moment

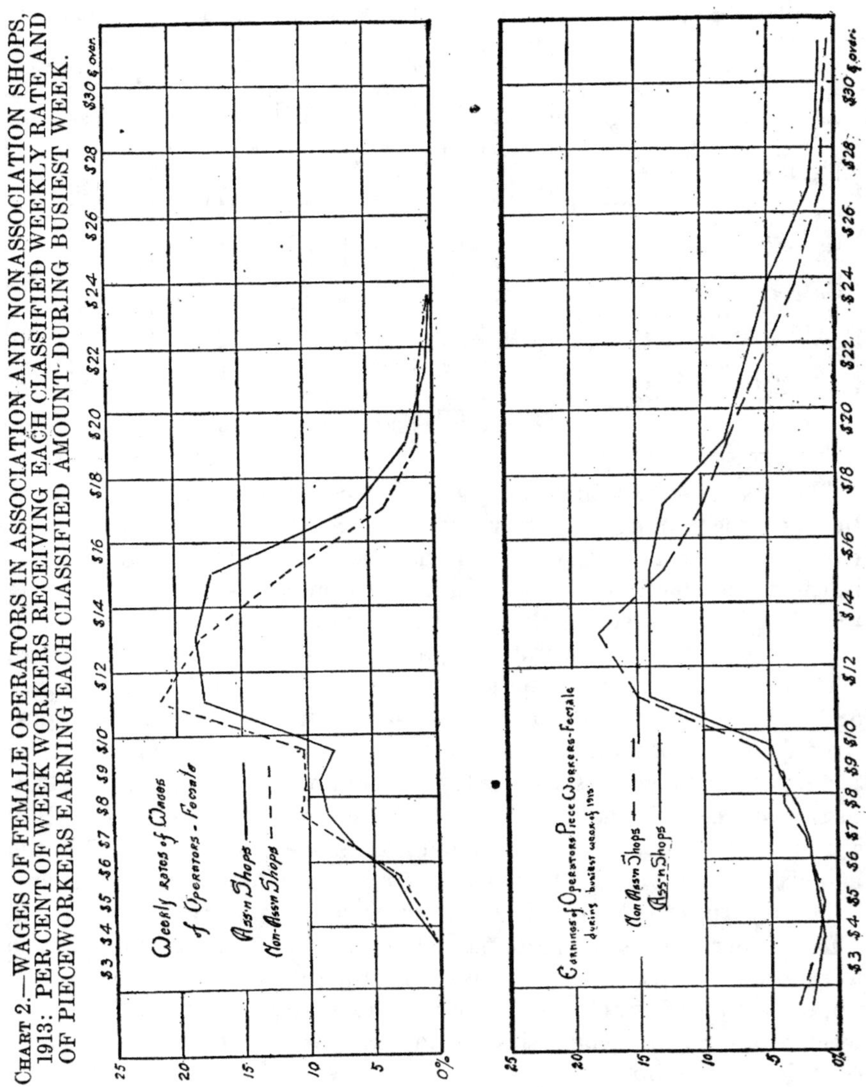

CHART 2.—WAGES OF FEMALE OPERATORS IN ASSOCIATION AND NONASSOCIATION SHOPS, 1913: PER CENT OF WEEK WORKERS RECEIVING EACH CLASSIFIED WEEKLY RATE AND OF PIECEWORKERS EARNING EACH CLASSIFIED AMOUNT DURING BUSIEST WEEK.

to those concerned in the industry, both employers and employees. The question will naturally arise: Are these differences due to a higher standard of wages being enforced in the association shops than in the nonassociation shops, a condition which would be equivalent to discrimination against the interests of manufacturers belonging to the association; or are they due to economic differences prevailing in the association and the nonassociation shops, respectively, as a result of the difference in the character of the garments they produce? It will be recalled from what was said in the first section of this report, that the association shops are chiefly large shops, while the nonassociation shops are mainly small shops; also that the association shops have a much larger percentage of shops manufacturing high-grade garments than have the nonassociation shops. If the differences in wages shown to exist in the association and nonassociation shops, respectively, are due merely to their affiliation or nonaffiliation with the association, then we should find the wages in association A and B shops more or less the same and considerably higher than in the nonassociation A and B shops, which likewise should not differ much from each other. On the other hand, if the difference between the wages which we have found prevailing in the association and nonassociation shops is due to the fact that the association has a much larger percentage of shops manufacturing high-grade garments than the nonassociation shops, then we should find nearly the same rates prevailing in the association B and nonassociation B shops, which should be considerably higher than those in the association A and nonassociation A shops.

COMPARISON OF WAGES OF MEN AND WOMEN OPERATORS IN SHOPS MAKING CHEAP AND HIGH-GRADE GARMENTS.

Week workers.

In Tables 21 and 22, which follow, are shown the differences in the wages of female and male operators, week workers, in four classes of shops designated as association A, association B, nonassociation A, and nonassociation B. As already explained, the A shops are those making the cheaper grades of garments and the B shops those making the higher grades.

TABLE 21.—NUMBER AND PER CENT OF OPERATORS, FEMALE, WEEK WORKERS, RECEIVING EACH CLASSIFIED RATE OF WAGES PER WEEK, 1912 AND 1913, IN ASSOCIATION AND NONASSOCIATION SHOPS MAKING THE CHEAPER AND THE HIGHER GRADES OF GARMENTS.

NUMBER.

Classified rates of wages per week.	Association A.		Nonassociation A.		Association B.		Nonassociation B.		Total.	
	1912	1913	1912	1913	1912	1913	1912	1913	1912	1913
Under $3	4	....	....	....	5	....	....	....	9	....
$3 to $3.99	43	11	7	4	3	....	....	....	53	15
$4 to $4.99	156	72	18	26	30	21	....	2	204	121
$5 to $5.99	219	149	21	59	57	18	2	2	299	228
$6 to $6.99	294	261	72	126	60	67	6	3	432	457
$7 to $7.99	362	374	84	188	83	50	12	9	541	621
$8 to $8.99	354	355	89	174	102	88	19	16	564	633
$9 to $9.99	381	332	102	182	107	80	25	12	615	606
$10 to $11.99	620	645	155	347	319	243	67	49	1,161	1,284
$12 to $13.99	464	479	103	269	496	443	73	73	1,136	1,264
$14 to $15.99	252	345	43	164	336	495	41	52	672	1,056
$16 to $17.99	52	102	14	43	116	184	14	33	196	362
$18 to $19.99	17	34	4	7	61	80	10	15	92	136
$20 to $22.49	5	13	2	6	12	15	5	13	24	47
$22.50 to $24.99	2	2	....	....	2	....	2	2	6	4
$25 to $27.49	....	....	....	....	3	1	1	3	4	4
$27.50 to $29.99	....	....	....	....	1	....	....	....	1	....
$30 and over	....	....	....	....	1	1	....	1	1	2
Total	3,225	3,174	714	1,595	1,794	1,786	277	285	6,010	6,840

PER CENT.

Classified rates of wages per week.	Association A.		Nonassociation A.		Association B.		Nonassociation B.		Total.	
	1912	1913	1912	1913	1912	1913	1912	1913	1912	1913
Under $3	0.1	....	....	....	0.3	....	....	....	0.1	....
$3 to $3.99	1.3	0.3	1.0	0.3	.2	....	....	....	.9	0.2
$4 to $4.99	4.8	2.3	2.5	1.6	1.7	1.2	....	0.7	3.4	1.8
$5 to $5.99	6.8	4.7	2.9	3.7	3.2	1.0	0.7	.7	5.0	3.3
$6 to $6.99	9.1	8.2	10.1	7.9	3.3	3.8	2.2	1.0	7.2	6.7
$7 to $7.99	11.2	11.8	11.8	11.8	4.6	2.8	4.3	3.1	9.0	9.1
$8 to $8.99	11.0	11.2	12.5	10.9	5.7	4.9	6.8	5.6	9.4	9.2
$9 to $9.99	11.8	10.5	14.3	11.4	6.0	4.5	9.0	4.2	10.2	8.9
$10 to $11.99	19.2	20.3	21.7	21.8	17.8	13.6	24.2	17.2	19.3	18.8
$12 to $13.99	14.4	15.1	14.4	16.9	27.6	24.8	26.4	25.6	18.9	18.5
$14 to $15.99	7.8	10.9	6.0	10.3	18.7	27.7	14.8	18.3	11.2	15.4
$16 to $17.99	1.6	3.2	2.0	2.7	6.5	10.3	5.1	11.6	3.3	5.3
$18 to $19.99	.5	1.1	.6	.4	3.4	4.5	3.6	5.3	1.5	2.0
$20 to $22.49	.2	.4	.3	.4	.7	.8	1.8	4.6	.4	.7
$22.50 to $24.99	(1)	(1)	....	....	.1	....	.7	.7	.1	.1
$25 to $27.49	....	....	....	....	.2	.1	.4	1.0	.1	.1
$27.50 to $29.99	....	....	....	....	.1	....	....	....	(1)	....
$30 and over	....	....	....	....	.1	.1	....	.4	(1)	(1)
Total	100.0	100.0	100.0	100.0	100.0	100.0	100.0	100.0	100.0	100.0

1 Less than one-tenth of 1 per cent.

TABLE 22.—NUMBER AND PER CENT OF OPERATORS, MALE, WEEK WORKERS, RECEIVING EACH CLASSIFIED RATE OF WAGES PER WEEK, 1912 AND 1913, IN ASSOCIATION AND NONASSOCIATION SHOPS MAKING THE CHEAPER AND THE HIGHER GRADES OF GARMENTS.

Classified rates of wages per week.	Association A.		Nonassociation A.		Association B.		Nonassociation B.[1]		Total.	
	1912	1913	1912	1913	1912	1913	1912	1913	1912	1913
NUMBER.										
$3 to $3.99	1	1			2				3	1
$4 to $4.99	8	4	2	2					10	6
$5 to $5.99	8	5	3	7	4	1			15	13
$6 to $6.99	6	16	4	10	2	6			12	32
$7 to $7.99	11	20	2	5	4	3	1	2	18	30
$8 to $8.99	21	13	4	15	8	7		1	33	36
$9 to $9.99	13	18	8	8	12	8	1		34	34
$10 to $11.99	41	24	19	25	22	24	2	1	84	74
$12 to $13.99	87	51	21	55	35	28	3	5	146	139
$14 to $15.99	86	84	33	51	55	58	7	6	181	199
$16 to $17.99	42	69	15	49	22	22	4	3	83	143
$18 to $19.99	39	45	5	41	14	21	3	4	61	111
$20 to $22.49	16	28	12	25	9	11		5	37	69
$22.50 to $24.99	5	1		7	4	6		3	9	17
$25 to $27.49	1	4	1	1	3	1			5	6
$27.50 to $29.99		3								3
$30 and over	2							1	2	1
Total	387	386	129	301	196	196	21	31	733	914
PER CENT.										
$3 to $3.99	0.3	0.3			1.0				0.4	0.1
$4 to $4.99	2.1	1.0	1.6	0.7					1.4	.7
$5 to $5.99	2.1	1.3	2.3	2.3	2.0	0.5			2.0	1.4
$6 to $6.99	1.6	4.1	3.1	3.3	1.0	3.1			1.6	3.5
$7 to $7.99	2.8	5.2	1.5	1.7	2.0	1.5			2.5	3.3
$8 to $8.99	5.4	3.4	3.1	5.0	4.1	3.6			4.5	3.9
$9 to $9.99	3.4	4.7	6.3	2.7	6.2	4.1			4.6	3.7
$10 to $11.99	10.6	6.2	14.7	8.3	11.2	12.2			11.5	8.1
$12 to $13.99	22.5	13.2	16.3	18.3	17.9	14.3			19.9	15.2
$14 to $15.99	22.2	21.8	25.6	16.9	28.1	29.6			24.7	21.8
$16 to $17.99	10.9	17.9	11.6	16.3	11.2	11.2			11.3	15.6
$18 to $19.99	10.1	11.7	3.9	13.6	7.1	10.7			8.3	12.1
$20 to $22.49	4.1	7.3	9.3	8.3	4.6	5.6			5.0	7.5
$22.50 to $24.99	1.3	.3		2.3	2.0	3.1			1.2	1.9
$25 to $27.49	.3	1.0	.8	.3	1.5	.5			.7	.7
$27.50 to $29.99		.8								.3
$30 and over	.5								.3	.1
Total	100.0	100.0	100.0	100.0	100.0	100.0			100.0	100.0

[1] Percentages for nonassociation B not computed on account of small number of employees.

Taking first the wages of women week workers as shown in Table 21, it is found that there is a greater difference between the high-grade and the low-grade garment shops, whether inside or outside of the association, than there is between the association and the nonassociation shops manufacturing the same grade of garments. Thus in 1913 the percentage of women earning $10 a week and over was as follows in the separate branches of the industry: Association B shops, 81.8 per cent; nonassociation B shops, 84.7 per cent; association A shops, 51.0 per cent; nonassociation A shops, 52.5 per cent. In other words, the figures for the association B and the nonassociation B shops are almost the same, but greatly different from those for the association A and the nonassociation A shops, which are very close to each other.

CHART 3.—WAGES OF FEMALE OPERATORS (WEEK WORKERS) IN ASSOCIATION AND NONASSOCIATION SHOPS MAKING LOW AND HIGH GRADE GARMENTS, 1913: PER CENT RECEIVING EACH CLASSIFIED WEEKLY WAGE RATE AND OVER.

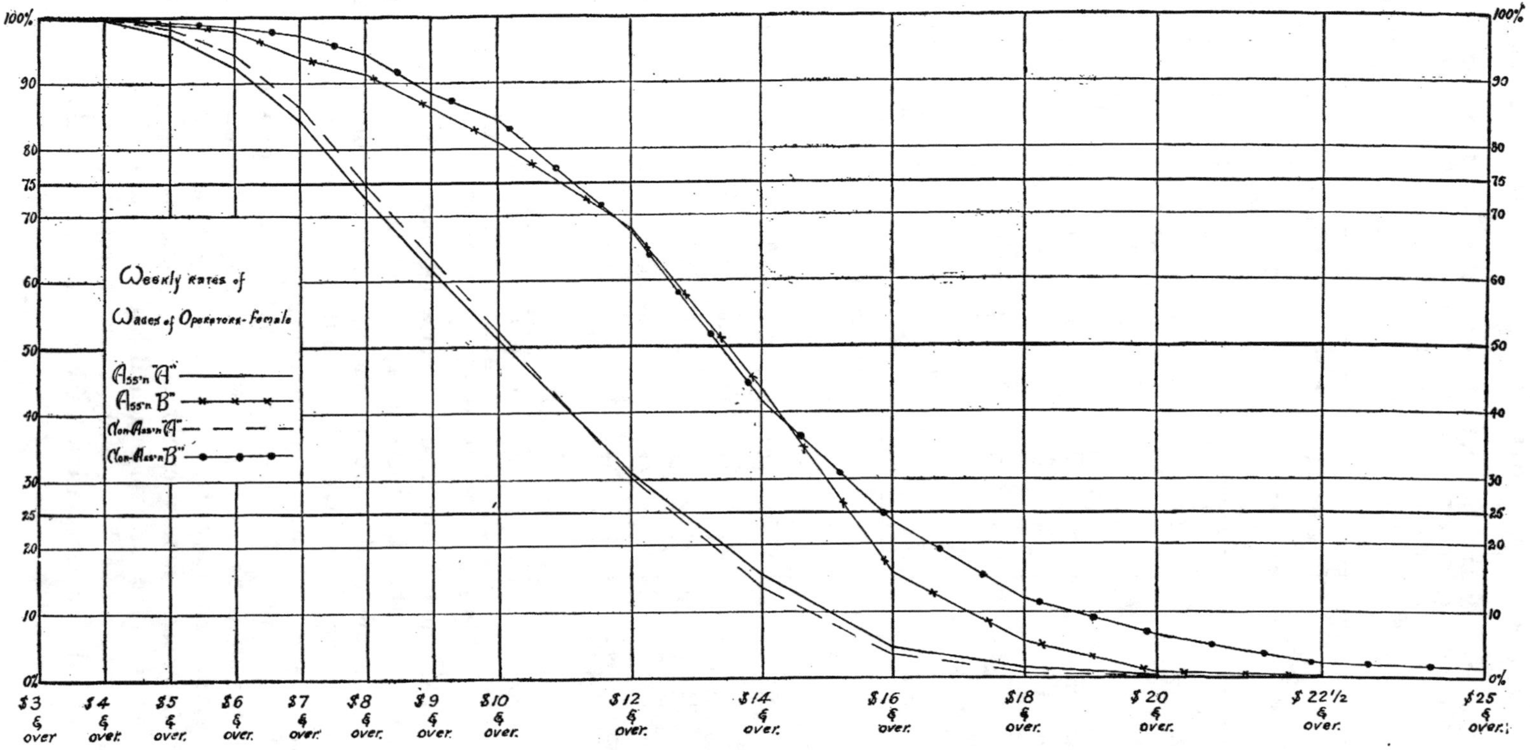

This difference is made clear to the eye in Chart 3, where the association B and the nonassociation B lines lie very close to each other, entirely coinciding in some parts and where, on the other hand, the association A and the nonassociation A shops likewise lie close to each other, coinciding in some parts but lying at a considerable distance from the B lines. It will be interesting to note at the same time that of the two curves, representing the B or high-grade garment shops, the one representing the nonassociation shops lies above that representing the association shops, showing that the proportion of workers receiving the higher wages is larger in the nonassociation than in the association shops, while in the A shops (manufacturing the lower-grade garments) the proportion of the higher-paid workers is higher in the association shops than in the nonassociation shops. This furnishes additional proof that there is no strict line of demarcation between the association and the nonassociation shops but that there is always a very marked difference between the A and B shops irrespective of their affiliation or nonaffiliation with the association.

Pieceworkers.

The differences in the wages of female and male operators working by the piece are shown for the four classes of shops in Tables 23 and 24 which follow:

TABLE 23.—NUMBER AND PER CENT OF OPERATORS, FEMALE, PIECEWORKERS, EARNING EACH CLASSIFIED AMOUNT DURING THE BUSIEST WEEK OF THE YEAR, 1912 AND 1913.

NUMBER.

Classified earnings per week.	Association A.		Nonassociation A.		Association B.		Nonassociation B.		Total.	
	1912	1913	1912	1913	1912	1913	1912	1913	1912	1913
Under $3	90	78	20	30	84	51	1	1	195	160
$3 to $3.99	52	47	9	13	41	20	3	3	105	83
$4 to $4.99	78	49	14	12	47	38	3	2	142	101
$5 to $5.99	81	76	22	16	68	40	10	4	181	136
$6 to $6.99	118	85	25	20	95	55	4	6	242	166
$7 to $7.99	155	123	29	34	100	69	8	10	292	236
$8 to $8.99	185	163	39	35	152	101	8	11	384	310
$9 to $9.99	231	182	36	54	191	129	9	9	467	374
$10 to $11.99	422	463	76	114	388	354	26	43	912	974
$12 to $13.99	668	463	60	131	386	393	20	57	1,134	1,044
$14 to $15.99	268	454	43	105	346	374	27	35	684	968
$16 to $17.99	178	352	27	72	221	404	18	37	444	865
$18 to $19.99	117	202	22	54	211	301	12	33	362	590
$20 to $22.49	58	164	3	41	156	264	14	22	231	491
$22.50 to $24.99	78	112	3	17	95	179	2	13	178	321
$25 to $27.49	24	55	1	7	47	93	3	4	75	159
$27.50 to $29.99	15	33	....	4	29	52	1	7	45	96
$30 and over	13	30	....	4	32	44	....	1	45	79
Total	2,831	3,131	429	763	2,689	2,961	169	298	6,118	7,153

PER CENT.

Classified earnings per week.	Association A.		Nonassociation A.		Association B.		Nonassociation B.		Total.	
	1912	1913	1912	1913	1912	1913	1912	1913	1912	1913
Under $3	3.2	2.5	4.7	3.9	3.1	1.7	0.6	0.3	3.2	2.2
$3 to $3.99	1.8	1.5	2.1	1.7	1.5	.7	1.8	1.0	1.7	1.2
$4 to $4.99	2.8	1.6	3.3	1.6	1.7	1.3	1.8	.7	2.3	1.4
$5 to $5.99	2.9	2.4	5.1	2.1	2.5	1.4	5.9	1.3	3.0	1.9
$6 to $6.99	4.2	2.7	5.8	2.6	3.5	1.9	2.4	2.0	4.0	2.3
$7 to $7.99	5.5	3.9	6.8	4.5	3.7	2.3	4.7	3.4	4.8	3.3
$8 to $8.99	6.5	5.2	9.1	4.6	5.7	3.4	4.7	3.7	6.3	4.3

TABLE 23.—NUMBER AND PER CENT OF OPERATORS, FEMALE, PIECEWORKERS, EARNING EACH CLASSIFIED AMOUNT DURING THE BUSIEST WEEK OF THE YEAR, 1912 AND 1913—Concluded.

PER CENT—Concluded.

Classified earnings per week.	Association A.		Nonassociation A.		Association B.		Nonassociation B.		Total.	
	1912	1913	1912	1913	1912	1913	1912	1913	1912	1913
$9 to $9.99	8.2	5.8	8.4	7.1	7.1	4.4	5.3	3.0	7.6	5.2
$10 to $11.99	14.9	14.8	17.7	14.9	14.4	12.0	15.4	14.4	14.9	13.6
$12 to $13.99	23.6	14.8	14.0	17.2	14.4	13.3	11.8	19.1	18.5	14.6
$14 to $15.99	9.5	14.5	10.0	13.8	12.9	12.6	16.0	11.7	11.2	13.5
$16 to $17.99	6.3	11.2	6.3	9.4	8.2	13.6	10.7	12.4	7.3	12.1
$18 to $19.99	4.1	6.5	5.1	7.1	7.8	10.2	7.1	11.1	5.9	8.2
$20 to $22.49	2.0	5.2	.7	5.4	5.8	8.9	8.3	7.4	3.8	6.9
$22.50 to $24.99	2.8	3.6	.7	2.2	3.5	6.0	1.2	4.4	2.9	4.5
$25 to $27.49	.8	1.8	.2	.9	1.7	3.1	1.8	1.3	1.2	2.2
$27.50 to $29.99	.5	1.1	....	.5	1.1	1.8	.6	2.3	.7	1.3
$30 and over	.5	1.0	....	.5	1.2	1.5	....	.3	.7	1.1
Total	100.0	100.0	100.0	100.0	100.0	100.0	100.0	100.0	100.0	100.0

TABLE 24.—NUMBER AND PER CENT OF OPERATORS, MALE, PIECEWORKERS, EARNING EACH CLASSIFIED AMOUNT DURING THE BUSIEST WEEK OF THE YEAR, 1912 AND 1913.

NUMBER.

Classified earnings per week.	Association A.		Nonassociation A.		Association B.		Nonassociation B.[1]		Total.	
	1912	1913	1912	1913	1912	1913	1912	1913	1912	1913
Under $3	8	5	2	2	2	1	2	....	14	8
$3 to $3.99	2	3	3	11	3	....	....	....	8	14
$4 to $4.99	2	5	5	6	....	2	....	....	7	13
$5 to $5.99	4	2	6	3	1	1	....	....	11	6
$6 to $6.99	5	8	4	9	1	....	....	....	10	17
$7 to $7.99	13	9	4	6	4	2	1	....	22	17
$8 to $8.99	19	17	5	10	5	5	3	....	32	32
$9 to $9.99	19	20	7	5	4	4	1	2	31	31
$10 to $11.99	49	56	14	30	14	8	....	3	77	97
$12 to $13.99	40	61	13	38	15	12	1	1	69	112
$14 to $15.99	49	86	15	41	22	27	3	3	89	157
$16 to $17.99	54	102	15	43	16	20	3	5	88	170
$18 to $19.99	51	106	14	36	19	22	3	3	87	167
$20 to $22.49	55	124	19	34	19	19	2	9	95	186
$22.50 to $24.99	33	99	11	43	20	20	1	8	65	170
$25 to $27.49	42	63	9	20	20	26	1	5	72	114
$27.50 to $29.99	29	34	7	16	12	13	3	2	51	65
$30 and over	38	78	7	20	37	32	....	5	82	135
Total	512	878	160	373	214	214	24	46	910	1,511

PER CENT.

Classified earnings per week.	Association A.		Nonassociation A.		Association B.		Nonassociation B.[1]		Total.	
	1912	1913	1912	1913	1912	1913	1912	1913	1912	1913
Under $3	1.6	0.6	1.3	0.5	0.9	0.5	....	....	1.5	0.5
$3 to $3.99	.4	.3	1.9	2.9	1.4	....	....	....	.9	.9
$4 to $4.99	.4	.6	3.1	1.6	....	.9	....	....	.8	.9
$5 to $5.99	.8	.2	3.8	.8	.5	.5	....	....	1.2	.4
$6 to $6.99	1.0	.9	2.5	2.4	.5	....	....	....	1.1	1.1
$7 to $7.99	2.5	1.0	2.5	1.6	1.9	.9	....	....	2.4	1.1
$8 to $8.99	3.7	1.9	3.1	2.7	2.3	2.3	....	....	3.5	2.1
$9 to $9.99	3.7	2.3	4.4	1.3	1.9	1.9	....	....	3.4	2.1
$10 to $11.99	9.6	6.4	8.8	8.0	6.5	3.7	....	....	8.5	6.4
$12 to $13.99	7.8	6.9	8.1	10.2	7.0	5.6	....	....	7.6	7.4
$14 to $15.99	9.6	9.8	9.4	11.0	10.3	12.6	....	....	9.8	10.4
$16 to $17.99	10.5	11.6	9.4	11.5	7.5	9.3	....	....	9.7	11.3
$18 to $19.99	10.0	12.1	8.8	9.7	8.9	10.3	....	....	9.6	11.1
$20 to $22.49	10.7	14.1	11.9	9.1	8.9	8.9	....	....	10.4	12.3
$22.50 to $24.99	6.4	11.3	6.9	11.5	9.3	9.3	....	....	7.1	11.3
$25 to $27.49	8.2	7.2	5.6	5.4	9.3	12.1	....	....	7.9	7.5
$27.50 to $29.99	5.7	3.9	4.4	4.3	5.6	6.1	....	....	5.6	4.3
$30 and over	7.4	8.9	4.4	5.4	17.3	15.0	....	....	9.0	8.9
Total	100.0	100.0	100.0	100.0	100.0	100.0	....	....	100.0	100.0

[1] Percentages for nonassociation B not computed on account of small number of employees.

The same tendency is observed in the wages of women operators working by the piece as in the wages among the week workers. The percentage of women pieceworkers earning $10 and over during the busiest week in 1913 was 78.2 per cent for the industry as a whole. Taking the separate branches of the industry, it is found that in the B shops the percentage was 84.4 per cent for the nonassociation shops and 83.0 per cent for the association shops, while in the A shops it was 71.9 per cent in the nonassociation shops and 74.5 per cent in the association shops. As in the case of the week workers, there is found here a close similarity of conditions in the shops manufacturing the same grades of garments, whether they belong to the association or not, and a considerable difference between the shops manufacturing high and low grade garments, respectively, both among those affiliated with the association and those outside of it; but there is a much smaller difference between the A and B shops' figures among the pieceworkers than there is in the case of the week workers. Thus, as will be recalled, Table 21 showed the percentage of those earning $10 a week or more to be from 82 to 85 per cent for the B shops, and from 51 to 52 per cent for the A shops; whereas, as shown by Table 23, the number of the same class of workers among the pieceworkers is from 83 to 84 per cent for the B shops, and from 72 to 74 per cent for the A shops (disregarding decimals). This is apparently due to the fact that, among week workers, the differences in rates of wages between A and B shops are due largely to difference in skill, the B shops requiring operators capable of turning out high-grade garments, who can therefore command a considerably higher rate of wages than the less skilled and more recently apprenticed workers in the low-grade garment shops. Among pieceworkers on the other hand, the differences in the high-grade and the low-grade garment shops are more nearly equalized. In the high-grade garment shops the rate per garment is higher, but the garment can not be made so rapidly as a low-grade garment. The result is that what a less skilled worker in the low-grade garment shop loses on the rate per garment, she makes up, to a large extent, on the speed with which she can turn it out and the earnings of the pieceworkers in the two types of shops come close together.

This fact is likewise shown in Chart 4. It will be observed that, as in the previous chart, the two lines representing the B groups lie near one another and that the two lines representing the A groups constitute the other pair; but unlike the showing in Chart 3 there is not the same close coincidence between lines of each pair, and, on the other hand, the two pairs come closer to one another than they do in Chart 3, for the reasons just explained.

In Tables 22 and 24 the wages of the men operators are shown in the same detail as are those of the women operators just considered.

CHART 4.—WAGES OF FEMALE OPERATORS (PIECEWORKERS) IN ASSOCIATION AND NONASSOCIATION SHOPS MAKING LOW AND HIGH GRADE GARMENTS, 1913: PER CENT EARNING EACH CLASSIFIED AMOUNT AND OVER DURING BUSIEST WEEK.

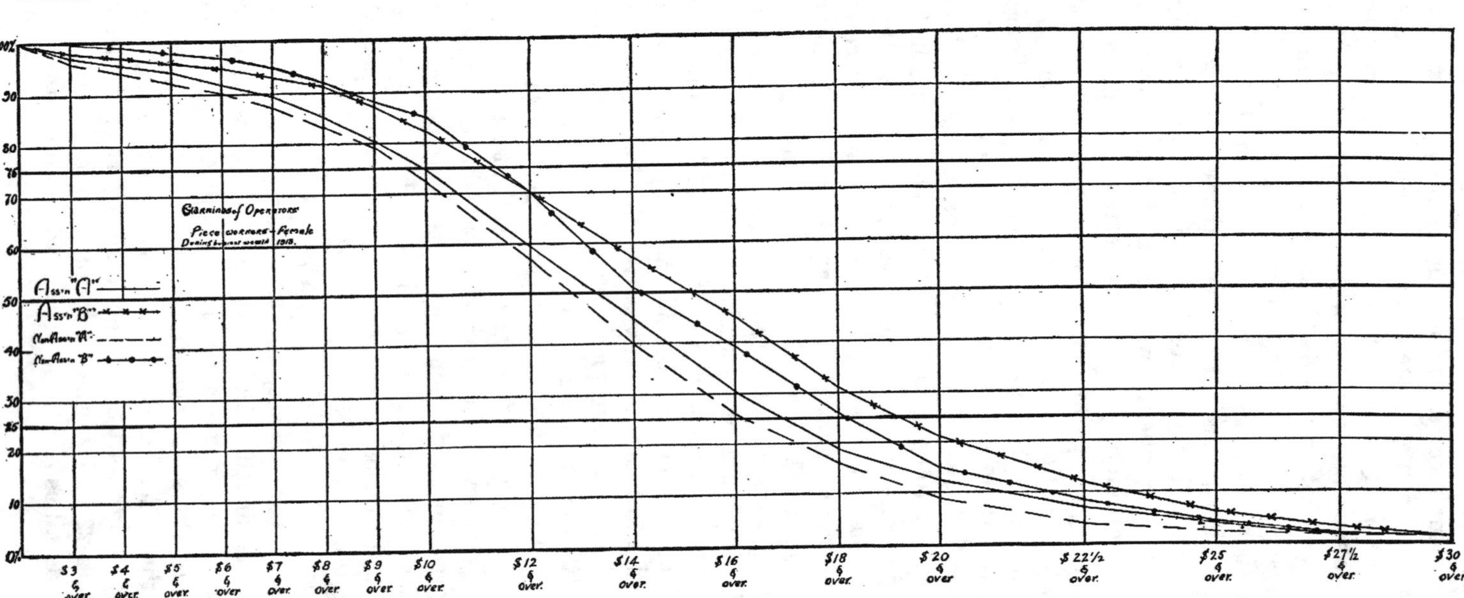

Table 22 shows the wages of the week workers and Table 24 the wages of the pieceworkers. The same general tendencies will be observed in the case of the men week workers as in the case of the women week workers. The number of workers being very small, the percentages were not worked out for the nonassociation shops at all and are less conclusive in the case of the other shops than they are in connection with the women week workers. In 1913 the male operators, pieceworkers (Table 24), earning $14 a week and over, constituted 77.1 per cent of all such operators in the industry as a whole, and in the four branches of the industry the percentages were as follows: Nonassociation B shops, 87 per cent; association B, 83.6 per cent; nonassociation A, 67.9 per cent; association A, 78.9 per cent. Again, there is found to be a close resemblance of conditions in the association B and the nonassociation B shops on the one hand, and in the association A and the nonassociation A shops on the other, and also it is noted that the wages are somewhat higher in the nonassociation shops in the B group [1] and in the association shops in the A group.

The difference in the earnings of men and women operators is illustrated in Chart 5. This chart consists of diagrams, illustrating the difference between men's and women's earnings in the A (those manufacturing lower-grade garments) and B (those manufacturing higher-grade garments) shops, respectively. The upper section of the chart shows the wages of week workers and the lower section those of pieceworkers. Since the majority of the workers are employed in association shops, this chart has been prepared to illustrate the difference between the high-grade and low-grade garment shops belonging to the association.

In both sections of the chart the contrast between the lines representing the A and B shops is remarkable. Taking, first, the upper section relating to week workers, it is found that in the A shops the two curves representing the wages of men and women, respectively, run almost parallel to each other except at the point near the middle, where they intersect, while in the B shops the two lines come very close to one another, the line representing men's wages showing an appreciable excess of men over women only in the upper ranks, beginning with $18 a week, in which there is a comparatively small number.

The same thing is true of the lower section relating to pieceworkers. Here, too, the women's earnings are seen to lag behind those of the men in the A shops except at the point of intersection above $16, while in the B shops there is no such uniformity, although on the whole men's earnings are seen to be above women's. The reason for this is clear. In the A shops, where the lower-grade garments are

[1] It must be pointed out, however, that the percentages for the nonassociation B group are based on too small numbers to warrant comparison in fine detail.

manufactured, quantity of output is the chief requirement, and the men, therefore, have a distinct advantage over the women, with the result that there is a larger percentage of men in the higher-paid wage groups, which begin with $12 to $13.99 a week for week workers, and

CHART 5.—WAGES OF MALE AND FEMALE OPERATORS IN ASSOCIATION SHOPS MAKING LOW AND HIGH GRADE GARMENTS, 1913: PER CENT OF WEEK WORKERS RECEIVING EACH CLASSIFIED WEEKLY RATE AND OF PIECEWORKERS EARNING EACH CLASSIFIED AMOUNT DURING BUSIEST WEEK.

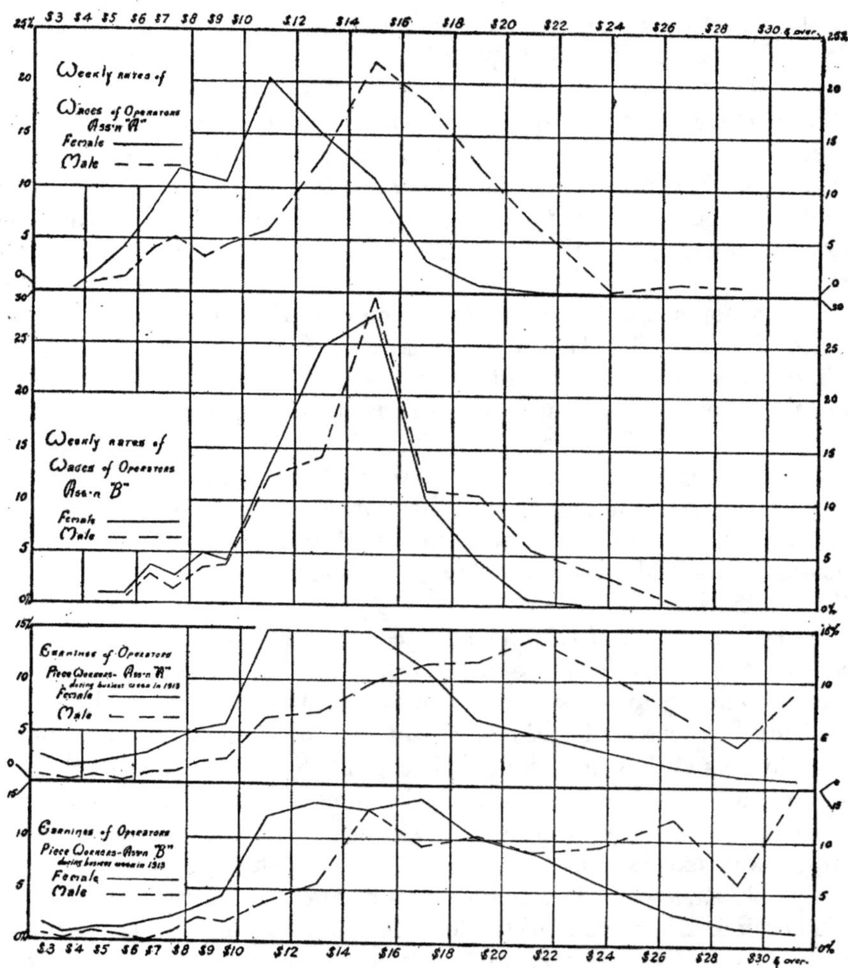

in the group of $16 to $17.99 among the pieceworkers. In the higher-grade shops skill and quality of work is as important and frequently much more important than quantity of output, and in these cases men have frequently less of an advantage over the women than in the lower-grade shops and in some cases have none.

It is also interesting to compare the wages of week workers and pieceworkers in the same branch of the industry, as brought out by this chart. In the upper section, representing the week workers, the curves for both A and B shops are seen to rise to points between 20 per cent and 30 per cent, while in the lower section, representing the pieceworkers, the high points do not rise above 15 per cent. That is to say, while from 20 per cent to 30 per cent of the week workers receive a certain rate of pay, the number of pieceworkers earning the same amount does not exceed 15 per cent of the total. This shows that in all branches of the industry, irrespective of the grade of goods manufactured, the tendency under the week-work system is for weekly rates of wages to concentrate about a certain rate which may be called the customary, if not the standard, rate of pay to workers of average skill; hence the rise of the curve representing weekly rates to a more or less high point. This is less the case among pieceworkers. While here, too, workers of average skill should earn similar wages under similar conditions, conditions as between shop and shop and between worker and worker in the same shop are never exactly alike, and each individual variation, whether in the physical condition of the workers at any moment or lack or accumulation of work or condition of each worker's machine, etc., is automatically reflected in his or her earnings, which is not the case with workers paid by the week. Hence the curves for the pieceworkers, whether in the A or B shops and whether male or female, do not rise to as high a point as in the case of week workers, thus indicating a wider variation in individual earnings and less uniformity among pieceworkers than among week workers.

COMPARISON OF WAGES IN 1912 AND 1913.

The effect of the protocol on the wages of operators will be seen by comparing the wages in 1912 and 1913. The usual course will be followed, comparing first the wages of week workers during the two years, taking the female and male workers separately, and then the earnings of the pieceworkers.

Week workers.

Table 15 shows the wages of all the operators working by the week in the entire industry, their number in 1913 being 6,840 women and 914 men, which constitutes about a thousand more workers in 1913 than in 1912. An examination of the figures showing the percentages of workers in the different wage groups shows that there has been a uniform increase in the proportion of women operators earning $14 a week and over and a corresponding reduction in the number of operators earning less than $14. In the case of the men operators, the dividing line begins at $16. It must be borne in mind, however, that the number of both men and women receiving $22.50 and over is too small to warrant a discussion of percentages. The increase in the number of higher-paid workers is shown by the following figures: The proportion of women receiving $14 a week and over increased from 16.6 per cent in 1912 to 23.5 per cent in 1913. Although there was a much larger increase in the percentage of women earning $14 a week and over than of men, the fact still remains that there were only 23.5 per cent of the women receiving $14 a week and over as against 60 per cent of the men.

It is interesting to see to what extent this increase affected the nonassociation and association shops, respectively. Table 19 and Chart 6 contain the answer to this question. The wages of women only are shown on the chart, since the number of men is comparatively small. Looking at the upper section of Chart 6, in which the solid line represents the wages in association shops in 1913 and the broken line the wages in 1912, the 1913 line is seen to be higher than the 1912 line for the groups of $12 a week and upward, showing the increase in the proportion of workers receiving the higher rates of pay. Corresponding to this, the 1912 line is a little above the 1913 line for the wage groups below the $12 rate. The lower section of the chart shows practically the same state of affairs in the nonassociation shops with some variation in details. The 1912 and 1913 lines meet in the group of $12 to $13.99, and the 1913 line is above the 1912 line for the wage groups above that figure. For the wage groups below the $12 rate, the 1912 line is in some cases above and in others below the 1913 line, the two lines alternating as they pass from group to group. This shows that, as the number of people in a lower group was reduced, it caused an increase in the next higher group in excess of the number of people transferred from that group to the next higher one. The details as to the exact number of people in each wage group, both men and women in the association and nonassociation shops, will be found in Table 19, but they may be briefly summed up here: Thus, in the association shops, the percentage of women operators, week workers, receiving $14 a week and over increased from 17.1 per cent to 25.7 per cent, and in the nonassociation shops, from 13.7 per cent in 1912 to 18 per cent in 1913. The percentage of men operators, week workers, receiving $14 a week and over in association shops increased from 51.1 per cent in 1912 to 60.6 per cent in 1913, and in the nonassociation shops from 53.3 per cent to 59.1 per cent. All of these figures show a fairly uniform increase in wages since the protocol went into effect both in association and nonassociation shops.

Pieceworkers.

The protocol had no less an effect in causing an advance of wages among the operators working by the piece than it had among the week workers. Table 17 shows what has happened among the pieceworkers in the industry as a whole, giving the wages of 7,153 women and 1,511 men operators working in 1913, and showing an excess of over 1,600 workers in 1913 over those for whom data were obtained for 1912.

As in the case of the week workers, so with the pieceworkers, the increase in percentages begins with the $14 group, while for those earn-

CHART 6.—WAGES OF FEMALE OPERATORS (WEEK WORKERS) IN ASSOCIATION AND NONASSOCIATION SHOPS, 1912 AND 1913: PER CENT RECEIVING EACH CLASSIFIED WEEKLY RATE.

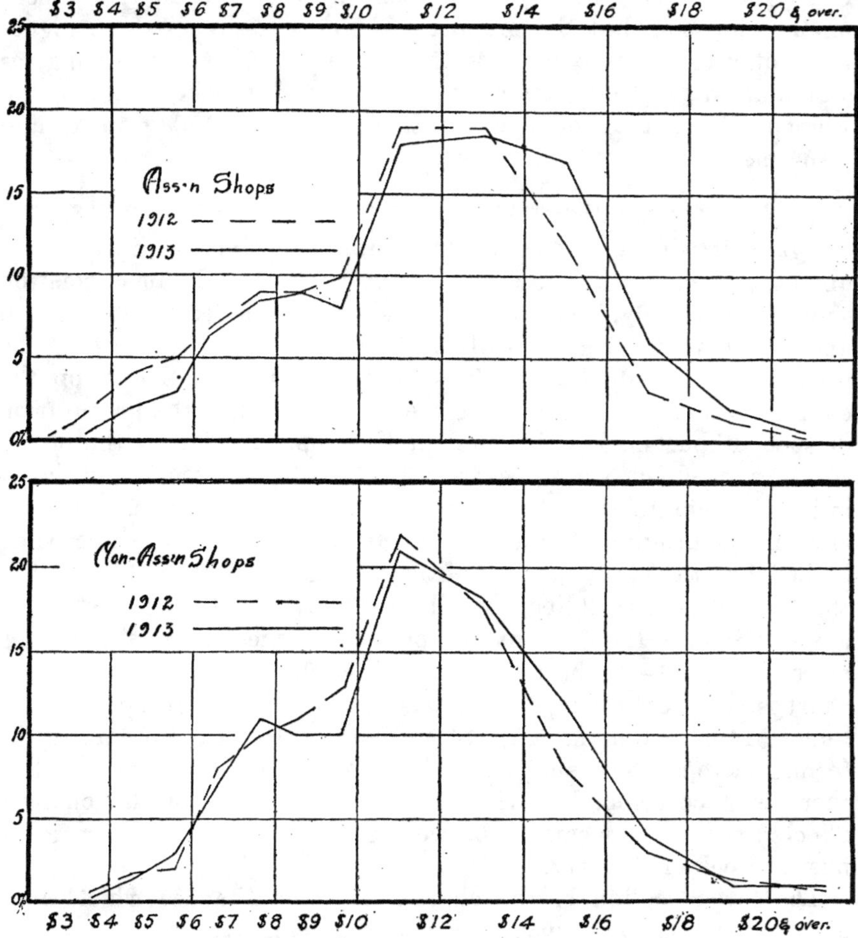

ing under $14 a week there is a decline in every wage group among the women, and in most wage groups among the men, some of the groups of men operators showing the same percentage as the groups of women operators. Thus, the number of women operators receiving $14 a week and over increased from 33.7 per cent of the total in 1912 to 50.0 per cent in 1913. In the case of men, the number of those receiving $14 a week and over increased from 69 per cent in 1912 to 77.1 per cent in 1913. That is to say, one-half of all the women operators and more than three-fourths of all the men operators earned $14 and over a week during the busiest week of 1913.

As in the case of the week workers, so among the pieceworkers the increase in the proportion of workers receiving $14 a week and over was greater among the women than among the men, amounting to nearly 50 per cent among the women and to less than 12 per cent among the men, but the proportion of men receiving these higher rates of wages greatly exceeds the proportion of women, being, as stated above, 77.1 per cent among the men and 50 per cent among the women. In actual numbers, this represents 3,570 women and 1,164 men.

Increase in earnings of pieceworkers in association and nonassociation shops.

Again, it will be interesting to compare the increase in earnings among the operators employed in association and nonassociation shops, respectively. The figures are shown in Tables 20, 23, and 24, and are reproduced graphically in Chart 7. As in the case of the week workers, only the earnings of the women are shown on the chart, the number of men being too small to justify the preparation of special charts. Looking first at the upper section of the chart, showing the changes in wages from 1912 to 1913 in association shops, it is seen that the two lines, representing 1913 and 1912 earnings, cross in the group of $14 and under $16 a week, the 1913 line being higher than the 1912 line in all of the wage groups above $14. Below the $14 rate, the 1912 line is in all cases above the 1913 line, showing a reduction in the percentages of women pieceworkers receiving wages below $14. The most striking feature in this section of the chart is the great change which has occurred in the groups $12 and under $14 on one hand, and $14 and under $18 on the other; in the former there is a very sharp drop from 1912 to 1913, and in the latter there is a corresponding rise, showing that most of the changes affected the workers earning between $12 and $18 a week during the busiest week of the year.

The lower section of the chart shows the changes which have occurred among the women piece operators employed in the nonassociation shops. Here the same general tendency is shown as in association shops. The increase of 1913 over 1912 occurs in the group $12 and under $14 a week, but is not so great as in the association shops. Both sections of the chart show a decline in the percentage of workers receiving under $12 a week.

The changes in wages brought out in Chart 7 are shown in detail for each wage group in the tables. A summary of all the tables quoted points to one conclusion which constitutes the most salient finding of the investigation covered by this report, namely: A general increase in the proportion of those earning the higher rates of wages and a reduction in the proportion of those earning the lower rates. How

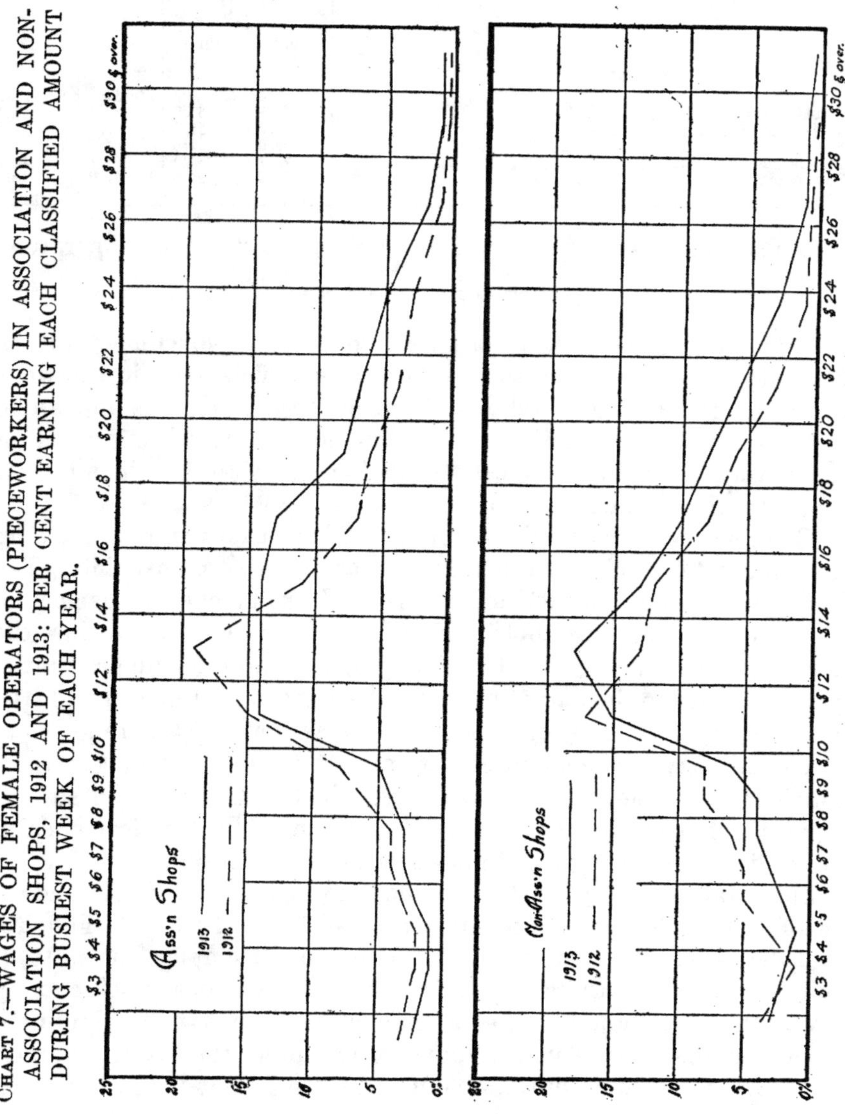

CHART 7.—WAGES OF FEMALE OPERATORS (PIECEWORKERS) IN ASSOCIATION AND NON-ASSOCIATION SHOPS, 1912 AND 1913: PER CENT EARNING EACH CLASSIFIED AMOUNT DURING BUSIEST WEEK OF EACH YEAR.

general this change was will be seen from the following summary. The proportion of women week workers receiving $10 a week and over in 1912 and in 1913 and the proportion of women pieceworkers earning $10 and over in the busiest week of the years 1912 and 1913 follows.

TABLE 25.—PER CENT OF WOMEN WEEK WORKERS AND PIECEWORKERS RECEIVING $10 A WEEK AND OVER 1912, AND 1913.

	Week workers receiving $10 or more per week.		Pieceworkers earning $10 or more per week.	
	1912	1913	1912	1913
	Per cent.	*Per cent.*	*Per cent.*	*Per cent.*
Industry as a whole	54.8	60.8	67.1	78.1
Association A	43.8	51.1	65.0	74.4
Nonassociation A	45.0	52.4	54.8	71.9
Association B	75.1	81.9	71.1	83.2
Nonassociation B	76.9	84.6	72.8	84.6

Similar changes have occurred in the earnings of the men operators.

BUTTONHOLE MAKERS.

Buttonholes are made on a special buttonhole machine. In the majority of shops one buttonhole maker is sufficient to do the work on all the garments in the shop. In most of the shops it is impossible to keep a buttonhole maker busy all the time and he is employed on other work when there is no buttonhole making to do. The largest shops employ from one to three buttonhole makers.

There are two types of buttonhole-making machines, one made by the Singer Co. and the other known as the Reece machine. The Reece is a very rapid machine and is used on the cheaper garments. The skill of the buttonhole maker lies not only in operating the machine and in being able to space properly the buttonholes on the garment, but in his ability to do the necessary repairing of the machine, which is subject to frequent breakdowns. Where girls are employed they are not expected to attend to this part of the work, which falls on the machinist employed in the factory. In several shops the buttonhole maker acts also as a machinist and attends to the ordinary repairing of all machines on the premises.

The total number of workers found recorded as buttonhole makers on the pay rolls of the different firms was 145 in 1913. Although a considerable proportion of the 520 shops do not employ any buttonhole makers at all, there are, on the other hand, shops which employ two or three buttonhole makers. It is probable that the total number of buttonhole makers in the industry is double the above number, those not reported as buttonhole makers being included in the group "operators not specified;" in this group were included all workers designated on the pay rolls as "operators" but concerning whose particular work the agents of the wage scale board could obtain no information. Since in the majority of shops the buttonhole maker is employed on other work also, it is but natural that he should be entered on the pay roll as "operator" instead of buttonhole maker.

SEX.

As will be seen from Table 9, of the 145 buttonhole makers reported in 1913, 79 were men and 66 women, this being one of the few occupations in the dress and waist industry in which the number of men exceeds that of women.

WAGES.

As will be seen from Table 11, the extent of piecework has been increased considerably among buttonhole makers; in 1912 the week workers constituted 60 per cent and the pieceworkers 40 per cent, while in 1913 the pieceworkers were nearly one-half of the total or 48 per cent, and the week workers 52 per cent.

Week workers.—Among the buttonhole makers working by the week, as will be seen from Table 26 which follows, the wages in 1913 ranged from $6 to $14 and over among the women, and from $8 to $25 a week and over among the men. Of the 31 men working by the week the great majority earned $12 and less than $20 a week. Of the 45 women more than half earned $9 and less than $14 a week. Among both men and women there was an increase in the number of people receiving the higher rates of wages and a reduction in the number of those receiving the lower rates.

Pieceworkers.—Among women pieceworkers the lowest earnings during the busiest week in 1913 were less than $3 while the highest were in the group $22.50 and under $25; the men earned from less than $3 a week to $30 a week and over; 25, or over one-half of the men, earned $18 a week and over; 15, or about one-third of the men, earned $10 and under $18 a week. About half of the women earned $9 and under $14 a week. The same tendency toward an increase in the number of those receiving higher rates of wages since the protocol went into effect is noticeable among the pieceworkers as among the week workers. In view of the small number no conclusions can be drawn as to the difference in wages in the nonassociation and association shops.

TABLE 26.—NUMBER OF BUTTONHOLE MAKERS (WEEK WORKERS AND PIECEWORKERS) RECEIVING EACH CLASSIFIED RATE OF WAGES OR EARNINGS PER WEEK, 1912 AND 1913, BY SEX.

Classified rates of wages or earnings per week, and classes of shops.	Week workers receiving each classified rate of wages.				Pieceworkers earning each classified amount during busiest week of year.			
	Females.		Males.		Females.		Males.	
	1912	1913	1912	1913	1912	1913	1912	1913
Under $3	1					1	1	2
$3 to $3.99					2			
$4 to $4.99	1					1	2	2
$5 to $5.99					2	2	2	1
$6 to $6.99	3	1				1	1	
$7 to $7.99	7	3	1		1	1	1	1
$8 to $8.99	7	7		2	4	1	2	2
$9 to $9.99	7	8	1	1	5	2	2	
$10 to $11.99	11	11	3	1	2	5	3	5
$12 to $13.99	9	13	7	7		3	3	1
$14 to $15.99		2	5	8		2	4	5
$16 to $17.99			4	4	1	1	1	4
$18 to $19.99			2	6			2	7
$20 to $22.49							2	5
$22.50 to $24.99						1		8
$25 to $27.49				2			1	2
$27.50 to $29.99							1	1
$30 and over			1				1	2
Total	46	45	24	31	17	21	29	48
	Workers in specified classes of shops.							
Association A	33	24	21	22	10	9	14	25
Association B	9	15	3	3	6	8	3	2
Nonassociation A	4	6		6		2	12	21
Nonassociation B					1	2		

BUTTON SEWERS.

What has been said about the number of buttonhole makers applies also to button sewers. Only 155 persons were found on the pay rolls under the latter designation. Button sewing is a much easier operation to learn than buttonhole making. The women predominate in this, there being 136 women and only 19 men button sewers, and the rates of wages are less than for buttonhole making. Week work is much more common than piecework. In 1912, 78.4 per cent of the women button sewers were week workers and 21.6 per cent pieceworkers. In 1913 the proportion of week workers was still greater, being 83.1 per cent as against 16.9 per cent of pieceworkers. This was due to the fact that the number of week workers increased much faster than that of pieceworkers, the week workers having increased from 81 in 1912 to 127 in 1913, while the pieceworkers increased from 22 to only 28 during the same period.

WAGES.

As will be seen from Table 27, which follows, the largest single group of button sewers were the women week workers, who in 1913 numbered 113 out of a total of 155, or 72.9 per cent. The wages of these women week workers ranged from $4 to less than $16 a week; 15 per cent of these earned less than $6 a week; 41.6 per cent earned $6 and less than $9 a week, and 43.4 per cent earned $9 a week and over. There was a noticeable increase in 1913 over 1912 in the proportion of those earning $9 a week and over and a corresponding decrease in the proportion of those receiving less than $9 a week. The earnings of the women pieceworkers do not differ much from those of the week workers. The wages of the few men employed in this trade are larger than those of the women.

TABLE 27.—NUMBER AND PER CENT OF BUTTON SEWERS (WEEK WORKERS AND PIECEWORKERS) RECEIVING EACH CLASSIFIED RATE OF WAGES OR EARNINGS PER WEEK, 1912 AND 1913, BY SEX.

Classified rates of wages or earnings per week, and classes of shops.	Week workers receiving each classified rate of wages.						Pieceworkers earning each classified amount during busiest week of year.			
	Females.				Males.[1]		Females.[1]		Males.[1]	
	Number.		Per cent.							
	1912	1913	1912	1913	1912	1913	1912	1913	1912	1913
Under $3								1		
$3 to $3.99							2	1		
$4 to $4.99	9	13	13.0	11.5			3			
$5 to $5.99	7	4	10.1	3.5		1	1	2		
$6 to $6.99	10	9	14.5	8.0		1	1	4		
$7 to $7.99	15	17	21.7	15.0			3	3	3	
$8 to $8.99	14	21	20.3	18.6			1		1	
$9 to $9.99	5	20	7.2	17.7	1	1	1			
$10 to $11.99	7	17	10.1	15.0	5	2	4	6	1	2
$12 to $13.99	2	11	2.9	9.7	2	6	1	3	1	1
$14 to $15.99		1		.9			2	3	1	
$16 to $17.99										1
$18 to $19.99										
$20 to $22.49										1
$22.50 to $24.99										1
$25 to $27.49										1
$27.50 to $29.99										1
Total	69	113	100.0	100.0	[2] 8	[3] 11	19	23	[4] 7	[5] 8
Association A	68	85			8	6	11	9	6	6
Association B							8	9	1	1
Nonassociation A	1	27				5		4		1
Nonassociation B		1						1		

[1] Percentages not computed on account of small number of employees.
[2] Not including 4 for whom earnings but not weekly rates of wages could be ascertained.
[3] Not including 3 for whom earnings but not weekly rates of wages could be ascertained.
[4] Including 4 week workers for whom earnings but not weekly rates of wages could be ascertained.
[5] Including 3 week workers for whom earnings but not weekly rates of wages could be ascertained.

CLOSERS AND HEMMERS.

The operation of closing consists in sewing together the front and back parts of the waist, forming the seam on each side of the waist. On cheap waists this work is done on the Union Special machine. This machine works very fast, and since it automatically cuts off the raw edge and finishes off the seam on the wrong side all in one operation, it offers the least expensive way of doing this work. Another machine is the Metropolitan, which automatically puts on a binding on the wrong side of the waist. On the better grade garments the so-called French seam is used, which involves three operations: First, the sewing together of the two parts of the waist on the right side; second, the cutting off of the raw edges; third, the turning over and sewing of the second seam on the wrong side. Some machines are equipped with a knife which automatically cuts off the raw edge, but most of the factories still do without the automatic knife, and scissors are employed instead.

The hemming consists in hemming the bottom of the waist by means of an attachment known as "the hemmer," which automatically turns the garment so that the turning in of the hem and the stitching it over is all done in one operation.

The number of closers and hemmers in 1913 is given in Table 8 at only 134, which is manifestly less than the total number employed in the shops, the majority of the closers and hemmers being included in the group "Operators not specified," for reasons explained under that head. The number of pieceworkers was practically the same both years, being 53 in 1912 and 56 in 1913 (Table 11). Week workers, on the other hand, increased from 51 to 78, which makes the proportion of pieceworkers smaller in 1913 than in 1912, namely, 42 per cent in 1913, as against 51 per cent in 1912. Of the 134 closers and hemmers reported, 104 were women and 30 were men.

SEX.

Most of the closers are women, while most of the hemmers are men, since speed is the chief consideration in hemming. Where the Metropolitan machine is used for closing, men are preferred because the machine is a very fast and complicated one and requires the handling of the binding tape at the same time when the sewing proper is being done.

Prior to the conclusion of the protocol, most of the closing and hemming was done by subcontractors. Since subcontracting has been prohibited under the protocol, the work is being done as a rule by two partners, who frequently have one assistant. Under this system one of the partners attends to the hemming and the other to the closing. If an assistant is employed in addition, the partner who does the closing puts in the first seam, leaving the assistant to cut off the raw edge and put in the second seam.

WAGES.

As will be seen from Table 28, in 1913, of the 64 women closers working by the week, 35, or nearly 55 per cent, received $10 and less than $18 a week; 28, or nearly 44 per cent, received less than $10; one-fourth of all the women received $6 and less than $9 a week; one-fourth received $12 and less than $18 a week. A little less than one-half received $9 and less than $12.

A slight change is noticeable in the earnings between 1912 and 1913, the most noticeable increase occurring in the proportion of those receiving from $9 to $9.99 a week.

The number of men workers and women workers working by the piece was too small to warrant any general conclusions. Details will be found in Table 28.

TABLE 28.—NUMBER OF CLOSERS AND HEMMERS (WEEK WORKERS AND PIECEWORKERS) RECEIVING EACH CLASSIFIED RATE OF WAGES OR EARNINGS PER WEEK, 1912 AND 1913, BY SEX.

Classified rates of wages or earnings per week, and classes of shops.	Week workers receiving each classified rate of wages.				Pieceworkers earning each classified amount during busiest week of year.			
	Females.		Males.		Females.		Males.	
	1912	1913	1912	1913	1912	1913	1912	1913
Under $3					1			
$3 to $3.99								
$4 to $4.99					3			
$5 to $5.99	2	2	1		2	2	1	
$6 to $6.99	3	5			4	3		
$7 to $7.99	5	2			3	4		
$8 to $8.99	2	9		1	6	4	1	
$9 to $9.99	3	10	1	2	4	6		1
$10 to $11.99	12	19	1	2	7	4		1
$12 to $13.99	6	7	2	2	7	6		1
$14 to $15.99	6	8	4	2	3	5	3	2
$16 to $17.99		1	2	2	4	1	1	4
$18 to $19.99		1		1		1	1	1
$20 to $22.49				2	1	3		2
$22.50 to $24.99							2	1
$25 to $27.49						1		1
$27.50 to $29.99								1
$30 and over								1
Total	[1] 39	64	11	14	[2] 45	40	9	16
	Workers in specified classes of shops.							
Association A	26	35	10	10	19	17	1	1
Association B	9	15		2	23	20	4	4
Nonassociation A	4	10	1	2	3	3	4	11
Nonassociation B		4						

[1] Not including 1 for whom earnings but not weekly rate of wages could be ascertained.
[2] Including 1 week worker for whom earnings but not weekly rate of wages could be ascertained.

DRESSMAKERS.

Dressmakers are operators of the highest skill, for they are required to make an entire dress including both the hand and machine sewing as well as the draping. Dressmakers are employed on high-grade dresses and gowns only. Most of the dressmakers employed have learned their trade in Europe. Those who have learned the trade in this country come into the industry fully apprenticed outside. Good dressmakers are promoted to positions of high-class examiners at wages running from $16 to $20 a week and of high-class drapers at similar wages.

Of late years, since cheap dresses have come to be produced in large quantities, operators engaged in making lingerie and cheap dresses have also come to be known as dressmakers. This class of dressmakers likewise works on the entire dress, but confines its work chiefly to machine operating, the hand sewing being done by the finishers and the draping by the drapers.

If we are to understand dressmaking in this broader sense, there are probably a few thousand of these workers, most of them appearing in Table 8 as "operators not specified," of whom 6,455 are given in that table (these are discussed more fully on pp. 99–104), while only 440 were found described as dressmakers on the pay rolls of the factories investigated.

SEX.

Women predominate among dressmakers. Of the 440 dressmakers reported for 1913, 350, or 80 per cent, were women and 90, or 20 per cent, were men. In high-grade dressmaking men are employed mostly on dresses of heavy material, such as velvets, serges, woolens, ratines, etc., while the women are employed on light materials, such as silks, chiffons, voiles, etc.

WAGES.

Of the 440 dressmakers found on the pay rolls for 1913, 369, or 84 per cent, worked by the piece and only 71, or 16 per cent, worked by the week. The percentage of pieceworkers in 1912, before the protocol went into effect, was somewhat less—namely, 81 per cent. As will be seen from Table 29, the largest single group of dressmakers consisted of women pieceworkers, of whom there were 294, or 67 per cent of the total. Of these 4.1 per cent were found earning less than $6 a week in 1913; 5.8 per cent earned $6 and less than $9 a week; 22.8 per cent, or almost one-fourth, earned less than $12; 19.7 per cent, or almost one-fifth, earned $20 a week and over; 57.5 per cent, or more than one-half, earned $12 and less than $20 a week.

The men pieceworkers' earnings are, as usual, much higher than those of the women. Thus, there were no men dressmakers earning less than $6 a week, 2.7 per cent earned $6 and less than $9 a week, or nearly one-half of the percentage of women. Of those earning $9 and less than $14 a week there were over 9 per cent among men as against more than 27 per cent among women. While only 20 per cent of the women pieceworkers earned $20 a week and over, 72 per cent of the men earned that amount. Both the men and the women pieceworkers show a higher percentage of workers in the higher-wage groups in 1913 as compared with 1912 and a lower percentage in the lower-wage groups.

The number of week workers both in 1912 and 1913 is too small to serve as the basis of any general conclusions. The details will be found in Table 29, which follows:

TABLE 29.—NUMBER AND PER CENT OF DRESSMAKERS (WEEK WORKERS AND PIECEWORKERS) RECEIVING EACH CLASSIFIED RATE OF WAGES OR EARNINGS PER WEEK, 1912 AND 1913, BY SEX.

Classified rates of wages or earnings per week, and classes of shops.	Week workers receiving each classified rate of wages.				Pieceworkers earning each classified amount during busiest week of year.							
	Females.[1]		Males.[1]		Females.				Males.			
					Number.		Per cent.		Number.		Per cent.	
	1912	1913	1912	1913	1912	1913	1912	1913	1912	1913	1912	1913
Under $3					5	4	1.8	1.4				
$3 to $3.99	1				1		.4					
$4 to $4.99					2	5	.7	1.7				
$5 to $5.99	1				7	3	2.5	1.0				
$6 to $6.99	1	1			7	4	2.5	1.4		1		1.3
$7 to $7.99	1	3			4	5	1.5	1.7	1	1	2.3	1.3
$8 to $8.99	3	2			11	8	3.9	2.7	1		2.3	
$9 to $9.99	4	2			17	11	6.2	3.7	2		4.5	
$10 to $11.99	18	10	1		40	27	14.4	9.2	1	5	2.3	6.7
$12 to $13.99	17	18	1	1	43	42	15.5	14.3	2	2	4.5	2.7
$14 to $15.99	8	7	1		41	50	14.8	17.0	2	1	4.5	1.3
$16 to $17.99	8	10		1	36	44	13.0	15.0	3	4	6.8	5.3
$18 to $19.99	3	1	2	11	24	33	8.7	11.2	2	7	4.5	9.3
$20 to $22.49	3	2	2	2	18	33	6.5	11.2	6	13	13.6	17.3
$22.50 to $24.99					14	17	5.0	5.8	2	8	4.5	10.7
$25 to $27.49					4	3	1.5	1.0	6	8	13.6	10.7
$27.50 to $29.99					2	3	.7	1.0	3	7	6.8	9.3
$30 and over					1	2	.4	.7	13	18	29.5	24.0
Total	68	56	7	15	277	294	100.0	100.0	44	75	100.0	100.0
	Workers in specified classes of shops.											
Association A	34	37	4	5	69	132			12	49		
Association B	14	11			195	151			15	21		
Nonassociation A	13	7	3	10	10	1			14	2		
Nonassociation B	7	1			3	10			3	3		

[1] Percentages not computed on account of small number of employees.

HEMSTITCHERS.

The hemstitching machine is one of the most difficult to operate. Instead of the one needle which the operator has to watch in an ordinary sewing machine, there are two needles and the so-called "plunger," which makes the holes in the material that is hemstitched. It requires great skill and patience to operate the machine and to handle the material. At every turn and change of direction the threads easily get tangled, and the machine breaks down frequently. As hemstitching is always done for decorative purposes, it generally takes the form of intricate designs, curves, and other figures, which are frequently carried out on the edge of laces or fine embroideries.

Most of the hemstitchers graduate into that work after they have been operating a machine or doing simpler kinds of work, such as repairing, lace running, etc. In some cases, girls who show sufficient intelligence are put to work on a hemstitching machine from the very start and are taught the trade. It takes about a week to train a worker to handle a hemstitching machine. The skill of the worker, however, naturally increases as time goes on, resulting in an increase of output as well as in better work.

Only a few shops, comparatively, employ hemstitchers. In most shops, there is insufficient work to keep a hemstitching machine busy all the time, and the hemstitching is contracted out to special shops.

SEX.

The peculiarity of the hemstitcher's occupation, as just explained, makes it distinctly a woman's trade, for, as explained before in discussing the work of operators, men, as a rule, are more adapted for work which requires either greater physical endurance or speed. Of the 180 hemstitchers reported for 1913 only 10 were men.

WAGES.

The nature of the hemstitcher's work is not favorable to compensation on a piece basis. It is impossible for an operator to do the work any faster than the machine and the character of the work will permit. Patience and skill are the chief requirements. There is, therefore, a general consensus of opinion in the trade, both among the workers and the employers, that hemstitchers should be paid on a weekly basis. Therefore, although no provision has been made in the protocol for a minimum weekly rate, more than eight-tenths of all the hemstitchers were employed on a weekly basis, the exact proportion in 1913 being 86 per cent of week workers and 14 per cent of pieceworkers. Of the 180 hemstitchers, only 8 were found employed in nonassociation shops. Of the 172 hemstitchers employed in the association shops, 155 were week workers (including 7 men) and 25 were pieceworkers (including 3 men). The bulk of the hemstitchers were, therefore, women week workers whose wages will now be considered.

As will be seen from Table 30, the largest single group among the women week workers were those receiving $12 and less than $14 a week, who constituted 33.8 per cent, or one-third, of all the women week workers. Over one-fourth of the women received $10 and less than $12 a week; over 9 per cent of the women received $9 and less than $10 a week; over 12 per cent received $6 and less than $9; 2 girls received less than $6 a week, and 26 women, constituting less than 18 per cent of the total, received $14 a week and over.

As in the case of most other workers, the hemstitchers show a decided improvement in wages since the protocol went into effect. The percentage of those receiving $6 and less than $10 a week declined from 25.9 per cent to 21.5 per cent; and of those getting from $10 to $11.99 from nearly 39 per cent to less than 26 per cent.

On the other hand, the percentage of those getting from $12 to $13.99 increased from 21.5 per cent to 33.8 per cent, and of those receiving $14 a week and over from 8.6 per cent to 17.6 per cent. Further details as to the earnings of hemstitchers will be found in Table 30.

TABLE 30.—NUMBER AND PER CENT OF HEMSTITCHERS (WEEK WORKERS AND PIECEWORKERS) RECEIVING EACH CLASSIFIED RATE OF WAGES OR EARNINGS PER WEEK, 1912 AND 1913, BY SEX.

Classified rates of wages or earnings per week, and classes of shops.	Week workers receiving each classified rate of wages.						Pieceworkers earning each classified amount during busiest week of year.			
	Females.				Males.[1]		Females.[1]		Males.[1]	
	Number.		Per cent.							
	1912	1913	1912	1913	1912	1913	1912	1913	1912	1913
Under $3	......	......	......	......	......	......	......	1	......	......
$3 to $3.99	......	......	......	......	......	......	......	......	......	......
$4 to $4.99	2	1	2.1	0.7	......	......	......	......	......	......
$5 to $5.99	3	1	3.2	.7	......	......	......	1	......	......
$6 to $6.99	5	4	5.4	2.7	......	......	......	1	......	......
$7 to $7.99	4	5	4.3	3.4	......	1	......	2	......	......
$8 to $8.99	9	9	9.7	6.0	......	......	1	1	......	......
$9 to $9.99	6	14	6.5	9.4	......	......	......	......	......	......
$10 to $11.99	36	38	38.7	25.7	......	......	......	6	......	1
$12 to $13.99	20	50	21.5	33.8	1	3	2	2	......	......
$14 to $15.99	7	20	7.5	13.5	1	2	1	4	......	1
$16 to $17.99	1	5	1.1	3.4	......	1	......	1	......	......
$18 to $19.99	......	1	......	.7	......	......	......	2	......	......
$20 to $22.49	......	......	......	......	......	......	1	1	......	......
$22.50 to $24.99	......	......	......	......	......	......	......	......	......	1
Total	93	148	100.0	100.0	2	7	5	22	......	3
	Workers in specified classes of shops.									
Association A	14	27	......	......	......	1	1	6	......	3
Association B	75	115	......	......	2	4	4	16	......	......
Nonassociation A	1	1	......	......	......	......	......	......	......	......
Nonassociation B	3	5	......	......	......	2	......	......	......	......

[1] Percentages not computed on account of small number of employees.

LACE RUNNERS.

Lace running is one of the least skilled occupations among the operators. It is the first work given to young girls who are put to work at a machine. The work of "lace running" consists in joining strips of lace to strips of cloth or other lace of various widths. Most lace running is done in long strips which may run into the hundreds of yards, but there is also considerable work done on short pieces which go into individual waists. The skill of the lace runner consists in handling the lace carefully and running the material and the lace in such a manner that the machine is operated steadily without a break and so that the unraveling of the lace and the cloth, which are wound up in rolls, takes place almost automatically without requiring the stopping of the machine on the part of the operator.

Although it takes only a few days to learn lace running, the operator acquires greater skill and therefore greater productive capacity in the course of time, which accounts for the fact that the wages of lace runners vary all the way from $5 to $16 a week and over.

SEX.

Practically all the lace running is done by girls. Of the 113 lace runners reported in Table 8, only 10 were men, the remainder being girls.

WAGES.

Most lace runners are paid by the week. Of the 113 reported, as will be seen from Table 11, four-fifths were week workers in 1913. In 1912 only 17 per cent were pieceworkers.

As will be seen from Table 31, which follows, more than one-half of the 83 women lace runners paid by the week received $10 and less than $14 a week. More than one-tenth received $14 a week and over. Nearly one-fifth of the workers received $6 and less than $9; 2 lace runners received less than $6 a week. Of the 7 men lace runners, 1 received from $8 to $8.99 a week and 6 received $14 and less than $18 a week. The earnings of the pieceworkers as well as further details as to the week workers will be found in Table 31.

Both the week workers and the pieceworkers show a marked increase since the protocol went into effect in the number of those earning $9 and less than $20 a week, with a corresponding decline in the number of those receiving less than $9.

TABLE 31.—NUMBER OF LACE RUNNERS (WEEK WORKERS AND PIECEWORKERS) RECEIVING EACH CLASSIFIED RATE OF WAGES OR EARNINGS PER WEEK, 1912 AND 1913, BY SEX.

Classified rates of wages or earnings per week, and classes of shops.	Week workers receiving each classified rate of wages.				Pieceworkers earning each classified amount during busiest week of year.			
	Females.		Males.		Females.		Males.	
	1912	1913	1912	1913	1912	1913	1912	1913
$3 to $3.99	......	......	......	......	2	......	......	......
$4 to $4.99	3	1	......	......	1	......	......	......
$5 to $5.99	1	1	1	......	1	......	......	......
$6 to $6.99	13	2	......	......	......	......	......	......
$7 to $7.99	12	7	......	......	1	1	......	......
$8 to $8.99	7	7	......	1	2	1	......	......
$9 to $9.99	8	14	......	......	1	3	......	......
$10 to $11.99	8	21	2	......	3	5	......	......
$12 to $13.99	19	21	......	......	......	4	......	......
$14 to $15.99	7	6	2	4	1	1	......	1
$16 to $17.99	......	3	1	2	2	2	......	1
$18 to $19.99	......	......	1	......	......	2	......	......
$20 to $22.49	......	......	1	......	3	1	......	1
Total	8	83	8	7	17	20	......	3
	Workers in specified classes of shops.							
Association A	52	57	1	3	14	18	......	......
Association B	23	25	6	2	3	......	......	2
Nonassociation A	3	1	1	2	......	2	......	1

SAMPLE MAKERS.

Sample makers are operators who are engaged in making samples of new garments from models furnished by the designer. They also assist the designer in the preparation of new models. This work naturally calls for operators of the highest skill. Most of the sample makers are experienced dressmakers or waist operators and are drawn from those classes of workers. Sample makers who have acquired considerable experience in their work and have a bent for original designing graduate into designers.

SEX.

Practically all sample makers are women. Of the 580 sample makers reported in Table 9 for 1913, only 21, or 3.6 per cent, were men.

WAGES.

The nature of the sample maker's work makes the piece-rate system impractical. Of the 580 sample makers only 8 were found to be doing piecework in 1913. As will be seen from Table 32, the largest single group of sample makers were those receiving $14 and less than $16 a week, most of whom received the minimum protocol rate of $14. This group constituted more than 42 per cent of the total. Those getting $16 and less than $20 a week exceeded 27 per cent of the total. The number of those receiving less than the protocol rate of $14 a week exceeded 26 per cent of the total. The number of those receiving less than $6 a week was very small, amounting to 1.5 per cent of all the sample makers. The number of those receiving $20 a week and over was nearly 4 per cent of the total.

An examination of the figures showing the wages of sample makers in the four branches of the industry shows that, in each case, the largest number falls in the group of $14 and less than $16 a week with the exception of the nonassociation B shops in which the largest number is in the group of $18 and less than $20 a week. However, the number of sample makers in the nonassociation shops is so small as hardly to warrant any general conclusions.

The figures in the two columns of Table 32 showing the percentage of the total number of sample makers receiving different rates of wages in 1912 and 1913 and Chart 8 which presents these figures in graphic form are very instructive. The largest group both in 1912 and 1913 consisted of employees receiving $14 and under $16 a week, the minimum protocol rate being $14, but the percentage in this group was much larger in 1913 than in 1912, being nearly 43 per cent in 1913 and only 30 per cent in 1912. In 1912 the percentage receiving $12 and under $14 was almost as high as for those receiving $14 and under $16, being nearly 28 per cent, but fell to a little over 15 per cent in 1913. Beginning with the $14 rate the figures, in all cases but one, show a larger percentage of sample makers receiving the higher rates in 1913 as compared with 1912. The reverse is true of those receiving rates below $14 a week where the 1913 percentages are in nearly all cases below those in 1912.

TABLE 32.—NUMBER AND PER CENT OF SAMPLE MAKERS, FEMALE, WEEK WORKERS,[1] RECEIVING EACH CLASSIFIED RATE OF WAGES PER WEEK, 1912 AND 1913, BY CLASS OF SHOPS.

NUMBER.

Classified rates of wages per week.	Association A.		Nonassociation A.[2]		Association B.		Nonassociation B.[2]		Total.	
	1912	1913	1912	1913	1912	1913	1912	1913	1912	1913
$4 to $4.99					4	3			4	3
$5 to $5.99		1			4	4			4	5
$6 to $6.99			1		1	3			2	3
$7 to $7.99	2				1	1	1		4	1
$8 to $8.99	1	2	1		7	3			9	5
$9 to $9.99	6	2	1		13	13	1		21	15
$10 to $11.99	11	9	5	1	20	17		1	36	28
$12 to $13.99	43	25	6	1	95	55	1	2	145	83
$14 to $15.99	56	94	4	20	91	113	6	5	157	232
$16 to $17.99	22	30	5	5	50	48	3	8	80	91
$18 to $19.99	10	19	1	2	32	25	2	11	45	57
$20 to $22.49	2	5			7	5	2	6	11	16
$22.50 to $24.99	1						1	2	2	2
$25 to $27.49					2	1	1	3	3	4
Total	154	187	24	29	327	291	18	38	[3] 523	[4] 545

PER CENT.

Classified rates of wages per week.	Association A. 1912	Association A. 1913	Nonassociation A. 1912	Nonassociation A. 1913	Association B. 1912	Association B. 1913	Nonassociation B. 1912	Nonassociation B. 1913	Total 1912	Total 1913
$4 to $4.99					1.2	1.0			0.8	0.6
$5 to $5.99		0.5			1.2	1.3			.8	.9
$6 to $6.99					.3	1.0			.4	.6
$7 to $7.99	1.3				.3	.3			.8	.2
$8 to $8.99	.6	1.0			2.1	1.0			1.7	.9
$9 to $9.99	3.9	1.0			4.0	4.5			4.0	2.8
$10 to $11.99	7.2	4.8			6.1	5.9			6.9	5.1
$12 to $13.99	28.0	13.4			29.1	19.0			27.8	15.3
$14 to $15.99	36.4	50.3			27.9	38.9			30.0	42.6
$16 to $17.99	14.2	16.1			15.3	16.5			15.3	16.7
$18 to $19.99	6.5	10.2			9.8	8.6			8.6	10.5
$20 to $22.49	1.3	2.7			2.1	1.7			2.1	2.9
$22.50 to $24.99	.6								.4	.3
$25 to $27.49					.6	.3			.6	.7
Total	100.0	100.0			100.0	100.0			100.0	100.0

SUMMARY OF PERCENTAGES.

Classified rates of wages per week.	Association A. 1912	Association A. 1913	Nonassociation A. 1912	Nonassociation A. 1913	Association B. 1912	Association B. 1913	Nonassociation B. 1912	Nonassociation B. 1913	Total 1912	Total 1913
Under $14	41.0	20.7			44.3	34.0			43.0	26.4
$14 to $15.99	36.4	50.3			27.9	38.9			30.0	42.6
$16 and over	22.6	29.0			27.8	27.1			27.0	31.2
Total	100.0	100.0			100.0	100.0			100.0	100.0

[1] In addition to the week workers shown in this table there were 2 pieceworkers, female, and 1 pieceworker, male, in 1912, and 8 pieceworkers, female, in 1913.
[2] Percentages not computed on account of small number of employees.
[3] Not including 17 week workers, female, and 14 week workers, male, for whom weekly rates of wages could not be ascertained.
[4] Not including 6 week workers, female, and 21 week workers, male, for whom weekly rates of wages could not be ascertained.

SKIRT OPERATORS.

The work of skirt operators consists chiefly in sewing together parts of skirts in long vertical seams and, the work being quite simple, the quantity of output is the chief consideration. This enables men to compete to a large extent with women in this trade, especially in making skirts of heavy materials. In lingerie dresses, where the material is light and where there is a good deal of lace inserting to be done, women are fully as competent as men and in many cases are preferred. A skirt operator is apprenticed usually by working as assistant to an experienced operator. He is first shown how to make the simpler seams on the wrong side of the skirt and

CHART 8.—PER CENT OF SAMPLE MAKERS, FEMALE (WEEK WORKERS) RECEIVING EACH CLASSIFIED RATE OF WAGES PER WEEK, 1912 AND 1913.

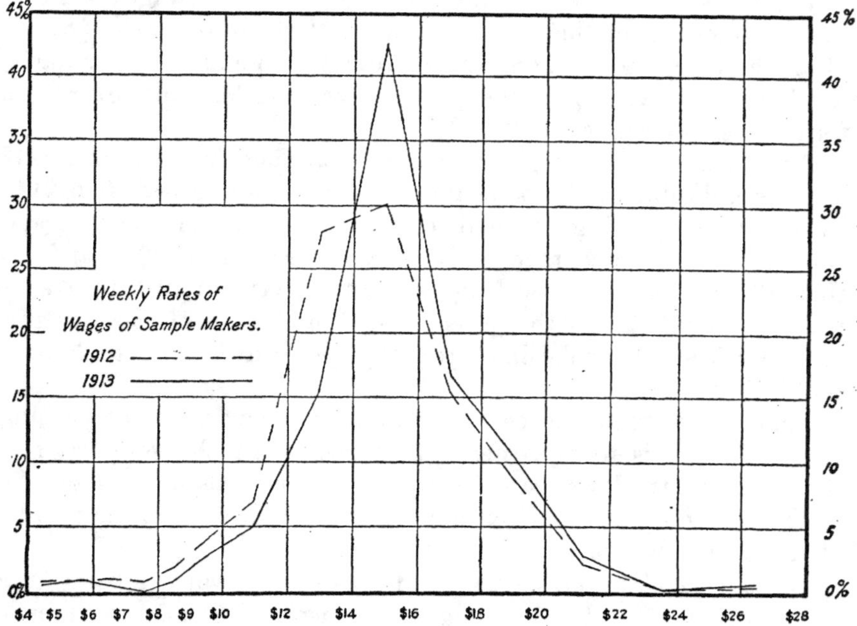

gradually is taught the more difficult parts of the work. It takes about the length of a season to train a fairly skilled skirt operator.

SEX.

Of the 399 skirt operators reported for 1913, 228, or a little over 57 per cent, were women and 171, or almost 43 per cent, were men.

WAGES.

Speed being the chief factor in making skirts, it is natural that the work should be paid by the piece. During 1913 two-thirds of all the skirt operators reported were paid by the piece. In 1912 the percentage of piece workers was slightly larger, namely, 72 per cent.

Of the 399 skirt operators, 340, or 85 per cent, were employed in association shops and only 59, or 15 per cent, in nonassociation shops.

Earnings of pieceworkers.—As will be seen from Table 33, over 51 per cent, or more than one-half of the 170 women paid by the piece, earned from $18 a week to $30 a week or over during the busiest week of 1913; more than one-fifth of all the women pieceworkers earned from $22.50 to $24.99; 17.5 per cent, or about one-sixth, earned $9 and less than $14 a week; only 3 per cent earned less than $9 a week.

The proportion of men earning the higher rates of wages was even higher than that of the women. Nearly three-fourths (73 per cent) of all the men pieceworkers earned from $18 to $30 and over during the busiest week; the number of those earning less than $9 a week formed less than 4 per cent of the total.

Comparing the earnings of men pieceworkers in 1912 and 1913, there is a decline in the percentage of those earning less than $14 a week. Those earning $14 and less than $18 a week show practically the same percentage both years; those earning $18 and less than $25 a week increased from over 34 per cent in 1912 to over 52 per cent in 1913. On the other hand, the number of those earning $25 a week and over declined from 29.5 per cent in 1912 to 20.6 per cent in 1913.

Among the women pieceworkers, similar changes in the earnings occurred; that is to say, there was a decline in the proportion of those earning the lower rates of wages and an increase in the number of those earning the medium amounts and a decline in the number of those earning $25 a week or more.

Wages of week workers.—The number of week workers being comparatively small, only 58 among the women and 64 among the men, no general conclusions can be drawn. It is interesting to note, however, that of the 64 men week workers, 38, or more than one-half, received from $16 to $22.49 a week; 18, or more than one-fourth, received $20 a week and over. Only 1 received $4 and less than $5 a week and 2 received $6 and less than $7 a week.

Of the 58 women week workers, 22 received $9 and less than $14; 15 received $14 and less than $18 a week; 4 girls received less than $6 a week, and 14 received $6 and less than $9. Further details as to the wages of skirt operators will be found in Table 33.

TABLE 33.—NUMBER AND PER CENT OF SKIRT OPERATORS (WEEK WORKERS AND PIECEWORKERS) RECEIVING EACH CLASSIFIED RATE OF WAGES OR EARNINGS PER WEEK, 1912 AND 1913, BY SEX.

Classified rates of wages or earnings per week, and classes of shops.	Week workers receiving each classified rate of wages.				Pieceworkers earning each classified amount during busiest week of year.							
	Females.[1]		Males.[1]		Females.				Males.			
					Number.		Per cent.		Number.		Per cent.	
	1912	1913	1912	1913	1912	1913	1912	1913	1912	1913	1912	1913
Under $3					11	1	6.1	0.6		1		0.9
$3 to $3.99			2									
$4 to $4.99		2		1								
$5 to $5.99	1	2			3		1.7		1		2.3	
$6 to $6.99	4	2	1	2	5	2	2.8	1.2	1	2	2.3	1.8
$7 to $7.99	4	8				1		.6	1		2.3	
$8 to $8.99	5	4	2		5	1	2.8	.6	1	1	2.3	.9
$9 to $9.99	8	5		1	6		3.3					
$10 to $11.99	15	8		3	14	10	7.8	5.8	2	3	4.5	2.8
$12 to $13.99	9	9	6	5	19	20	10.5	11.7	3	5	6.8	4.7
$14 to $15.99	5	9	9	9	21	18	11.7	10.6	3	9	6.8	8.4
$16 to $17.99	1	6	6	15	12	30	6.6	17.6	4	8	9.1	7.5
$18 to $19.99			7	10	23	18	12.8	10.6	5	21	11.4	19.7
$20 to $22.49		3	3	13	13	21	7.2	12.4	7	23	15.9	21.5
$22.50 to $24.99				1	30	36	16.7	21.2	3	12	6.8	11.2
$25 to $27.49				3	10	7	5.5	4.1	7	12	15.9	11.2
$27.50 to $29.99				1	5	4	2.8	2.4	4	5	9.1	4.7
$30 and over			1		3	1	1.7	.6	2	5	4.5	4.7
Total	52	[2] 58	37	64	180	[3] 170	100.0	100.0	44	107	100.0	100.0
	Workers in specified classes of shops.											
Association A	46	26	21	34	42	69			24	80		
Association B	5	10	13	11	138	101			18	9		
Nonassociation A	1	20	3	15								
Nonassociation B		2		4					2	18		

[1] Percentages not computed on account of small number of employees.
[2] Not including 11 for whom earnings but not weekly rates of wages could be ascertained.
[3] Including 11 week workers for whom earnings but not weekly rates of wages could be ascertained.

SLEEVE MAKERS.

It takes about the same kind of skill in making sleeves as in making waists. Sleeve makers and waist or body makers are regarded as operators of equal skill and practically equal earning capacity. It takes about the length of a season to train a sleeve maker, although he or she, no doubt, continues to gain in skill as time goes on. The chief skill of the sleeve maker is in sewing the lace and trimmings to the material of which the waist is made. Experienced sleeve makers sometimes graduate into waist makers and trimmers.

SEX.

Of the 344 sleeve makers reported for 1913, only 44 were men; 300, or 87 per cent, were women.

WAGES.

The sleeve makers work almost equally on a piece and a week basis (Table 11). In 1913, 54 per cent, or a little over one-half of all the sleeve makers, were week workers and 46 per cent were pieceworkers. The number of pieceworkers increased considerably in 1913, for in 1912 they numbered only 35 per cent of all the sleeve makers.

The largest single group of sleeve makers in 1913 were the women week workers, who numbered 173. Of these, as will be seen from Table 34, nearly one-fourth received $7 and less than $8 a week; a little over 28 per cent received $8 and less than $10 a week; a little over one-fifth received less than $7. Nine girls received less than $6 a week.

In 1912 there were 23 girls receiving less than $6 a week. In general, there was a reduction in the number of those receiving less than $7 a week and a slight increase in the proportion of those receiving $7 a week and over.

The next largest group were the women pieceworkers, who numbered 127 in 1913. Of these, 21.3 per cent, or a little over one-fifth, earned $10 and less than $12 during the busiest week in 1913; 21.9 per cent earned $8 and less than $10; and 23.6 per cent earned $12 and less than $16. The number of these receiving $16 a week and over constituted 12.7 per cent; 9.5 per cent earned less than $6. As compared with 1912, there was an increase in the percentage of those earning $12 a week and over. The percentage of those earning $10 and less than $12 a week remained the same, and of those earning under $10 a week declined from 57 in 1912 to 42 in 1913.

The number of male sleeve makers, both week workers and pieceworkers, is too small to require any discussion of their wages. The figures will be found in Table 34.

TABLE 34.—NUMBER AND PER CENT OF SLEEVE MAKERS (WEEK WORKERS AND PIECEWORKERS) RECEIVING EACH CLASSIFIED RATE OF WAGES OR EARNINGS PER WEEK, 1912 AND 1913, BY SEX.

Classified rates of wages or earnings per week, and classes of shops.	Week workers receiving each classified rate of wages.						Pieceworkers earning each classified amount during busiest week of year.					
	Females.				Males.[1]		Females.				Males.[1]	
	Number.		Per cent.		1912	1913	Number.		Per cent.		1912	1913
	1912	1913	1912	1913			1912	1913	1912	1913		
Under $3							2	1	3.1	0.8		
$3 to $3.99	1	2	0.7	1.2	1	1		1		.8		
$4 to $4.99	8	3	5.5	1.7			2	3	3.1	2.4		
$5 to $5.99	14	4	9.7	2.3			7	7	10.8	5.5		
$6 to $6.99	29	26	20.1	15.0			1	7	1.6	5.5		2
$7 to $7.99	24	43	16.7	24.8		2	3	7	4.6	5.5		
$8 to $8.99	17	25	11.8	14.5		1	9	13	13.8	10.1	2	1
$9 to $9.99	26	24	18.0	13.9		1	13	15	20.0	11.8	1	
$10 to $11.99	15	25	10.5	14.5	2		14	27	21.5	21.3	4	4
$12 to $13.99	3	11	2.1	6.4	4	3	6	15	9.2	11.8	2	5
$14 to $15.99	4	5	2.8	2.9	2	3	2	15	3.1	11.8	1	5
$16 to $17.99	1	3	.7	1.7	2	1	4	8	6.2	6.3	3	3
$18 to $19.99	1		.7				1	6	1.5	4.5	1	6
$20 to $22.49		1		.6			1	1	1.5	.5	4	4
$22.50 to $24.99	1		.7									
$25 to $27.49												
$27.50 to $29.99								1		.8		2
$30 and over		1		.6								
Total	144	173	100.0	100.0	11	12	65	127	100.0	100.0	18	32
	Workers in specified classes of shops.											
Association A	96	93			8	10	35	79			12	20
Association B	14	14			1	1	15	19			4	3
Nonassociation A	31	61			2	1	4	18				9
Nonassociation B	3	5					11	11			2	

[1] Percentages not computed on account of small number of employees.

SLEEVE SETTERS.

The work of the sleeve setter consists in sewing the sleeves to the waists. There are two ways of doing this work. In the waists which were in style prior to 1913, the sleeves were closed by the sleeve maker and set into the armhole of the waist by the sleeve setter. The setting of the closed sleeve requires great skill. As a rule, the sleeve is larger than the armhole and while it is being set into the waist it has to be gathered into folds, the sleeve setter knowing practically by instinct just how much to gather in so that the sleeve will fit perfectly into the armhole and will "hang right" from the body of the waist. The work is usually done on a Union Special machine, which with a knife attachment trims off the raw edges on the wrong side as fast as the sleeve is sewed on to the waist and then fells the seam. It is also done on a Metropolitan machine which automatically binds the seam on the wrong side instead of felling it.

In the style that has been in vogue since 1913 the sleeves are not closed before being attached to the waist, being sewed on to the body of the waist before being closed. The closer then closes the sleeves and the sides of the waist in one operation. The change in style left the sleeve setters with but little sleeve setting to do and they have been employed mostly on other work requiring the use of the Union Special machine.

SEX.

Of the 139 sleeve setters reported in 1913, 86, or 62 per cent, were women and 53 were men.

WAGES.

Of all the sleeve setters reported, 59 per cent were week workers and 41 per cent were pieceworkers. The proportion of pieceworkers has increased considerably, having constituted only 30 per cent during the preceding year. Taking the sleeve setters as reported for the entire industry for 1913, there were 57 women working by the week, 29 women working by the piece, 25 men working by the week, and 28 men working by the piece. These numbers are too small to justify any detailed conclusions as to the trend of wages.

It is interesting to note, however, that of the 57 women week workers, 40, or more than two-thirds of them, received $10 and less than $16 a week. None received less than $7 a week, while during the preceding year there were 4 girls receiving less than that amount. There was a decided reduction in the number of those receiving less than $10 a week and an increase from the preceding year in the number of those receiving the higher rates of wages.

Among the men sleeve setters, week workers, the lowest wage group reported in 1913 was $12 to $13.99 a week and the highest $27.50 to $29.99 a week, the men as a rule receiving higher wages than the women. This is ven more noticeable of the pieceworkers, where the men earned considerably in excess of the women. Further details as to the wages of sleeve setters will be found in Table 35.

TABLE 35.—NUMBER OF SLEEVE SETTERS (WEEK WORKERS AND PIECEWORKERS) RECEIVING EACH CLASSIFIED RATE OF WAGES OR EARNINGS PER WEEK, 1912 AND 1913, BY SEX.

Classified rates of wages or earnings per week, and classes of shops.	Week workers receiving each classified rate of wages.				Pieceworkers earning each classified amount during busiest week of year.			
	Females.		Males.		Females.		Males.	
	1912	1913	1912	1913	1912	1913	1912	1913
Under $3						1		
$3 to $3.99								
$4 to $4.99	1					1		
$5 to $5.99	1							
$6 to $6.99	2					2		
$7 to $7.99	5	1	1		1	1		
$8 to $8.99	2	5	1				1	
$9 to $9.99	14	8	1		3	3		
$10 to $11.99	8	13	1		2	5	3	5
$12 to $13.99	18	11		5	2	3		1
$14 to $15.99	4	16	7	8		5	1	1
$16 to $17.99		2	3	7	2	3	3	3
$18 to $19.99			1	3	1	3	2	1
$20 to $22.49		1		1			2	4
$22.50 to $24.99						1	4	8
$25 to $27.49			1			1	3	2
$27.50 to $29.99				1				2
$30 and over							1	1
Total	55	57	16	25	11	29	20	28
	Workers in specified classes of shops.							
Association A	30	24	11	16	7	23	11	13
Association B	5	12	5	6	2	2		1
Nonassociation A	8	18		3	2	4	9	14
Nonassociation B	12	3						

TRIMMERS.

Trimmers form the group of operators of the highest skill. Their work consists in sewing on the trimmings, laces, embroideries, silks, etc. It requires delicate touch, patience, and skill in handling delicate materials, such as laces, embroideries, chiffons, and nets. Girls are promoted to be trimmers after they have proved to be good waist or dress makers. It takes about the length of a season to learn trimming, but the trimmer gains in skill as she goes on working from season to season.

SEX.

The nature of a trimmer's work is such as to give women a decided advantage over men. Of the 634 trimmers reported for 1913, 612, or 96.5 per cent, were women and only 22, or 3.5 per cent, were men.

WAGES.

Wages of week workers.—The great majority of the female trimmers were found employed in association shops, only 37 being reported in the nonassociation shops, as will be seen from Table 36. Of the 333 women week workers the largest single group were those receiving $12 and less than $14 a week, these constituting about one-third of the entire number; the next largest single group were those receiving $10 and less than $12 who constituted a little less than 29 per cent of the total, these two groups making up more than one-half of all the women trimmers working by the week. A little over 14 per cent of the women received $14 a week and over and nearly one-fifth received under $9 a week. Three girls received under $6 a week.

Earnings of pieceworkers.—Of the 279 women pieceworkers, over 19 per cent, or nearly one-fifth, earned $14 and less than $16 during the busiest week of 1913. Nearly 34 per cent, or a little over one-third, earned $10 and less than $14 a week; over 16 per cent earned under $10 a week; a little less than 9 per cent, or nearly one-tenth, earned $18 and less than $20 a week, and the remaining 8.5 per cent earned $20 a week and over.

Comparison of wages in 1912 and 1913.—The wages of all classes of trimmers show a marked improvement since the protocol went into effect. In the case of the women trimmers working by the week, there is a general increase in the proportion of workers receiving $12 a week and over, who constituted 30 per cent of all the women week workers in 1912 and nearly 47 per cent in 1913, with a corresponding decline in the relative number of women week workers receiving less than $12 a week. In the case of women pieceworkers, a similar change has occurred, except that the increase begins not with the $12 but with the $14 a week workers. The proportion of those earning $14 a week and over was less than 19 per cent in 1912 and nearly 50 per cent in 1913, with a corresponding decline in the number of those earning under $14 a week.

TABLE 36.—NUMBER AND PER CENT OF TRIMMERS, FEMALE,[1] WEEK WORKERS, RECEIVING EACH CLASSIFIED RATE OF WAGES PER WEEK, 1912 AND 1913, BY CLASS OF SHOPS.

NUMBER.

Classified rates of wages per week.	Association A.		Nonassociation A.		Association B.		Nonassociation B.		Total.	
	1912	1913	1912	1913	1912	1913	1912	1913	1912	1913
$4 to $4.99	3				1				4	
$5 to $5.99	9	2			4	1			13	3
$6 to $6.99	7	3			4	5			11	8
$7 to $7.99	8	9		2	8	8			16	19
$8 to $8.99	11	11		1	14	23			25	35
$9 to $9.99	17	13	1	3		1			18	17
$10 to $11.99	43	43	5	9	54	43			102	95
$12 to $13.99	23	44	7	16	29	49			59	109
$14 to $15.99	4	14	5	5	6	17			15	36
$16 to $17.99		3			6	2			6	5
$18 to $19.99	1			1	2	3			3	4
$20 to $22.49		1				1				2
Total	126	143	18	37	128	153			[2] 272	[3] 333

[1] There were 8 trimmers, male, week workers, in 1912, and 9 in 1913.
[2] Not including 14, for whom earnings but not weekly rates of wages could be ascertained.
[3] Not including 10, for whom earnings but not weekly rates of wages could be ascertained.

TABLE 36.—NUMBER AND PER CENT OF TRIMMERS, FEMALE, WEEK WORKERS, RECEIVING EACH CLASSIFIED RATE OF WAGES PER WEEK, 1912 AND 1913, BY CLASS OF SHOPS—Concluded.

PER CENT.

Classified rates of wages per week.	Association A.		Nonassociation A.[1]		Association B.		Nonassociation B.[1]		Total.	
	1912	1913	1912	1913	1912	1913	1912	1913	1912	1913
$4 to $4.99	2.4				0.8				1.4	
$5 to $5.99	7.1	1.4			3.1	0.7			4.8	0.9
$6 to $6.99	5.6	2.1			3.1	3.3			4.0	2.4
$7 to $7.99	6.3	6.3			6.3	5.2			5.9	5.7
$8 to $8.99	8.7	7.6			10.9	15.0			9.2	10.5
$9 to $9.99	13.5	9.1				.7			6.6	5.1
$10 to $11.99	34.1	30.1			42.2	28.1			37.6	28.6
$12 to $13.99	18.3	30.8			22.6	32.0			21.7	32.7
$14 to $15.99	3.2	9.8			4.7	11.1			5.5	10.8
$16 to $17.99		2.1			4.7	1.3			2.2	1.5
$18 to $19.99	.8				1.6	1.9			1.1	1.2
$20 to $22.49		.7				.7				.6
Total	100.0	100.0			100.0	100.0			100.0	100.0

TABLE 37.—NUMBER AND PER CENT OF TRIMMERS, FEMALE,[2] PIECEWORKERS, EARNING EACH CLASSIFIED AMOUNT, DURING THE BUSIEST WEEK OF THE YEAR, 1912 AND 1913, BY CLASS OF SHOPS.

NUMBER.

Classified earnings per week.	Association A.		Nonassociation A.[1]		Association B.		Nonassociation B.[1]		Total.	
	1912	1913	1912	1913	1912	1913	1912	1913	1912	1913
Under $3	3	1			4	2			7	3
$3 to $3.99	2				3				5	
$4 to $4.99	7	1			3	2			10	3
$5 to $5.99	1	1			3	2			4	3
$6 to $6.99	6	3			9	3			15	6
$7 to $7.99	10	3			8	3			18	6
$8 to $8.99	12	6			11	4			23	10
$9 to $9.99	8	9			22	6	1		31	15
$10 to $11.99	18	24	1		38	21	1	3	58	48
$12 to $13.99	23	23			27	21	1	2	51	46
$14 to $15.99	11	26		1	10	27			21	54
$16 to $17.99	4	13			7	24			11	37
$18 to $19.99	1	6			6	18			7	24
$20 to $22.49		2			6	9			6	11
$22.50 to $24.99		2			4	7			4	9
$25 to $27.49					1	2			1	2
$27.50 to $29.99		1			1	1			1	2
$30 and over					1				1	
Total	106	121	1	1	164	152	3	5	[3] 274	[4] 279

PER CENT.

Classified earnings per week.	Association A.		Nonassociation A.[1]		Association B.		Nonassociation B.[1]		Total.	
	1912	1913	1912	1913	1912	1913	1912	1913	1912	1913
Under $3	2.9	0.8			2.4	1.3			2.6	1.0
$3 to $3.99	1.9				1.8				1.8	
$4 to $4.99	6.6	.8			1.8	1.3			3.6	1.0
$5 to $5.99	1.0	.8			1.8	1.3			1.5	1.0
$6 to $6.99	5.7	2.5			5.5	2.0			5.5	2.2
$7 to $7.99	9.4	2.5			4.9	2.0			6.6	2.2
$8 to $8.99	11.3	5.0			6.7	2.6			8.4	3.6
$9 to $9.99	7.5	7.4			13.4	3.9			11.3	5.4
$10 to $11.99	17.0	19.8			23.2	13.8			21.2	17.3
$12 to $13.99	21.7	19.0			16.5	13.8			18.6	16.5
$14 to $15.99	10.3	21.5			6.1	17.8			7.7	19.4
$16 to $17.99	3.7	10.7			4.3	15.8			4.0	13.3
$18 to $19.99	1.0	5.0			3.7	11.8			2.6	8.6
$20 to $22.49		1.7			3.7	5.9			2.2	3.9
$22 50 to $24.99		1.7			2.4	4.6			1.5	3.2
$25 to $27.49					.6	1.3			.3	.7
$27.50 to $29.99		.8			.6	.7			.3	.7
$30 and over					.6				.3	
Total	100.0	100.0			100.0	100.0			100.0	100.0

[1] Percentages not computed on account of small number of employees.
[2] There were 4 trimmers, male, pieceworkers, in 1912 and 13 in 1913.
[3] Including 14 week workers, for whom earnings but not weekly rates of wages could be ascertained.
[4] Including 10 week workers, for whom earnings but not weekly rates of wages could be ascertained.

TUCKERS.

Tucking consists of folding certain parts of the waist or cloth into plaits or tucks which are stitched down on the machine. Much of the tucking is so-called strip tucking consisting of the making of tucks on long strips of material which run sometimes into the hundreds of yards. The width of the tuck is regulated by the so-called knife, which is an attachment put on the machine for that purpose. The skill of the operator is in getting the cloth under the knife, guiding the cloth under the needle of the machine, in regulating the spaces between the rows of stitching, and in knowing how to handle the machine. More skill is required in "short tucking," which consists in making tucks of various lengths and widths on the body of the waist. This requires frequent starting and stopping of the machine and getting the waist under the machine, which can be easily damaged by an unskillful operator. Some of the tucking is done free hand without any knife to regulate the width of the tuck. This is especially the case with tucks on skirts which are made to taper from a considerable width at the waist line down to a point at the end of the tuck. Tucking of this kind requires the highest skill. There are a number of shops which do nothing but make tucking for other manufacturers, for the reason that in shops of moderate size there is not enough tucking to do to keep one or more tuckers busy continuously. This was especially the case in 1913, when tucking was not much in demand on account of changes in style and when tuckers were unemployed much of the time.

SEX.

Men formed a considerable proportion of the tuckers in 1913. Out of 875 tuckers, 248, or more than one-fourth, were men, and 627 were women.

WAGES.

About half of the tucking is done at piece rates; but contrary to the tendency observed in most of the other operating work, the proportion of pieceworkers has declined since the protocol went into effect. Thus, in 1913, 46 per cent, or less than one-half of all the tuckers, worked by the piece; while in 1912 the proportion of pieceworkers among tuckers was 54 per cent, or more than one-half.

Wages of week workers, women.—Among the women working by the week, the largest group, which numbered 125 women and constituted nearly 35 per cent of the total, received $12 and less than $14 a week; a little over one-fifth of the women received $14 and less than $16, and a little over one-fifth received $10 and less than $12, these three groups of women—that is, those receiving $10 and less than $16 a week—constituting 75.5 per cent or more than three-fourths of all the women. Less than one-fifth or nearly 19 per cent received under $10 a week and three girls received under $6 a week; nearly 6 per cent received $16 a week and over.

Wages of week workers, men.—The largest single group among the 109 men week workers were those receiving $14 and less than $16 a week, constituting over 42 per cent of the total; nearly 14 per cent received $16 and less than $18; over 10 per cent received $18 and less than $20 and less than 5 per cent received $20 a week and over. Only one boy tucker received under $6 a week and three received $6 a week. It will be seen from these figures that the men received, on the whole, higher wages than the women. Thus, there were no women receiving $20 a week, while nearly 5 per cent of the men received $20 a week and over. While the number of women receiving $14 a week and over constituted only one-fourth of the total, the number of men receiving these wages constituted nearly three-fourths.

Earnings of pieceworkers.—Sixty-one of the 267 women pieceworkers constituting 23 per cent, or nearly one-fourth of the total, earned $18 a week and over during the busiest week of 1913; nearly 34 per cent or more than one-third earned $14 and less than $18 a week; over 14 per cent earned from $12 to $13.99 a week; over 11 per cent earned $10 and less than $12 a week, and over 18 per cent, or less than one-fifth, earned under $10 a week. As is usually the case, men earned much higher wages than the women. Over one-fourth of the pieceworkers, male, earned $22.50 a week and over during the busiest week of the year; over one-fifth earned from $18 to $22.49; over 30 per cent, or a little less than one-third, earned $14 and less than $18; more than 24 per cent, or nearly one-fourth, earned under $14 a week. Of the men, less than 4 per cent earned under $6 a week.

Comparison of wages in 1912 and 1913.—There was a noticeable increase in the earnings of the tuckers, both week and pieceworkers, from 1912 to 1913. An examination of Tables 38, 39, and 40 will show that among the women week workers, those receiving $12 a week and over constituted a larger proportion in 1913 as compared with 1912, while those receiving under $12 a week were reduced in numbers. The same is true of the men week workers except that the line is to be drawn at $14 a week instead of $12 as in the case of the women. Among the pieceworkers this is likewise true. Thus, the number of women pieceworkers earning $14 a week and over has increased from 21.9 per cent in 1912 to 56.5 per cent in 1913. Among the men, the number of those earning $14 a week and over during the busiest week of the year increased from 52.8 per cent in 1912 to 75.6 per cent in 1913.

No great differences appear in the wages paid to tuckers in the different branches of the industry. The details as to the wages paid in association and nonassociation shops will be found in Tables 38, 39, and 40.

TABLE 38.—NUMBER AND PER CENT OF TUCKERS, FEMALE, WEEK WORKERS, RECEIVING EACH CLASSIFIED RATE OF WAGES PER WEEK, 1912 AND 1913, BY CLASS OF SHOPS.

NUMBER.

Classified rates of wages per week.	Association A.		Nonassociation A.		Association B.		Nonassociation B.[1]		Total.	
	1912	1913	1912	1913	1912	1913	1912	1913	1912	1913
$3 to $3.99	1		2	1					3	1
$4 to $4.99	2		1	1					3	1
$5 to $5.99	1		1	1	2				4	1
$6 to $6.99	2	3	4		1				7	3
$7 to $7.99	4	6	5	15	1	2			10	23
$8 to $8.99	7	3	7	6	3	4			17	13
$9 to $9.99	9	8	12	13	5	3		1	26	25
$10 to $11.99	21	30	11	28	27	12		4	59	74
$12 to $13.99	24	43	7	41	25	27	2	14	59	125
$14 to $15.99	9	26	3	15	23	30	1	2	36	73
$16 to $17.99	2	6		5	2	3		4	4	18
$18 to $19.99		2			1	1			1	3
$20 to $22.49										
Total	82	127	53	126	90	82	3	25	229	360

PER CENT.

Classified rates of wages per week.	Association A. 1912	Association A. 1913	Nonassociation A. 1912	Nonassociation A. 1913	Association B. 1912	Association B. 1913	Nonassociation B.[1] 1912	Nonassociation B.[1] 1913	Total. 1912	Total. 1913
$3 to $3.99	1.2		3.8	0.8					1.3	0.3
$4 to $4.99	2.4		1.9	.8					1.3	.3
$5 to $5.99	1.2		1.9	.8	2.2				1.7	.3
$6 to $6.99	2.4	2.4	7.5		1.1				3.0	.9
$7 to $7.99	4.9	4.7	9.4	11.9	1.1	2.4			4.4	6.4
$8 to $8.99	8.6	2.4	13.2	4.8	3.3	4.9			7.4	3.6
$9 to $9.99	11.0	6.3	22.6	10.3	5.6	3.7			11.3	6.9
$10 to $11.99	25.6	23.6	20.8	22.2	30.0	14.6			25.9	20.5
$12 to $13.99	29.3	33.8	13.2	32.5	27.8	32.9			25.9	34.7
$14 to $15.99	11.0	20.5	5.7	11.9	25.6	36.6			15.7	20.3
$16 to $17.99	2.4	4.7		4.0	2.2	3.7			1.7	4.9
$18 to $19.99		1.6			1.1	1.2			.4	.9
Total	100.0	100.0	100.0	100.0	100.0	100.0			100.0	100.0

[1] Percentages not computed on account of small number of employees.

TABLE 39.—NUMBER AND PER CENT OF TUCKERS, FEMALE, PIECEWORKERS, EARNING EACH CLASSIFIED AMOUNT, DURING THE BUSIEST WEEK OF THE YEAR, 1912 AND 1913, BY CLASS OF SHOPS.

NUMBER.

Classified earnings per week.	Association A.		Nonassociation A.[1]		Association B.		Nonassociation B.[1]		Total.	
	1912	1913	1912	1913	1912	1913	1912	1913	1912	1913
Under $3	2		1	3	2	1			5	4
$3 to $3.99	2	1	1		6	1			9	2
$4 to $4.99	4	1			1	1			5	2
$5 to $5.99	1	3	1	1	3	1			5	5
$6 to $6.99	2	2	2	1	4	1			8	4
$7 to $7.99	6	2	5		7	4		1	18	7
$8 to $8.99	9	9	8	1	10	2	1		23	12
$9 to $9.99	12	4	7	4	10	4	1		30	12
$10 to $11.99	14	14	11	9	29	7			54	30
$12 to $13.99	24	10	5	16	33	12			62	38
$14 to $15.99	8	19	1	6	13	20			27	45
$16 to $17.99	5	17	2	6	7	21		1	14	45
$18 to $19.99	5	8		7	6	16	1	3	12	34
$20 to $22.49	2	3			5	10	1		8	13
$22.50 to $24.99					1	8			1	8
$25 to $27.49		1				1	1		1	2
$27.50 to $29.99						2		1		3
$30 and over						1				1
Total	96	94	44	54	142	113	5	6	287	267

[1] Percentages not computed on account of small number of employees.

TABLE 39.—NUMBER AND PER CENT OF TUCKERS, FEMALE, PIECEWORKERS, EARNING EACH CLASSIFIED AMOUNT, DURING THE BUSIEST WEEK OF THE YEAR, 1912 AND 1913, BY CLASS OF SHOPS—Concluded.

PER CENT.

Classified earnings per week.	Association A.		Nonassociation A.		Association B.		Nonassociation B.		Total.	
	1912	1913	1912	1913	1912	1913	1912	1913	1912	1913
Under $3	2.1				1.4	0.9			1.7	1.5
$3 to $3.99	2.1	1.1			4.2	.9			3.1	.8
$4 to $4.99	4.1	1.1			.7	.9			1.7	.8
$5 to $5.99	1.0	3.2			2.1	.9			1.7	1.9
$6 to $6.99	2.1	2.1			2.8	.9			2.8	1.5
$7 to $7.99	6.3	2.1			4.9	3.5			6.3	2.6
$8 to $8.99	9.4	9.6			7.1	1.8			9.8	4.5
$9 to $9.99	12.5	4.2			7.1	3.5			10.4	4.5
$10 to $11.99	14.6	14.9			20.4	6.2			18.8	11.2
$12 to $13.99	25.0	10.6			23.3	10.6			21.6	14.2
$14 to $15.99	8.3	20.2			12.7	17.7			9.4	16.8
$16 to $17.99	5.2	18.1			4.9	18.6			4.9	16.8
$18 to $19.99	5.2	8.5			4.2	14.1			4.2	12.7
$20 to $22.49	2.1	3.2			3.5	8.8			2.8	4.9
$22.50 to $24.99					.7	7.1			.3	3.0
$25 to $27.49		1.1				.9			.3	.8
$27.50 to $29.99						1.8				1.1
$30 and over						.9				.4
Total	100.0	100.0			100.0	100.0			100.0	100.0

TABLE 40.—NUMBER AND PER CENT OF TUCKERS, MALE (WEEK WORKERS AND PIECEWORKERS), RECEIVING EACH CLASSIFIED RATE OF WAGES OR EARNINGS PER WEEK, 1912 AND 1913, FOR THE INDUSTRY AS A WHOLE.

Classified rates of wages or earnings per week.	Week workers (male) receiving each classified rate of wages.				Pieceworkers (male) receiving each classified amount during busiest week of year.			
	Number.		Per cent.		Number.		Per cent.	
	1912	1913	1912	1913	1912	1913	1912	1913
Under $3					2		2.8	
$3 to $3.99					1	3	1.4	2.2
$4 to $4.99	1		1.2		1	2	1.4	1.4
$5 to $5.99		1		1.0				
$6 to $6.99	2	3	2.4	2.7		2		1.4
$7 to $7.99	1		1.2		1	2	1.4	1.4
$8 to $8.99	3	2	3.6	1.8	1	3	1.4	2.2
$9 to $9.99	5	1	6.0	1.0	7	6	9.7	4.3
$10 to $11.99	17	8	20.5	7.3	11	6	15.2	4.3
$12 to $13.99	30	17	36.2	15.6	10	10	13.9	7.2
$14 to $15.99	12	46	14.5	42.2	7	20	9.7	14.4
$16 to $17.99	5	15	6.0	13.7	7	22	9.7	15.9
$18 to $19.99	4	11	4.8	10.1	6	16	8.3	11.5
$20 to $22.49	2	4	2.4	3.6	4	12	5.6	8.6
$22.50 to $24.99	1		1.2		4	12	5.6	8.6
$25 to $27.49		1		1.0	4	12	5.6	8.6
$27.50 to $29.99					1	3	1.4	2.2
$30 and over					5	8	6.9	5.8
Total	83	109	100.0	100.0	72	139	100.0	100.0

WAIST OPERATORS.

By "waist operators" are generally meant operators who make a complete waist. The work consists of the following processes: 1, The preparation of the so-called trimmings, which includes the making of the collars, the sewing on of laces or embroideries on the fronts, the sewing on of the trimmings on the sleeves, etc.; 2, the joining of the shoulders, that is, sewing together the front and back parts of the waists along the shoulder lines; 3, "collar setting," that is, sewing the collar on to the waist; 4, "making facings," that is, preparing the buttonhole and button pieces which are narrow strips of folded cloth, on one of which the buttons are sewed and on the other the buttonholes are made; 5, "closing sides," that is, joining the front and back parts of the waist along the sides; 6, "shirring" or "tacking" the fronts and backs, that is, gathering the front and back parts of the waist into folds and stitching these down along the waist line; 7, "setting little skirts," that is, sewing on at the waist line the bottom part of the waist; 8, "hemming," that is, hemming the lower edge of the waist; 9, "setting sleeves," that is, sewing the sleeves to the waist.

As a rule, however, the work of making the waist is divided between the "body maker" and those who specialize in making certain parts, such as sleeve setters, buttonhole makers, etc. The body maker is practically a waist operator, relieved of certain of the processes in the making of the waist. Where body makers are employed they may do the trimming or the work may be done by "trimmers." The same is true of setting the collars. The work of the "body makers" proper is confined to joining the shoulders, setting the collar, closing the sleeves and sides, making the facings, shirring or tacking the front and back, and setting the little skirt to the waist. Occasionally, also, they may make some of the tucks on the waist. The change in fashion in 1913, which did away with the seamed shoulders and substituted kimono sleeves for the old style and did away with lace trimming in most cases, resulted in the body makers' making practically the whole waist.

In Tables 41, 42, 43, and 44, which give the wages of waist operators, it was found necessary to include not only the body makers and waist operators as just defined, but also a number of other operators, in view of the indiscriminate manner in which operators are described on the pay rolls of the different shops. The following were included among "waist operators" in classifying the different classes of operators: First, all operators described as "waist operators" or "body makers" on the pay rolls; second, persons described as operators on the pay rolls of shops manufacturing waists exclusively. These may include buttonhole makers, hemstitchers, tuckers, or any other branch of operators, as well as waist makers strictly speaking, so long as they were found working in shops manufacturing waists exclusively and were not described more definitely under any one of the occupations mentioned in Table 7.

SEX.

The great majority of waist operators are women. Of the 5,825 waist operators reported in Table 9, 5,061, or 87 per cent, were women, and only 764, or 13 per cent, of the total were men.

WAGES.

As is shown in Table 11, the proportion of week workers and pieceworkers among waist operators was practically the same in 1912 and 1913. The pieceworkers are slightly in excess of the week workers, the former constituting in 1913 51.6 per cent of the total and the latter 48.4 per cent, as shown in the following table, which also gives corresponding figures for each branch of the industry.

	Number.		Per cent.	
	Week workers.	Pieceworkers.	Week workers.	Pieceworkers.
Association A	1,729	1,398	55.3	44.7
Association B	357	1,187	23.1	76.9
Nonassociation A	646	387	62.5	37.5
Nonassociation B	17	104	14.0	86.0
Total	[1] 2,820	[1] 3,005	48.4	51.6

[1] The figures for association and nonassociation shops shown in this table are derived from Tables 41 to 44, which give the number of waist operators according to classified earnings or wage rates. In those tables 71 week workers for whom earnings but not weekly rates were ascertained were included among pieceworkers. This accounts for the discrepancy between this total and the sum of the items.

The following table shows what per cent the week workers and the pieceworkers in each branch were of all the waist operators in the industry:

	Week workers.	Pieceworkers.
	Per cent.	*Per cent.*
Association A	30.8	22.9
Association B	6.1	20.4
Nonassociation A	11.2	6.5
Nonassociation B	.3	1.8
Total	48.4	51.6

Wages of week workers.—If we draw the line at $12 a week, we shall find that in the wage groups of $12 and over, the percentage of men waist operators exceeds that of women; below the $12 a week line the relation is reversed. Thus, only a little over 20 per cent of all women waist operators, week workers, received $12 a week and over, while the corresponding group of men constituted over 59 per cent of all the men week workers. In other words, only one-fifth of the women week workers received $12 a week and over, while nearly three-fifths of the men week workers received these wages. The number of women week workers receiving under $6 a week in 1913 was 9.6 per cent of the total, while the number of men was 3.3 per cent. Those receiving $6 and less than $9 a week included nearly 39 per cent of the women and only a little over 19 per cent of the men; those receiving $9 and less than $12 constituted over 31 per cent of the women and 18.4 per cent of the men. While on the whole there is a slight improvement over 1912 in the wages of waist operators working by the week, the increase in the proportion of workers receiving higher wages with a corresponding reduction in the number of those receiving lower rates is not as clearly perceptible among the waist operators as has been the case in the other occupations noted in this report.

Earnings of pieceworkers.—As is the case with the week workers, the earnings of the men working by the piece are greater than those of the women, except that the line has to be drawn at $18 a week among the pieceworkers instead of $12, as among the week workers. The number of those earning $18 a week and over during the busiest week of 1913 constituted 18 per cent of all the women pieceworkers and nearly 49 per cent of all the men pieceworkers. The number of those earning $16 and less than $18 constituted 12.5 per cent of all women pieceworkers, and almost the same percentage of the men pieceworkers. Below that wage group the proportion of women exceeds that of men in nearly every case.

The increase over 1912 in earnings among the waist operators working by the piece was more perceptible than among those working by the week; it was also greater among the women than among the men pieceworkers. Thus, the proportion of women earning $16 a week and over during the busiest week of the year increased from less than 18 per cent in 1912 to 30.5 per cent in 1913, while among the men it increased from 54 per cent in 1912 to nearly 62 per cent in 1913.

Further details as to wages of waist operators will be found in Tables 41, 42, 43, and 44.

TABLE 41.—NUMBER AND PER CENT OF WAIST OPERATORS, FEMALE, WEEK WORKERS, RECEIVING EACH CLASSIFIED RATE OF WAGES PER WEEK, 1912 AND 1913, BY CLASS OF SHOPS.

NUMBER.

Classified rates of wages per week.	Association A.		Nonassociation A.		Association B.		Nonassociation B.[1]		Total.	
	1912	1913	1912	1913	1912	1913	1912	1913	1912	1913
Under $3	3								3	
$3 to $3.99	29	6	4	3					33	9
$4 to $4.99	115	45	11	13	14	13			140	71
$5 to $5.99	148	117	8	25	27	10		1	183	153
$6 to $6.99	202	182	41	55	19	40			262	277
$7 to $7.99	213	255	46	59	33	13	4	1	296	328
$8 to $8.99	202	221	37	74	29	30	8	4	278	329
$9 to $9.99	181	184	42	70	41	15	8	3	272	272
$10 to $11.99	225	314	80	127	60	37	17	7	380	485
$12 to $13.99	119	145	35	80	92	61	14		260	286
$14 to $15.99	48	69	18	46	35	43			101	158
$16 to $17.99	3	19	1	11	3	7			7	37
$18 to $19.99	1	1	1	3	2	3			4	7
$20 to $22.49		2				2				4
$22.50 to $24.99		1								1
Total	1,489	1,561	324	566	355	274	51	16	[2] 2,219	[3] 2,417

[1] Percentages not computed, on account of small number of employees.
[2] Not including 44, for whom earnings but not weekly rates of wages could be ascertained.
[3] Not including 71, for whom earnings but not weekly rates of wages could be ascertained.

TABLE 41.—NUMBER AND PER CENT OF WAIST OPERATORS, FEMALE, WEEK WORKERS, RECEIVING EACH CLASSIFIED RATE OF WAGES PER WEEK, 1912 AND 1913, BY CLASS OF SHOPS—Concluded.

PER CENT.

Classified rates of wages per week.	Association A.		Nonassociation A.		Association B.		Nonassociation B.		Total.	
	1912	1913	1912	1913	1912	1913	1912	1913	1912	1913
Under $3	0.2								0.1	
$3 to $3.99	1.9	0.4	1.2	0.5					1.5	0.4
$4 to $4.99	7.7	2.9	3.4	2.3	3.9	4.8			6.3	2.9
$5 to $5.99	9.9	7.5	2.5	4.4	7.6	3.6			8.3	6.3
$6 to $6.99	13.6	11.7	12.6	9.7	5.3	14.6			11.8	11.5
$7 to $7.99	14.3	16.3	14.2	10.4	9.3	4.8			13.3	13.6
$8 to $8.99	13.6	14.1	11.4	13.1	8.2	10.9			12.5	13.6
$9 to $9.99	12.2	11.8	13.0	12.4	11.5	5.5			12.3	11.2
$10 to $11.99	15.1	20.1	24.7	22.5	16.9	13.5			17.1	20.1
$12 to $13.99	8.1	9.3	10.8	14.2	25.9	22.3			11.7	11.9
$14 to $15.99	3.2	4.4	5.6	8.1	9.9	15.7			4.6	6.5
$16 to $17.99	.2	1.2	.3	1.9	.9	2.5			.3	1.5
$18 to $19.99		.1	.3	.5	.6	1.1			.2	.3
$20 to $22.49		.1				.7				.2
$22.50 to $24.99		.1								(1)
Total	100.0	100.0	100.0	100.0	100.0	100.0			100.0	100.0

1 Less than one-tenth of 1 per cent.

TABLE 42.—WAIST OPERATORS, MALE, WEEK WORKERS, RECEIVING EACH CLASSIFIED RATE OF WAGES PER WEEK, 1912 AND 1913, BY CLASS OF SHOPS.

Classified rates of wages per week.	Association A.		Nonassociation A.		Association B.		Nonassociation B.		Total.			
									Number.		Per cent.	
	1912	1913	1912	1913	1912	1913	1912	1913	1912	1913	1912	1913
Under $3												
$3 to $3.99		1		1						2		0.6
$4 to $4.99	7	2	1	1					8	3	2.9	.9
$5 to $5.99	7	4		2	1				8	6	2.9	1.8
$6 to $6.99	5	11	2	3		6			7	20	2.6	6.0
$7 to $7.99	8	17		3	4	3			12	23	4.4	6.9
$8 to $8.99	11	10	1	7	6	4			18	21	6.6	6.3
$9 to $9.99	7	10	2	3	8	7	1		18	20	6.6	6.0
$10 to $11.99	22	13	2	9	14	19	1		39	41	14.3	12.4
$12 to $13.99	37	22	3	19	8	13			48	54	17.6	16.4
$14 to $15.99	38	30	10	16	30	30	1		79	76	28.9	22.9
$16 to $17.99	13	25	2	12	3				18	37	6.6	11.1
$18 to $19.99	10	12		1	1			1	11	14	4.0	4.2
$20 to $22.49	4	11	2	3		1			6	15	2.2	4.5
$22.50 to $24.99	1								1		.4	
Total	170	168	25	80	75	83	3	1	1 273	332	100.0	100.0

1 Not including 4 for whom earnings but not weekly rates of wages could be ascertained.

TABLE 43.—NUMBER AND PER CENT OF WAIST OPERATORS, FEMALE, PIECEWORKERS, EARNING EACH CLASSIFIED AMOUNT DURING THE BUSIEST WEEK OF THE YEAR, 1912 AND 1913, BY CLASS OF SHOPS.

NUMBER.

Classified earnings per week.	Association A.		Nonassociation A.		Association B.		Nonassociation B.		Total.	
	1912	1913	1912	1913	1912	1913	1912	1913	1912	1913
Under $3	19	31	9	11	31	13	1	1	60	56
$3 to $3.99	14	22	3	6	13	12	1	3	31	43
$4 to $4.99	32	19	6	5	13	15	1	....	52	39
$5 to $5.99	29	31	11	5	23	11	2	....	65	47
$6 to $6.99	45	39	9	5	38	17	1	3	93	64
$7 to $7.99	51	42	8	11	36	23	6	3	101	79
$8 to $8.99	56	76	19	13	73	47	4	2	152	138
$9 to $9.99	80	71	13	24	84	63	4	2	181	160
$10 to $11.99	165	195	27	47	143	165	11	21	346	428
$12 to $13.99	420	190	23	41	152	177	10	22	605	430
$14 to $15.99	107	173	18	40	135	127	11	13	271	353
$16 to $17.99	49	125	10	30	73	165	9	11	141	331
$18 to $19.99	33	66	4	16	69	108	6	8	112	198
$20 to $22.49	16	37	1	17	42	72	2	4	61	130
$22.50 to $24.99	10	21	....	5	36	39	1	2	47	67
$25 to $27.49	5	17	....	1	12	17	1	2	18	37
$27.50 to $29.99	5	9	....	1	10	13	....	....	15	23
$30 and over	....	4	....	1	19	16	....	....	19	21
Total	1,136	1,168	161	279	1,002	1,100	71	97	[1] 2,370	[2] 2,644

PER CENT.

Classified earnings per week.	Association A.		Nonassociation A.		Association B.		Nonassociation B.		Total.	
	1912	1913	1912	1913	1912	1913	1912	1913	1912	1913
Under $3	1.7	2.6	5.6	3.9	3.1	1.2	1.4	1.0	2.5	2.1
$3 to $3.99	1.3	1.9	1.9	2.1	1.3	1.1	1.4	3.1	1.3	1.6
$4 to $4.99	2.8	1.6	3.7	1.8	1.3	1.4	1.4	....	2.2	1.5
$5 to $5.99	2.5	2.6	6.8	1.8	2.3	1.0	2.8	....	2.8	1.8
$6 to $3.99	4.0	3.3	5.6	1.8	3.8	1.5	1.4	3.1	3.9	2.4
$7 to $7.99	4.5	3.6	4.9	3.9	3.6	2.1	8.5	3.1	4.3	3.0
$8 to $8.99	5.0	6.5	11.8	4.7	7.3	4.3	5.6	2.1	6.4	5.2
$9 to $9.99	7.1	6.1	8.1	8.6	8.4	5.7	5.6	2.1	7.6	6.1
$10 to $11.99	14.5	16.7	16.8	16.9	14.2	15.1	15.5	21.6	14.6	16.2
$12 to $13.99	36.9	16.3	14.3	14.7	15.1	16.1	14.1	22.7	25.6	16.3
$14 to $15.99	9.4	14.8	11.2	14.3	13.5	11.5	15.5	13.4	11.4	13.3
$16 to $17.99	4.3	10.7	6.2	10.7	7.3	15.1	12.7	11.3	6.0	12.5
$18 to $19.99	2.9	5.7	2.5	5.7	6.9	9.8	8.5	8.2	4.7	7.5
$20 to $22.49	1.4	3.2	.6	6.1	4.2	6.5	2.8	4.1	2.6	4.9
$22.50 to $24.99	.9	1.8	....	1.8	3.6	3.5	1.4	2.1	2.0	2.5
$25 to $27.49	.4	1.5	....	.4	1.2	1.5	1.4	2.1	.7	1.4
$27.50 to $29.99	.4	.8	....	.4	1.0	1.2	....	....	.6	.9
$30 and over	....	.3	....	.4	1.9	1.4	....	....	.8	.8
Total	100.0	100.0	100.0	100.0	100.0	100.0	100.0	100.0	100.0	100.0

[1] Including 44 week workers for whom earnings but not weekly rates of wages could be ascertained.
[2] Including 71 week workers for whom earnings but not weekly rates of wages could be ascertained.

TABLE 44.—NUMBER OF WAIST OPERATORS, MALE, PIECEWORKERS, EARNING EACH CLASSIFIED AMOUNT DURING THE BUSIEST WEEK OF THE YEAR, 1912 AND 1913, BY CLASS OF SHOPS.

Classified earnings per week.	Association A.		Nonassociation A.		Association B.		Nonassociation B.		Total.			
									Number.		Per cent.	
	1912	1913	1912	1913	1912	1913	1912	1913	1912	1913	1912	1913
Under $3		1					1		1	1	0.3	0.2
$3 to $3.99	1	2	1	5					2	7	.7	1.6
$4 to $4.99	1		3	2		1			4	3	1.4	.7
$5 to $5.99	1	1	3	1		1			4	3	1.4	.7
$6 to $6.99	3	1	2	3					5	4	1.7	.9
$7 to $7.99	1	5	3	2	1	1			5	8	1.7	1.9
$8 to $8.99	7	10	1	5	1	2	2		11	17	3.9	3.9
$9 to $9.99	7	2	1	1	1	3		1	9	7	3.1	1.6
$10 to $11.99	23	10	1	9	5	6			29	25	10.0	5.8
$12 to $13.99	14	18	6	16	5	6			25	40	8.7	9.2
$14 to $15.99	25	27	2	15	9	9	2		38	51	13.1	11.8
$16 to $17.99	19	32	1	12	7	11	1		28	55	9.7	12.8
$18 to $19.99	16	21	1	8	9	15	2	1	28	45	9.7	10.4
$20 to $22.49	19	27	2	11	7	5	1	1	29	44	10.0	10.2
$22.50 to $24.99	10	27	1	11	9	8		1	20	47	6.9	10.9
$25 to $27.49	8	18	1	2	7	6		1	16	27	5.6	6.3
$27.50 to $29.99	8	10	1	4	6	3			15	17	5.2	3.9
$30 and over	7	18		1	13	10		2	20	31	6.9	7.2
Total	170	230	30	108	80	87	9	7	[1] 289	432	100.0	100.0

[1] Including 4 week workers for whom earnings but not weekly rates of wages could be ascertained.

OPERATORS, NOT SPECIFIED.

Under this heading were included all operators employed in shops manufacturing dresses, who were found designated on the pay rolls as "operators." This includes operators who can make an entire dress, as well as any one of the 13 classes of operators enumerated in Table 8, such as buttonhole makers, hemstitchers, tuckers, trimmers, etc.

SEX.

Of the 6,455 "operators, not specified," reported in Table 8 for 1913, 5,591, or 87 per cent, were women and 864, or 13 per cent, were men.

WAGES.

In 1912, 47 per cent of all the "operators, not specified," were week workers and 53 per cent pieceworkers. The extent of piecework has increased since the adoption of the protocol, the pieceworkers in 1913 comprising 59 per cent and the week workers 41 per cent.

Earnings of pieceworkers.—As will be seen from Tables 45, 46, 47, and 48, the largest single group among the "operators, not specified," were women pieceworkers, who numbered 3,205 in 1913. The next largest group were the women week workers, who numbered 2,386. The men numbered 607 among the pieceworkers and 257 among the week workers.

Considering the earnings of the largest group, namely, the women pieceworkers, we find a uniform increase in the proportion of those earning $14 a week and over since the adoption of the protocol. These constituted less than 39 per cent in 1912 and nearly 54 per cent in 1913. The number of those earning $12 and less than $14 constituted about the same percentage both years, namely, over 13 per cent, while the percentage of those earning under $12 a week declined from over 48 per cent in 1912 to less than 33 per cent in 1913. The percentage of men pieceworkers earning higher rates of wages was larger than that of the women. Thus the number of those earning $20 and over during the busiest week of 1913 constituted 48 per cent, or nearly one-half, of all the men and less than 21 per cent, or a little over one-fifth, of all the women.

The changes in the earnings of men pieceworkers since the adoption of the protocol are not so conspicuous as in the case of the women. Among those earning under $10 a week, there was a decline, namely, from over 14 per cent in 1912 to nearly 8 per cent in 1913. The proportion of those earning $10 and less than $16 a week increased from 18 per cent in 1912 to 23 per cent in 1913. The number of those receiving $16 and less than $20 a week formed practically the same percentage of the total number of male workers both years, namely, 20 and 20.3 per cent. Those earning $20 and less than $25 increased from a little over 19 per cent in 1912 to nearly 24 per cent in 1913, while those earning $25 a week and over declined from more than 28 per cent in 1912 to nearly 24 per cent in 1913.

Wages of week workers.—Among the women week workers there was an increase in the proportion of those receiving $14 and over, which constituted less than 22 per cent in 1912 and nearly 31 per cent in 1913. The proportion of those receiving under $14 a week declined during that period. The same is true of the men week workers, except that the line has to be drawn at $16 a week, the percentage of those earning $16 a week and over having increased from 43.5 in 1912 to 56.6 in 1913.

Comparing the men's and women's earnings during 1913, the general rule is observed here of the men receiving considerably higher wages than the women. The number of those receiving $16 a week and over constituted less than 11 per cent among the women and nearly 57 per cent among the men. That is to say, while only a little over one-tenth of the women week workers received $16 a week and over, considerably more than one-half of the men received those wages. The differences between the earnings of operators in the different branches of the industry have been fully discussed in speaking of the operators as a whole. The details as to "operators, not specified," will be found in Tables 45, 46, 47, and 48.

TABLE 45.—NUMBER AND PER CENT OF OPERATORS NOT SPECIFIED, FEMALE, WEEK WORKERS, RECEIVING EACH CLASSIFIED RATE OF WAGES PER WEEK, 1912 AND 1913, BY CLASS OF SHOPS.

NUMBER.

Classified rates of wages per week.	Association A.		Nonassociation A.		Association B.		Nonassociation B.		Total.	
	1912	1913	1912	1913	1912	1913	1912	1913	1912	1913
Under $3	1				2				3	
$3 to $3.99	11	3	1		3				15	3
$4 to $4.99	17	11	5	12	8	1		2	30	26
$5 to $5.99	38	18	10	31	14	1	2		64	50
$6 to $6.99	37	56	17	50	20	9	6	2	80	117
$7 to $7.99	77	55	28	86	25	12	7	7	137	160
$8 to $8.99	85	66	35	71	37	14	10	9	167	160
$9 to $9.99	111	57	34	73	37	33	13	8	195	171
$10 to $11.99	251	161	46	157	108	91	46	31	451	440
$12 to $13.99	204	151	37	117	221	186	48	55	510	509
$14 to $15.99	112	120	10	66	167	245	32	42	321	473
$16 to $17.99	20	28	6	19	54	113	9	19	89	179
$18 to $19.99	5	10		1	25	46	6	4	36	61
$20 to $22.49	3	2	1	3	6	5	1	6	11	16
$22.50 to $24.99	1				2				3	
$25 to $27.49										
$27.50 to $29.99										
$30 and over					1	1			1	1
Total	973	738	230	686	730	757	180	185	[1] 2,113	[2] 2,366

PER CENT.

Classified rates of wages per week.	Association A.		Nonassociation A.		Association B.		Nonassociation B.		Total.	
	1912	1913	1912	1913	1912	1913	1912	1913	1912	1913
Under $3	0.1				0.3				0.1	
$3 to $3.99	1.1	0.4	0.4		.4				.7	0.1
$4 to $4.99	1.8	1.5	2.1	1.7	1.1	0.1		1.1	1.4	1.1
$5 to $5.99	3.9	2.4	4.3	4.5	1.9	.1	1.1		3.0	2.1
$6 to $6.99	3.8	7.6	7.4	7.3	2.7	1.1	3.3	1.1	3.8	4.9
$7 to $7.99	7.9	7.5	12.2	12.5	3.4	1.6	3.9	3.8	6.5	6.8
$8 to $8.99	8.7	8.9	15.2	10.4	5.1	1.9	5.6	4.9	7.9	6.8
$9 to $9.99	11.4	7.7	14.8	10.6	5.1	4.4	7.2	4.3	9.2	7.2
$10 to $11.99	25.8	21.8	20.0	22.9	14.8	12.0	25.5	16.7	21.4	18.6
$12 to $13.99	21.0	20.4	16.1	17.0	30.3	24.6	26.7	29.7	24.2	21.5
$14 to $15.99	11.5	16.3	4.3	9.6	22.9	32.4	17.8	22.7	15.2	20.0
$16 to $17.99	2.1	3.8	2.8	2.8	7.4	14.9	5.0	10.3	4.2	7.6
$18 to $19.99	.5	1.4		.2	3.4	6.1	3.3	2.2	1.7	2.6
$20 to $22.49	.3	.3	.4	.5	.8	.7	.6	3.2	.5	.7
$22.50 to $24.99	.1				.3				.2	
$25 to $27.49										
$27.50 to $29.99										
$30 and over					.1	.1			(3)	(3)
Total	100.0	100.0	100.0	100.0	100.0	100.0	100.0	100.0	100.0	100.0

[1] Not including 113 for whom earnings but not weekly rates of wages could be ascertained.
[2] Not including 2[illegible] for whom earnings but not weekly rates of wages could be ascertained.
[3] Less than one-tenth of 1 per cent.

TABLE 46.—NUMBER AND PER CENT OF OPERATORS NOT SPECIFIED, MALE, WEEK WORKERS, RECEIVING EACH CLASSIFIED RATE OF WAGES PER WEEK, 1912 AND 1913, BY CLASS OF SHOPS.

NUMBER.

Classified rates of wages per week.	Association A.		Nonassociation A.		Association B.[1]		Nonassociation B.[1]		Total.	
	1912	1913	1912	1913	1912	1913	1912	1913	1912	1913
Under $3										
$3 to $3.99										
$4 to $4.99			1	1					1	1
$5 to $5.99			3	4	2	1			5	5
$6 to $6.99		3	2	3					2	6
$7 to $7.99		1	2	2			1	1	3	4
$8 to $8.99	5	2	3	3		1		1	8	7
$9 to $9.99		3	4	4	2				6	7
$10 to $11.99	4	2	8	8	1	3	1	1	14	14
$12 to $13.99	19	5	13	22	7	3	3	4	42	34
$14 to $15.99	20	9	16	16	12	5	6	3	54	33
$16 to $17.99	10	10	8	26	15	12	4	2	37	50
$18 to $19.99	19	17	4	18	14	14	2	2	39	51
$20 to $22.49	10	6	6	18	5	3		1	21	28
$22.50 to $24.99	3	1		5	1	6			4	12
$25 to $27.49	1		1	1	1	1			3	2
$27.50 to $29.99		1								1
$30 and over								1		1
Total	91	60	71	131	60	49	17	16	[2] 239	[3] 256

PER CENT.

Classified rates of wages per week.	Association A. 1912	Association A. 1913	Nonassociation A. 1912	Nonassociation A. 1913	Association B.[1] 1912	Association B.[1] 1913	Nonassociation B.[1] 1912	Nonassociation B.[1] 1913	Total. 1912	Total. 1913
Under $3										
$3 to $3.99										
$4 to $4.99			1.4	0.8					0.4	0.4
$5 to $5.99			4.2	3.0					2.1	2.0
$6 to $6.99		5.0	2.8	2.3					.8	2.3
$7 to $7.99		1.7	2.8	1.6					1.3	1.6
$8 to $8.99	5.5	3.3	4.2	2.3					3.3	2.7
$9 to $9.99		5.0	5.6	3.0					2.5	2.7
$10 to $11.99	4.4	3.3	11.3	6.1					5.9	5.5
$12 to $13.99	20.9	8.3	18.3	16.8					17.6	13.3
$14 to $15.99	22.0	15.0	22.6	12.2					22.6	12.9
$16 to $17.99	11.0	16.6	11.3	19.9					15.5	19.5
$18 to $19.99	20.9	28.4	5.6	13.7					16.3	19.9
$20 to $22.49	11.0	10.0	8.5	13.7					8.8	10.9
$22.50 to $24.99	3.3	1.7		3.8					1.6	4.7
$25 to $27.49	1.0		1.4	.8					1.3	.8
$27.50 to $29.99		1.7								.4
$30 and over										.4
Total	100.0	100.0	100.0	100.0					100.0	100.0

1 Percentages not computed on account of small number of employees.
2 Not including 6 for whom earnings but not weekly rates of wages could be ascertained.
3 Not including 1 for whom earnings but not weekly rate of wages could be ascertained.

TABLE 47.—NUMBER AND PER CENT OF OPERATORS NOT SPECIFIED, FEMALE, PIECEWORKERS, EARNING EACH CLASSIFIED AMOUNT DURING THE BUSIEST WEEK OF THE YEAR, 1912 AND 1913, BY CLASS OF SHOPS.

NUMBER.

Classified earnings per week.	Association A.		Nonassociation A.		Association B.		Nonassociation B.		Total.	
	1912	1913	1912	1913	1912	1913	1912	1913	1912	1913
Under $3	60	36	9	13	35	33	....	....	104	82
$3 to $3.99	29	22	5	7	17	6	2	....	53	35
$4 to $4.99	28	22	8	6	26	19	2	1	64	48
$5 to $5.99	45	33	10	9	27	20	2	3	84	65
$6 to $6.99	63	34	13	12	29	24	3	....	108	70
$7 to $7.99	79	64	15	19	43	31	1	5	138	119
$8 to $8.99	86	55	9	17	43	43	3	6	141	121
$9 to $9.99	107	76	15	24	52	45	1	2	175	147
$10 to $11.99	189	178	36	47	130	133	11	14	366	372
$12 to $13.99	173	185	31	74	120	140	9	30	333	429
$14 to $15.99	122	191	23	56	130	146	16	22	291	415
$16 to $17.99	102	168	11	35	93	142	9	24	215	369
$18 to $19.99	71	95	14	28	92	126	4	22	181	271
$20 to $22.49	35	106	2	24	72	130	10	17	119	277
$22.50 to $24.99	40	49	1	12	40	111	1	11	82	183
$25 to $27.49	18	35	1	6	21	64	1	2	41	107
$27.50 to $29.99	10	21	....	3	11	30	....	6	21	60
$30 and over	15	26	....	3	11	25	....	1	26	55
Total	1,272	1,396	203	395	992	1,268	75	166	[1] 2,542	[2] 3,225

PER CENT.

Classified earnings per week.	Association A.		Nonassociation A.		Association B.		Nonassociation B.		Total.	
	1912	1913	1912	1913	1912	1913	1912	1913	1912	1913
Under $3	4.7	2.6	4.4	3.3	3.5	2.6	....	....	4.0	2.5
$3 to $3.99	2.3	1.6	2.5	1.7	1.7	.5	2.7	....	2.1	1.1
$4 to $4.99	2.2	1.6	3.9	1.5	2.6	1.5	2.7	0.6	2.5	1.5
$5 to $5.99	3.5	2.4	4.9	2.3	2.8	1.6	2.7	1.8	3.3	2.0
$6 to $6.99	4.9	2.4	6.4	3.0	2.9	1.9	4.0	....	4.3	2.2
$7 to $7.99	6.2	4.6	7.4	4.8	4.3	2.4	1.3	3.0	5.4	3.7
$8 to $8.99	6.7	3.9	4.4	4.3	4.3	3.4	4.0	3.6	5.5	3.8
$9 to $9.99	8.4	5.4	7.4	6.1	5.3	3.5	1.3	1.2	6.9	4.5
$10 to $11.99	14.9	12.8	17.8	11.9	13.1	10.5	14.7	8.4	14.4	11.5
$12 to $13.99	13.6	13.2	15.3	18.7	12.1	11.0	12.0	18.1	13.1	13.3
$14 to $15.99	9.6	13.7	11.3	14.2	13.1	11.5	21.4	13.3	11.4	12.9
$16 to $17.99	8.0	12.0	5.4	8.9	9.4	11.2	12.0	14.5	8.5	11.4
$18 to $19.99	5.6	6.8	6.9	7.1	9.3	9.9	5.3	13.3	7.1	8.4
$20 to $22.49	2.8	7.6	1.0	6.1	7.3	10.3	13.3	10.2	4.7	8.6
$22.50 to $24.99	3.2	3.5	.5	3.0	4.0	8.8	1.3	6.6	3.2	5.7
$25 to $27.49	1.4	2.5	.5	1.5	2.1	5.0	1.3	1.2	1.6	3.3
$27.50 to $29.99	.8	1.5	....	.8	1.1	2.4	....	3.6	.8	1.9
$30 and over	1.2	1.9	....	.8	1.1	2.0	....	.6	1.2	1.7
Total	100.0	100.0	100.0	100.0	100.0	100.0	100.0	100.0	100.0	100.0

[1] Including 113 week workers for whom earnings but not weekly rates of wages could be ascertained.
[2] Including 20 week workers for whom earnings but not weekly rates of wages could be ascertained.

TABLE 48.—NUMBER AND PER CENT OF OPERATORS NOT SPECIFIED, MALE, PIECE-WORKERS, EARNING EACH CLASSIFIED AMOUNT DURING THE BUSIEST WEEK OF THE YEAR, 1912 AND 1913, BY CLASS OF SHOPS.

NUMBER.

Classified earnings per week.	Association A.		Nonassociation A.		Association B.[1]		Nonassociation B.[1]		Total.	
	1912	1913	1912	1913	1912	1913	1912	1913	1912	1913
Under $3	8	3	1		1	1			10	4
$3 to $3.99	1	1	1	3	3				5	4
$4 to $4.99		3		3						6
$5 to $5.99	2			2	1				3	2
$6 to $6.99	1	1	1	5	1				3	6
$7 to $7.99	8	2	1	3	1				10	5
$8 to $8.99	5	4	4	2	2	1			11	7
$9 to $9.99	6	13	3	3	1			1	10	17
$10 to $11.99	13	19	3	14	3	2			19	35
$12 to $13.99	14	23	2	20	4	2		1	20	46
$14 to $15.99	14	28	10	17	4	13		2	28	60
$16 to $17.99	23	35	6	21	6	5		2	35	63
$18 to $19.99	23	38	8	16	7	5		2	38	61
$20 to $22.49	22	49	12	14	5	9	1	2	40	74
$22.50 to $24.99	16	42	7	19	6	5	1	4	30	70
$25 to $27.49	23	27	6	12	5	11			34	50
$27.50 to $29.99	17	13	4	7	4	6	2		27	26
$30 and over	26	45	3	15	13	11		1	42	72
Total	222	346	72	176	67	71	4	15	[2] 365	[3] 608

PER CENT.

Classified earnings per week.	Association A.		Nonassociation A.		Association B.[1]		Nonassociation B.[1]		Total.	
	1912	1913	1912	1913	1912	1913	1912	1913	1912	1913
Under $3	3.6	0.9	1.4						2.7	0.7
$3 to $3.99	.4	.3	1.4	1.7					1.4	.7
$4 to $4.99		.9		1.7						1.0
$5 to $5.99	.9			1.1					.8	.3
$6 to $6.99	.4	.3	1.4	2.8					.8	1.0
$7 to $7.99	3.6	.6	1.4	1.7					2.7	.8
$8 to $8.99	2.3	1.2	5.5	1.1					3.0	1.1
$9 to $9.99	2.7	3.8	4.2	1.7					2.7	2.8
$10 to $11.99	5.8	5.5	4.2	8.0					5.2	5.8
$12 to $13.99	6.3	6.6	2.8	11.4					5.5	7.6
$14 to $15.99	6.3	8.1	13.9	9.7					7.7	9.9
$16 to $17.99	10.4	10.1	8.3	11.9					9.6	10.4
$18 to $19.99	10.4	10.9	11.1	9.1					10.4	9.9
$20 to $22.49	9.9	14.1	16.7	8.0					11.0	12.2
$22.50 to $24.99	7.2	12.1	9.7	10.8					8.3	11.5
$25 to $27.49	10.4	7.8	8.3	6.8					9.3	8.2
$27.50 to $29.99	7.7	3.8	5.5	4.0					7.4	4.3
$30 and over	11.7	13.0	4.2	8.5					11.5	11.8
Total	100.0	100.0	100.0	100.0					100.0	100.0

[1] Percentages not computed on account of small number of employees.
[2] Including 6 week workers for whom earnings but not weekly rates of wages could be ascertained.
[3] Including 1 week worker for whom earnings but not weekly rate of wages could be ascertained.

EMPLOYEES OTHER THAN OPERATORS.

ASSORTERS.

Assorters are employed only in large shops. Their work consists in the preparation of bundles of work for the operators. Taking up a bundle (which consists of a certain number of parts that go to make up the waist or dress) as it comes from the cutter, the assorter adds to it all the necessary parts which the operator will require in his work, such as laces, embroideries, belts, and other kinds of trimmings. The assorters must be intelligent and understand all the parts that go to make up a waist. They have to match the laces and understand how to substitute a lace of a given kind when the supply of the original lace is exhausted. A mistake made by the assorter will result in serious delay in the work of the operator and may also cause serious loss through the sewing on of the wrong lace or trimmings.

SEX.

Assorters are usually girls. Out of the total of 151 assorters given in Table 49, only 4 were men. The source of supply of assorters is cleaners and "cutting-out-lace" girls. The brightest among these two classes of girls, those who show the most intelligence and the keenest perception of color and lace design, are allowed to graduate into the class of assorters

WAGES.

As will be seen from Table 49, wage records were obtained for only 151 assorters. There are probably more than that number of assorters employed in the industry, although the number is hardly much larger, since only the large shops can afford to employ this class of workers. Of the total number, 142, or 94 per cent, were employed in association shops, leaving but 9, or 6 per cent, employed in the nonassociation shops, which are mostly small shops. Assorters are paid by the week. As will be seen from the table, the wages of assorters both in 1912 and 1913 ranged between $4 and $18 per week. The number of those who received under $6 a week constituted over 8 per cent of the total number employed. More than one-fourth of all the assorters received under $8 a week, and less than one-fifth of the workers (18.5 per cent) received $6 and less than $8 a week. A little over one-half, or 51.8 per cent, received $9 and less than $14 a week. Five women and one man were found receiving $14 and less than $18 a week. These workers, in addition to being assorters, acted as forewomen and foreman, distributing work as well as preparing it. In general, the higher-grade assorters act as assistants to the foremen and forewomen in distributing work to the operators.

TABLE 49.—NUMBER AND PER CENT OF ASSORTERS, WEEK WORKERS, RECEIVING EACH CLASSIFIED RATE OF WAGES PER WEEK, 1912 AND 1913, BY SEX.

Classified rates of wages or earnings, per week, and classes of shops.	Females.				Males.	
	Number.		Per cent.		1912	1913
	1912	1913	1912	1913		
$4 to $4.99	2	2	1.5	1.4		
$5 to $5.99	11	10	8.5	6.8		
$6 to $6.99	10	13	7.8	8.8		
$7 to $7.99	16	15	12.4	10.2		
$8 to $8.99	17	26	13.2	17.7		
$9 to $9.99	17	18	13.2	12.3		
$10 to $11.99	32	37	24.8	25.2		
$12 to $13.99	20	21	15.5	14.3		3
$14 to $15.99	3	3	2.3	2.0	1	1
$16 to $17.99	1	2	.8	1.3		
Total	129	147	100.0	100.0	1	4
	Workers in specified classes of shops.					
Association A	51	64			1	1
Association B	77	74				3
Nonassociation A		9				
Nonassociation B	1					

CLEANERS.

Cleaning forms the lowest step in the industrial ladder in the dress and waist shops. It is the first occupation of young girls without industrial training. Their work consists in cutting off loose threads with the aid of scissors. Very little skill is required, although carelessness may result in great damage, since the thread has to be cut close to the garment and an unskilled cleaner may cut into the waist or dress in trying to cut off the thread. Cleaners who show aptitude for more important work are graduated into other kinds of work, such as finishing, assorting, operating, and even examining.

SEX.

Only girls are employed in this work, and 2,086 cleaners were found working in the industry during 1913.

WAGES.

Table 50 gives the wages of cleaners in 1912 and 1913 in each of the four branches of the industry and also for the industry as a whole. As will be seen from that table, weekly rates were obtained for 2,006 cleaners in 1913. Of the remaining 80 cleaners, 20 were pieceworkers and 60 were week workers for whom no wage data could be obtained. As the number of pieceworkers is very small, only week workers are considered in analyzing the earnings of the cleaners. Only a little over 2 per cent of the cleaners were getting $3 and under $4 a week in 1913, but those receiving under $6 a week exceeded one-third of all the cleaners, or over 37 per cent. Nearly one-half of the girls, over 47 per cent, received $6 and less than $8 a week; nearly 16 per cent received $8 a week and over; and a few received $12.

Comparison of wages in 1912 and 1913.—A comparison of the wages earned during 1913 with those earned during the preceding year before the adoption of the protocol shows a uniform decline in the percentage of workers receiving less than $6 a week and an increase in the percentage of those receiving $6 a week and over. In 1912 over 60 per cent of the cleaners received under $6 a week as compared with 37.3 per cent in 1913. On the other hand, those receiving $6 and less than $8 constituted less than 29 per cent in 1912 and over 47 per cent in 1913. Those earning $8 a week and over comprised 11 per cent in 1912 and nearly 16 per cent in 1913. These facts are brought out in Table 50 and are shown graphically in Chart 9, in which the broken line (representing the percentage of workers receiving specified wages in 1912) is above the solid line (representing 1913) in the case of all wage groups below $6 and is below the solid line for wages of $6 and over, showing the shifting of the workers from the lower to the higher paid groups.

Wages in association and nonassociation shops.—The figures in Table 50 show the varying percentages of workers getting specified rates of wages in the high-grade and low-grade shops belonging to the association as well as in those not members of the association. The most noticeable point in the table is the fact that 38 per cent of the cleaners employed in nonassociation A shops, manufacturing the cheaper garments, received $6 per week and under $7. The proportion receiving that rate in the nonassociation B shops was 26.9 per cent. In the association shops the same situation is found, namely, that the wages in the A shops are higher than in the B shops. Thus the percentage of cleaners receiving $6 to $6.99 per week in the association A shops was 29.3, while in the association B shops it was 25.8. The percentage of cleaners receiving under $6 a week was nearly

CHART 9.—PER CENT OF CLEANERS, FEMALE (WEEK WORKERS), RECEIVING EACH CLASSIFIED RATE OF WAGES PER WEEK, 1912 AND 1913.

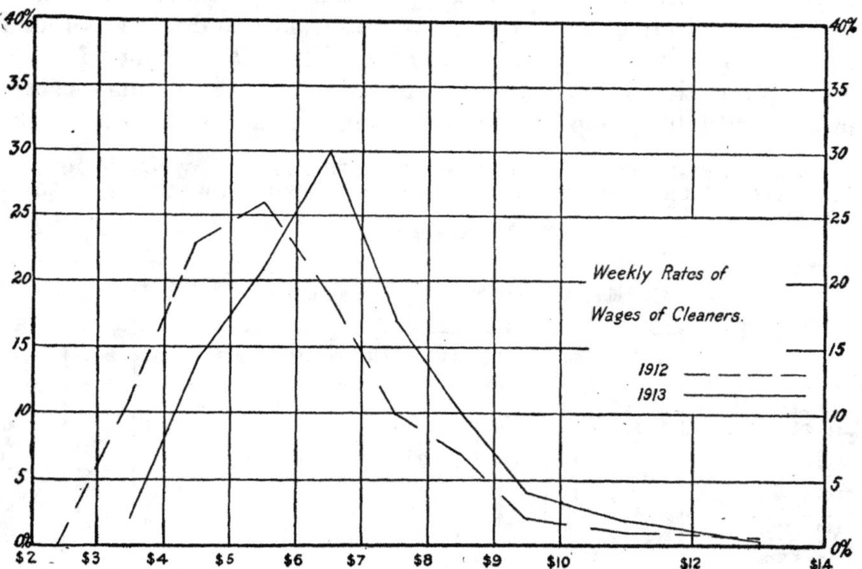

26 in the nonassociation A shops and over 35 in the association A shops. This indicates a higher percentage of cleaners receiving less than the minimum rate in the association shops manufacturing the cheaper garments than in the nonassociation shops. In the B shops, i. e., those manufacturing the higher-grade garments, the percentage receiving under $6 a week was 36.5 in the nonassociation shops and 48.9 in the association shops. On the other hand, for those receiving $7 and over per week, the percentages in the nonassociation A shops and in the association A shops were practically the same. In the B shops, the percentage in the nonassociation shops was less than 37 and in the association shops over 25.

In other words, the proportion of experienced cleaners getting more than the minimum scale is about the same whether the shops are those manufacturing high-grade or low-grade garments, whether belonging to the association or not. The proportion of those receiving the minimum scale of $6 a week is practically the same in all except the nonassociation shops making the cheaper garments. On the other hand the cleaners receiving less than the minimum scale are more numerous in the association than in the nonassociation shops, irrespective of whether high-grade or low-grade garments are manufactured. As the association shops include mostly large establishments while the nonassociation shops are mostly of a small size, the difference is apparently due to the fact that in large shops there are quite a number of so-called floor girls and errand girls employed who are not needed at all in the small shops. As the errand girls are not always kept apart from the cleaners on the pay rolls and, moreover, are made to work on cleaning when they have no errands to do, it was found necessary to enter them all as cleaners. This may account for the larger proportion of "cleaners" receiving less than the minimum scale in the association shops as compared with the nonassociation shops.

TABLE 50.—NUMBER AND PER CENT OF CLEANERS, FEMALE, WEEK WORKERS,[1] RECEIVING EACH CLASSIFIED RATE OF WAGES PER WEEK, 1912 AND 1913, BY CLASS OF SHOPS.

NUMBER.

Classified rates of wages per week.	Association A.		Nonassociation A.		Association B.		Nonassociation B.		Total.	
	1912	1913	1912	1913	1912	1913	1912[2]	1913	1912	1913
Under $3	5	....	....	....	....	....	....	....	5	....
$3 to $3.99	84	30	21	4	65	11	1	1	171	46
$4 to $4.99	212	141	28	30	116	119	....	2	356	292
$5 to $5.99	247	198	30	62	116	135	8	16	401	411
$6 to $6.99	188	305	35	141	67	140	3	14	293	600
$7 to $7.99	81	198	25	57	46	79	....	10	152	344
$8 to $8.99	68	94	22	52	21	43	1	4	112	193
$9 to $9.99	18	55	4	16	6	7	....	2	28	80
$10 to $11.99	17	16	1	8	2	6	1	2	21	32
$12 to $13.99	8	4	1	1	....	2	....	1	9	8
Total	928	1,041	167	371	439	542	14	52	[3]1,548	[4]2,006

PER CENT.

Classified rates of wages per week.	Association A.		Nonassociation A.		Association B.		Nonassociation B.		Total.	
	1912	1913	1912	1913	1912	1913	1912[2]	1913	1912	1913
Under $3	0.5	....	....	....	....	....	....	....	0.3	....
$3 to $3.99	9.1	2.9	12.6	1.1	14.8	2.0	....	1.9	11.0	2.3
$4 to $4.99	22.9	13.5	16.7	8.1	26.4	22.0	....	3.9	23.0	14.5
$5 to $5.99	26.6	19.0	18.0	16.7	26.4	24.9	....	30.7	25.9	20.5
$6 to $6.99	20.3	29.3	20.9	38.0	15.3	25.8	....	26.9	18.9	30.0
$7 to $7.99	8.7	19.0	15.0	15.3	10.4	14.6	....	19.2	9.8	17.1
$8 to $8.99	7.3	9.0	13.2	14.0	4.8	7.9	....	7.7	7.2	9.6
$9 to $9.99	1.9	5.3	2.4	4.3	1.4	1.3	....	3.9	1.8	4.0
$10 to $11.99	1.8	1.6	.6	2.2	.5	1.1	....	3.9	1.4	1.6
$12 to $13.99	.9	.4	.6	.3	....	.4	....	1.9	.6	.4
Total	100.0	100.0	100.0	100.0	100.0	100.0	....	100.0	100.0	100.0

[1] In addition to the week workers shown in this table, there were 45 pieceworkers in 1912 and 20 in 1913.
[2] Percentages not computed for the year 1912 on account of small number of employees.
[3] Not including 44, for whom weekly rates could not be ascertained.
[4] Not including 60, for whom weekly rates could not be ascertained.

TABLE 50.—NUMBER AND PER CENT OF CLEANERS, FEMALE, WEEK WORKERS, RECEIVING EACH CLASSIFIED RATE OF WAGES PER WEEK, 1912 AND 1913, BY CLASS OF SHOPS—Concluded.

SUMMARY OF PERCENTAGES.

Classified rates of wages per week.	Association A.		Nonassociation A.		Association B.		Nonassociation B.		Total.	
	1912	1913	1912	1913	1912	1913	1912	1913	1912	1913
Under $6	59.1	35.4	47.3	25.9	67.6	48.9	....	36.5	60.3	37.3
$6 to $6.99	20.3	29.3	20.9	38.0	15.3	25.8	....	26.9	18.9	29.9
$7 and over	20.6	35.3	31.8	36.1	17.1	25.3	....	36.6	20.8	32.7
Total	100.0	100.0	100.0	100.0	100.0	100.0	....	100.0	100.0	100.0

CUTTERS.

The occupation of cutter is one of the most skilled and most responsible in the industry. Upon the cutter depends not only the fit and appearance of the garment, but, also, to a considerable extent, the cost of it. An error made by the cutter may result in the partial or total damage of the goods cut. Apart from that, a slight error or failure to cut the goods to the exact size required, sometimes within a fraction of an inch, or the notching of the cloth a fraction of an inch out of the way, may cause the operators endless trouble in the sewing together of the different pieces and result in the necessity of ripping the work already done and the duplication of the work on the part of the operators as well as of the cutters. In a shop in which operators are paid by the week this may entail a very serious loss to the manufacturer. In those in which the work is done by the piece this may likewise be the case, if the blame can be clearly placed on the cutter, for in that case the pieceworkers would be entitled to pay on the spoiled garments. It happens very frequently, however, that the cutting or notching, while not distinctly wrong, is done in so careless or crude a fashion as to cause much trouble without compensation for loss of time to the operator working by the piece.

The skill of the cutter also affects the cost of the garment so far as the ability of the cutter to lay out his pattern economically is concerned; a cutter who is thoroughly familiar with his work will know how to lay out his pattern on the cloth in such a way as to utilize every available part of the cloth and reduce waste to a minimum; a less skilled cutter will waste a great deal of the cloth, being unable to utilize comparatively large pieces of cloth. This may account for the seemingly long period of apprenticeship which the cutters' union requires before admitting a worker to the class of full-fledged cutters. It is the only trade in the industry for which the protocol has provided a graduated scale of compensation.

Under the protocol cutters are divided into full-fledged cutters and apprentices. The apprentices are divided into three grades, thus making four grades in all. The three grades of apprentices are known as: Grade A, to which are admitted apprentices of less than one year's standing; grade B, which includes apprentices of more than one year and less than two years' standing; and grade C, consisting of apprentices of more than two years' and less than three years' time. The protocol provides that on or about the 15th day of June and November in each year the cutters' union, known as Local No. 10, shall hold an examination for the purpose of admitting apprentices of grade C to the class of full-fledged cutters. The protocol also provides that "after January 1, 1914, the following rule shall be adopted: In each shop there shall be not more than one apprentice for each five cutters employed, but in case there shall be less than five cutters employed one apprentice may be employed." It also provides that "at least one cutter shall be employed in the shops of members of the association."

The method of cutting the goods varies with the character of the garments manufactured in the industry. In shops manufacturing high-grade dresses and gowns of silk in which one garment is made at a time the cutter may cut only one or a very few garments of the same style and uses shears for that purpose. Where cheaper garments are manufactured, a knife or a cutting machine is employed instead of shears. This is done to enable the cutter to cut as many as 400 garments at once. It is done by stretching out bolts of material on a long table, placing one layer on top of another until the necessary thickness has been reached. The number of layers or thicknesses of cloth depends on the character of the material and on the size of the order. In shops making a medium grade and a high grade of garments where no stock is ever made up the amount cut will depend entirely on the size of the order received, while in shops manufacturing cheaper waists and dresses made of lingerie and other light cotton material, for which orders are usually received in large quantities and where there is no hesitation in making up garments in excess of the order so as to have stock in readiness, the cloth is piled high to the limit of the capacity of the knife and to the limit of the ability of the cutter to do his work without damage to the goods.

In the case of lawns, about 20 or 22 dozen layers are stretched one on top of the other and cut with a long knife or machine. When lingerie, cotton voile, and similar light cottons are used, the number of layers may reach about 300. In heavy linens about four dozen, sometimes eight dozen, layers are cut. In ratines, six to eight dozen is the largest number. In case of silks, a short knife is used because the number of layers that can be cut at once is much smaller than in cotton. This is due to the fact that silk being very slippery and very light, it is exceedingly difficult for the cutter to keep the layers in a fixed, steady position. The highest number of layers cut at one time does not exceed 90 when a cutting machine is employed and 40 if a short knife is used. The long knife is never used on silks.

Woolen goods are easier to handle than silks, but not so easy to cut as cotton. The cutting machine is usually employed in cutting out the cloth. In the case of heavy woolen cloths, about 60 layers are usually regarded as the maximum. For light serges and worsteds, as many as 96 layers are cut at a time.

In large shops, where more than one cutter is employed, there is more or less division of labor. The assistants or apprentices do the stretching of the cloth, other cutters do the cutting, while the most responsible work, namely, the marking of the outline of the pattern on the top layer of the cloth is done by the most experienced cutter, who is also called the marker.

The apprenticing of a cutter.—During the first year (grade A), the cutter's apprentice is taught how to stretch the cloth, preparing it for the marker and the cutter. He is also taught to cut out small parts such as cuffs and other odd parts with a short knife. An opportunity is also given him to cut "repairs"; that is, to correct outlines in garments which through an error of the cutter or the operator have to be repaired. The repair cutting is done with shears on single garments.

During the second year (grade B) the apprentice gradually learns to do more and more cutting. He assists the cutter in cutting out those parts which do not have to be cut to the exact size but merely in rough outline. These are parts that are cut much larger than the final size in order to allow for plaits, tucks, etc., and which are later "sloped" to the right size. He is also given smaller parts to cut and odd parts like strips for tucking, binding, etc.

Sloping.—The grade B cutter also does the sloping which consists in cutting down parts of the garment such as a front or back of a waist to the exact size after the plaits, tucks, or insertions have been put in by the operator.

During the third year (grade C), the apprentice assists in laying out the patterns and marking out the lays. He also does the general cutting under the supervision of the cutter. After the third year, upon passing an examination, he is admitted to the standing of a full-fledged cutter.

SEX.

Only men are employed in cutting. In some shops, however, women are employed as slopers. As will be seen from Table 8 only 6 women slopers were found employed in the 520 shops under investigation. It will also be seen from the same table that there were 13 male slopers. This does not mean that there were only 13 men slopers in the industry; the other slopers were in all probability entered on the pay rolls as cutters.

WAGES.

Information was obtained as to 1,701 cutters in 1913 and 1,397 in 1912. All of these were paid by the week. As will be seen from Table 51, they were distributed among the four branches of the industry as follows: Association A (lower-grade garments) 830; nonassociation A, 213; association B, 560; nonassociation B, 61, making a total of 1,664. For the remaining 37 cutters no information was obtainable as to their weekly rates of wages, but merely of their total earnings during the busiest week.

Over 67 per cent or two-thirds of all the cutters in 1913 were in those groups which included the protocol rates of $6, $12, $18, $25, and over. In 1912 less than 38 per cent of all the cutters received these rates. The proportion of cutters receiving these rates in the different branches of the industry was as follows: Association B, nearly 78 per cent; nonassociation B, over 72 per cent; association A, over 62 per cent; nonassociation A, over 56 per cent. It will be seen from these figures that the enforcement of the protocol rates does not depend so much on whether the shops belong to members of the association or to nonmembers as on the grade of garments manufactured in the various shops. The higher the grade, the greater the skill of the cutter required, the higher the pay he can command, and the greater, therefore, the proportion of those receiving protocol rates. On the other hand, the detailed comparison of rates prevailing in association and nonassociation shops of the same grade which follows, indicates that in some cases the association shops make a better showing, while in other cases it is the nonassociation shops.

Comparing the figures in Table 51 showing the proportion of workers receiving different rates of wages in association and nonassociation A shops (those manufacturing lower-grade garments), we find a higher percentage of cutters receiving $25 a week and over in the nonassociation shops than in the association shops and a lower percentage of cutters receiving under $25 a week. Thus, the number of cutters receiving $6 and less than $7 a week constituted more than 5 per cent of all the cutters in the association A shops and more than 3 per cent in the nonassociation A shops. Those getting $12 and less than $14 a week were nearly 11 per cent of the total in the association shops and nearly 10 per cent in the nonassociation shops. Those getting $18 and less than $20 a week constituted nearly 14 per cent in the association and 8.5 per cent in the nonassociation shops, and those getting $25 and less than $27.50 were almost 28 per cent in the association and over 32 per cent in the nonassociation shops.

The contrary is true of the B shops (those manufacturing the higher-grade garments). Thus the proportion of cutters receiving the highest protocol rate ($25) and over was 64 per cent in the association B shops and only a little over 49 per cent in the nonassociation B shops. On the other hand, in the groups including two of the protocol rates under $25 ($18 and $12) the nonassociation shops had a higher percentage of cutters than the association shops. Thus, in the group $18 to $19.99 were found 13.1 per cent of the cutters in nonassociation B shops as against 7.4 per cent of those in association B shops and in the group $12 to $13.99 were found 9.8 per cent of the cutters in nonassociation shops as against 4.6 per cent of those in association shops. In the group $6 to $6.99, that is, the group containing the lowest protocol rate ($6), there were only 11 cutters in the association B shops and none in the nonassociation B shops. In fact, there were no cutters in the nonassociation B shops receiving under $8, while in the association B shops nearly 5 per cent of all the cutters received $4 and less than $8 a week.

A comparison of Table 51 and Chart 10, showing the rates for cutters, with Tables 50, 52, 54, and 55, and Charts 9, 11, 12, and 13, representing the wages of cleaners, drapers, examiners, and finishers, respectively, shows the striking effect of providing only one rate of wages, as has been done in the protocol for those occupations and four different rates as is the case with the cutters. In the trades mentioned there is always only one high peak showing that the largest single group of workers is the group receiving the minimum protocol rate, while in the case of the cutters there are four distinct peaks showing that wages tend to concentrate at the rates provided in the protocol.

Table 51 shows the difference in the wages paid in the two classes of association shops, A and B. In the higher-grade (B) shops the proportion of cutters receiving $25 a week and under $27.50 rises to 56.2 per cent, while for the line representing the lower-grade (A) shops it goes up only to 27.8 per cent. In the lower wage groups, the relative position of the percentages is reversed, that is to say, the proportion of cutters in the group receiving $18, $12, and $6 a week, as well as of those receiving the intermediate rates not fixed in the protocol, is in every case higher in the lower-grade shops than in the higher-grade shops.

Wages in 1912 and 1913.—Table 51 throws an interesting light on the changes which have occurred in the wages of the cutters since the protocol has gone into effect. As will be seen from the last two columns in the table, the percentage of those receiving the lower rates of wages has uniformly declined, while the proportion of those receiving $25 a week and over has increased from less than 19 per cent of all the cutters in 1912 to 44 per cent in 1913.

This fact is shown even more strikingly when we look at the absolute numbers of cutters receiving different rates of wages as shown in Table 51, for we find an increase in the number of workers receiving protocol rates of wages and a decline in the number of those receiving less than the protocol rates, in spite of the increase of the total number of cutters from 1,328 in 1912 to 1,664 in 1913. Thus, the number of those receiving $6 and less than $7 a week increased from 36 in 1912 to 63 in 1913, while the number of those receiving under $6 declined from 27 to 20. The number of cutters receiving $12 and less than $14 a week increased from 113 to 142, while the number of those receiving $7 and less than $12 a week declined from 210 to 165. The number of those receiving $18 and less than $20 a week increased from 117 in 1912 to 182 in 1913, while those receiving $14 and less than $18 a week declined from 223 to 196. Finally, the number of those receiving $25 a week and over increased from 250 in 1912 to 731 in 1913, while those receiving $20 and less than $25 declined from 352 to 165.

The changes in the rates of wages paid to cutters since the protocol went into effect are shown in Chart 10, in which the broken line represents the wages in 1912 and the solid line those for 1913. The great rise in the number of those in the group receiving $25 a week is the most conspicuous feature on that chart. The smaller increase in the number of those in the groups receiving $18 and $6 a week and the decline in the number of those receiving the intermediate rates is likewise clearly shown.

TABLE 51.—NUMBER AND PER CENT OF CUTTERS, WEEK WORKERS, RECEIVING EACH CLASSIFIED RATE OF WAGES PER WEEK, 1912 AND 1913, BY CLASS OF SHOPS.

NUMBER.

Classified rates of wages per week.	Association A.		Nonassociation A.		Association B.		Nonassociation B.		Total.	
	1912	1913	1912	1913	1912	1913	1912	1913	1912	1913
$3 to $3.99	1	1	1	....	....	....	....	....	2	1
$4 to $4.99	3	3	1	3	4	3	....	....	8	9
$5 to $5.99	9	4	2	2	6	4	....	....	17	10
$6 to $6.99	21	45	7	7	8	11	....	....	36	63
$7 to $7.99	24	27	4	4	6	10	1	....	35	41
$8 to $8.99	25	20	6	6	9	2	1	1	41	29
$9 to $9.99	24	25	5	4	10	5	1	3	40	37
$10 to $11.99	65	37	13	10	16	10	....	1	94	58
$12 to $13.99	68	89	16	21	28	26	1	6	113	142
$14 to $15.99	72	67	12	25	30	28	3	3	117	123
$16 to $17.99	57	39	9	16	37	17	3	1	106	73
$18 to $19.99	63	115	11	18	33	41	10	8	117	182
$20 to $22.49	115	67	17	18	118	33	4	5	254	123
$22.50 to $24.99	28	22	2	5	64	12	4	3	98	42
$25 to $27.49	53	230	9	69	114	314	4	22	180	635
$27.50 to $29.99	3	7	2	1	3	8	....	2	8	18
$30 and over	29	32	4	4	24	36	5	6	62	78
Total	660	830	121	213	510	560	37	61	[1] 1,328	[2] 1,664

[1] Not including 69, for whom weekly rates could not be ascertained.
[2] Not including 37, for whom weekly rates could not be ascertained.

TABLE 51.—NUMBER AND PER CENT OF CUTTERS, WEEK WORKERS, RECEIVING EACH CLASSIFIED RATE OF WAGES PER WEEK, 1912 AND 1913, BY CLASS OF SHOPS—Concluded.

PER CENT.

Classified rates of wages per week.	Association A.		Nonassociation A.		Association B.		Nonassociation B.		Total.	
	1912	1913	1912	1913	1912	1913	1912	1913	1912	1913
$3 to $3.99	0.2	0.1	0.8	....	....	....	....	....	0.2	0.1
$4 to $4.99	.5	.4	.8	1.4	0.8	0.5	....	....	.6	.5
$5 to $5.99	1.4	.5	1.7	.9	1.2	.7	....	....	1.3	.6
$6 to $6.99	3.2	5.4	5.8	3.3	1.6	1.9	....	....	2.7	3.8
$7 to $7.99	3.6	3.3	3.3	1.9	1.2	1.8	2.7	....	2.6	2.5
$8 to $8.99	3.8	2.4	5.0	2.8	1.8	.4	2.7	1.6	3.1	1.7
$9 to $9.99	3.6	3.0	4.1	1.9	2.0	.9	2.7	4.9	3.0	2.2
$10 to $11.99	9.9	4.5	10.7	4.7	3.1	1.8	....	1.6	7.1	3.5
$12 to $13.99	10.3	10.7	13.2	9.8	5.5	4.6	2.7	9.8	8.5	8.5
$14 to $15.99	10.9	8.1	9.9	11.7	5.9	5.0	8.1	4.9	8.8	7.4
$16 to $17.99	8.6	4.7	7.4	7.5	7.3	3.0	8.1	1.6	8.0	4.4
$18 to $19.99	9.5	13.9	9.1	8.5	6.5	7.4	27.1	13.1	8.8	10.9
$20 to $22.49	17.4	8.1	14.1	8.5	23.1	5.9	10.8	8.2	19.1	7.4
$22.50 to $24.99	4.2	2.7	1.7	2.3	12.5	2.1	10.8	4.9	7.3	2.5
$25 to $27.49	8.0	27.7	7.4	32.4	22.3	56.1	10.8	36.1	13.6	38.2
$27.50 to $29.99	.5	.8	1.7	.5	.6	1.4	....	3.3	.6	1.1
$30 and over	4.4	3.9	3.3	1.9	4.7	6.4	13.5	9.8	4.6	4.7
Total	100.0	100.0	100.0	100.0	100.0	100.0	100.0	100.0	100.0	100.0

DRAPERS.

Draping is one of the most skilled occupations in the trade in connection with the making of dresses and waists. Most of the drapers graduate into that class of work after having worked as dressmakers or examiners.

The drapers are roughly divided into two classes, those working on comparatively simple dresses and waists, and the high-grade dressmaker drapers. A lower-grade draper through practice and years of experience gradually works up to the higher grades. To do this she must have, however, a native taste for the beautiful in dress. The lower-grade drapers usually confine their attention to the simple draping of waists, which consists in arranging the plaits, joining the skirt to the waist with the aid of pins, seeing that the skirt hangs properly from the waistline, and draping the skirt. Drapers of this class are usually promoted to this work after they have been working as examiners or as plain dressmakers. They receive about $14 a week.

The high-grade draper or dressmaker draper, as she is sometimes called, works on high-class dresses and gowns. In many cases she makes practically the whole dress. After taking the cloth as it comes from the cutter, she joins the different pieces of cloth and, fixing them by means of pins, she drapes the cloth around the figure in graceful folds, sewing together with the needle the different parts where necessary. In many such cases there is but little work left for the operator to do after the draper removes the garment from the figure, most of the remaining work being done by hand by the finisher. Drapers of this class get all the way from $14 to $20 a week, although but few get more than $18.

CHART 10.—PER CENT OF CUTTERS (WEEK WORKERS) RECEIVING EACH CLASSIFIED RATE OF WAGES PER WEEK, 1912 AND 1913.

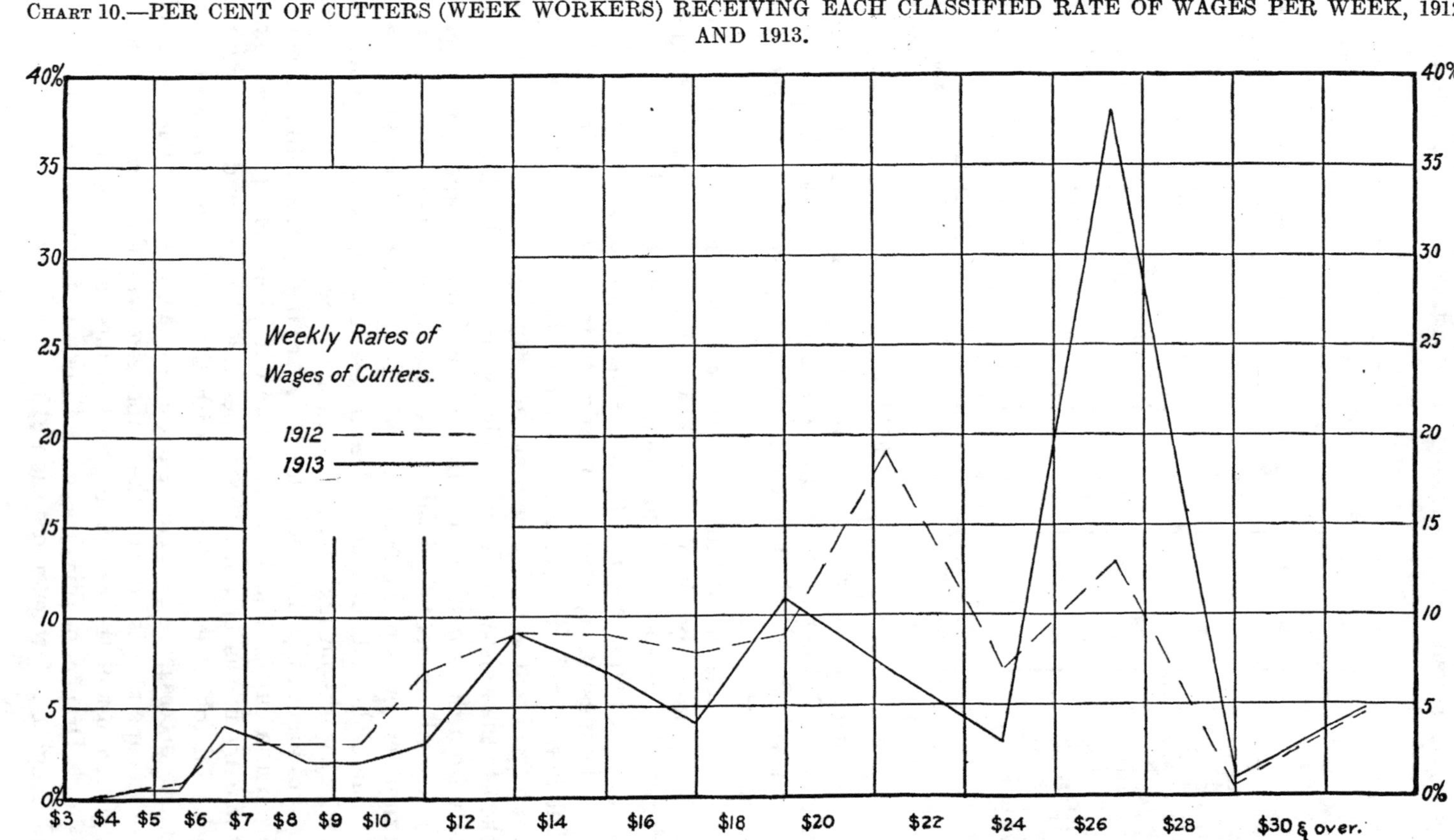

SEX.

Women are employed almost exclusively in this work. As will be seen from Table 8, out of 1,321 drapers for whom wages were found on the pay rolls in 1913, 1,315 were women and only 6 were men.

WAGES.

Draping is done almost entirely on a week basis. The protocol recognizes this fact by providing a weekly rate of wages which is fixed at a minimum of $14. Out of 1,321 drapers (Table 11), 1,273, or 96 per cent of all the drapers, were found working by the week and only 48, or 4 per cent, were pieceworkers.

Table 52 gives the wages of drapers in 1912 and 1913 in each of the four branches of the industry as well as for the industry as a whole, and also the percentage of the workers receiving various rates of wages. Of the 1,259 drapers for whom weekly rates of wages were obtained, 1,058, or 84 per cent, worked in association shops and only 201, or 16 per cent, were found employed in nonassociation shops.

Taking the minimum rate of wages as fixed in the protocol, $14, we find that in association shops producing low-grade garments (A), nearly 49 per cent of all the workers were in the wage group including this rate and in the corresponding nonassociation shops over 47 per cent, or practically the same proportion. On the other hand, in the high-grade shops (B) belonging to the association nearly 57 per cent were in the group receiving the minimum protocol rate, while in the corresponding nonassociation shops only about 35 per cent were in the group receiving the minimum rate. It must be borne in mind, however, that the percentages just quoted include not only those receiving $14 a week but also those receiving from $14 to $15.99, although the great majority of them were receiving $14. Taking those receiving $16 and over a week, we find that in the high-grade (B) association shops less than 15 per cent belong to that class, while in the high-grade nonassociation shops the percentage was practically the same, namely, over 16. In the shops manufacturing lower-grade garments (A), the proportion of drapers receiving $16 a week and over was over 10 per cent in the association and 12.5 per cent in the nonassociation shops.

As will be seen from Table 52, the largest group after the $14 to $15.99 was that of drapers receiving from $12 to $13.99 a week, which constituted 25.5 per cent of all the drapers employed in the association (A) shops (manufacturing low-grade garments) and over 18 per cent in the corresponding nonassociation shops, while in the B shops it constituted more than 20 per cent in the association branch and nearly 37 per cent in the nonassociation. A comparatively large proportion of drapers receiving $12 a week and less than $14, as well as the drapers receiving under $12 a week, consist of the lower-grade drapers and those whom the manufacturers regard more or less as apprentices in this kind of work. A personal investigation after the figures were compiled has also disclosed the fact that in some shops little or no distinction is made between joiners and drapers; sometimes those who do joining work are called drapers and are paid the wages of joiners, while in other shops workers who do real draping are called joiners.

An examination of Table 52 shows that association shops manufacturing high-grade (B) and low-grade (A) goods employed 84 per cent of all the drapers in the industry. As will be seen from the table, the group of $14 to $15.99 workers is the largest of all, reaching nearly 57 per cent in the association B shops and nearly 49 per cent in the A shops. Below the $14 rate it will be seen that the A shops in every wage group have a higher percentage than the B shops. That is to say, the proportion of workers receiving $5 and less than $14 a week is greater in the low-grade shops than in the high grade. At $14 and over the relative position is reversed.

Still more interesting is a consideration of the changes in the wages of all drapers since the adoption of the protocol shown in the last two columns of Table 52 and also in graphic form in Chart 11. The most conspicuous fact is the high peak representing the $14 to $15.99 group for 1913, at over 51 per cent, while in 1912 this group is less than 33 per cent. In 1912, the percentage of workers receiving $12 and less than $14 a week was almost as high as that of those receiving $14 and less than $16, while in 1913, the $12 to $13.99 group was only about 23 per cent, or 10 points below the 1912 line. The shifting that has occurred in the industry by way of the increase of the compensation to drapers is shown very clearly in this table and chart. For wage groups below $14 the percentages in 1912 are in almost all cases above those for 1913, while at $14 and above the position is reversed, showing that in every wage group from $14 to $22.50 there was a greater proportion of drapers in 1913 than in 1912.

An examination of the summary part of Table 52, in which these facts are brought out not only for the industry as a whole, but also for the different branches of the industry, shows, first, for the industry as a whole, that the number of drapers receiving under $12 a week declined from 27.5 per cent in 1912 to 13 per cent in 1913. Those getting $12 and less than $14 a week declined from 32.6 per cent in 1912 to less than 23 per cent in 1913. This makes the total number of drapers receiving less than the minimum protocol rate in 1913, 36 per cent of all the drapers. On the other hand, those getting $14 and less than $16 increased from nearly 33 per cent in 1912 to 51.5 per cent, or more than half of the entire number of drapers, in 1913, and those getting $16 and over increased from 7.1 per cent to nearly 13 per cent.

Taking the different branches of the industry, we find that the B (high-grade) shops belonging to the association lead all the others in the advance in wages for drapers, the proportion of those getting $14 and over in 1913 being 71.3 per cent, or nearly three-fourths of all

CHART 11.—PER CENT OF DRAPERS (WEEK WORKERS) RECEIVING EACH CLASSIFIED RATE OF WAGES PER WEEK, 1912 AND 1913.

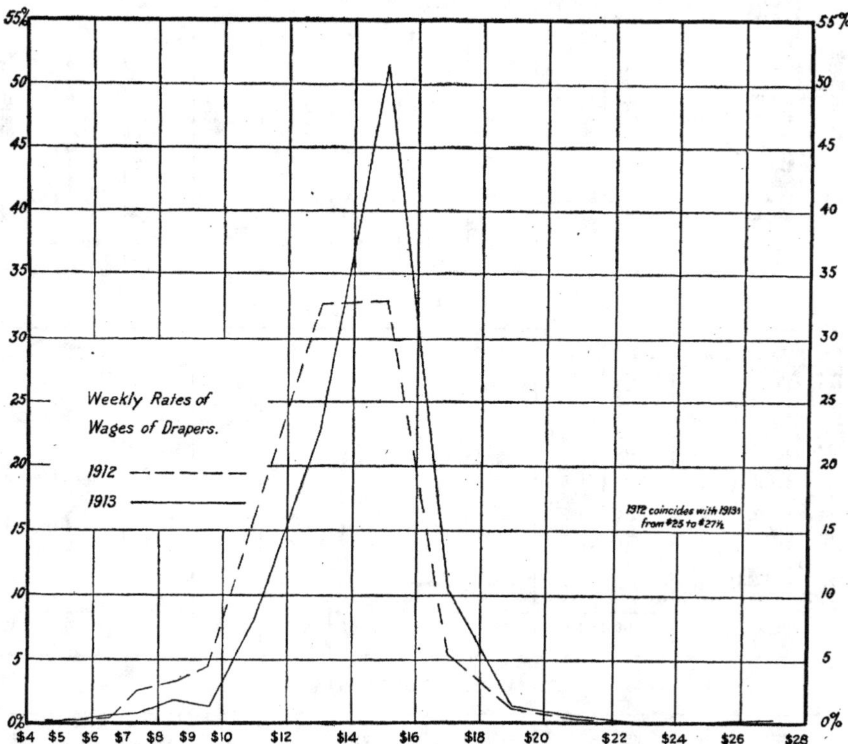

the drapers employed in those shops, as against 46.3 per cent during the preceding year. In the lower-grade association shops the percentage of those receiving $14 and over was 58.9 per cent as compared with 36.1 per cent the year before, and in the corresponding nonassociation shops it was 59.9 per cent, as compared with 26 per cent the year before.

TABLE 52.—NUMBER AND PER CENT OF DRAPERS, WEEK WORKERS,[1] RECEIVING EACH CLASSIFIED RATE OF WAGES PER WEEK, 1912 AND 1913, BY CLASS OF SHOPS.

NUMBER.

Classified rates of wages per week.	Association A.		Nonassociation A.		Association B.		Nonassociation B.[2]		Total.	
	1912	1913	1912	1913	1912	1913	1912	1913	1912	1913
Under $3										
$3 to $3.99										
$4 to $4.99	1	1			2				3	1
$5 to $5.99	2	2	1	2					3	4
$6 to $6.99	3	4	1	4			1		5	8
$7 to $7.99	13	5		2	9	2	2	1	24	10
$8 to $8.99	13	13	3	5	14	5	2		32	23
$9 to $9.99	19	10	1	3	21	5	1		42	18
$10 to $11.99	67	45	13	17	61	33	7	5	148	100
$12 to $13.99	132	131	30	28	128	111	13	18	303	288
$14 to $15.99	121	251	15	72	163	308	6	17	305	648
$16 to $17.99	16	46	2	17	28	62	4	6	50	131
$18 to $19.99	3	2		2	8	12		2	11	18
$20 to $22.49	1	4			3	5			4	9
$22.50 to $24.99										
$25 to $27.49					1	1			1	1
Total	391	514	66	152	438	544	33	49	[3] 931	[4] 1,259

PER CENT.

Classified rates of wages per week.	Association A. 1912	Association A. 1913	Nonassociation A. 1912	Nonassociation A. 1913	Association B. 1912	Association B. 1913	Nonassociation B. 1912	Nonassociation B. 1913	Total. 1912	Total. 1913
Under $3										
$3 to $3.99										
$4 to $4.99	0.2	0.2			0.5				0.3	0.1
$5 to $5.99	.5	.4	1.5	1.3					.3	.3
$6 to $6.99	.8	.8	1.5	2.6					.5	.6
$7 to $7.99	3.3	1.0		1.3	2.1	0.4			2.6	.8
$8 to $8.99	3.3	2.5	4.6	3.3	3.2	.9			3.4	1.8
$9 to $9.99	4.9	1.9	1.5	2.0	4.8	.9			4.5	1.4
$10 to $11.99	17.1	8.7	19.7	11.2	13.9	6.1			15.9	8.0
$12 to $13.99	33.8	25.5	45.5	18.4	29.2	20.4			32.6	22.9
$14 to $15.99	31.0	48.8	22.7	47.4	37.2	56.6			32.8	51.5
$16 to $17.99	4.1	9.0	3.0	11.2	6.4	11.4			5.4	10.4
$18 to $19.99	.8	.4		1.3	1.8	2.2			1.2	1.4
$20 to $22.49	.2	.8			.7	.9			.4	.7
$22.50 to $24.99										
$25 to $27.49					.2	.2			.1	.1
Total	100.0	100.0	100.0	100.0	100.0	100.0			100.0	100.0

SUMMARY OF PERCENTAGES.

Classified rates of wages per week.	Association A. 1912	Association A. 1913	Nonassociation A. 1912	Nonassociation A. 1913	Association B. 1912	Association B. 1913	Nonassociation B. 1912	Nonassociation B. 1913	Total. 1912	Total. 1913
Under $12	30.1	15.6	28.8	21.7	24.5	8.3			27.5	13.0
$12 to $13.99	33.8	25.5	45.5	18.4	29.2	20.4			32.6	22.9
$14 to $15.99	31.0	48.8	22.7	47.4	37.2	56.6			32.8	51.5
$16 and over	5.4	10.1	3.0	12.5	9.1	14.7			7.1	12.6
Total	100.0	100.0	100.0	100.0	100.0	100.0			100.0	100.0

[1] In addition to the week workers shown in this table there were 26 pieceworkers in 1912 and 48 in 1913.
[2] Percentages not computed on account of small number of employees.
[3] Not including 21 females, 1 male, for whom weekly rates of wages could not be ascertained.
[4] Not including 9 females, 5 males, for whom weekly rates of wages could not be ascertained.

EMBROIDERERS.

The work of embroiderers is too well known to need any explanation. The embroiderers for whom information is given in Table 8 and Table 53 are all handworkers skilled in the use of the needle. The majority of them are Italians. The skill of the embroiderer calls not only for the deft use of the needle, but for keen perception of colors and their different shadings, since colored thread is used to a very large extent. The great majority of the embroiderers working in the industry come with their skill previously acquired in their home country. There is an increasing number of embroiderers working on machines in some of the dress and waist making shops, but no mention of them appeared on the pay rolls of 1913 and therefore they are not included in these tables.

Only 184 embroiderers were found mentioned as such on the pay rolls of the shops investigated. A much larger number are actually employed in the industry. On the pay rolls, many of these are probably described as finishers, since they do their work by hand, and a great many are not mentioned at all, because the embroidery department is frequently in charge of a subcontractor, who pays his help directly and is compensated by the firm on a piece basis.

SEX.

Only 1 man was found among the 184 embroiderers covered by this report.

WAGES.

Of the 184 embroiderers reported in Table 11, 87, or a little less than one-half, were paid by the week, and 97 were paid by the piece. In 1912 the proportion was reversed, more than half being paid by the week and 74, out of a total of 167, being paid by the piece.

The 184 embroiderers were distributed as follows among three branches of the industry: Association A, 36; association B, 133; nonassociation B, 15. From this it will be seen that 169, or more than nine-tenths of all the embroiderers, were employed in association shops, leaving less than one-tenth in the nonassociation shops. The number being very small, no conclusions can be safely drawn as to the wages for the separate branches of the industry. They are, therefore, analyzed for the industry as a whole.

Wages of week workers.—The largest single group of week workers were those getting $8 a week and less than $9. These constituted more than 29 per cent of all the week workers. Nearly one-half of all the week workers received $9 and less than $14 a week. Only 1 girl received under $6 a week. More than one-tenth of all the week workers received $6 and less than $8 a week.

Earnings of pieceworkers.—Of the 97 pieceworkers, 16.5 per cent earned under $6 during the busiest week of the year. Nearly 29 per cent earned $6 and less than $9 a week. Over 42 per cent, or a little over four-tenths of the workers, earned $9 and less than $14, and more than 12 per cent, or about one-eighth, earned $14 and less than $18 a week.

Wages in 1912 and 1913.—No provision has been made in the protocol in regard to the wages of embroiderers. So far as the week workers are concerned, there is no marked change in the rates of wages from 1912 to 1913, with the exception of one group, namely, those earning $8 and less than $9 a week, which increased from over 17 per cent in 1912 to more than 29 per cent in 1913. The total number of embroiderers working by the week declined from 95 in 1912 to 87 in 1913, showing a loss of 8 workers. On the other hand, the number of pieceworkers increased from 74 to 97, an increase of 23 workers. A dropping off is noticeable in the number of week workers receiving under $8 a week, who numbered 23 in 1912 and only 11, or less than one-half of the former number, in 1913. On the other hand, the number of those receiving $8 and less than $9 increased from 16 to 25, showing a gain of 9, which may account for most of the decline in the lower groups. From $9 and over there is also a decline in every group except those getting $14 and less than $16 a week which may be accounted for by their passing into the group of pieceworkers where greater earnings are possible.

Earnings of pieceworkers in 1912 and 1913.—The proportion of pieceworkers earning under $6 during the busiest week of the year declined from 20.2 per cent in 1912 to 16.5 per cent in 1913. Those earning $6 and less than $9 a week formed practically the same proportion of the total both years, namely, 29.8 per cent and 28.9 per cent, respectively. Those earning $9 and less than $14 a week declined from 46 per cent in 1912 to 42.2 per cent in 1913, while those earning $14 a week and over increased from 4 per cent in 1912 to 12.4 per cent in 1913.

Summing up the changes in the wages of embroiderers, it may be said that among the week workers the number of those receiving under $8 a week declined; those receiving $8 to $8.99 increased perceptibly, and the number of those earning $9 and over remained practically the same. Among pieceworkers, while no radical changes in earnings occurred, there was a general tendency upward.

TABLE 53.—NUMBER AND PER CENT OF EMBROIDERERS (WEEK WORKERS AND PIECEWORKERS) RECEIVING EACH CLASSIFIED RATE OF WAGES OR EARNINGS PER WEEK, 1912 AND 1913, BY SEX.

Classified rates of wages or earnings per week, and classes of shops.	Week workers receiving each classified rate of wages.						Pieceworkers earning each classified amount during busiest week of year.			
	Females.				Males.		Females.			
	Number.		Per cent.		1912	1913	Number.		Per cent.	
	1912	1913	1912	1913			1912	1913	1912	1913
Under $3							8	7	10.8	7.2
$3 to $3.99							3	4	4.0	4.1
$4 to $4.99	3		3.2				2	1	2.7	1.1
$5 to $5.99	2	1	2.1	1.2			2	4	2.7	4.1
$6 to $6.99	8	2	8.6	2.3			4	10	5.4	10.3
$7 to $7.99	10	8	10.8	9.3			7	7	9.5	7.2
$8 to $8.99	16	25	17.2	29.1			11	11	14.9	11.4
$9 to $9.99	17	16	18.3	18.6	1		13	4	17.6	4.1
$10 to $11.99	19	15	20.5	17.4		1	15	17	20.3	17.5
$12 to $13.99	11	10	11.8	11.6			6	20	8.1	20.6
$14 to $15.99	3	6	3.2	6.9	1		2	5	2.7	5.2
$16 to $17.99		1		1.2				7		7.2
$18 to $19.99	1	1	1.1	1.2			1		1.3	
$20 to $22.49	1		1.1							
$22.50 to $24.99										
$25 to $27.49	2	1	2.1	1.2						
Total	93	86	100.0	100.0	2	1	74	97	100.0	100.0
	Workers in specified classes of shops.									
Association A	8	6			1		15	30		
Association B	72	66			1	1	53	66		
Nonassociation A										
Nonassociation B	13	14					6	1		

EXAMINERS.

The duty of an examiner consists in examining the garments after they have been completely finished by the workers. There are two distinct classes of examiners; first, those who examine the garments on a figure; second, those who examine the garments without the use of a figure. The former are the examiners of higher-grade garments, the latter of the cheap and medium grades of waists. The class 2 examiners are usually promoted from among the more intelligent and capable cleaners and finishers. They very seldom get more than $10 a week, which is the minimum rate fixed under the protocol. Those among this class of examiners who show capacity for better work are promoted to draping at which they can earn higher wages. The high-grade examiners are engaged on dresses and on waists selling at wholesale for $48 per dozen and over. These garments have to be put on a figure in order to be examined. It is the duty of the examiner to see that the garment thoroughly fits the figure and that the measurements at the waist line are correct. They carefully go over the entire garment to see that the sleeves hang right, that the collar fits properly, and that the laces on the corresponding sides of the garment "match"; in other words, that the garment is properly made as to fit, measurement, and "matching" of the corresponding parts and that there is no flaw in the work of the different workers who made up the garment. Examiners of this class are promoted from draping and dressmaking and receive all the way from $14 to $19.99 a week. It is seldom that they are promoted to any other occupation, although occasionally a high-class examiner, in changing factories, may go into high-class draping. Once in a while one is promoted to the position of forewoman.

SEX.

As a rule, only women are employed as examiners. Among the 852 examiners, reported in 1913, there were only 10 men, or but little over 1 per cent of the total.

WAGES.

Examiners are always paid by the week. Of the 790 women examiners (Table 54) whose weekly rates in 1913 could be ascertained, the largest single group were those receiving $10 and less than $12 a week, who constituted nearly 38 per cent of the total. The next largest group were those getting $12 and less than $14, who constituted almost 18 per cent of the total. A little less than 12 per cent received $14 and less than $16 a week, and only 3.2 per cent received $16 a week and over. Only 3 examiners in the entire industry were found receiving $20 a week and over. The number of those earning less than the minimum protocol rate of $10 a week was 235, or nearly 30 per cent of the total in 1913. Sixteen examiners, or 2 per cent, received under $6 per week.

Nearly one-half (370) of the 790 women examiners worked in association A shops; 323 worked in association B shops, leaving only 76 in nonassociation A shops and 21 in nonassociation B shops.

A comparison of the earnings of the women workers in the association A and nonassociation A shops in 1913 shows that the number of those receiving $10 a week and over formed a larger percentage of the total in the nonassociation shops than in the association shops, namely, over 67 per cent as against nearly 62 per cent. This is also true for each of the following separate groups: $10 and less than $12, $12 and less than $14, $14 and less than $16, $16 and less than $18. In the case of those earning $8 and less than $10, the percentage is likewise larger in the nonassociation shops as compared with the association shops, being 25 per cent in the former and less than 19 per cent in the latter. Those earning under $8 constituted nearly 8 per cent in the nonassociation A shops and nearly 20 per cent in the association shops of the same class.

Comparing the A and B association shops, the percentage of those earning $12 a week and over is found to be larger in the B shops (those manufacturing the higher grade garments), while of those receiving under $12 a week there is a larger percentage in the A shops. This is easily explained by the fact that the B shops require examiners of greater skill, who naturally command higher wages entirely apart from the protocol provision which specifies only the minimum rate. The difference in the compensation of examiners in the A and B shops can be clearly seen by reference to Table 54. Both groups rise to a high point in the class of $10 to $11.99 a week workers, which includes the minimum protocol rate of $10, the percentage of those getting the minimum rate being higher in the lower-grade shops than in the higher-grade. Above this rate, the group percentages in the high-grade shops are in each case higher than those in the lower-grade shops, while in the group below $9 a week the reverse is true.

Comparison of wages in 1912 and 1913.—A glance at Table 54 and Chart 12 will show a uniform improvement in the earnings of examiners which has taken place since the protocol went into effect. Although during both years the $10 to $11.99 group forms the highest peak, it does not rise as high in 1912 as in 1913. The 1913 percentages are higher than the 1912 at all points representing wages of $10 and over, while the reverse is true for wages below $10. The greatest rise, however, occurred in the $10 to $11.99 group containing the rate fixed by the protocol ($10), and a corresponding decline occurred in the two groups from $8 to $9.99 a week. The percentage of those receiving $10 a week and over increased from less than 58 in 1912 to over 70 in 1913 and correspondingly declined in the case of those receiving under $10 a week.

TABLE 54.—NUMBER AND PER CENT OF EXAMINERS, WEEK WORKERS, RECEIVING EACH CLASSIFIED RATE OF WAGES PER WEEK, 1912 AND 1913, BY CLASS OF SHOPS.

NUMBER.

Classified rates of wages per week.	Association A.		Nonassociation A.		Association B.		Nonassociation B.[1]		Total.	
	1912	1913	1912	1913	1912	1913	1912	1913	1912	1913
Under $3										
$3 to $3.99		1								1
$4 to $4.99	5	4			3				8	4
$5 to $5.99	4	8	2	2	4	1			10	11
$6 to $6.99	9	19	2	2	7	1	1		19	22
$7 to $7.99	22	41	3	2	14	6			39	49
$8 to $8.99	38	30	7	9	32	14			77	53
$9 to $9.99	39	39	13	10	37	42	1	4	90	95
$10 to $11.99	79	146	15	32	74	110	4	10	172	298
$12 to $13.99	38	56	3	12	56	68	2	4	99	140
$14 to $15.99	15	23	2	5	35	61		3	52	92
$16 to $17.99	1	1	1	2	6	11			8	14
$18 to $19.99	1				1	8			2	8
$20 to $22.49		2				1				3
$22.50 to $24.99										
$25 to $27.49										
$27.50 to $29.99										
$30 and over										
Total	251	370	48	76	269	323	8	21	[2] 576	[3] 790

[1] Percentages for nonassociation B shops not computed on account of small number of employees.
[2] Not including 64 females for whom weekly rates could not be ascertained.
[3] Not including 52 females and 10 males for whom weekly rates could not be ascertained.

TABLE 54.—NUMBER AND PER CENT OF EXAMINERS, WEEK WORKERS, RECEIVING EACH CLASSIFIED RATE OF WAGES PER WEEK, 1912 AND 1913, BY CLASS OF SHOPS—Concluded.

PER CENT.

Classified rates of wages per week.	Association A.		Nonassociation A.		Association B.		Nonassociation B.		Total.	
	1912	1913	1912	1913	1912	1913	1912	1913	1912	1913
Under $3										
$3 to $3.99		0.3								0.1
$4 to $4.99	2.0	1.1			1.1				1.4	.5
$5 to $5.99	1.6	2.2	4.2	2.6	1.5	0.3			1.7	1.4
$6 to $6.99	3.6	5.1	4.2	2.6	2.6	.3			3.3	2.8
$7 to $7.99	8.9	11.1	6.2	2.6	5.2	1.9			6.8	6.2
$8 to $8.99	15.1	8.1	14.6	11.8	12.0	4.3			13.4	6.7
$9 to $9.99	15.5	10.5	27.1	13.2	13.7	13.0			15.6	12.0
$10 to $11.99	31.4	39.5	31.2	42.1	27.5	34.1			29.9	37.7
$12 to $13.99	15.1	15.1	6.2	15.8	20.8	21.0			17.0	17.7
$14 to $15.99	6.0	6.2	4.2	6.6	13.0	18.9			9.0	11.7
$16 to $17.99	.4	.3	2.1	2.6	2.2	3.4			1.4	1.8
$18 to $19.99	.4				.4	2.5			.3	1.0
$20 to $22.49		.5				.3				.4
$22.50 to $24.99										
$25 to $27.49										
$27.50 to $29.99										
$30 and over										
Total	100.0	100.0	100.0	100.0	100.0	100.0			100.0	100.0

SUMMARY OF PERCENTAGES.

Classified rates of wages per week.	Association A. 1912	Association A. 1913	Nonassociation A. 1912	Nonassociation A. 1913	Association B. 1912	Association B. 1913	Nonassociation B. 1912	Nonassociation B. 1913	Total. 1912	Total. 1913
Under $10	46.7	38.4			36.1	19.8			42.2	29.7
$10 to $11.99	31.4	39.5			27.5	34.1			29.9	37.7
$12 and over	21.9	22.1			36.4	46.1			28.0	32.5
Total	100.0	100.0			100.0	100.0			100.0	100.0

FINISHERS.

The protocol distinguishes between two kinds of finishers—dressmaker finishers and plain finishers. For the former, a weekly rate of not less than $8 a week is provided; for the latter, piece rates are established with a provision as to the minimum earnings of $8 a week if the worker is retained after one week's trial.

Finishers do most of the sewing that has to be done by hand. The plain finishers sew on hooks and eyes, buttons, belts; they baste the bottoms of skirts, etc. Any girl who can use a needle can be put to work as a finisher. Dressmaker finishers are employed on the higher grade of dresses. In addition to doing the same work as the plain finishers, they do the other work that has to be done by hand on higher-grade dresses, such as sewing on the trimmings, ornaments, sashes, rosettes, bows, ties, etc. This class of finishers is obtained from among plain finishers and dressmakers who have previously worked in custom dressmaking establishments in this country or abroad.

SEX.

Only women are employed as finishers.

WAGES.

For 1913 5,363 finishers were reported (Table 11), while for 1912 records were obtained for only 4,352. Of those employed in 1913, 3,334, or 62 per cent, worked by the week and 2,029, or 38 per cent, worked by the piece. That is to say, only a little over one-third were pieceworkers.

Wages of week workers.—Of the 3,249 finishers working by the week (Table 55), those receiving the minimum rate of $8 a week

CHART 12.—PER CENT OF EXAMINERS (WEEK WORKERS) RECEIVING EACH CLASSIFIED RATE OF WAGES PER WEEK, 1912 AND 1913.

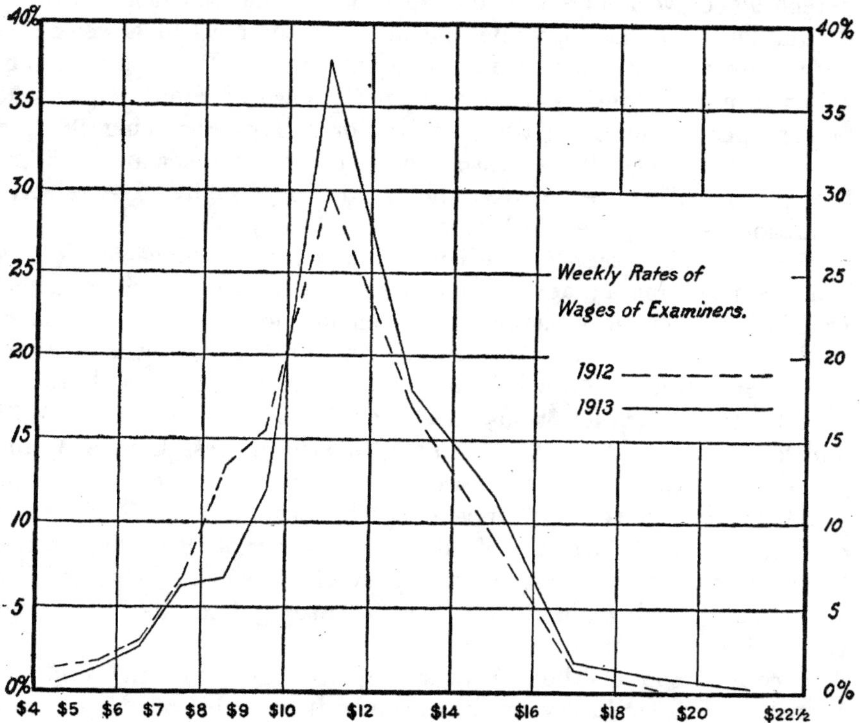

and less than $9 numbered 1,148, constituting the largest single group, namely, over 35 per cent of the total. The next largest group were those receiving $9 and less than $10 a week, who formed nearly one-fifth of the total, the two together constituting more than 55 per cent of the total, or considerably more than one-half of all the women finishers working by the week. Nearly 16 per cent received $10 and less than $12 a week, and a little less than 12 per cent received $7 and less than $8 a week. The percentage of those receiving $12 a week and over was 5.5. The percentage of those earning less than the minimum protocol rate of $8 a week was less than 24, or nearly one-fourth of all the finishers working by the week, and the number of those earning under $6 a week formed a little less than 5 per cent of the total.

A comparison of the wages of week-working finishers in the different branches of the industry can be made from the figures of percentages given in Table 55. This table shows that the number of those receiving more than the minimum protocol rate of $8 a week is higher in the nonassociation B shops (high-grade garments) than in the association B shops and is higher in nonassociation A shops than in the association A shops. The only exception is in the case of those receiving $12 and less than $14 a week, in which the percentage of workers in the nonassociation B and association B shops is practically the same, while of workers receiving $14 a week and over there is only 1 person in the nonassociation B shops and only 4 in the nonassociation A shops. In the case of the A shops, the percentages in nonassociation shops for groups receiving $8 and over are in practically all cases above those for association shops, though the difference between the two is very small. The relative conditions are reversed for wages below $8 a week.

Earnings of pieceworkers.—There was no such concentration of workers receiving a single rate of wages in the case of the finishers working by the piece as we have seen in the case of the finishers working by the week, where more than one-third of the workers earned $8 a week. As will be seen from Table 56, six wage groups, namely, those earning $6 and less than $7, $7 and less than $8, $8 and less than $9, $9 and less than $10, $10 and less than $12, and $12 and less than $14, contributed each about 10 per cent in round numbers to the total of finisher pieceworkers in 1913, together embracing over 61 per cent of all. The number of those who earned $14 a week or more during the busiest week of 1913 slightly exceeded 9 per cent, leaving about 30 per cent earning less than $6 during the busiest week of the year.

A comparison of the earnings of pieceworkers in the different branches of the industry can be obtained from Table 56. This table shows that no such clear line of demarcation can be drawn between the earnings of pieceworkers in the different branches of the industry as in the case of the week workers. The nonassociation B shops (higher-grade garments) contain the highest peak of all, 19 per cent in the $8 and under $9 group, as against a little over 8 per cent for the association B shops. In practically all the wage groups below $9 the nonassociation B shops are above the association B shops; on the other hand, above the $9 group the association B is considerably above the nonassociation B, showing a larger percentage of the higher-paid finishers in the association shops.

The same is true in general of the association A and nonassociation A shops, although the distinction between these two is not so clear and so much in favor of the association as is the case with the B shops. The highest peak in the association A shops reaches less than 12 per cent in the $9 and under $10 group while the nonassociation A shops reach the highest point at 16.5 per cent in the $10 and under $12 group. If we draw the line at $10, the proportion of finishers earning $10 a week or more in the association A shops is less than 24 per cent, while in the nonassociation A shops it exceeds 29 per cent, showing a slight advantage in favor of the nonassociation shops.

COMPARISON OF WAGES IN 1912 AND 1913.

Changes in wages of week workers.—A glance at the last two columns in Table 55 and at Chart 13 will show a uniform increase in the number of week workers receiving $8 a week or more and a reduction in the relative number of those receiving less than $8. The percentage of those receiving the minimum protocol rate of $8 and under $9 rose from 21.2 to 35.3 per cent. The percentage of those receiving $8 a week or more increased from less than 51 in 1912 to over 76 in 1913. In every group below $8 a week there was a larger percentage in 1912 than in 1913.

Changes in the earnings of pieceworkers.—No such striking change is seen in the case of the pieceworkers (see Table 56). The percentage of finishers earning $8 and less than $10 during the busiest week of the year was practically the same during both years, namely, a little less than 20 in 1912 and a little less than 21 in 1913. The percentage of those earning $10 and less than $12 declined from 14 in 1912 to nearly 11 in 1913. Of those earning $12 a week and over, there was an increase from less than 15 per cent in 1912 to nearly 19 per cent in 1913. Of those earning less than $8 a week there was a decline from 51.5 per cent in 1912 to 49 per cent in 1913. The drop is clearly shown to be in the $4 and under $6 and $10 and under $12 groups, with a consequent increase in the number of those earning $6 and under $9 and $12 and over a week.

Summary.—The figures in Tables 55 and 56 may be summed up as follows: First, that there has been, on the whole, an increase in the wages of finishers which was much more effective among the week workers than among the pieceworkers; second, that there was a larger percentage of higher paid workers in the high-grade shops than in the low-grade shops; third, that in each of these classes of shops the percentage of the higher paid week workers was greater in the nonassociation than in the association shops; fourth, among the pieceworkers, the highest percentage of finishers earning $8 a week and up was in the high-grade association shops, where they numbered 58 per cent, followed by the low-grade nonassociation shops where they numbered nearly 52 per cent, while in the high-grade nonassociation shops and in the low-grade association shops it was practically the same, nearly 46 per cent. In other words, where the wages were paid by the week, they were determined, in the long run, by the skill

CHART 13.—PER CENT OF FINISHERS (WEEK WORKERS) RECEIVING EACH CLASSIFIED RATE OF WAGES PER WEEK, 1912 AND 1913.

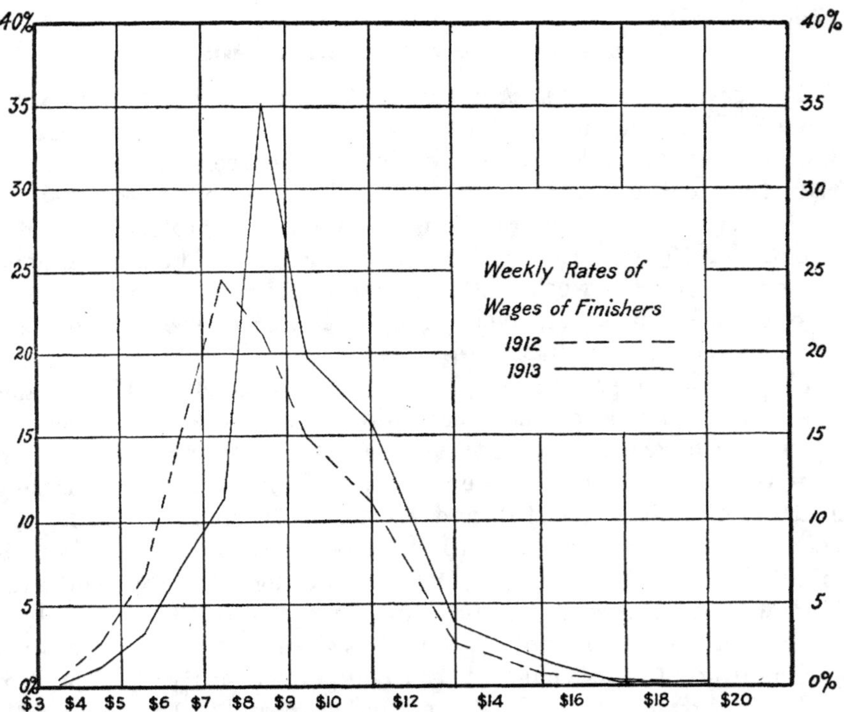

of the worker. The workers were enabled to command higher wages in the shops manufacturing high-grade garments than in those manufacturing low-grade garments and requiring less skilled workers. On the other hand, where the work was paid for by the piece, the earnings were determined not only by the skill but by the speed of the workers, and the rates paid, not being uniform in the different shops, resulted in great differences in earnings without regard to the character of the goods manufactured.

TABLE 55.—NUMBER AND PER CENT OF FINISHERS, WEEK WORKERS, RECEIVING EACH CLASSIFIED RATE OF WAGES PER WEEK, 1912 AND 1913, BY CLASS OF SHOPS.

NUMBER.

Classified rates of wages per week.	Association A.		Nonassociation A.		Association B.		Nonassociation B.		Total.	
	1912	1913	1912	1913	1912	1913	1912	1913	1912	1913
Under $3	1	....	1	....	....	....	....	....	2	....
$3 to $3.99	11	1	2	1	1	....	....	1	14	3
$4 to $4.99	35	15	5	5	23	17	3	4	66	41
$5 to $5.99	92	53	14	17	61	34	12	7	179	111
$6 to $6.99	180	100	25	40	160	79	17	17	382	236
$7 to $7.99	234	170	65	58	295	122	41	22	635	372
$8 to $8.99	218	402	43	166	233	518	54	62	548	1,148
$9 to $9.99	141	221	32	89	165	264	45	69	383	643
$10 to $11.99	82	168	24	76	163	225	18	45	287	514
$12 to $13.99	20	34	6	21	34	59	7	10	67	124
$14 to $15.99	7	13	....	4	9	32	3	1	19	50
$16 to $17.99	....	....	1	....	3	3	....	....	4	3
$18 to $19.99	2	1	....	....	....	3	....	....	2	4
Total	1,023	1,178	218	477	1,147	1,356	200	238	[1] 2,588	[2] 3,249

PER CENT.

Classified rates of wages per week.	Association A. 1912	Association A. 1913	Nonassociation A. 1912	Nonassociation A. 1913	Association B. 1912	Association B. 1913	Nonassociation B. 1912	Nonassociation B. 1913	Total. 1912	Total. 1913
Under $3	0.1	....	0.5	....	....	....	....	....	0.1	....
$3 to $3.99	1.0	0.1	.9	0.2	0.1	....	....	0.5	.5	0.1
$4 to $4.99	3.4	1.3	2.3	1.0	2.0	1.3	1.5	1.7	2.6	1.3
$5 to $5.99	9.0	4.5	6.4	3.6	5.3	2.5	6.0	2.9	6.9	3.4
$6 to $6.99	17.6	8.5	11.5	8.4	13.9	5.8	8.5	7.1	14.8	7.3
$7 to $7.99	22.9	14.4	29.8	12.1	25.7	9.0	20.5	9.2	24.5	11.5
$8 to $8.99	21.3	34.1	19.7	34.9	20.3	38.2	27.0	26.1	21.2	35.3
$9 to $9.99	13.8	18.8	14.7	18.7	14.4	19.5	22.5	29.0	14.8	19.8
$10 to $11.99	8.0	14.2	11.0	15.9	14.2	16.6	9.0	18.9	11.1	15.8
$12 to $13.99	2.0	2.9	2.7	4.4	3.0	4.3	3.5	4.2	2.6	3.8
$14 to $15.99	.7	1.1	....	.8	.8	2.4	1.5	.4	.7	1.5
$16 to $17.99	....	....	.5	....	.3	.2	....	....	.2	.1
$18 to $19.99	.2	.1	....	....	....	.2	....	....	.1	.1
Total	100.0	100.0	100.0	100.0	100.0	100.0	100.0	100.0	100.0	100.0

SUMMARY OF PERCENTAGES.

Classified rates of wages per week.	Association A. 1912	Association A. 1913	Nonassociation A. 1912	Nonassociation A. 1913	Association B. 1912	Association B. 1913	Nonassociation B. 1912	Nonassociation B. 1913	Total. 1912	Total. 1913
Less than $8	54.0	28.8	51.4	25.3	47.1	18.6	36.5	21.4	49.3	23.6
$8 to $8.99	21.3	34.1	19.7	34.9	20.3	38.2	27.0	26.1	21.2	35.3
$9 and over	24.7	37.1	28.9	39.8	32.6	43.2	36.5	52.5	29.5	41.1
Total	100.0	100.0	100.0	100.0	100.0	100.0	100.0	100.0	100.0	100.0

[1] Not including 196, for whom earnings but not weekly rates of wages could be ascertained.
[2] Not including 85, for whom earnings but not weekly rates of wages could be ascertained.

TABLE 56.—NUMBER AND PER CENT OF FINISHERS, PIECEWORKERS, EARNING EACH CLASSIFIED AMOUNT DURING THE BUSIEST WEEK OF THE YEAR, 1912 AND 1913, BY CLASS OF SHOPS.

NUMBER.

Classified earnings per week.	Association A.		Nonassociation A.		Association B.		Nonassociation B.[1]		Total.	
	1912	1913	1912	1913	1912	1913	1912	1913	1912	1913
Under $3	125	122	18	34	117	76	2	5	262	237
$3 to $3.99	38	59	7	15	41	41	2	10	88	125
$4 to $4.99	46	54	13	14	57	37	2	13	118	118
$5 to $5.99	70	66	16	24	46	38	2	8	134	136
$6 to $6.99	64	95	15	37	55	56	2	11	136	199
$7 to $7.99	79	96	20	40	68	69	2	16	169	221
$8 to $8.99	78	91	28	44	66	63	2	22	174	220
$9 to $9.99	76	106	18	31	73	75	5	9	172	221
$10 to $11.99	104	55	28	56	114	117	2	10	248	238
$12 to $13.99	54	86	7	28	79	85	6	5	146	204
$14 to $15.99	26	55	8	12	42	55	1	5	77	127
$16 to $17.99	14	17	4	4	10	24		2	28	47
$18 to $19.99	4	3	1		3	14			8	17
$20 to $22.49					1	4			1	4
$22.50 to $24.99	2				1				3	
Total	780	905	183	339	773	754	28	116	[2]1,764	[3]2,114

PER CENT.

Classified earnings per week.	Association A.		Nonassociation A.		Association B.		Nonassociation B.[1]		Total.	
	1912	1913	1912	1913	1912	1913	1912	1913	1912	1913
Under $3	16.0	13.5	9.8	10.0	15.1	10.1		4.3	14.9	11.2
$3 to $3.99	4.9	6.5	3.8	4.4	5.3	5.4		8.6	5.0	5.9
$4 to $4.99	5.9	6.0	7.1	4.1	7.4	4.9		11.2	6.7	5.6
$5 to $5.99	9.0	7.3	8.8	7.1	6.0	5.0		6.9	7.6	6.4
$6 to $6.99	8.2	10.5	8.2	10.9	7.1	7.4		9.5	7.7	9.4
$7 to $7.99	10.1	10.6	10.9	11.8	8.8	9.2		13.8	9.6	10.5
$8 to $8.99	10.0	10.0	15.3	13.0	8.5	8.3		19.0	9.9	10.4
$9 to $9.99	9.7	11.7	9.8	9.2	9.5	10.0		7.8	9.7	10.5
$10 to $11.99	13.4	6.1	15.3	16.5	14.8	15.5		8.6	14.0	11.3
$12 to $13.99	6.9	9.5	3.8	8.3	10.2	11.3		4.3	8.3	9.6
$14 to $15.99	3.3	6.1	4.4	3.5	5.4	7.3		4.3	4.4	6.0
$16 to $17.99	1.8	1.9	2.2	1.2	1.3	3.2		1.7	1.6	2.2
$18 to $19.99	.5	.3	.6		.4	1.9			.4	.8
$20 to $22.49					.1	.5			.1	.2
$22.50 to $24.99	.3				.1				.2	
Total	100.0	100.0	100.0	100.0	100.0	100.0		100.0	100.0	100.0

[1] Percentages for 1912 not computed on account of small number of employees.
[2] Including 196 week workers for whom earnings but not weekly rates of wages could be ascertained.
[3] Including 85 week workers for whom earnings but not weekly rates of wages could be ascertained.

IRONERS AND PRESSERS.

The protocol provided for different rates of wages for ironers and pressers without defining what was meant by each. Considerable difference of opinion has developed between the workers and the manufacturers as to where the exact line is to be drawn between the two classes of workers.

By pressers are meant those who work with a heavy flatiron, placing a wet cloth between the iron and the garment that is pressed. By ironers are meant those working with a light iron without the use of a wet cloth. The heavy iron is used on serges and other woolen and worsted cloths, heavy linens, ratines, and, sometimes, silks. The light iron is used mostly on lingerie and light cotton cloth and most silks. So far, there is complete agreement on both sides. The difference arises in determining where the light iron ends and the heavy iron begins. The workers are inclined to consider an iron weighing 8 pounds or more as a heavy iron. Among the manufacturers, some draw the line at 12 pounds. There is a tendency to an agreement on 10 pounds as the line of demarcation.

In view of the contention as to the designation of pressers and ironers, respectively, it was found impossible to account for each separately. Several manufacturers call their workers pressers, although they work with light irons; others call their people uniformly ironers, although the majority of them may be pressers; while in some shops the relative number of pressers and ironers changes with the seasons and with the changes in the character of the garments manufactured. It was, therefore, found necessary to combine pressers and ironers into one class.

SEX.

With but rare exceptions pressers are all men, while ironers are mostly women. Of the pressers and ironers, 1,119 are reported in Table 8 for 1913 and 816 for 1912. Of those in 1913, 537 were males and 582 were females.

WAGES.

Although the protocol provides for weekly rates of wages for ironers and pressers, nearly one-third of all the ironers and pressers found on the pay rolls of the shops investigated were working by the piece (see Table 11). The exact percentage of pieceworkers was 32 per cent in 1913 and 37 per cent in 1912. Although the proportion of pieceworkers declined from 1912 to 1913, the actual number of pieceworkers increased, being 298 in 1912 and 357 in 1913.

Wages of week workers, women.—The minimum rates of wages provided by the protocol for ironers are $12 a week for women and $15 for men and $20 for pressers, who are all men. The number of women week workers receiving a wage of $12 and under $14 a week was 115 out of the total of 387, or nearly 30 per cent (Table 57). Nearly 13 per cent of the women ironers received $14 and less than $16; over 4 per cent received $16 and less than $18; 5 women ironers received $18 and under $20, and 2 women received $20 a week and over. That is to say, less than 49 per cent of all the women ironers working by the week received $12 a week or more, while over 51 per cent, or more than half, received less than the minimum protocol rate. Of these, nearly 21 per cent, or more than one-fifth of all the women week workers, received $10 and less than $12 a week, and nearly 12 per cent, or more than one-tenth, received $9 and less than $10. The remainder, over 18 per cent, received $4 and less than $9 a week. Of these, 4 workers received $4 and less than $5 a week and 5 workers received $5 and less than $6.

Wages of week workers, men.—On the whole the men week workers have fared better than the women in receiving the protocol rates.

The number of men ironers or pressers receiving $12 a week or more constituted nearly 82 per cent of the total of 352 men ironers and pressers (Table 58). Those in the groups getting $15 (the minimum protocol rate of ironers) or more constituted more than 69 per cent of the total; those receiving the minimum protocol rate of pressers ($20) and more than that amount constituted over 28 per cent of the total. This does not mean that 28 per cent of the pressers received the minimum pressers' rate of $20, since the pressers and ironers are combined. On the other hand, there is no doubt that the number of those who received $15 and less than $20 a week includes not only ironers but also pressers.

Earnings of pieceworkers, women.—Since pieceworkers are presumed to work harder than week workers, especially during the busy season, and since the figures here given for pieceworkers cover their total earnings, including overtime, while the figures for the week workers are the weekly rates, not including overtime, it is natural to expect that the pieceworkers' earnings will exceed the weekly rates of wages for the corresponding workers. A comparison of the piecework earnings and the weekly rates bears this out for the women, but not so strongly, if at all, for the men.

Earnings of pieceworkers, men.—Thus, the proportion of men (Table 60) earning $12 a week and over by piecework was over 83 per cent as compared with nearly 82 per cent of men receiving these rates by the week (Table 58). The proportion of men earning $14 a week or more was more than 74 per cent as compared with more than 69 per cent receiving these rates by the week.

In the case of women pieceworkers (Table 59), nearly 67 per cent earned $12 a week or more, while among the women week workers less than 49 per cent received that rate, and the proportion of women pieceworkers earning $14 a week or more was over 57 per cent as compared with less than 20 per cent of women earning this amount by the week. Among the women week workers, the highest wage group was that of $20 and less than $22.50, while among the women pieceworkers nearly 9 per cent earned $20 and less than $22.50 a week, over 9 per cent earned $22.50 and less than $25, nearly 3 per cent earned $25 and less than $27.50, nearly 4 per cent earned $27.50 and less than $30, and 1 woman earned over $30.

The inference from these figures is clear that where women and men are compensated strictly on their respective merits—that is, in proportion to the work turned out, receiving the same compensation for equal quantities of work—women come much nearer earning the same wages as the men than where the compensation is fixed according to the sex as is the case with the weekly rates.

While the proportion of men earning $12 a week and over is practically the same among pieceworkers and week workers, namely, over

83 per cent in the former and nearly 82 per cent in the latter, the difference between the two classes increases as the scale of wages increases. Thus those receiving $16 a week or more constitute over 66 per cent among the pieceworkers and only 52.5 per cent among the week workers; those receiving $20 a week or more form nearly 49 per cent among pieceworkers and less than 29 per cent among the week workers; those receiving $25 a week or more constitute over 29 per cent among the pieceworkers and less than 4 per cent among the week workers.

A comparison of the wages in the high-grade and low-grade shops is made in Table 57, giving the wages of the women ironers working by the week, this being the largest group in the occupation of ironers and pressers. This table shows for a few of the lower wage groups an excess of workers in the low-grade shops as compared with the high grade. Corresponding to this is an excess in the proportion of workers in the high-grade shops over the low-grade for the next group of higher-paid workers. Thus there is a greater percentage of workers receiving less than $8 a week in the A shops than in the B shops. In the next three succeeding wage groups ($8 and under $12 a week) the percentage for the B shops rises slightly above that for the A shops. Again, for the group $12 and under $14 a week there is a high peak above 32 per cent for the A shops, while the percentage for B shops rises to a little over 23 per cent; and for the group $14 and under $16 the percentage for B shops is higher than that for the A shops, showing that there is a greater percentage of the higher-paid workers in the high-grade shops than in the shops manufacturing the cheaper garments.

Wages in 1912 and 1913.—The effect of the protocol upon the wages of female ironers, week workers, is shown in Table 57 and in Chart 14. The usual high peak is shown for the group containing the protocol rate ($12), as is the case with week workers in all occupations for which there is only one protocol rate. The number of those receiving $12 to $13.99 a week has risen from less than 20 per cent of all the women ironers to nearly 30 per cent, and those receiving less than $12 formed a much larger proportion in 1912 than in 1913, while those receiving $12 a week or more are relatively more numerous in 1913. There is a clear shifting of the entire force from lower-paid positions to higher-paid.

Table 58 and Chart 15 show the changes in the wages of men pressers and ironers, week workers, in the two years 1912 and 1913. The change here does not show the same uniform movement upward as in Chart 14. On the whole, however, it shows an improvement and a decided increase in the number of those receiving $20 a week or more and a slight increase in the number of those receiving $14 to $15.99 a week. The $20 to $22.49 group forms the highest peak, rising to nearly 22 per cent, as against only 4 per cent in the year 1912. All the other groups above $20 show an increase with the exception of the group of those receiving $30 and over, which has declined from more than 5 per cent in 1912 to a little more than 1 per cent in 1913. This represents, however, only 11 persons in 1912 and 5 persons in 1913. With the exception of those receiving $7 and under $8 a week, all the wage groups below $15 show a falling off since 1912. The percentage of ironers receiving $10 and under $12

CHART 14.—PER CENT OF IRONERS, FEMALE (WEEK WORKERS), RECEIVING EACH CLASSIFIED RATE OF WAGES PER WEEK, 1912 AND 1913.

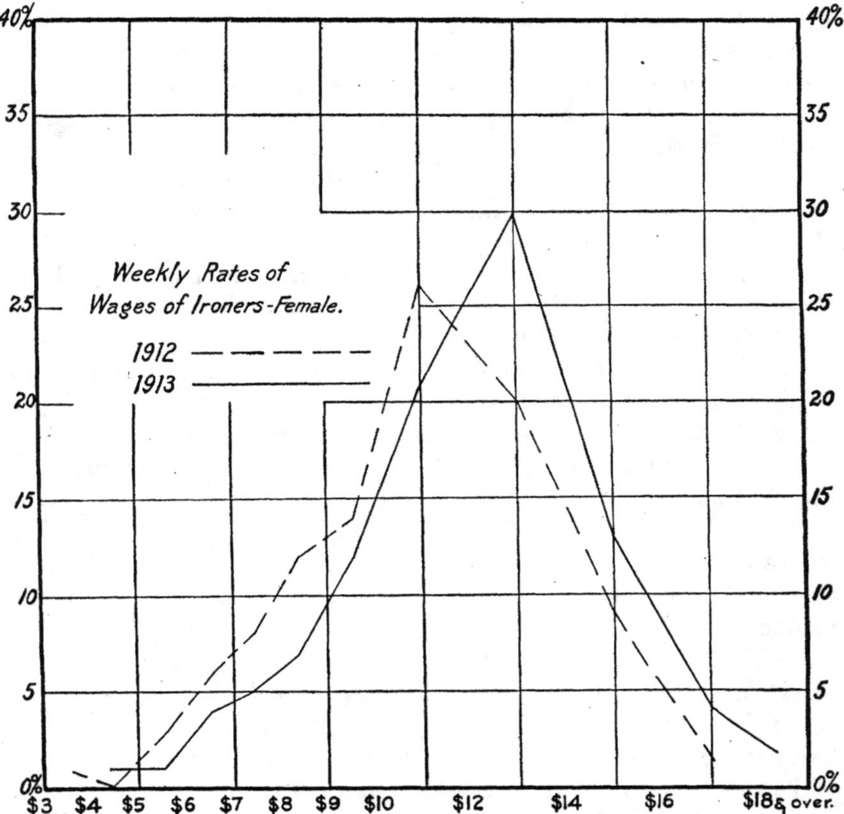

is practically the same for both years, namely, 8 and 7.4. All these reductions have been accompanied by an increase in the number of people receiving the protocol rate of $15, and especially in the number of those receiving $20 a week and more.

Tables 59 and 60 show clearly the changes that have occurred in the earnings of pressers and ironers working by the piece. Looking first at the figures of percentages of female pieceworkers in these tables, an almost uniform decline is found in the proportion of those

CHART 15.—PER CENT OF PRESSERS AND IRONERS, MALE (WEEK WORKERS), RECEIVING EACH CLASSIFIED RATE OF WAGES PER WEEK, 1912 AND 1913.

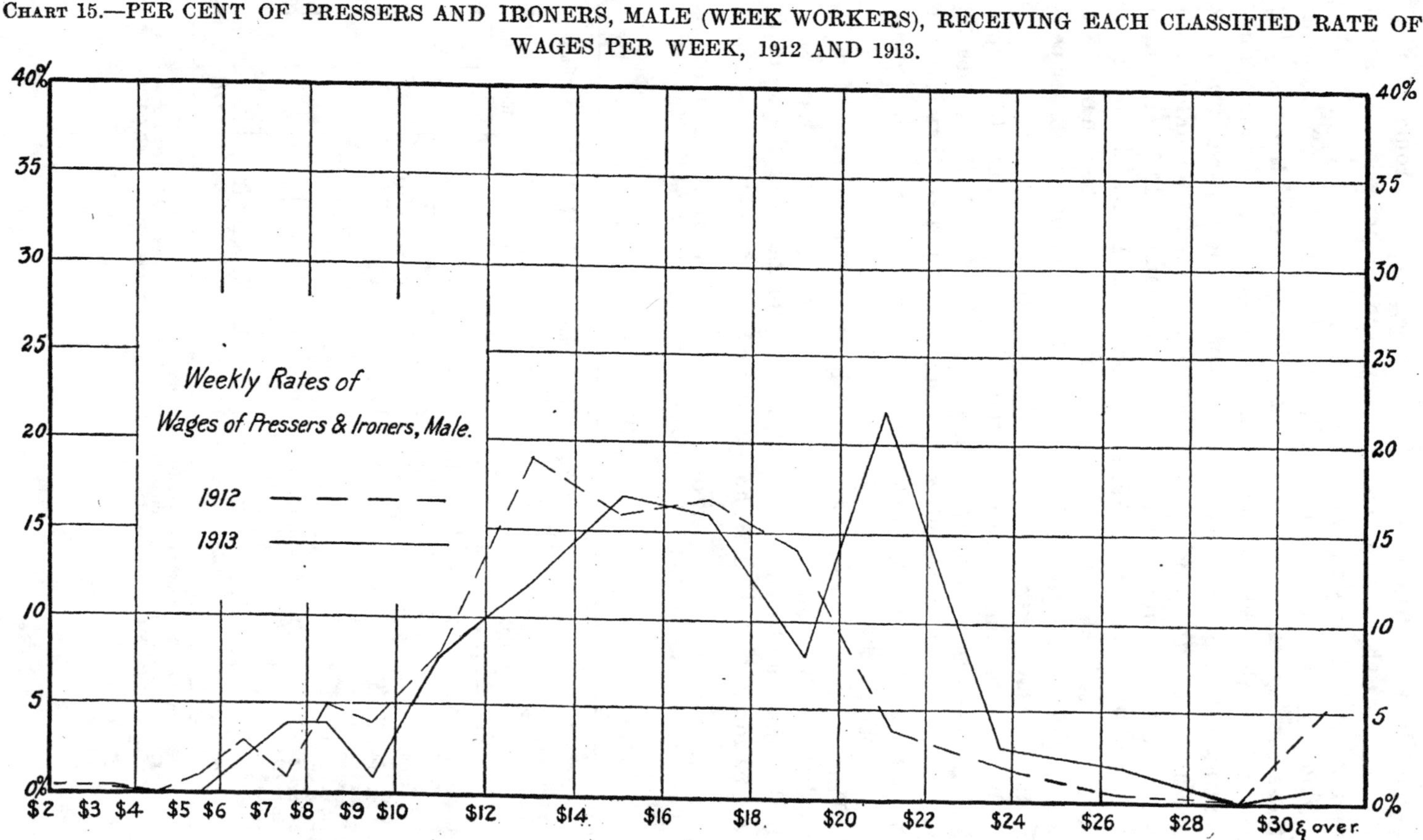

earning less than $18 a week. The changes in the earnings of men pieceworkers show the same tendency, though not with the same uniformity as among the women ironers.

The only exception to this uniform decline in the proportion of those earning less than $18 a week is in the case of those earning $8 and less than $9, the proportion of whom increased from 2.3 per cent in 1912 to 3.1 per cent in 1913 (representing 6 persons in 1912 and 6 in 1913), the proportion of those who earned $10 and less than $12 a week remaining practically the same, namely, 14.5 per cent in 1912 and 13.4 per cent in 1913 (38 workers in 1912 and only 26 in 1913). This is also true of those earning $16 and less than $18 a week, who constituted 13.5 per cent in 1912 and nearly 13 per cent in 1913 (35 workers in 1912 and only 25 in 1913).

On the other hand, the proportion of those receiving $18 a week and more increased from less than 19 per cent in 1912 to over 33 per cent in 1913. The inference from this would be that like the week rates, the piecework earnings have advanced since the adoption of the protocol.

Further details as to the changes in the rates of wages of week workers and earnings of pieceworkers among ironers and pressers, both women and men, in each of the four branches of the industry will be found in Tables 57, 58, 59, and 60, which follow:

TABLE 57.—NUMBER AND PER CENT OF IRONERS, FEMALE, WEEK WORKERS, RECEIVING EACH CLASSIFIED RATE OF WAGES PER WEEK, 1912 AND 1913, BY CLASS OF SHOPS.

NUMBER.

Classified rates of wages per week.	Association A.		Nonassociation A.[1]		Association B.		Nonassociation B.[1]		Total.	
	1912	1913	1912	1913	1912	1913	1912	1913	1912	1913
Under $3										
$3 to $3.99	2				1				3	
$4 to $4.99	1	4							1	4
$5 to $5.99	6	2			2	3			8	5
$6 to $6.99	13	11		1	4	4			17	16
$7 to $7.99	13	14			8	5			21	19
$8 to $8.99	18	17	1		13	9		1	32	27
$9 to $9.99	23	27	1	2	12	17	1		37	46
$10 to $11.99	39	50		3	32	28	2		73	81
$12 to $13.99	22	77		2	32	31		5	54	115
$14 to $15.99	14	24			11	25		1	25	50
$16 to $17.99	1	9			3	8			4	17
$18 to $19.99		2				2		1		5
$20 to $22.49		1				1				2
Total	152	238	2	8	118	133	3	8	[2] 275	[3] 387

[1] Percentages not computed on account of small number of employees.
[2] Not including 30 for whom earnings but not weekly rates of wages could be ascertained.
Not including 20 for whom earnings but not weekly rates of wages could be ascertained.

TABLE 57.—NUMBER AND PER CENT OF IRONERS, FEMALE, WEEK WORKERS, RECEIVING EACH CLASSIFIED RATE OF WAGES PER WEEK, 1912 AND 1913, BY CLASS OF SHOPS—Concluded.

PER CENT.

Classified rates of wages per week.	Association A.		Nonassociation A.		Association B.		Nonassociation B.		Total.	
	1912	1913	1912	1913	1912	1913	1912	1913	1912	1913
Under $3	....	....	....	....	....	....	....	....	....	....
$3 to $3.99	1.3	....	....	....	0.8	....	....	....	1.1	....
$4 to $4.99	.7	1.7	....	....	....	....	....	....	.4	1.0
$5 to $5.99	3.9	.8	....	....	1.7	2.3	....	....	2.9	1.3
$6 to $6.99	8.6	4.6	....	....	3.4	3.0	....	....	6.2	4.1
$7 to $7.99	8.6	6.9	....	....	6.8	3.8	....	....	7.6	4.9
$8 to $8.99	11.8	7.1	....	....	11.0	6.8	....	....	11.6	7.0
$9 to $9.99	15.1	11.3	....	....	10.2	12.8	....	....	13.5	11.9
$10 to $11.99	25.7	21.0	....	....	27.1	21.1	....	....	26.5	20.9
$12 to $13.99	14.5	32.4	....	....	27.1	23.3	....	....	19.6	29.7
$14 to $15.99	9.2	10.1	....	....	9.3	18.8	....	....	9.1	12.9
$16 to $17.99	.7	3.8	....	....	2.5	6.0	....	....	1.5	4.4
$18 to $19.99	....	.8	....	....	....	1.5	....	....	....	1.3
$20 to $22.49	....	.4	....	....	....	.8	....	....	....	.5
Total	100.0	100.0	....	....	100.0	100.0	....	....	100.0	100.0

SUMMARY OF PERCENTAGES.

Classified rates of wages per week.	Association A. 1912	Association A. 1913	Nonassociation A. 1912	Nonassociation A. 1913	Association B. 1912	Association B. 1913	Nonassociation B. 1912	Nonassociation B. 1913	Total. 1912	Total. 1913
Under $12	75.7	52.5	....	....	61.0	49.6	....	....	69.8	51.2
$12 to $13.99	14.5	32.4	....	....	27.1	23.3	....	....	19.6	29.7
$14 and over	9.9	15.1	....	....	11.9	27.1	....	....	10.5	19.1
Total	100.0	100.0	....	....	100.0	100.0	....	....	100.0	100.0

TABLE 58.—NUMBER AND PER CENT OF PRESSERS AND IRONERS, MALE, WEEK WORKERS, RECEIVING EACH CLASSIFIED RATE OF WAGES PER WEEK, 1912 AND 1913, BY CLASS OF SHOPS.

NUMBER.

Classified rates of wages per week.	Association A.		Nonassociation A.[1]		Association B.		Nonassociation B.[1]		Total.	
	1912	1913	1912	1913	1912	1913	1912	1913	1912	1913
Under $3	....	....	1	....	....	....	....	....	1	....
$3 to $3.99	....	....	....	....	1	1	....	....	1	1
$4 to $4.99	....	....	....	....	....	....	....	....	....	....
$5 to $5.99	1	....	....	....	2	....	....	....	3	....
$6 to $6.99	5	5	....	....	2	1	....	....	7	6
$7 to $7.99	2	11	....	1	....	1	....	1	2	14
$8 to $8.99	8	9	....	1	2	2	....	....	10	12
$9 to $9.99	6	4	....	1	2	....	....	....	8	5
$10 to $11.99	10	17	3	3	4	5	....	1	17	26
$12 to $13.99	22	24	5	7	11	12	2	1	40	44
$14 to $15.99	20	38	3	3	11	17	....	1	34	59
$16 to $17.99	13	28	6	9	16	17	2	2	37	56
$18 to $19.99	18	18	1	6	8	4	1	2	28	30
$20 to $22.49	5	45	1	11	2	18	1	2	9	76
$22.50 to $24.99	3	7	....	1	....	2	....	....	3	10
$25 to $27.49	1	5	....	....	....	2	....	....	1	7
$27.50 to $29.99	....	1	....	....	....	....	....	....	....	1
$30 and over	6	2	....	....	5	3	....	....	11	5
Total	120	214	20	43	66	85	6	10	[2] 212	[3] 352

[1] Percentages not computed on account of small number of employees.
[2] Not including 1 for whom earnings but not weekly rate of wages could be ascertained.
[3] Not including 3 for whom earnings but not weekly rates of wages could be ascertained.

TABLE 58.—NUMBER AND PER CENT OF PRESSERS AND IRONERS, MALE, WEEK WORKERS, RECEIVING EACH CLASSIFIED RATE OF WAGES PER WEEK, 1912 AND 1913, BY CLASS OF SHOPS—Concluded.

PER CENT.

Classified rates of wages per week.	Association A.		Nonassociation A.		Association B.		Nonassociation B.		Total.	
	1912	1913	1912	1913	1912	1913	1912	1913	1912	1913
Under $3									0.5	
$3 to $3.99					1.5	1.2			.5	0.3
$4 to $4.99										
$5 to $5.99	0.8				3.0				1.4	
$6 to $6.99	4.2	2.3			3.0	1.2			3.3	1.7
$7 to $7.99	1.7	5.1				1.2			1.0	4.0
$8 to $8.99	6.7	4.2			3.0	2.3			4.7	3.4
$9 to $9.99	5.0	1.9			3.0				3.8	1.4
$10 to $11.99	8.3	8.0			6.1	6.0			8.0	7.4
$12 to $13.99	18.3	11.2			16.7	14.1			18.9	12.5
$14 to $15.99	16.7	17.8			16.7	20.0			16.0	16.8
$16 to $17.99	10.8	13.1			24.3	20.0			17.4	15.9
$18 to $19.99	15.0	8.4			12.1	4.7			13.2	8.5
$20 to $22.49	4.2	21.0			3.0	21.2			4.2	21.6
$22.50 to $24.99	2.5	3.3				2.3			1.4	2.8
$25 to $27.49	.8	2.3				2.3			.5	2.0
$27.50 to $29.99		.5								.3
$30 and over	5.0	.9			7.6	3.5			5.2	1.4
Total	100.0	100.0			100.0	100.0			100.0	100.0

TABLE 59.—NUMBER AND PER CENT OF IRONERS, FEMALE, PIECEWORKERS, EARNING EACH CLASSIFIED AMOUNT DURING THE BUSIEST WEEK OF THE YEAR, 1912 AND 1913, BY CLASS OF SHOPS.

NUMBER.

Classified earnings per week.	Association A.		Nonassociation A.[1]		Association B.		Nonassociation B.[1]		Total.	
	1912	1913	1912	1913	1912	1913	1912	1913	1912	1913
Under $3	5	2		3	4	2			9	7
$3 to $3.99	4								4	
$4 to $4.99	3	2			1				4	2
$5 to $5.99	6	1			2				8	1
$6 to $6.99	11	1							11	1
$7 to $7.99	6	4			4	1			10	5
$8 to $8.99	5	5			1	1			6	6
$9 to $9.99	13	13	1	1	15	2		1	29	17
$10 to $11.99	31	18			7	8			38	26
$12 to $13.99	18	11			8	7	2		28	18
$14 to $15.99	20	12		2	11	6		2	31	22
$16 to $17.99	23	12		1	12	11		1	35	25
$18 to $19.99	8	11		1	6	5			14	17
$20 to $22.49	19	13			1	4			20	17
$22.50 to $24.99	10	15		1		2			10	18
$25 to $27.49	1	5			1				2	5
$27.50 to $29.99		6		1	3				3	7
$30 and over						1				1
Total	183	131	1	10	76	50	2	4	[2] 262	[3] 195

[1] Percentage not computed on account of small number of employees.
[2] Including 30 week workers for whom earnings but not weekly rates of wages could be ascertained.
[3] Including 20 week workers for whom earnings but not weekly rates of wages could be ascertained.

TABLE 59.—NUMBER AND PER CENT OF IRONERS, FEMALE, PIECEWORKERS, EARNING EACH CLASSIFIED AMOUNT, DURING THE BUSIEST WEEK OF THE YEAR, 1912 AND 1913, BY CLASS OF SHOPS—Concluded.

PER CENT.

Classified earnings per week.	Association A.		Nonassociation A.		Association B.		Nonassociation B.		Total.	
	1912	1913	1912	1913	1912	1913	1912	1913	1912	1913
Under $3	2.7	1.5			5.3	4.0			3.4	3.6
$3 to $3.99	2.2								1.5	
$4 to $4.99	1.6	1.5			1.3				1.5	1.0
$5 to $5.99	3.3	.8			2.6				3.1	.5
$6 to $6.99	6.0	.8							4.2	.5
$7 to $7.99	3.3	3.1			5.3	2.0			3.8	2.6
$8 to $8.99	2.7	3.8			1.3	2.0			2.3	3.1
$9 to $9.99	7.1	9.9			19.8	4.0			11.1	8.7
$10 to $11.99	17.0	13.7			9.2	16.0			14.5	13.4
$12 to $13.99	9.8	8.4			10.5	14.0			10.7	9.2
$14 to $15.99	10.9	9.2			14.5	12.0			11.8	11.3
$16 to $17.99	12.6	9.2			15.8	22.0			13.5	12.8
$18 to $19.99	4.4	8.4			7.9	10.0			5.3	8.7
$20 to $22.49	10.4	9.8			1.3	8.0			7.6	8.7
$22.50 to $24.99	5.5	11.5				4.0			3.8	9.2
$25 to $27.49	.5	3.8			1.3				.8	2.6
$27.50 to $29.99		4.6			3.9				1.1	3.6
$30 and over						2.0				.5
Total	100.0	100.0			100.0	100.0			100.0	100.0

TABLE 60.—NUMBER AND PER CENT OF PRESSERS AND IRONERS, MALE, PIECEWORKERS, EARNING EACH CLASSIFIED AMOUNT DURING THE BUSIEST WEEK OF THE YEAR, 1912 AND 1913, BY CLASS OF SHOPS.

Classified earnings per week.	Association A.		Nonassociation A.		Association B.		Nonassociation B.		Total.			
									Number.		Per cent.	
	1912	1913	1912	1913	1912	1913	1912	1913	1912	1913	1912	1913
Under $3	1			1					1	1	1.5	0.5
$3 to $3.99												
$4 to $4.99		2		1						3		1.6
$5 to $5.99		3		1			1		1	4	1.5	2.2
$6 to $6.99	1			1					1	1	1.5	.5
$7 to $7.99	2	4		2					2	6	3.0	3.2
$8 to $8.99	1	1		5					1	6	1.5	3.2
$9 to $9.99		1						2		3		1.6
$10 to $11.99	2	3		3		1			2	7	3.0	3.8
$12 to $13.99	5	3	2	12	2	2			9	17	13.4	9.2
$14 to $15.99	3	5	3	5	2	4		1	8	15	12.0	8.0
$16 to $17.99	4	6		7		3	1		5	16	7.4	8.6
$18 to $19.99	3	5		9		2			4	16	6.0	8.6
$20 to $22.49	9	15	3	4	1	7		3	13	29	19.4	15.7
$22.50 to $24.99		3	2	2	2	2	1		5	7	7.4	3.8
$25 to $27.49	3	5	1	8				1	4	14	6.0	7.6
$27.50 to $29.99	1	5	2	3	1		1	1	5	9	7.4	4.9
$30 and over	4	13	2	16	1			2	6	31	9.0	16.8
Total	39	74	15	80	9	21	4	10	[1] 67	[2] 185	100.0	100.0

[1] Including 1 week worker for whom earnings but not weekly rate of wages could be ascertained.
[2] Including 3 week workers for whom earnings but not weekly rates of wages could be ascertained.

JOINERS.

In the dress and waist industry there are two classes of workers known under the name of joiners. One is the class of operators who join the waist to the skirt and stitch the belt over the two on the sewing machine. The other class of workers known as joiners is but one degree removed from that of drapers. Their work consists in joining the waist, skirt, and belt together on the figure by means of pins. They are not supposed to do any draping beyond seeing that the skirt hangs right from the waist and that the waist is properly pinned to the skirt so as to fit the figure uniformly.

The source of supply of joiners is dressmakers and examiners. After joiners have attained sufficient skill through experience, they are graduated into the class of drapers and high-grade examiners.

SEX.

Only women are employed as joiners on figures. Machine or operator joiners are, as a rule, women, though a few men are found among this class of workers. It was impossible to ascertain from the pay rolls whether the joiners mentioned there were of one or the other class. The overwhelming majority of them, however, are undoubtedly of the class who work on figures, though a few may be operators. This may account for the presence of 11 men among the total of 207 joiners in 1913, for whom information was secured.

WAGES.

Most joiners are paid by the week, the minimum weekly rate of wages under the protocol being $12. As will be seen from Table 11, out of 207 joiners for whom wages were obtained, only 12 were found to be working by the piece.

The 207 joiners were distributed as follows among three of the branches of the industry: Association A (lower-grade garments), 113; association B (higher-grade garments), 56; nonassociation A, 38. The numbers are too small to permit of analysis of the percentage of workers receiving various rates of wages in the different branches of the industry. Of the 166 women joiners (Table 61) whose weekly rates were obtained, 74, or nearly 45 per cent, were in the group including the minimum protocol rate of $12 a week; 14, or over 8 per cent of the total, received more than the protocol rate, so that the proportion of those receiving the protocol rate and over was 53 per cent, or more than one-half of the total.

Wages in 1912 and 1913.—Comparing the wages of joiners working by the week in 1912 and 1913, a general reduction is found in the proportion of workers receiving the lower rates of wages and an increase among those receiving the higher rates. Thus, the number of female workers receiving less than the protocol rate of $12 a week declined from nearly 56 per cent in 1912 to 47 per cent in 1913. Those in the group receiving the minimum protocol rate increased from over 39 per cent to nearly 45 per cent; those receiving $14 or more increased from less than 5 per cent to over 8 per cent, so that the proportion of joiners receiving $12 and over was 53 per cent in 1913 as against more than 44 per cent in 1912. Table 61, which follows, shows the number of joiners receiving each classified rate, and Chart 16 presents the figures in graphic form.

TABLE 61.—NUMBER AND PER CENT OF JOINERS, WEEK WORKERS,[1] RECEIVING EACH CLASSIFIED RATE OF WAGES PER WEEK, 1912 AND 1913, BY SEX.

Classified rates of wages per week, and classes of shops.	Female.				Male.	
	Number.		Per cent.		1912	1913
	1912	1913	1912	1913		
$6 to $6.99	6	16	9.8	9.6		
$7 to $7.99	6	6	9.8	3.6		
$8 to $8.99	3	16	4.9	9.6		1
$9 to $9.99	11	14	18.1	8.4		
$10 to $11.99	8	26	13.1	15.8		2
$12 to $13.99	24	74	39.4	44.6	2	1
$14 to $15.99	3	13	4.9	7.8		1
$16 to $17.99		1		.6		1
$18 to $19.99						1
Total	[2] 61	[3] 166	100.0	100.0	2	7
	Workers in specified classes of shops.					
Association A	30	79				1
Association B	30	54				2
Nonassociation A	1	33			2	4

[1] In addition to the week workers shown in this table there were 2 pieceworkers, female, in 1912, and 8 in 1913, and 3 pieceworkers, male, in 1912 and 4 in 1913.
[2] Not including 1 for whom weekly rate of wages could not be ascertained.
[3] Not including 22 for whom weekly rates of wages could not be ascertained.

MARKERS.

Markers are usually young girls who mark with a pencil the spot opposite the buttonhole where the button is to be sewed on the waist. There is no skill required for this work and any young beginner who comes into the factory may be put to mark buttons.

As will be seen from Table 8, only 18 markers were found on the pay rolls of the 520 shops during the year 1913. Of these, 15 were girls and 3 were boys. There were, no doubt, a great many more markers in the industry, but in all probability they were entered on the pay rolls as cleaners. This is quite natural, since a girl will be put either on cleaning work or marking, according to the needs of the shop.

As will be seen from Table 62, the lowest wage which markers received in 1913 was $5 to $5.99 a week, as against $4 to $4.99 in 1912. Altogether there were only 3 markers receiving less than $6 a week during 1913, while 4 received $10 a week or more, the remainder receiving $6 and less than $10 a week. Nine out of 18, or exactly one-half, received $6 and less than $8 a week.

CHART 16.—PER CENT OF JOINERS, FEMALE (WEEK WORKERS), RECEIVING EACH CLASSIFIED RATE OF WAGES PER WEEK, 1912 AND 1913.

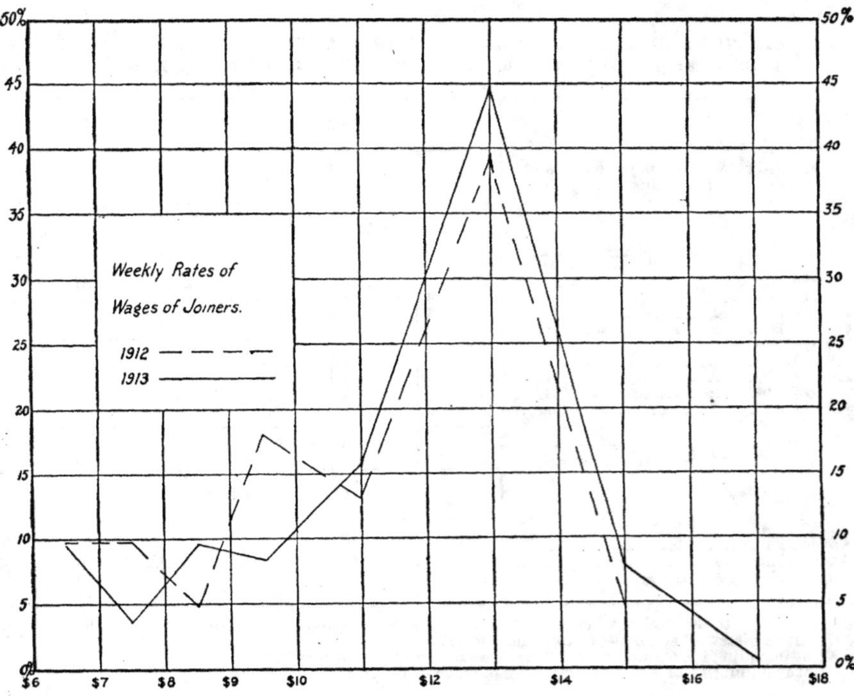

TABLE 62.—MARKERS, RECEIVING EACH CLASSIFIED RATE OF WAGES PER WEEK 1912 AND 1913, BY SEX.

Classified rates of wages per week, and classes of shops.	Females.		Males.	
	1912	1913	1912	1913
$4 to $4.99	2			
$5 to $5.99	1	2		1
$6 to $6.99	2	4		
$7 to $7.99	1	5		
$8 to $8.99		1		
$9 to $9.99	1	1		
$10 to $11.99		1		2
$12 to $13.99		1		
Total	7	15		3
	Workers in specified classes of shops.			
Association A	6	12		3
Association B	1	1		
Nonassociation A		2		

SLOPERS.

Slopers are assistant cutters, whose work is described under the heading cutters (see, especially, that part entitled "The apprenticing of a cutter," "sloping," and "sex").

The wages of slopers, so far as they have been found designated as such on the pay rolls, are given in Table 63.

TABLE 63.—SLOPERS, WEEK WORKERS, RECEIVING EACH CLASSIFIED RATE OF WAGES PER WEEK, 1912 AND 1913, BY SEX.

Classified rates of wages per week, and classes of shops.	Females.		Males.	
	1912	1913	1912	1913
$6 to $6.99	1			
$7 to $7.99		1	1	
$8 to $8.99	1			
$9 to $9.99	1	1		
$10 to $11.99	4	3		2
$12 to $13.99	2		8	3
$14 to $15.99		1	2	4
$16 to $17.99				1
$18 to $19.99				3
Total	9	6	11	13
	Workers in specified classes of shops.			
Association A	4		2	1
Association B	5	6	8	11
Nonassociation A			1	1

SUBCONTRACTING AND PARTNERSHIPS.

Article XV of the protocol reads as follows: "All inside subcontracting shall be abolished." No definition of subcontracting is given in the protocol.

Subcontracting is practiced, as a rule, in shops in which workers are paid on a piece basis. Manufacturers find it to their advantage in certain cases to allow their skilled workers, mostly operators, to employ assistants who are directly responsible to these workers and who receive their wages from them. These assistants receive no official recognition from the manufacturer and are not carried on the pay roll of the factory. They receive their pay from the workers, who employ them either on a weekly basis or on a basis of a percentage of the earnings of their employer. The latter method is used only when a worker employs but one assistant of sufficient skill to be acceptable as a partner, though not necessarily an equal partner.

The term subcontracting does not apply to partnerships, by which are meant combinations of two workers of practically the same skill who divide their earnings equally, or nearly so.

42132°—Bull. 146—14——10

ADVANTAGES OF SUBCONTRACTING TO MANUFACTURERS.

The advantages of subcontracting to manufacturers who maintain such a system in their shops are as follows:

1. It reduces the work of supervision to a minimum; it is easier to run a factory with, say, one hundred operators of whom ten or a dozen are subcontractors and the remaining number working for these subcontractors than it is to have a factory of the same size where each worker is subject to the direct supervision of the manufacturer. In the former case, he practically has 10 foremen who receive no wages for this work of supervision and are at the same time responsible for the work of their respective teams or "sets," as they are generally called in the dress and waist industry.

2. It does away with the necessity of hiring assistant foremen or forewomen for the instruction of new and inexperienced help.

3. There is a further saving in the clerical work in the shop and in the office. Instead of distributing work among a hundred workers and keeping track of them in order to keep them busy, the work is now given out to only 10 people, leaving it to them to look out for the rest. This not only means less distributive handling of the work by the supervisory and clerical force of the establishment, but also saves loss of time on the part of the individual workers in the intervals when they have completed their tasks and are waiting for new work, and to that extent it is a saving to the manufacturer in the number of hours his plant is partly or wholly idle. This loss of time is common in all shops to a greater or less extent.

4. The problem of securing help during the height of the season is greatly simplified. During this period there is great rivalry among manufacturers to secure necessary help, causing much annoyance and a great deal of lost effort on the part of the management. Under the subcontracting system, the subcontractors attend to the hiring of their own help, and as they are workmen themselves and mingle with the working people, they secure their assistants more readily than the manufacturer. Frequently they enroll their relatives and personal friends and thereby secure more personal loyalty and steadiness in employment among their assistants than is possible for the manufacturer.

5. In a large number of cases, the subcontractors attend to the repair of the machines used by their help and thereby save the manufacturer the cost of employing machinists or of taking the time of the foreman for that purpose.

6. Subcontracting secures a maximum of output from each worker. As their own earnings depend directly upon the output of their assistants, it is to the interest of the subcontractors to get the greatest possible output out of them. This is done in a number of ways: (*a*) Extreme subdivision of labor is introduced, each worker in the set doing only a small part of the work in which he quickly special-

izes and attains great speed. (*b*) Under this system, the subcontractor, who is himself a skillful and very rapid worker, sets the pace for his assistants, who must keep up with him in order to keep him supplied with the parts which he needs for his work. (*c*) This system coupled with the fact that the assistants in the sets are working under the very eye of their employer, who is constantly with them, insures an application to their tasks and intensity of labor such as can not be secured under any other system. (*d*) The advantages set forth above result in so great an output per worker that it enables the manufacturer to reduce gradually the piece rate per garment. As the assistants employed by the subcontractors are paid by the week, they are not concerned in this matter, so that the manufacturer meets only with the resistance of the few subcontractors, if there be any resistance at all, instead of the workers of the entire shop. On their part, the subcontractors are not greatly inclined to resist such reductions of pay, expecting to be able to make up for the loss by further speeding up their help and by introducing new devices for increasing the output.

7. The system of subcontracting results in an indirect saving, inasmuch as it does away with the necessity of paying a higher rate for overtime and of paying wages to week workers for certain holidays, since these provisions of the protocol, which are generally enforced with regard to week workers employed directly by the manufacturers, have not been enforced in the case of employees of subcontractors.

8. The great increase in output secured from each machine under the subcontracting system results in further savings to the manufacturer, inasmuch as the overhead expenses per garment are greatly reduced thereby—first, through the saving in the supervisory and clerical force already mentioned; and, secondly, through the fact that the total overhead expense, such as rent, power, wear and tear of machinery, office expense, etc., is now distributed over a much larger number of garments than would otherwise be possible.

DISADVANTAGES OF SUBCONTRACTING.

Such were the advantages, from the point of view of the manufacturer, which were responsible for the existence and spread of the subcontracting system. On the other hand, it was but natural that the workers should find it objectionable, since the speeding up was frequently carried to a point that injured their health. Through the extreme subdivision of labor which this system always carried with it, it also reduced the opportunity for the workers of learning the trade sufficiently to enable them to be graduated into shops manufacturing a better grade of garments, and thus made it impossible for them to work up to a higher standard of wages.

The workers were not the only ones injured by the subcontracting system. The general interests of the industry as a whole were likewise injured, for the system prevented the new recruits in the industry from becoming skilled operators, without a sufficient supply of which the industry in New York can not retain its commanding position in the growing market of ready-made high-grade and medium-grade women's dresses and waists. The fact that 85 per cent of the operators are women, most of them young, a very large portion of whom (roughly estimated by those in the industry to amount to one-fifth of the total) marry each year and leave the industry, calls for a constant recruiting of new workers who must be taught the trade of dressmaking as it is carried on in the shops. This may have furnished one of the reasons which prompted the association to agree to the demand of the union in incorporating article 15 in the protocol calling for the abolition of all inside subcontracting.

DECLINE OF SUBCONTRACTING.

One of the objects of the present investigation was to ascertain the extent to which subcontracting has been abolished or reduced. The only source of information was furnished by the pay rolls in the shops investigated. The task, however, proved much more difficult than was at first anticipated. The difficulty arises from the fact that there is nothing on the pay rolls to indicate whether a worker has earned the amount he is credited with by his own efforts or with the assistance of others. The only guide in this matter is the amount of the worker's earnings. When a worker appeared on the pay roll with weekly earnings of $50 or $100 or more, such a figure at once attracted the attention of the investigator and inquiries were made as to whether the worker is an employer of additional labor. It happens, however, especially at times when work is more or less slack, that the combined earnings of a worker and his assistant may be below $25 or, in some instances, even below $20, and thus fail to attract any attention. The agents of the board were instructed to inquire of the manufacturer or his representative as to whether a worker had assistants, in all cases where the weekly earnings exceeded $20.

Supplementary inquiries, which were made after the figures for the industry were tabulated, disclosed the fact that, in some cases, correct information was not obtained, so that some of the individual earnings of $20 a week and over appearing in the tables as earnings of individual workers may in reality represent the earnings of two partners or of a worker with one or more assistants.

The figures relating to subcontracting are summed up in Tables 64, 65, and 66, which are presented in the following pages. Table 64 gives the number of sets found working in 1912 and 1913, tabulated according to the occupation of the workers and the number of workers in each set, both for the industry as a whole and for the association and the nonassociation shops separately. Table 65 shows the number of individual workers employed in the sets tabulated by sex, so far as known. Table 66 gives the earnings of these sets in the busiest week of 1912 and of 1913, arranged according to occupation, extent of earnings, and character of shop.

SIZE OF SETS.

The "sets" may be of three kinds: First, partnerships, pure and simple, consisting of two workers dividing their earnings according to their respective skill; second, two partners employing one or more assistants; third, one worker employing one or more assistants. In all cases of sets an effort was made to ascertain the exact number of people employed in the set, but as the assistants are seldom entered on the pay rolls, it was not always possible to obtain the information.

TABLE 64.—NUMBER AND COMPOSITION OF PARTNERSHIPS AND SETS IN VARIOUS OCCUPATIONS IN ASSOCIATION AND NONASSOCIATION SHOPS.

Occupation and year.	Association shops.																	Nonassociation shops.							
	Sets or teams having each specified number of persons.																	Sets or teams having each specified number of persons.							
	2	3	4	5	6	7	8	9	12	14	15	17	18	20	35	45	Total.	2	3	4	5	6	7	8	Total.
Buttonhole makers:																									
Sets or teams—1912	6	2															8	2							2
1913	7	1															8	3							3
Cleaners:																									
Sets or teams—1912	1																1								
1913	2																2								
Closers and hemmers:																									
Sets or teams—1912	4																4								
1913	6		3														9								
Drapers:																									
Sets or teams—1912	1																1	1							1
1913	3		1														4								
Finishers:																									
Sets or teams—1912	19	1	1														21	3	1	1		2			7
1913	12																12	10	2						12
Embroiderers:																									
Sets or teams—1912											1						1								
1913										1							1								
Joiners:																									
Sets or teams—1912																									
1913																		1							1
Ironers and pressers:																									
Sets or teams—1912	18	8	6	4	2	1											39	13	8		2		1		24
1913	19	9	3		1												32	24	11	1				1	37
Lace runners:																									
Sets or teams—1912																									
1913	2																2								
Operators—N. S.:																									
Sets or teams—1912	124	33	10	3	4		1	2					1	1	1	1	181	45	8	1	2	1			57
1913	242	17	4	2	1	1	1										268	112	8	1	1	1			123
Body makers:																									
Sets or teams—1912	0	5		1													26	1							1
1913	68	5	1								1						75	20	1						21
Skirt makers:																									
Sets or teams—1912	15	2	1	3	1		1				1						24	5							5
1913	22		3		1												26	8	2	1	1				12
Dressmakers:																									
Sets or teams—1912	17	1		1		1	1	1									22	1							1
1913	18	2													1		21	3							3
Sleeve makers:																									
Sets or teams—1912	2	2			1												5								
1913	6			2													8		1						1
Sleeve setters:																									
Sets or teams—1912	3	1															4			1					1
1913	7	2															9	6	1						7
Sample makers:																									
Sets or teams—1912																									
1913		1															1								
Trimmers:																									
Sets or teams—1912																									
1913	5																5								
Tuckers:																									
Sets or teams—1912	8	4	2	3	1		1		1								20	2	1					1	4
1913	8	4	1				1		2			1					17	3	1						4
Total:																									
Sets or teams—1912	238	59	20	15	9	2	4	3	1		2		1	1	1	1	357	73	18	3	4	3	1	1	103
1913	427	41	16	4	3	1	2		2	1	1	1			1		500	190	27	3	2	1		1	224

TABLE 64.—NUMBER AND COMPOSITION OF PARTNERSHIPS AND SETS IN VARIOUS OCCUPATIONS IN ASSOCIATION AND NONASSOCIATION SHOPS—Concluded.

Occupation and year.	Total.																		Earnings (number of persons in sets unknown).	
	Sets or teams having each specified number of persons.																			
	2	3	4	5	6	7	8	9	12	14	15	17	18	20	35	45	No. unkn.	Total.	Lowest.	Highest.
Buttonhole makers:																				
Sets or teams—1912	8	2															2	12	$55.22	$69.48
1913	10	1																11		
Cleaners:																				
Sets or teams—1912	1																	1		
1913	2																	2		
Closers and hemmers:																				
Sets or teams—1912	4																1	5		23.79
1913	6		3															9		
Drapers:																				
Sets or teams—1912	2																1	3		58.53
1913	3		1															4		
Finishers:																				
Sets or teams—1912	22	2	2		2												2	30	44.65	360.81
1913	22	2																24		
Embroiderers:																				
Sets or teams—1912											1						4	[1] 5	56.70	445.12
1913										1							1	[1] 2		126.32
Joiners:																				
Sets or teams—1912																				
1913	1																	1		
Ironers and pressers:																				
Sets or teams—1912	31	16	6	6	2	2											4	67		
1913	43	20	4		1		1										4	73	42.93	81.17
Lace runners:																				
Sets or teams—1912																				
1913	2																	2		
Operators—N. S.:																				
Sets or teams—1912	169	41	11	5	5		1	2					1	1	1	1	71	309	23.55	196.40
1913	354	25	5	3	2	1	1										38	429	30.41	118.92
Body makers:																				
Sets or teams—1912	21	5		1													3	30	43.82	57.03
1913	88	6	1								1							96		
Skirt makers:																				
Sets or teams—1912	20	2	1	3	1		1				1						1	30		763.80
1913	30	2	4	1	1												1	39		144.90
Dressmakers:																				
Sets or teams—1912	18	1		1		1	1	1									1	24		77.30
1913	21	2													1		1	25		50.68
Sleeve makers:																				
Sets or teams—1912	2	2			1												1	6		73.28
1913	6	1		2													1	10		45.31
Sleeve setters:																				
Sets or teams—1912	3	1	1															5		
1913	13	3																16		
Sample makers:																				
Sets or teams—1912																				
1913		1																1		
Trimmers:																				
Sets or teams—1912																				
1913	5																	5		
Tuckers:																				
Sets or teams—1912	10	5	2	3	1		2		1								5	29	42.35	126.82
1913	11	5	1				1		2			1					2	23	56.20	120.63
Total:																				
Sets or teams—1912	311	77	23	19	12	3	5	3	1		2		1	1	1	1	96	556	23.55	763.80
1913	617	68	19	6	4	1	3		2	1	1	1			1		48	772	30.41	144.90

[1] Including 1 hemstitcher.

In many cases, the number of people in a set had to be estimated with the aid of the manufacturer or the bookkeeper on the basis of the earnings and his knowledge of the conditions prevailing in the shop. In a number of cases, however, no reliable estimate could be made, and these sets are entered in Table 64 in the column headed "Number unknown."

As will be seen from the table, the number of such sets was 96 in 1912 and 48, or exactly one-half that number, in 1913. Of the 48 sets, 38 were "operators not specified," 4 were pressers and ironers, and the remainder were operators of various kinds, such as tuckers, sleeve makers, hemstitchers, etc. Some indication of the size of these sets may be obtained from their earnings, which are given in Table 66.

As will be seen from Table 64, the total number of sets in the industry increased from 556 in 1912 to 772 in 1913. These two numbers would seem to imply that not only has the provision of the protocol for the abolition of subcontracting failed to be carried out, but the evil has grown in extent. As a matter of fact such is not the case. An examination of the figures in Table 64 will disclose the fact that the increase occurred almost entirely in the number of sets consisting of two workers, while the number of sets consisting of three workers or more has been reduced. Thus, in the association shops there were 238 sets of two workers each in 1912 and 427 in 1913. In the nonassociation shops the number of those sets was 73 in 1912, and 190 in 1913. On the other hand, the number of sets of three or more was reduced from 149 in 1912 to 107 in 1913. When each group of sets is taken up separately, it will be found that the larger the number of workers in the group the greater, as a rule, has been the decline in the number of such sets. Thus, taking the association shops for an illustration, the number of sets consisting of three persons was reduced from 59 in 1912 to 41 in 1913; sets consisting of 4 each numbered 20 in 1912, and 16 in 1913; those consisting of 5 each numbered 15 in 1912, and 4 in 1913; those consisting of 6 each numbered 9 in 1912, and 3 in 1913, etc.

The increase in the number of sets consisting of two persons is explained by the following situation: After the adoption of the protocol it was found in a great many cases that not only was it not practicable to do away with the "sets," but permission had to be given for the introduction of the system of operators with assistants in shops where it had not prevailed before. This happened in shops in which the piecework system was for the first time introduced to take the place of week work which had prevailed before the signing of the protocol. In these shops generally the system of extreme subdivision of labor prevailed, known as the "section" system. The introduction of the piecework system was accompanied by the doing away with section work, most of the work being done henceforth by the body makers, and only certain parts, which represented distinct occupations, being left to separate workers, such as sleeve setting, tucking, buttonhole making, etc. The sudden introduction of the new system threatened many of the less skilled operators, who had been accustomed to section work, with the loss of their positions, since they were unable to do "body making." To prevent this hardship to many workers and to enable the manufacturer at the same time to train his employees gradually to the new system, the union officials joined the officials of the association in granting permission in such instances for the temporary introduction of the subcontracting system, under which the less skilled workers were enabled to remain in those factories as assistants to skilled operators, receiving their pay from these operators. Under this arrangement, the boss of the "set" becomes the instructor of his employees and derives his compensation for the services thus performed in the profit he makes on the work of his assistants.

Looking at the figures in Table 64 for 1913, it will be observed that by far the largest number of sets occurs in the occupation of "operators not specified" in which there were 268 in the association shops and 123 in the nonassociation shops. If to these be added the sets entered under "buttonhole makers," "closers and hemmers," "lace runners," "skirt operators," "waist operators," "dress operators," "sample makers," "sleeve makers," "sleeve setters," "trimmers," and "tuckers," all of whom are operators in the sense of operating sewing machines, it will be found that the combined occupation of operators totaled 666 sets. The other sets were distributed among the following occupations: "Ironers and pressers," of whom there were 32 sets in the association shops and 37 in the nonassociation shops in 1913, as compared with 39 and 24, respectively, in 1912; "finishers," of whom there were 12 sets in the association shops, all consisting of two workers each, and in the nonassociation shops 12 sets, of which 10 consisted of two workers each and 2 of three workers each. Those interested in further details as to the distribution of sets by occupations and by the number of people in a set are referred to Table 64.

SEX OF WORKERS IN SETS.

Table 65, which follows, gives the sex of the workers employed in sets, so far as it could be ascertained.

TABLE 65.—SEX OF EMPLOYEES WORKING IN PARTNERSHIPS AND SETS.

Occupation and year.	Association shops.					Nonassociation shops.					Total.				
	Number of persons.				Number of sets.	Number of persons.				Number of sets.	Number of persons.				Number of sets.
	M.	F.	Sex unknown.	Total.		M.	F.	Sex unknown.	Total.		M.	F.	Sex unknown.	Total.	
Buttonhole makers:															
1912	10	....	8	18	8	2	....	2	4	2	12	....	10	22	10
1913	8	1	8	17	8	4	....	2	6	3	12	1	10	23	11
Cleaners:															
1912	....	1	1	2	1	....	....	....	....	....	....	1	1	2	1
1913	....	4	....	4	2	....	....	....	....	....	....	4	....	4	2
Closers and hemmers:															
1912	4	....	4	8	4	....	....	....	....	....	4	....	4	8	4
1913	9	....	15	24	9	....	....	....	....	....	9	....	15	24	9
Drapers:															
1912	....	1	1	2	1	....	1	1	2	1	....	2	2	4	2
1913	1	7	2	10	4	....	....	....	....	....	1	7	2	10	4
Finishers:															
1912	1	35	9	45	21	....	12	13	25	7	1	47	22	70	28
1913	....	12	12	24	12	....	26	....	26	12	....	38	12	50	24
Embroiderers:															
1912	....	1	14	15	1	....	....	....	....	....	....	1	14	15	1
1913	....	1	13	14	1	....	....	....	....	....	....	1	13	14	1
Joiners:															
1912	....	....	....	....	....	....	....	....	....	....	....	....	....	....	....
1913	....	....	....	....	....	....	2	....	2	1	....	2	....	2	1
Ironers and pressers:															
1912	39	4	80	123	39	37	4	26	67	24	76	8	106	190	63
1913	37	2	44	83	32	40	5	48	93	37	77	7	92	176	69
Lace runners:															
1912	....	....	....	....	....	....	....	....	....	....	....	....	....	....	....
1913	1	1	2	4	2	....	....	....	....	....	1	1	2	4	2
Operators, not specified:															
1912	102	99	369	570	181	43	47	44	134	57	145	146	413	704	238
1913	138	192	252	582	268	90	97	76	263	123	228	289	328	845	391
Body makers:															
1912	27	15	18	60	26	1	1	....	2	1	28	16	18	62	27
1913	34	64	72	170	75	12	16	15	43	21	46	80	87	213	96
Skirt makers:															
1912	23	10	51	84	24	4	1	5	10	5	27	11	56	94	29
1913	20	7	35	62	26	16	....	15	31	12	36	7	50	93	38
Dressmakers:															
1912	20	20	26	66	22	....	1	1	2	1	20	21	27	68	23
1913	11	16	50	77	21	1	2	3	6	3	12	18	53	83	24
Sleeve makers:															
1912	5	2	9	16	5	....	....	....	....	....	5	2	9	16	5
1913	6	6	10	22	8	1	....	2	3	1	7	6	12	25	9
Sleeve setters:															
1912	3	3	3	9	4	2	2	....	4	1	5	5	3	13	5
1913	8	4	8	20	9	6	2	7	15	7	14	6	15	35	16
Sample makers:															
1912	....	....	....	....	....	....	....	....	....	....	....	....	....	....	....
1913	1	....	2	3	1	....	....	....	....	....	1	....	2	3	1
Trimmers:															
1912	....	....	....	....	....	....	....	....	....	....	....	....	....	....	....
1913	2	3	5	10	5	....	....	....	....	....	2	3	5	10	5
Tuckers:															
1912	21	8	48	77	20	4	....	11	15	4	25	8	59	92	24
1913	19	28	34	81	17	5	1	3	9	4	24	29	37	90	21
Total:															
1912	255	199	641	1,095	357	93	69	103	265	103	348	268	744	1,360	460
1913	295	348	564	1,207	500	175	151	171	497	224	470	499	735	1,704	724

As will be seen from the figures for 1913, out of 1,704 persons known to have been employed in the sets, 470 were men and 499 were women, the sex of the remaining 735 workers, who numbered nearly one-half of the total, being unknown. The women are thus seen to be in a majority in spite of the fact that in most instances the heads of sets are men. Were the sex of the remaining workers ascertainable, there is no doubt that the women would have been found greatly to outnumber the men.

EARNINGS OF SETS.

Table 66, which follows, shows the number of sets in the different occupations earning certain amounts during the busiest week in 1912 and in 1913, both in the association and the nonassociation shops.

TABLE 66.—NUMBER OF SETS IN VARIOUS OCCUPATIONS EARNING CLASSIFIED AMOUNTS OF WAGES IN THE BUSIEST WEEK IN 1912 AND IN 1913 IN ASSOCIATION AND NONASSOCIATION SHOPS.

ASSOCIATION SHOPS.

Occupation and year.	Under $20	$20 to $29	$30 to $39	$40 to $49	$50 to $59	$60 to $69	$70 to $79	$80 to $89	$90 to $99	$100 to $199	$200 to $299	$300 and over.	Total.
Buttonhole makers:													
Sets—1912		2	2	2	1				1				8
1913		1	4	2				1					8
Cleaners:													
Sets—1912	1												1
1913	1	1											2
Closers and hemmers:													
Sets—1912				2	2								4
1913	1		2	2	3	1							9
Drapers:													
Sets—1912				1									1
1913				1	2	1							4
Finishers:													
Sets—1912	5	10	4		2								21
1913	1	10		1									12
Embroiderers:													
Sets—1912										1			1
1913												1	1
Joiners:													
Sets—1912													
1913													
Ironers and pressers:													
Sets—1912	1	2	4	4	5	3	5	5		9	[1]1		39
1913			8	6	7	5	2	2	1	1			32
Lace runners:													
Sets—1912													
1913			2										2
Operators—N. S.:													
Sets—1912	5	29	47	47	17	11	5	4	4	8	2	2	181
1913	8	45	89	70	29	13	5	2		7			268
Body makers:													
Sets—1912	2	4	10	5		3	1			1			26
1913	3	25	29	10	4	3				1			75
Skirt makers:													
Sets—1912		3	6	4	1	1	1		2	4	2		24
1913	2	1	7	6	3	2			3	2			26
Dressmakers:													
Sets—1912	1	2	5	6	2	1	1			4			22
1913	3	2	5	7	1		1	1				[3]1	21
Sleeve makers:													
Sets—1912			2	1		1		1					5
1913	2	2	2	1					1				8
Sleeve setters:													
Sets—1912		1	1	1				1					4
1913		3	3	2		1							9
Sample makers:													
Sets—1912													
1913									1				1
Trimmers:													
Sets—1912													
1913			1	4									5
Tuckers:													
Sets—1912			2	2	4	2	2	1	1	5	1		20
1913		1	2	3	1	3	1	1		3	1	[4]1	17
Total:													
Sets—1912	15	53	83	75	34	22	15	12	8	32	6	2	357
1913	21	91	154	115	50	29	9	7	6	14	1	3	500

[1] $446.82. [2] $537.92 and $644.87. [3] $658.80. [4] $443.06.

TABLE 66.—NUMBER OF SETS IN VARIOUS OCCUPATIONS EARNING CLASSIFIED AMOUNTS OF WAGES IN THE BUSIEST WEEK IN 1912 AND IN 1913 IN ASSOCIATION AND NONASSOCIATION SHOPS—Continued.

NONASSOCIATION SHOPS.

Occupation and year.	Under $20	$20 to $29	$30 to $39	$40 to $49	$50 to $59	$60 to $69	$70 to $79	$80 to $89	$90 to $99	$100 to $199	$200 to $299	$300 and over.	Total.
Buttonhole makers:													
Sets—1912				1		1							2
1913		1	1	1									3
Cleaners:													
Sets—1912													
1913													
Closers and hemmers:													
Sets—1912													
1913													
Drapers:													
Sets—1912			1										1
1913													
Finishers:													
Sets—1912	1	2		1	2		1						7
1913	3	6	3										12
Embroiderers:													
Sets—1912													
1913													
Joiners:													
Sets—1912													
1913			1										1
Ironers and pressers:													
Sets—1912		2	6	4	3	2	1	2	1	3			24
1913		2	14	5	6	3	2		3	2			37
Lace runners:													
Sets—1912													
1913													
Operators—N. S.:													
Sets—1912	5	12	23	7	5	1			1	3			57
1913	4	24	50	25	10	6		1	1	2			123
Body makers:													
Sets—1912		1											1
1913	1	8	6	5	1								21
Skirt makers:													
Sets—1912		1	1	1	2								5
1913		1	1	1	2	5	1				1		12
Dressmakers:													
Sets—1912			1										1
1913			3										3
Sleeve makers:													
Sets—1912													
1913					1								1
Sleeve setters:													
Sets—1912							1						1
1913		2	4				1						7
Sample makers:													
Sets—1912													
1913													
Trimmers:													
Sets—1912													
1913													
Tuckers:													
Sets—1912		1	1		1					1			4
1913		1			2	1							4
Total:													
Sets—1912	6	19	33	14	13	4	3	2	2	7			103
1913	8	45	83	37	22	15	4	1	4	4	1		224

TOTAL.

Occupation and year.	Under $20	$20 to $29	$30 to $39	$40 to $49	$50 to $59	$60 to $69	$70 to $79	$80 to $89	$90 to $99	$100 to $199	$200 to $299	$300 and over.	Total.
Buttonhole makers:													
Sets—1912		2	2	3	1	1			1				10
1913		2	5	3				1					11
Cleaners:													
Sets—1912	1												1
1913	1	1											2
Closers and hemmers:													
Sets—1912				2	2								4
1913	1		2	2	3	1							9
Drapers:													
Sets—1912			1	1									2
1913				1	2	1							4

TABLE 66.—NUMBER OF SETS IN VARIOUS OCCUPATIONS EARNING CLASSIFIED AMOUNTS OF WAGES IN THE BUSIEST WEEK IN 1912 AND IN 1913 IN ASSOCIATION AND NONASSOCIATION SHOPS—Concluded.

TOTAL—Concluded.

Occupation and year.	Under $20	$20 to $29	$30 to $39	$40 to $49	$50 to $59	$60 to $69	$70 to $79	$80 to $89	$90 to $99	$100 to $199	$200 to $299	$300 and over.	Total
Finishers:													
Sets—1912	6	12	4	1	4		1						28
1913	4	16	3	1									24
Embroiderers:													
Sets—1912										1			1
1913												[1] 1	1
Joiners:													
Sets—1912													
1913			1										1
Ironers and pressers:													
Sets—1912	1	4	10	8	8	5	6	7	1	12	1		63
1913		2	22	11	13	8	4	2	4	3			69
Lace runners:													
Sets—1912													
1913			2										2
Operators—N. S.:													
Sets—1912	10	41	70	54	22	12	5	4	5	11	2	[2] 2	238
1913	12	69	139	95	39	19	5	3	1	9			391
Body makers:													
Sets—1912	2	5	10	5		3	1			1			27
1913	4	33	35	15	5	3				1			96
Skirt makers:													
Sets—1912		4	7	5	3	1	1		2	4	2		29
1913	2	2	8	7	5	7	1		3	2	1		38
Dressmakers:													
Sets—1912	1	2	6	6	2	1	1			4			23
1913	3	2	8	7	1		1	1				[3] 1	24
Sleeve makers:													
Sets—1912			2	1		1		1					5
1913	2	2	2	1	1				1				9
Sleeve setters:													
Sets—1912		1	1	1			1	1					5
1913		5	7	2		1	1						16
Sample makers:													
Sets—1912													
1913									1				1
Trimmers:													
Sets—1912													
1913			1	4									5
Tuckers:													
Sets—1912		1	3	2	5	2	2	1	1	6	1		24
1913		2	2	3	3	4	1	1		3	1	[4] 1	21
Total:													
Sets—1912	21	72	116	89	47	26	18	14	10	39	6	2	460
1913	29	136	237	152	72	44	13	8	10	18	2	3	724

No definite conclusions can be drawn from these figures, their chief value being that they furnish an indication of the size of the financial operations of the subcontractors and the changes that have occurred therein since the enactment of the protocol. From this point of view, it is significant to note in association shops the decline in the number of sets earning $200 or more from 8 to 4, and of those earning from $100 to $200 from 32 to 14, while the number has increased among those earning under $20 from 15 to 21; among those earning from $20 to $29, from 53 to 91, and among those earning from $30 to $39, from 83 to 154, etc. The increase in the number of sets earning less than $70 a week is undoubtedly due to the great increase in the number of sets consisting of two workers each, while the reduction in the number of sets earning from $70 a week up is due to the falling off in the number of large sets. A similar tendency is observed in the nonassociation shops.

REGULARITY OF EMPLOYMENT.

As already explained, the wages given in this report are for the busiest week of the year.

These figures are of no value, however, as an indication of the annual earnings of the men and women employed in the industry, unless it is known to what extent they are employed throughout the year. For the dress and waist industry, like other garment industries, fluctuates with the seasons, and very few workers are employed regularly throughout the year.

The reasons why earnings of individual workers could not be obtained for a whole year are explained at length on page 39 and need not be repeated here. In order to ascertain the extent to which the factories are busy throughout the year, and thereby lay a foundation for an approximate estimate of the annual earnings of the workers in the industry, the following method was employed: The total wages paid out each week during the year 1912 and the number of workers employed during those weeks were copied from the pay rolls of the factories investigated. As in the case of the wages for the busiest week, the wages paid to designers, foremen, forewomen, and office help, so far as possible, were eliminated.

Table 67, which follows, shows for each week of the year 1912 the number of employees in each branch of the industry and the total number in the 260 shops covered, and the per cent that the total number each week is of the number in the week showing maximum number employed. Table 68 shows the aggregate wages paid each week and the per cent these are of the maximum amount paid in any week. These figures are given for each of the four branches into which the industry has been divided, i. e.: (1) Association shops manufacturing low-grade garments, designated as association A; (2) Nonassociation A, i. e., nonassociation shops manufacturing low-grade garments; (3) Association B, including shops manufacturing high-grade garments; (4) Nonassociation B, manufacturing high-grade garments; and finally (5) for the industry as a whole.

TABLE 67.—NUMBER OF PERSONS EMPLOYED IN 260 SHOPS IN THE DRESS AND WAIST INDUSTRY IN 1912.

Week.	Number.				Total.	
	Group A.		Group B.			
	Association shops.	Nonassociation shops.	Association shops.	Nonassociation shops.	Number.	Per cent (busiest week=100).[1]
1	7,990	697	5,704	159	14,550	71
2	8,198	787	6,266	192	15,443	75
3	8,433	859	6,553	345	16,190	79
4	8,751	934	6,940	335	16,960	83
5	9,232	1,034	7,213	370	17,849	87
6	9,482	972	7,469	406	18,329	89
7	9,926	1,025	7,791	404	19,146	93
8	10,250	1,144	7,822	417	19,633	96
9	10,619	1,141	8,010	413	20,183	98
10	10,795	1,183	8,017	414	20,409	99
11	10,846	1,218	8,033	424	20,521	100
12	10,964	1,227	7,916	417	20,524	100
13	10,896	1,201	7,818	459	20,374	99
14	10,290	1,135	7,496	392	19,313	94
15	10,298	1,134	7,496	370	19,298	94
16	10,320	1,113	7,328	384	19,145	93
17	10,272	1,166	7,154	382	18,974	92
18	10,017	1,151	6,968	342	18,478	90
19	9,894	1,120	6,743	321	18,078	88
20	9,622	1,086	6,455	338	17,501	85
21	9,249	1,002	6,225	285	16,761	82
22	9,201	1,011	5,976	321	16,509	80
23	9,128	1,028	5,894	300	16,350	80
24	9,193	1,002	5,995	324	16,514	80
25	9,021	988	5,647	305	15,961	78
26	8,372	862	5,008	272	14,514	71
27	7,046	775	4,224	247	12,292	60
28	6,085	611	3,871	249	10,816	53
29	5,550	512	3,989	253	10,304	50
30	5,608	512	4,751	276	11,147	54
31	5,905	596	5,648	280	12,429	61
32	6,671	656	6,347	271	13,945	68
33	7,505	908	6,906	358	15,677	76
34	8,295	962	7,267	364	16,888	82
35	8,904	1,015	7,365	402	17,686	86
36	7,644	399	9,262	1,058	18,363	89
37	7,639	372	9,030	1,066	18,107	88
38	7,735	382	9,426	1,117	18,660	91
39	7,800	428	9,653	1,149	19,030	93
40	7,906	373	9,759	1,161	19,199	94
41	7,955	370	9,886	1,177	19,388	94
42	8,105	382	10,002	1,197	19,686	96
43	7,441	368	9,778	1,108	18,695	91
44	7,084	357	9,326	1,024	17,791	87
45	6,524	323	8,968	954	16,769	82
46	6,418	295	8,736	979	16,428	80
47	6,214	296	8,685	1,183	16,378	80
48	6,011	268	8,567	1,021	15,867	77
49	6,100	225	9,027	982	16,334	80
50	6,075	250	9,206	1,073	16,604	81
51	6,260	277	9,272	1,070	16,879	82
52	6,065	260	8,981	984	16,290	79
Total					889,159	
Average					17,100	83.3

[1] The busiest week means the week having the maximum number of employees. The figures in this column indicate the percentage which the number of employees each week constituted of the number of employees in the busiest week of the year.

TABLE 68.—AMOUNT OF WAGES PAID IN 260 SHOPS OF THE DRESS AND WAIST INDUSTRY IN 1912.

Week.	Wages.					Per cent (busiest week=100).[1]					Average weekly wage per employee.
	Group A.		Group B.		Total for the industry.	Group A.		Group B.		Total.	
	Association shops.	Nonassociation shops.	Association shops.	Nonassociation shops.		Association shops.	Nonassociation shops.	Association shops.	Nonassociation shops.		
1	$70,100	$5,526	$53,640	$1,218	$130,484	54	39	49	10	53	$8.97
2	80,464	7,046	64,287	1,801	153,598	62	50	58	14	63	9.95
3	85,830	7,598	68,841	3,280	165,549	67	54	62	26	67	10.23
4	92,555	8,975	75,852	3,291	180,673	72	64	69	26	74	10.65
5	98,272	10,175	80,107	3,828	192,382	76	72	73	30	78	10.78
6	102,949	10,313	85,069	4,175	202,506	80	73	77	33	82	11.05
7	109,959	10,675	88,056	4,282	212,972	85	76	80	34	87	11.12
8	115,652	11,292	90,636	4,349	221,929	90	80	82	34	90	11.30
9	124,085	12,713	99,246	4,570	240,614	96	90	90	36	98	11.92
10	127,342	13,033	99,652	4,954	244,981	99	93	90	39	100	12.00
11	127,850	14,068	98,757	4,819	245,494	99	100	89	38	100	11.96
12	129,018	13,579	97,846	4,734	245,177	100	97	89	37	100	11.95
13	125,223	12,688	94,828	4,212	236,951	97	90	86	33	97	11.63
14	100,318	10,575	80,182	3,508	194,583	78	75	73	28	79	10.08
15	105,556	11,173	80,746	3,796	201,271	82	79	73	30	82	10.43
16	110,020	11,908	82,191	3,934	208,053	85	85	74	31	85	10.87
17	112,467	11,925	75,413	3,790	203,595	87	85	68	30	83	10.73
18	104,383	11,597	73,889	2,566	192,435	81	82	67	20	78	10.41
19	100,280	10,777	71,103	3,475	185,635	76	77	64	27	76	10.27
20	96,123	10,695	67,973	3,326	178,117	75	76	62	26	73	10.18
21	91,061	8,921	63,912	3,011	166,905	71	63	58	24	68	9.96
22	86,579	9,753	57,558	2,973	156,863	67	69	52	23	64	9.50
23	91,821	10,411	62,154	2,998	167,384	71	74	56	24	68	10.24
24	95,471	10,114	62,748	3,154	169,487	72	72	57	25	69	10.26
25	89,335	9,497	57,559	3,143	159,534	69	68	52	25	65	10.00
26	81,026	7,381	50,296	2,703	141,406	63	52	46	21	58	9.74
27	59,793	6,118	37,451	2,197	105,559	46	43	34	17	43	8.59
28	51,732	4,615	36,528	2,404	95,279	40	33	33	19	39	8.81
29	48,473	3,813	39,235	2,628	94,149	38	27	36	21	38	9.14
30	50,898	4,204	47,693	2,495	105,290	39	30	43	20	43	9.45
31	54,477	5,151	52,919	2,832	115,379	42	37	48	22	47	9.28
32	63,551	5,707	66,271	2,807	138,336	49	41	60	22	56	9.92
33	73,276	8,443	73,964	3,639	159,322	57	60	67	29	65	10.16
34	83,809	9,537	80,485	3,971	177,802	65	68	73	31	72	10.53
35	95,116	10,675	86,409	3,767	195,967	74	76	78	30	80	11.08
36	80,076	4,128	97,040	10,727	191,971	62	29	88	84	78	10.45
37	76,047	3,694	81,113	9,665	170,519	59	26	73	76	69	9.42
38	87,923	4,374	94,324	10,844	197,465	68	31	85	85	80	10.58
39	94,776	4,384	105,315	11,521	215,996	73	31	95	90	88	11.35
40	94,462	4,621	104,255	11,813	215,151	73	33	94	93	88	11.21
41	94,882	4,269	108,907	12,751	220,809	74	30	99	100	90	11.39
42	89,188	4,503	110,458	12,477	216,626	69	32	100	98	88	11.00
43	85,534	4,035	101,692	10,887	202,148	66	29	92	85	82	10.81
44	79,049	3,580	95,908	9,578	188,115	61	25	87	75	77	10.57
45	68,186	3,141	86,024	8,385	165,736	53	22	78	66	68	9.88
46	68,872	2,970	86,903	9,008	167,753	53	21	79	71	68	10.21
47	64,844	2,963	85,020	9,475	162,302	50	21	77	74	66	9.91
48	57,267	2,558	80,086	9,217	149,128	44	18	73	72	61	9.40
49	61,616	2,475	89,165	9,199	162,455	48	18	81	72	66	9.93
50	63,897	2,425	92,208	10,470	169,000	50	17	83	82	69	10.18
51	64,065	2,339	93,922	10,136	170,462	50	17	85	79	69	10.10
52	57,594	2,014	82,091	9,128	150,827	45	14	74	72	61	9.26
Total	4,521,142	389,144	4,097,927	293,911	9,302,124						
Averages						67	53	71	44	73	10.46

[1] The busiest week in each of these columns means the week in which the maximum amount of wages was paid. The figures in this column indicate the percentage which the wages each week constituted of the wages in the busiest week of the year.

Table 69 which follows summarizes for the industry the figures presented in the two preceding tables and adds two columns showing the per cent of employees and of wages for each week as compared with the averages for the year:

TABLE 69.—FLUCTUATIONS OF EMPLOYMENT AND WAGES IN THE DRESS AND WAIST INDUSTRY FOR 1912.

Week.	Number of employees.	Amount of wages paid out.	Per cent (busiest week=100).[1]		Per cent (average for year=100).[2]	
			Employees.	Wages.	Employees.	Wages.
1	14,550	$130,484	71	53	85	73
2	15,443	153,568	75	63	90	86
3	16,190	165,549	79	67	95	93
4	16,960	180,673	83	74	99	101
5	17,849	192,382	87	78	104	108
6	18,329	202,506	89	82	107	113
7	19,146	212,972	93	87	112	119
8	19,633	221,929	96	90	115	124
9	20,183	240,614	98	98	118	135
10	20,409	244,981	99	100	119	137
11	20,521	245,494	100	100	120	137
12	20,524	245,177	100	100	120	137
13	20,374	236,951	99	97	119	132
14	19,313	194,583	94	79	113	109
15	19,298	201,271	94	82	113	113
16	19,145	208,053	93	85	112	116
17	18,974	203,595	92	83	111	114
18	18,478	192,435	90	78	108	108
19	18,078	185,635	88	76	106	104
20	17,501	178,117	85	73	102	100
21	16,761	166,905	82	68	98	93
22	16,509	156,863	80	64	97	88
23	16,350	167,384	80	68	96	94
24	16,514	169,487	80	69	97	95
25	15,961	159,534	78	65	93	89
26	14,514	141,406	71	58	85	79
27	12,292	105,559	60	43	72	59
28	10,816	95,279	53	39	63	53
29	10,304	94,149	50	38	60	53
30	11,147	105,290	54	43	65	59
31	12,429	115,379	61	47	73	64
32	13,945	138,336	68	56	82	77
33	15,677	159,322	76	65	92	89
34	16,888	177,802	82	72	99	99
35	17,686	195,967	86	80	103	110
36	18,363	191,971	89	78	107	107
37	18,107	170,519	88	69	106	95
38	18,660	197,465	91	80	109	110
39	19,030	215,996	93	88	111	121
40	19,199	215,151	94	88	112	120
41	19,388	220,809	94	90	113	123
42	19,686	216,626	96	88	115	121
43	18,695	202,148	91	82	109	113
44	17,791	188,115	87	77	104	105
45	16,769	165,736	82	68	98	93
46	16,428	167,753	80	68	96	94
47	16,378	162,302	80	66	96	91
48	15,867	149,128	77	61	93	83
49	16,364	162,455	80	66	96	91
50	16,604	169,000	81	69	97	94
51	16,879	170,462	82	69	99	95
52	16,290	150,827	79	61	95	84
Average	17,100	178,887	83.3	73	100	100

[1] In the column for employees the busiest week means the week in which the maximum number were employed; in the column for wages it means the week in which the maximum amount was paid.

[2] Percentage which employees or wages each week constituted of average employees or wages per week during year.

Taking the figures for the industry as a whole, it will be seen that the average employment through the year as shown by the number of employees each week was 83.3 per cent; expressed as a percentage of the amount of wages paid out each week, the annual average was 73 per cent. That is to say, if the 20,524 people, the maximum number employed in any week (Table 69), in the shops which had records for the entire year,[1] were all to be given an equal chance they would have employment 83.3 per cent of the year, or over 43 weeks. That does not mean, however, that they would be fully employed during those weeks; it means merely that they would be on the pay roll for that length of time, but the actual amount of work they would have an opportunity of doing is shown by the average annual wage percentage, which, as will be seen from Table 69, was 73 per cent. This percentage is based on the wages actually paid out from week to week and is necessarily smaller than the percentage of people employed, because workers, especially those paid by the piece, may be on the pay roll for a week, but be paid only for the work actually done by them, which may last only a few hours each day or a few hours for the entire week, especially when work is not plentiful.

The highest percentage of employment is, of course, 100, and occurred during the twelfth week (end of March), while the lowest was 50, found during the twenty-ninth week (early in August). On the other hand, taking the wages paid out (Table 68) it is found that the highest amount, $245,494, was paid out during the eleventh week, the lowest (in the twenty-ninth week) fell to $94,149, or 38 per cent of the highest, and the average for the year was $178,887. That is to say, if the work done during the year were spread out equally over every week of the year, the wages paid out by these shops would amount to $178,887 per week.

Another conclusion to be drawn from these figures is that employment is more steady than earnings in the industry; that is to say, when work slackens most of the people are retained at the factories, but there is less work to go around and in consequence less wages earned. For this reason the average wage per employee during one of the busiest weeks (tenth) was $12, while during the twenty-seventh week it dropped to $8.59, the weekly average for the year being $10.46. Taking the average annual percentage that wages for each of the four branches of the industry were of the maximum amount of wages of any week, it will be found that they differ widely, the lowest, 44 per cent, being for the high-grade (B) nonassociation shops, and the highest, 71 per cent, for the high-grade (B) association shops.

The fluctuations of employment in 1912, as expressed in the amount of wages paid and the number of people employed, can

[1] A very small number of shops has been included above in which wage records were missing for a few weeks. But the wages paid out for these shops constituted too small a fraction of the total to affect the results to any appreciable degree.

be easily traced from week to week in the following charts prepared for that purpose.

Chart 17 consists of two separate diagrams, the upper one showing the fluctuations in the industry as a whole, while the lower diagram shows the same facts for branch B, which consists of shops making high-grade garments. The solid line in each case represents the number of people employed, while the dotted shows the wages paid out. For the purpose of graphic presentation, the average number of people employed weekly throughout the year and the average weekly wages paid out in the industry for the whole year were designated as 100; and the number of people employed each week and the amount of wages paid out each week were expressed as percentages of those numbers.

SEASONAL RISE AND FALL IN NUMBER OF EMPLOYEES AND IN WAGES.

Looking at the upper diagram in Chart 17, two high peaks are found in the months of March and October, indicating the periods of greatest activity, while the lowest point falls in the month of July, showing the dullest month of the year for the industry. Between the high and low points there are several fluctuations of a minor character.

Examining the lines closely, the first point that strikes the eye is that while the two lines follow, as a rule, the same direction, they rarely coincide. The broken line, denoting wages, rises to greater heights and falls to lower depressions than the solid line, which shows the fluctuations in the number of people employed. Thus, in the month of March the wage line rises to 137 per cent, while the employment line stops at 120 per cent. This means that while during the busiest week in 1912, which occurred in March, there were 20 per cent more people employed in the shops than the average throughout the year, the wages at the same time rose to 37 per cent above the average. This is due to the fact that when factories are busy to their capacity, they can not increase the number of their employees beyond a certain limit, which is determined, first, by the number of machines at the factory, and, second, by the available supply of help which at that time of the year usually falls short of the demand. At the same time the people employed at the factories are kept more steadily at work than at other times in the year, and therefore the individual earnings per employee increase in greater proportion. This is especially true of pieceworkers, but is also true of week workers, who are able to command during those weeks higher rates of wages, which are further increased through working overtime.

A marked excess of the percentage of wages over the percentage of employees will be found at the other high peaks, viz, in February, in April, at the end of August (35th week), at the end of September

(39th week), and the middle of October. The only exceptions to this rule occur in the months of June, November, and December, when the employment peak is above the wage crest. These exceptions

CHART 17.—SEASONAL FLUCTUATIONS OF EMPLOYMENT AND WAGES IN WHOLE INDUSTRY AND IN 6 HIGH-GRADE SHOPS, 1912.

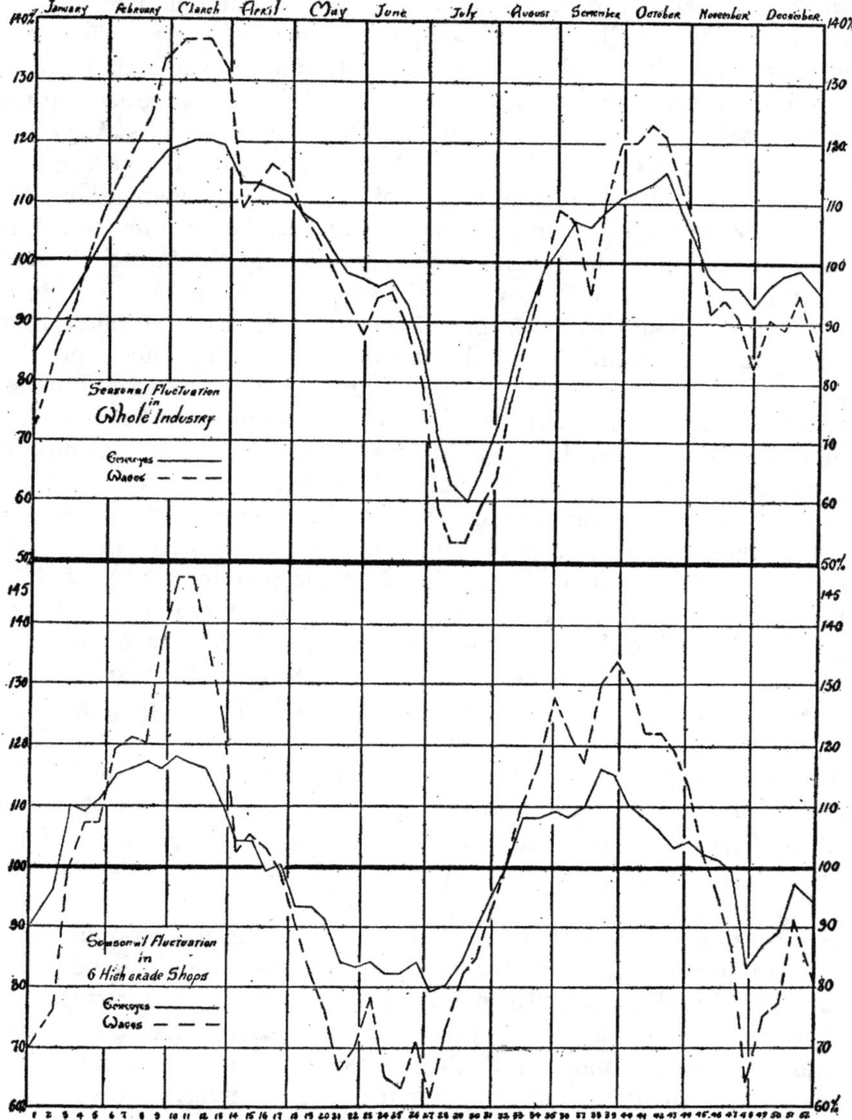

serve to confirm the rule as will be explained below, after considering the low points in the curves.

When the low points are examined it is found that here again the wage line goes to greater extremes than the employment line and therefore declines to lower points than the latter. Thus at the lowest ebb of the industry in July, the total wages paid out in the industry decline to 53 per cent of the average weekly wage paid through the year, while the per cent of employment goes down only to 60 per cent. The meaning of this is that when business drops off, the workers, especially those paid by the week, are not laid off in proportion to the decline in business, which leaves less work for each worker. In other words, while wages decline in proportion to the dropping off in business, the number of workers is not reduced to the same extent. What occurs in July will likewise be found at the other low points, such as April (14th week), end of May (22d week), middle of September, the three November points, and December. That the high peaks of wages in June, November, and December did not rise to the corresponding employment peaks was due to the fact that those are three comparatively slow months when there are more people at the factories than there is work to keep them all busy. When a temporary improvement in the situation occurs during those months, the wages rise more rapidly than the number of employees, but not sufficiently for the wage line to rise above the employment line. Thus before the rise in June the wage line was 88 per cent while the employment line was at 97 per cent, making a difference of 9 points between the two; the wages then rapidly increase in two weeks to 95 per cent (24th week), while the number of workers remains the same, at 97 per cent), making the difference between the two lines only 2 points, but not enough to send the wage line above the employment line. Exactly the same thing happened in November and December.

Following the rise and fall of the curves through the year, the first week of January is found to be at the lowest point of the year, with the exception of July. This is natural; it coincides with the New Year's holidays and the beginning of and the preparation for the new spring season. Wages are 73 per cent of the average, that is to say, 27 per cent below normal; employment is 85 per cent of the average, or 15 per cent below the normal. Both lines rise rapidly, indicating that orders are coming in; additional workers are taken on as fast as conditions warrant; wages are rising more rapidly than the number of new workers, which means that the old hands have more work to do; and at the end of the third week in January the two lines cross each other at 97 per cent, which means that wages have overtaken employment and the industry is nearly normal. The wheels of industry are now going faster and faster, the wage line mounts higher and higher, the employment line likewise rises but can not keep up with the wage line. This represents the time of the year when manufacturers complain of lack of skilled help and when the union can not meet the demand from the employers for more help. This keeps up for about two months, when the amount of weekly wages paid out in the middle of March reaches 137 per cent, that is to say, 37 per cent above normal; and the employment line is at 120 per cent, which means that the number of workers in the industry is 20 per cent above the average.

The highest point reached is maintained for two weeks and then the decline sets in, slowly at first, with temporary ups and downs through April, May, and June, but each subsequent rise finds the curves at a lower point than the preceding one, while each succeeding point of decline exceeds the preceding one. Noting now the course of the two lines, the first drop, both in the employment and in the wage lines, which occurs at the end of March, is much more precipitous than in the next few weeks. Up to this point everything was strained to the limit of endurance to meet the rush orders; workers were kept busy every minute of the day and made to work overtime; all the machines were in operation and anyone from outside the industry who could run a sewing machine was put to work. As soon as the rush is over, the last recruits and the less competent and the less desirable workers from the manufacturer's point of view are the first to go; hence the sudden decline of the employment line from the 12th to the 14th week (end of March and beginning of April). At the same time the wage line drops much more sharply than the employment line, because overtime is largely discontinued and there is less work during the regular work hours to go around among those who remain on the pay roll. After the line reaches bottom at the end of the first week in April there is a new rise in wages, although the number of people employed continues to decline slowly but surely. This temporary improvement is due to the fact that the preceding slump affected the entire industry, while from now on the factories making cheap waists and dresses are able to find a market for staple summer goods among the retail stores, and only those manufacturing fine dresses and gowns have but little to do.

The contrast between the two branches of the industry can be seen at a glance by looking at the lower diagram of Chart 8, which represents six shops making exclusively high-grade garments. Here the wage line is seen to decline much more rapidly in the months of April and May than in the upper diagram. At the end of May the wage line drops to 88 per cent in the upper diagram, while in the lower diagram it reaches the lowest point during that month at 66 per cent. In June and July the wage line for the whole industry (upper diagram) declines very rapidly, reaching bottom in the middle of July, when wages decline to 53, i. e. 47 per cent below normal (only a little over one-third of the wages paid out during the busiest week), while the line for the high-grade end of the industry (lower diagram) continues during the months of June and July (with some ups and downs) at about the same level as it reached at the end of May. This is due to the fact that after the slump in May the high-grade garment industry recovers part of the lost ground by making up garments at reduced prices offered at special sales in the stores and is thus able to keep moderately busy, while the manufacturers of low-priced garments, having satisfied the summer trade, are now only able to get mostly small supplementary orders "to fill sizes." As they are selling cheap goods regularly, they are not in the same position as the manufacturers of high-grade garments to make up special garments at reduced prices.

Having reached bottom in July, both branches of the industry begin to pick up for the fall season. The fall season is neither as long nor as active as the spring season, which a glance at the two diagrams in Chart 17 will show. Taking up first the upper diagram for the industry as a whole, we see that the highest point reached by the wage line is only 123 in October, as compared with 137 in March. While in the spring nearly four months are above the average line, in the fall only one and a half months are above that line. The rise in August is rapid, but as it starts from the bottom in July, it does not reach normal (100 per cent) until the last week in August. There is a big slump in the middle of September, due to the Jewish holidays. This explains why the solid line, representing the number of people employed, continues to rise in spite of the fall in the wage line: The people are all on the pay roll, but they earn but little on account of the holidays.

Both the upper and lower diagrams show the same tendency; but in the lower diagram (high-grade garment industry) the fall busy season (represented by the area above the normal 100 per cent line) is twice as large as in the upper diagram (representing the whole industry). That is to say, the high-grade garment industry is busy three months in the fall season as against one and a half months in the industry as a whole. Not only does the fall season last longer in the higher end of the industry, but it develops to a greater extent, the wage line rising to 134 per cent (beginning of October) in that branch and only to 123 per cent in the industry as a whole. In both diagrams the decline sets in during October, passing under the normal line in the early part of November, but here a change occurs in the relative positions of the high-grade branch of the industry and of the industry as a whole. In the former the wage line drops to 64 per cent at the end of November, while in the industry as a whole it does not go below 83 per cent. This is due to the fact that many of the shops manufacturing cheaper garments begin to get busy at this time on advance spring orders or are making up stock in anticipation of the rush order demand of the early spring months and the advance January sales, while the high-grade shops must still await the final developments in the style adjustments for the coming spring, and such a thing as making stock is entirely out of the question.

What has been said about the two branches of the industry is shown in Tables 70 and 71, which follow, and is strikingly brought out in Charts 18 and 19.

TABLE 70.—FLUCTUATIONS OF EMPLOYMENT AND WAGES IN 1912 IN SIX SHOPS MANUFACTURING HIGH-GRADE GARMENTS EXCLUSIVELY.

Week.	Number of persons employed.	Amount paid in wages.	Per cent (busiest week=100).[1]		Per cent (average for year=100).[2]	
			Employees.	Wages.	Employees.	Wages.
1	529	$4,701	77	48	90	70
2	561	5,107	81	52	95	76
3	646	6,647	93	67	110	99
4	642	7,181	93	72	109	107
5	651	7,216	94	73	111	107
6	677	7,999	98	81	115	119
7	681	8,114	99	82	116	121
8	685	8,050	99	81	116	119
9	684	9,185	99	93	116	136
10	691	9,907	100	100	118	147
11	685	9,885	99	100	117	147
12	681	9,216	99	93	116	137
13	647	8,332	94	84	110	124
14	611	6,846	88	69	104	102
15	612	7,030	89	71	104	104
16	581	6,953	84	70	99	103
17	586	6,659	85	67	100	99
18	545	6,024	79	61	93	89
19	544	5,525	79	56	93	82
20	533	5,117	77	52	91	76
21	493	4,467	71	45	84	66
22	489	4,676	71	47	83	69
23	493	5,218	71	53	84	77
24	483	4,364	70	44	82	65
25	482	4,253	70	43	82	63
26	495	4,804	72	48	84	71
27	461	4,073	67	41	78	60
28	473	4,927	68	50	80	73
29	493	5,496	71	55	84	82
30	528	5,738	76	58	90	85
31	560	6,216	81	63	95	92
32	589	6,742	85	68	100	100
33	632	7,405	91	75	107	110
34	635	7,878	92	80	108	117
35	639	8,582	92	87	109	127
36	634	8,183	92	83	108	121
37	646	7,845	93	79	110	116
38	679	8,764	98	88	115	130
39	675	9,043	98	91	115	134
40	647	8,777	94	89	110	130
41	633	8,217	92	83	108	122
42	624	8,195	90	83	106	122
43	602	8,017	87	81	102	119
44	609	7,588	88	77	104	113
45	601	6,863	87	69	102	102
46	596	6,386	86	64	101	95
47	584	5,858	85	59	99	87
48	488	4,284	71	43	83	64
49	509	5,062	74	51	87	75
50	523	5,199	76	52	89	77
51	569	6,149	82	62	97	91
52	550	5,360	80	54	94	80
Average	588	6,737	85.1	68	100	100

[1] In the column for employees the busiest week means the week in which the maximum number were employed; in the column for wages it means the week in which the maximum amount was paid.

[2] Percentage which employees or wages each week constituted of average employees or wages per week during year.

TABLE 71.—FLUCTUATIONS OF EMPLOYMENT AND WAGES IN 1912 IN SIX SHOPS MANUFACTURING LOW-GRADE WAISTS EXCLUSIVELY.

Week.	Number of persons employed.	Amount paid in wages.	Per cent (busiest week=100).[1]		Per cent (average for year=100).[2]	
			Employees.	Wages.	Employees.	Wages.
1	1,151	$9,616	79	66	95	84
2	1,175	10,752	81	74	97	94
3	1,148	11,333	79	78	95	99
4	1,189	12,112	81	83	98	106
5	1,199	11,847	82	82	99	104
6	1,235	12,204	85	84	102	107
7	1,248	12,548	85	86	103	110
8	1,264	12,768	87	88	104	112
9	1,251	13,411	86	92	103	117
10	1,263	13,497	87	93	104	118
11	1,214	13,129	83	90	100	115
12	1,257	13,701	86	94	104	120
13	1,250	14,260	86	98	103	125
14	1,191	11,092	82	76	98	97
15	1,237	11,944	85	82	102	104
16	1,269	13,002	87	89	105	114
17	1,272	13,604	87	94	105	119
18	1,290	13,083	88	90	107	114
19	1,290	13,066	88	90	107	114
20	1,296	12,848	89	88	107	112
21	1,298	12,768	89	88	107	112
22	1,282	11,151	88	77	106	98
23	1,257	11,664	86	80	104	102
24	1,235	11,504	85	79	102	101
25	1,205	10,646	83	73	100	93
26	1,136	9,322	78	64	94	82
27	1,070	7,154	73	49	88	63
28	847	5,275	58	36	70	46
29	720	5,250	49	36	59	46
30	744	5,270	51	36	61	46
31	864	6,018	59	41	71	53
32	904	6,917	62	48	75	60
33	975	7,915	67	54	81	69
34	997	8,905	68	61	82	78
35	1,048	10,044	72	69	87	88
36	1,106	10,389	76	72	91	91
37	1,104	8,049	76	55	91	70
38	1,180	9,584	81	66	97	84
39	1,224	11,956	84	82	101	105
40	1,283	12,930	88	89	106	113
41	1,329	13,633	91	94	110	119
42	1,360	13,940	93	96	112	122
43	1,407	13,881	96	96	116	121
44	1,422	14,256	97	98	117	125
45	1,416	13,907	97	96	117	122
46	1,446	14,528	99	100	119	127
47	1,459	14,291	100	98	120	125
48	1,446	13,159	99	91	119	115
49	1,441	13,927	99	96	119	122
50	1,413	13,040	97	90	117	114
51	1,413	12,867	97	89	117	113
52	1,272	10.596	87	73	105	93
Average	1,211	11,434	83	78.7	100	100

[1] In the column for employees the busiest week means the week in which the maximum number were employed; in the column for wages it means the week in which the maximum amount was paid.

[2] Percentage which employees or wages each week constituted of average employees or wages per week during year.

In view of the fact that many of the shops manufacture a wide range of goods and are therefore subject to conditions prevailing both in the cheap and expensive shops in the industry, a clear view of the conditions existing in each class of shops could be obtained only by selecting a few shops manufacturing exclusively high-grade garments and a few making exclusively cheap goods. The tables and charts

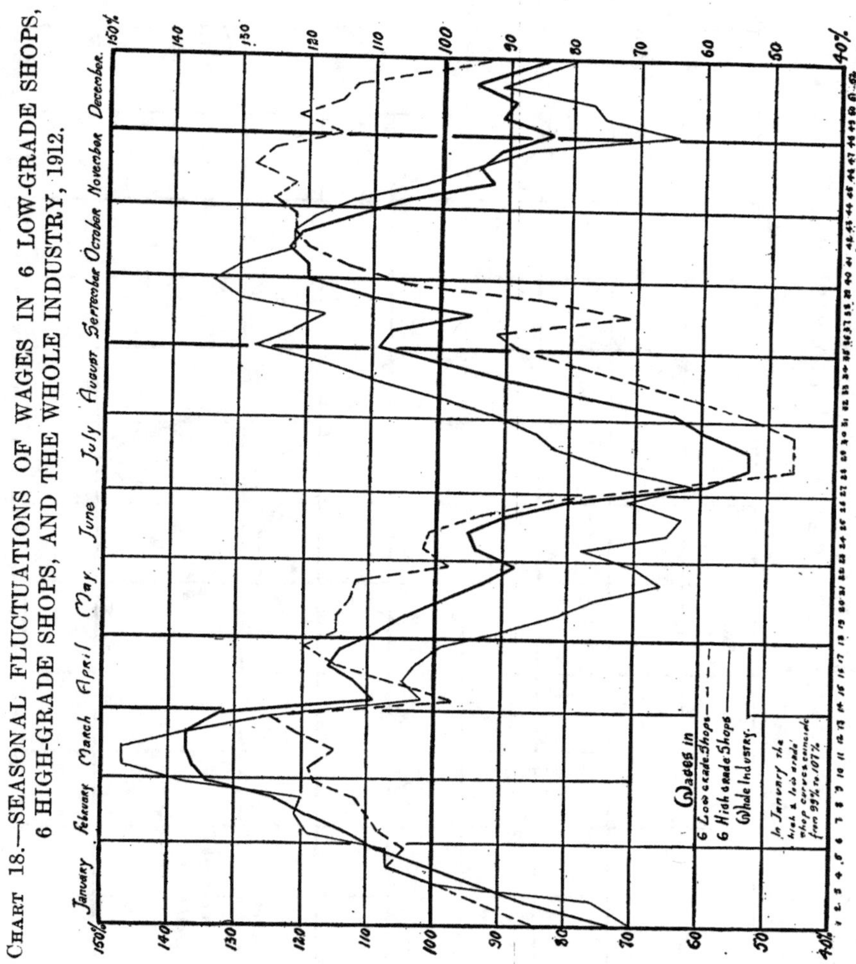

CHART 18.—SEASONAL FLUCTUATIONS OF WAGES IN 6 LOW-GRADE SHOPS, 6 HIGH-GRADE SHOPS, AND THE WHOLE INDUSTRY, 1912.

were prepared with this end in view. Chart 18 shows the fluctuations in wages prevailing in six high-grade shops (solid light lines), six large shops manufacturing cheap waists (broken line), and in the industry as a whole (heavy line). Chart 19 shows the fluctuation in employment for the same groups.

From these charts the contrast in the two ends of the industry can be seen at a glance. A more rapid rise in wages during the months of January, February, and March in the high-grade shops as compared with the cheap shops is apparent. At the climax in March the wage line for the high-grade shops rises to 147 per cent, while for the cheap shops it stops at 125 per cent. In the latter part of March both lines fall sharply and in the early part of April the line for the

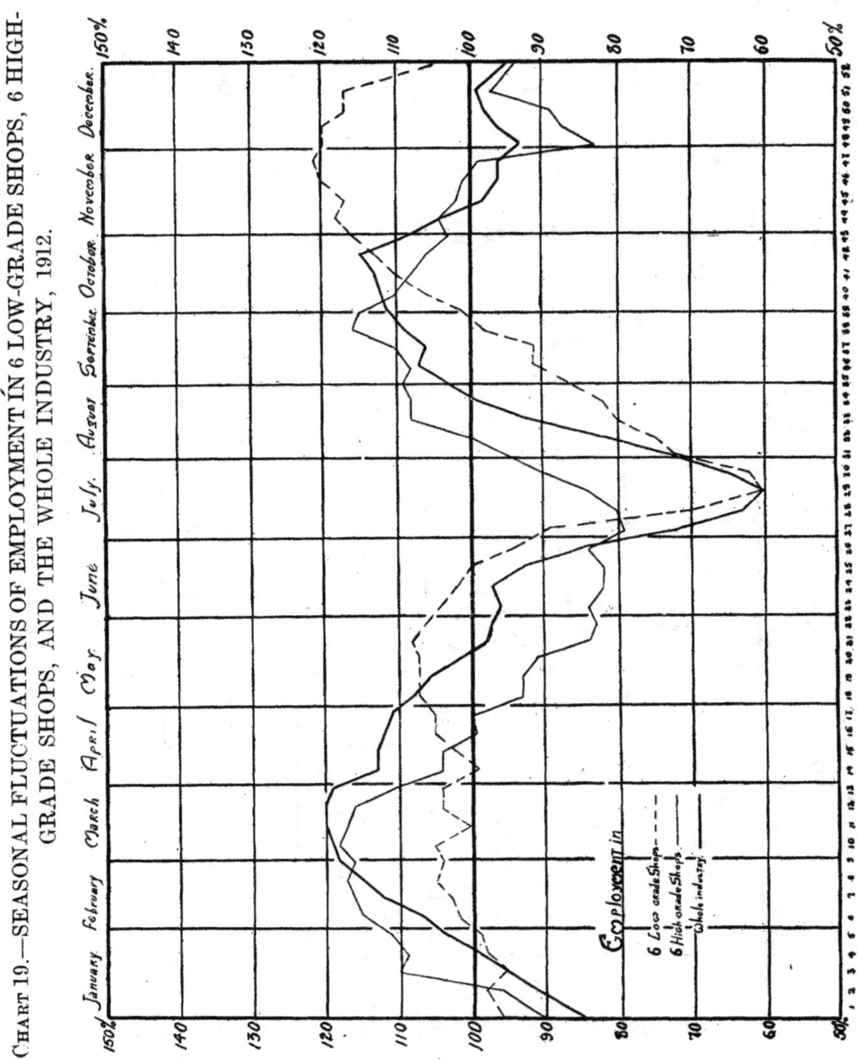

CHART 19.—SEASONAL FLUCTUATIONS OF EMPLOYMENT IN 6 LOW-GRADE SHOPS, 6 HIGH-GRADE SHOPS, AND THE WHOLE INDUSTRY, 1912.

low-grade shops drops to 3 per cent below normal and the line for the high-grade shops to 2 per cent above normal. From this drop the cheaper branch of the industry quickly recovers, rising to 120 per cent by the end of April, while the recovery in the high-grade is but slight (105 per cent), only 3 per cent above the low point and only lasts one week, after which there is a steady decline during the months of April and May. The line for the cheaper branch continues to rise all through April and fairly holds its own during May. In the latter part of May the low-grade line begins to decline, and from that time on there is an almost uninterrupted drop until it reaches the lowest point at 46 per cent, or 54 per cent below normal in July, while the high-grade line, in spite of fluctuations, practically holds its own through the month of June, for the reasons explained above, and early in July starts on a rapid and steady recovery.

This recovery, which marks the opening of the fall season, commences early in July in the high-grade line and a few weeks later at the cheap one. The two lines move in the same direction during August, which marks the period of rising activity, but while the high-grade line reaches the climax at the end of August at 128 per cent, the high-water mark of the cheap line halts at 91 per cent, or 9 per cent below normal. In September there is a perceptible drop in the wage curves of both ends of the industry, due to the Jewish holidays. That it is not due to a decline in business is shown by the lines in Chart 19, in which the curves representing employment show not only no decline, but on the contrary show a continuous increase. The end of September marks the culmination of the fall season in the high-grade line at 134 per cent, after which the curve takes a sudden and swift drop, which continues without interruption for two months, reaching bottom early in December at 64 per cent, or 36 per cent below normal.

The very opposite takes place at the cheap end of the industry. At the end of September, when the high-grade curve reaches the climax, the low-grade curve is at 105 per cent, or 29 points below the high-grade. But instead of declining from this time on, as the high-grade curve does, the low-grade continues to rise, overtaking the high-grade in the middle of October at 122, from which it continues to rise until it reaches the climax in the middle of November at 128. During these two months the waist manufacturers, especially at the cheaper end, have been busy supplying both an immediate fall demand and an advance spring demand, while the fine dress and gown shops have had little to do. In December there is a rapid decline both of employment (Chart 19) and of earnings (Chart 18), and a moderate rise in the expensive branch, which is beginning to work on sample orders for the early spring trade. A decline sets in in both curves in the second half of December, due to the Christmas holidays and end-of-the-year stock taking, in anticipation of the starting up of the wheels of industry after New Year's, as shown by the rising curves during the month of January.

In one respect the shops making exclusively cheap garments and those manufacturing high-grade garments are alike; both have a fairly long fall season, lasting about three months (see Chart 18), the only difference being that in the high-grade dress shops the season starts and ends at earlier dates than in the cheap waist shops. It seems strange, therefore, that the industry as a whole (represented by the heavy curve on Chart 18) should have a shorter season, lasting less than two months. One explanation for this is that the industry as a whole includes a large number of shops making a medium grade of waists and no dresses. These shops make too high a grade of waists to venture to make stock for advance spring sales as the cheap waist manufacturers do, and, on the other hand, have not the same demand for immediate fall deliveries as the dress manufacturers have. The result is a shorter season and a less active one while it lasts.

EMPLOYMENT AMONG WEEK WORKERS AND PIECEWORKERS.

An important question to those engaged in the industry is that of the comparative regularity of employment among pieceworkers and week workers. In compiling the wages paid each week throughout the year in the several shops, it was found impracticable to segregate the earnings of the pieceworkers from those of the week workers. This separation was made, however, in the case of two fairly large shops manufacturing exclusively $9 waists and two shops manufacturing a medium grade of waists ranging from $16.50 to $36 a dozen. These four shops may be considered as typical of the classes of shops which they represent.

The figures referring to these shops are given in Tables 72 and 73, which follow:

TABLE 72.—FLUCTUATIONS OF EMPLOYMENT AND WAGES OF WEEK WORKERS AND PIECEWORKERS IN TWO SHOPS MANUFACTURING $9-PER-DOZEN WAISTS EXCLUSIVELY.

Week.	Number of persons employed.		Amounts paid in wages.		Per cent of persons employed (busiest week = 100).[1]		Per cent paid in wages (busiest week = 100).[2]	
	Week work.	Piece-work.	Week work.	Piece-work.	Week work.	Piece-work.	Week work.	Piece-work.
1	116	110	$835	$1,291	89	87	57	62
2	118	110	990	1,341	91	87	68	65
3	115	112	1,021	1,592	88	88	70	77
4	114	114	1,046	1,615	88	90	72	78
5	115	111	987	1,343	88	87	68	65
6	115	115	1,098	1,566	88	91	75	75
7	119	111	1,061	1,490	92	87	73	72
8	114	107	1,077	1,422	88	84	74	69
9	119	111	1,190	1,716	92	87	81	83
10	121	116	1,289	1,765	93	91	88	85
11	122	119	1,320	2,011	94	94	90	97
12	122	118	1,462	2,062	94	93	100	99
13	123	118	1,362	2,075	95	93	93	100
14	123	108	1,104	1,873	95	85	76	90
15	120	112	1,171	1,459	92	88	80	70
16	122	117	1,244	1,953	94	92	85	94
17	124	110	1,271	1,775	95	87	87	86
18	123	109	1,189	1,604	95	86	81	77
19	124	110	1,218	1,605	95	87	83	77
20	130	104	1,251	1,552	100	82	86	75
21	127	106	1,190	1,549	98	83	81	75
22	124	102	971	1,277	95	80	66	62
23	120	105	1,034	1,362	92	83	71	66
24	116	105	992	1,375	89	83	68	66
25	116	103	1,004	1,275	89	81	69	61
26	114	107	967	1,398	88	84	66	67
27	110	89	746	1,056	85	70	51	51
28	106	84	558	663	82	66	38	32
29	100	80	623	656	77	63	43	32
30	87	84	461	740	67	66	32	36
31	77	76	365	324	59	60	25	16
32	85	81	503	478	65	64	34	23
33	82	92	668	696	63	72	46	34
34	95	96	826	917	73	76	56	44
35	96	102	908	924	74	80	62	45
36	98	103	894	1,009	75	81	61	49
37	96	99	698	719	74	78	48	35
38	101	102	816	963	78	80	56	46
39	99	104	980	1,273	76	82	67	61
40	100	102	1,116	1,303	77	80	76	63
41	104	107	1,197	1,478	80	84	82	72
42	122	108	1,404	1,612	94	85	96	78
43	111	117	1,304	1,611	85	92	89	78
44	108	126	1,228	1,926	83	99	84	93
45	108	126	1,166	1,875	83	99	80	90
46	108	124	1,389	1,710	83	98	95	82
47	111	127	1,190	1,859	85	100	81	90
48	110	121	1,082	1,684	85	95	74	81
49	110	124	1,108	1,658	85	98	76	80
50	112	119	1,092	1,514	86	94	75	73
51	110	121	1,096	1,482	85	95	75	71
52	109	121	1,050	1,561	84	95	72	75
Average	111	108	1,035	1,405	85	85	71	68

[1] The busiest week in each of these columns means the week having the maximum number of employees.
[2] The busiest week in each of these columns means the week in which the maximum amount of wages was paid.

TABLE 73.—FLUCTUATIONS OF EMPLOYMENT AND WAGES OF WEEK WORKERS AND PIECEWORKERS IN TWO SHOPS MANUFACTURING MEDIUM-GRADE WAISTS.

Week.	Number of persons employed.		Amounts paid in wages.		Per cent of persons employed (busiest week=100).[1]		Per cent paid in wages (busiest week=100).[2]	
	Week work.	Piecework.	Week work.	Piecework.	Week work.	Piecework.	Week work.	Piecework.
1	125	205	$984	$1,620	75	92	62	55
2	124	209	1,213	2,134	74	94	76	72
3	128	214	1,216	2,230	77	96	76	76
4	130	210	1,231	2,368	78	95	77	80
5	138	209	1,308	2,388	83	94	82	81
6	136	202	1,272	2,453	81	91	80	83
7	135	210	1,242	2,510	81	95	78	85
8	133	199	1,276	2,354	80	90	80	80
9	137	214	1,316	2,567	82	96	82	87
10	140	201	1,393	2,536	84	91	87	86
11	142	205	1,398	2,623	85	92	87	89
12	147	220	1,428	2,950	88	99	89	100
13	149	222	1,510	2,916	89	100	94	99
14	150	187	1,268	2,154	90	84	79	73
15	153	213	1,482	2,489	92	96	93	84
16	155	209	1,503	2,741	93	94	94	93
17	151	216	1,545	2,827	90	97	97	96
18	158	214	1,414	2,623	95	96	88	89
19	150	209	1,406	2,451	90	94	88	83
20	148	201	1,305	2,073	89	91	82	70
21	143	194	1,195	1,636	86	87	75	55
22	136	173	1,190	1,108	81	78	74	38
23	132	190	1,188	1,641	79	86	74	56
24	141	181	1,381	1,531	84	82	86	52
25	148	148	1,155	1,025	89	67	72	35
26	127	145	960	1,091	76	65	60	37
27	86	74	587	273	51	33	37	9
28	100	80	711	176	60	36	44	6
29	106	96	825	690	63	43	52	23
30	104	122	833	813	62	55	52	28
31	103	135	747	1,017	62	61	47	34
32	107	145	934	1,145	64	65	58	39
33	112	157	1,004	1,432	67	71	63	49
34	120	155	1,110	1,457	72	70	69	49
35	125	158	1,149	1,588	75	71	72	54
36	127	159	1,143	1,324	76	72	71	45
37	122	129	894	1,024	73	58	56	35
38	121	160	1,144	1,614	72	72	72	55
39	123	165	1,139	1,830	74	74	71	62
40	130	161	1,169	1,792	78	73	73	61
41	137	170	1,292	2,030	82	77	81	69
42	148	190	1,342	1,981	89	86	84	67
43	141	177	1,329	1,728	84	80	83	59
44	142	170	1,333	1,718	85	77	83	58
45	145	159	1,115	1,430	87	72	70	48
46	150	178	1,478	1,930	90	80	92	65
47	150	183	1,330	2,085	90	82	83	71
48	152	180	1,347	1,670	91	81	84	57
49	158	197	1,534	1,923	95	89	96	65
50	165	186	1,599	1,944	99	84	100	66
51	167	199	1,585	2,168	100	90	99	73
52	164	187	1,418	1,875	98	84	89	64
Average	137	178	1,228	1,840	82	80	77	62

[1] The busiest week in each of these columns means the week having the maximum number of employees.
[2] The busiest week in each of these columns means the week in which the maximum amount of wages was paid.

As will be seen from these figures the pieceworkers show practically the same average percentage of employment for the year as the week workers. The average weekly wage, however, forms a lower percentage for the pieceworkers than for the week workers. In the $9 group (Table 72) the week workers' average weekly wage is 71 per cent of the highest weekly wage, while in the case of the pieceworkers it is

68 per cent. In the shops manufacturing medium-grade garments the week workers' average weekly rate is 77 per cent of the highest weekly wage and that of the pieceworkers is only 62 per cent.

The shops to which the above figures refer are all conducted under the piecework system. In all piecework shops there are several occupations, however, that are paid by the week, such as cleaners, finishers, examiners, cutters, etc. In these shops pieceworkers and week workers do not compete with each other; on the contrary they supplement one another. When the operators are busy there is more work for the week workers; when the operators have little to do there is but little finishing, cleaning, and other operations to perform. How, then, is the fact to be explained that the average weekly wage of the pieceworkers forms a lower percentage of the wages of the busiest week of the year than in the case of the week workers? Two reasons may account for it: First, the manufacturers employ a relatively larger number of pieceworkers than they do of week workers in proportion to the quantity of work to be done during the rush weeks of the year. When work falls off the piecework operators are allowed to remain in the shop and divide whatever work there is among themselves. In the case of the week workers, one of the considerations in fixing the weekly rate of wages is the steadiness of employment, and it is to the interest of the manufacturer to have a smaller number of experienced workers who will be given steady employment, in consideration of which they will be willing to accept a smaller wage than they would if the manufacturer employed a large number of workers of various degrees of skill, a considerable part of whom would have to be laid off when work slackens. Second, during the busiest week of the year the pieceworkers work much harder, as compared with the rest of the year, than the week workers. The work is piled up beyond the capacity of the shop and, therefore, the loss of time which usually takes place in the intervals between the completion of one job and the beginning of another, is now reduced to a minimum. Moreover, the pieceworker, knowing that another "bundle" is awaiting him as soon as he is through with the one he has on hand, works much harder than at other times of the year and has a much greater incentive to do so than the week worker. All these facts combine to raise the pieceworkers' earnings during the busiest week of the year above the earnings during the rest of the year to a much greater extent than in the case of the week workers, and therefore make the average weekly earnings look much smaller in comparison with the busiest week in the case of the pieceworker than in that of the week worker.

The different policies in the treatment of pieceworkers and week workers come even more clearly to light when shops in which the piecework system prevails are compared with shops in which operators work by the week. In the former the tendency is to have as large a number of operators as possible during the rush season, most of whom are allowed to remain throughout the year sharing in what little work there is. In the week-work shops the tendency is to retain only the best workers during the slow season, so as to give them steady employment and thus retain a working nucleus throughout the year, ready to be enlarged as soon as the demands of the season warrant it. The policy of the union has been to oppose this system of employment in the week shops and to attempt as far as possible to retain all of the workers in the employ of the shops. In the shops manufacturing the cheaper garments, and especially in the smaller shops, the union has been fairly successful in having its policy adopted, and the week workers in those shops work by turns during the slow period. The workers are divided into two or more groups, which report for duty on alternating days or weeks or whatever other periods are agreed upon by the manufacturer and his employees.

HOURS OF LABOR.

It would have been interesting to secure information as to the number of hours actually worked by the employees at different times of the year. In some cases information on this point could not be obtained at all, and in others would have been exceedingly difficult and expensive to obtain. So far as pieceworkers are concerned, no record is kept of the time they work except in a few shops. Even in these shops a record is kept only of the time the workers spend in the factory, which is not necessarily the time they are actually at work, since pieceworkers frequently spend many hours a day in the factories without doing any work, especially during the slow season. The only employees for whom an accurate record of hours at work is kept are the week workers, but in the majority of the shops this record is not preserved throughout the year, and the time has to be recalculated from the wages paid out each week.

HOURS DURING BUSIEST WEEK IN THE YEAR.

From the records obtained for the busiest week of the year in each factory figures have been compiled as to the hours which the week workers worked during that week. The hours worked by the cutters have been separated from those worked by other employees, since the limitation as to overtime does not apply to them on the one hand, and on the other, cutters as a rule work more steadily than the rest of the force.

As has been seen in Table 2 (p. 17), which represents a summary for the entire industry, only a minority of the employees (not including the cutters), namely, 37.5 per cent, worked the normal number of

50 hours; 29.4 per cent, or almost one-third, worked less than 50 hours. On the other hand, over 33 per cent worked overtime, so that over 70 per cent of all the week workers, not including cutters, worked 50 hours or more. Of those who worked under 50 hours nearly three-fourths worked from 40 to 49 hours, leaving about 1,200 people, or less than 10 per cent of the total number of workers working less than 40 hours. Among these, as will be seen from the table, are some who worked less than 10 hours.

In the case of the cutters, more than 56 per cent worked the normal number of 50 hours and more than 87 per cent worked 50 hours or more, leaving but one-eighth of the people working less than 50 hours and less than 4 per cent working less than 40 hours.

OVERTIME.

So far as overtime is concerned, it is interesting to compare the figures of 1912 and 1913 when the protocol limited the overtime to four hours a week and the normal hours to 50. Taking first week workers other than cutters, in 1912, 66.8 per cent, or over two-thirds, worked more than 50 hours; in 1913 the percentage of those working more than 50 hours dropped to 33.1 per cent, or one-half of what it was the preceding year. This was due to the fact that during 1912 the normal hours in the various shops were from 50 to 54 per week. Taking the number of those working 55 hours and over, the percentage declined from nearly 33 per cent, or about one-third, of all the employees in 1912 to less than one-tenth in 1913.

In regard to the employees working overtime, it should be stated that the number given for 1913 is not entirely accurate, being in all probability an understatement of the actual facts. This was due to the fact that under the protocol week workers are entitled to double the regular rate when working overtime. In several instances it was not clear from the books whether a worker paid for, say, 58 hours, actually worked 54 hours, being paid double for overtime, or worked 58 hours, being paid for overtime at the regular hourly rate. In all such cases, unless there was clear proof that the protocol provision as to double rate for overtime was violated, the manufacturer was given the benefit of the doubt. But even allowing for this understatement, there can be no doubt that the number working in excess of 50 hours greatly declined during 1913, especially when it is borne in mind that the figures given here are for the busiest week in the year, when the number of hours worked is as a rule greater than at other times of the year.

Two tables follow, the first of which, Table 74, gives the number and per cent of cutters and of other employees (week workers) working each classified number of hours in the association and nonassociation shops, while the second, Table 75, gives separate figures for the factories manufacturing high-grade and low-grade garments in the nonassociation and the association groups.

TABLE 74.—NUMBER AND PER CENT OF WEEK WORKERS EMPLOYED EACH CLASSIFIED NUMBER OF HOURS DURING THE BUSIEST WEEK OF THE YEAR IN ASSOCIATION AND NONASSOCIATION SHOPS, 1912 AND 1913.

NUMBER.

Hours employed.	Association shops.				Nonassociation shops.			
	Cutters.		Other employees.		Cutters.		Other employees.	
	1912	1913	1912	1913	1912	1913	1912	1913
Under 10 hours	5	12	110	101	1	....	14	16
10 and under 20 hours	3	9	122	163	....	....	29	42
20 and under 30 hours	6	12	241	236	2	3	68	120
30 and under 40 hours	24	23	413	404	3	3	116	130
40 and under 50 hours	95	124	1,468	2,357	11	31	310	623
50 hours	184	804	1,161	4,608	21	165	191	744
51 and under 53 hours	260	160	2,027	1,385	39	18	401	292
53 and under 55 hours	179	152	1,678	1,418	28	13	245	228
55 and under 60 hours	172	117	2,263	860	16	14	372	246
60 and under 65 hours	140	31	1,022	178	6	3	113	70
65 and under 70 hours	91	10	322	30	3	3	17	8
70 hours and over	15	1	69	4	7	....	13	....
Total	1,174	1,455	10,896	11,744	137	253	1,889	2,519

PER CENT.

Hours employed.	Association shops: Cutters, 1912	Association shops: Cutters, 1913	Association shops: Other employees, 1912	Association shops: Other employees, 1913	Nonassociation shops: Cutters, 1912	Nonassociation shops: Cutters, 1913	Nonassociation shops: Other employees, 1912	Nonassociation shops: Other employees, 1913
Under 10 hours 10 and under 20 hours 20 and under 30 hours 30 and under 40 hours 40 and under 50 hours	11	12	22	28	12	15	28	37
50 hours	16	55	11	39	15	65	10	30
51 and under 53 hours 53 and under 55 hours	37	21	34	24	49	12	34	21
55 and under 60 hours 60 and under 65 hours 65 and under 70 hours 70 hours and over	36	11	34	9	23	8	27	13
Total	100	100	100	100	100	100	100	100

TABLE 75.—WEEK WORKERS EMPLOYED EACH CLASSIFIED NUMBER OF HOURS DURING THE BUSIEST WEEK OF THE YEAR, IN LOW-GRADE AND HIGH-GRADE ASSOCIATION AND NONASSOCIATION SHOPS, 1912 AND 1913.

Group A.

Hours employed.	Association.						Nonassociation.					
	Cutters.		Other employees.				Cutters.		Other employees.			
			Female.		Male.				Female.		Male.	
	1912	1913	1912	1913	1912	1913	1912	1913	1912	1913	1912	1913
Under 10 hours	4	9	56	60	1	2	......	......	8	13	......	2
10 and under 20 hours	2	7	83	100	......	1	......	......	20	28	4	5
20 and under 30 hours	4	8	158	129	10	5	2	3	56	107	1	5
30 and under 40 hours	18	17	250	232	7	8	2	3	85	85	11	14
40 and under 50 hours	46	78	812	1,240	45	60	5	24	241	469	15	30
50 hours	85	444	662	2,699	44	189	20	124	163	272	13	152
51 and under 53 hours	138	83	1,254	756	96	38	23	14	254	229	39	18
53 and under 55 hours	86	109	826	634	76	31	23	12	119	179	11	12
55 and under 60 hours	121	89	1,109	454	70	17	14	12	174	137	28	32
60 and under 65 hours	93	24	611	85	31	25	4	1	36	40	26	14
65 and under 70 hours	71	8	211	25	26	2	3	3	10	4	3	......
70 and over	9	1	21	3	1	......	3	......	12	......	......	......
Total	677	877	6,053	6,417	407	378	99	196	1,178	1,563	151	284

Group B.

Hours employed.	Association.						Nonassociation.					
	Cutters.		Other employees.				Cutters.		Other employees.			
			Female.		Male.				Female.		Male.	
	1912	1913	1912	1913	1912	1913	1912	1913	1912	1913	1912	1913
Under 10 hours	1	3	53	38	......	1	1	......	6	1	......	......
10 and under 20 hours	1	2	38	59	1	3	......	......	5	9	......	......
20 and under 30 hours	2	4	71	101	2	1	......	......	11	7	......	1
30 and under 40 hours	6	6	153	160	3	4	1	......	20	29	......	2
40 and under 50 hours	49	46	590	1,018	21	39	6	7	53	123	1	1
50 hours	99	360	443	1,616	12	104	1	41	15	304	......	16
51 and under 53 hours	122	77	650	563	27	28	16	4	103	44	5	1
53 and under 55 hours	93	43	752	735	24	18	5	1	110	36	5	1
55 and under 60 hours	51	28	995	378	89	11	2	2	166	75	4	2
60 and under 65 hours	47	7	370	67	10	1	2	2	47	15	4	1
65 and under 70 hours	20	2	82	3	3	......	......	......	4	4	......	......
70 and over	[1] 6	......	[2] 41	1	[3] 6	......	[4] 4	......	[5] 1	......	......	......
Total	497	578	4,238	4,739	198	210	38	57	541	647	19	25

[1] Highest 76½ hours.
[2] Highest 82¼ hours.
[3] Highest 75 hours.
[4] Highest 78 hours.
[5] Highest 73 hours.

Comparing the figures for 1912 with those for 1913, as shown in Table 74, it is found that both in the association and the nonassociation union shops the number of persons working more than 50 hours a week has been greatly reduced, while the number of those working 50 hours a week or less has increased. Excluding cutters, all of whom are men, the percentage of employees working 51 hours or more has been reduced from 68 per cent, or more than two-thirds, in association shops in 1912, to 33 per cent, or only one-third, in 1913, while in the nonassociation shops, the reduction has been from 61 per cent in 1912 to 34 per cent in 1913. Of those working 50 hours a week the proportion has increased in the association shops from 11 per cent to 39 per cent, and in the nonassociation shops from 10 per cent to 30 per cent. The percentage of those working less than 50 hours in the association shops has increased from 22 in 1912 to 28 in 1913, and in the nonassociation shops from 28 to 37.

The same tendency is observed in the case of the hours of the cutters except that a much smaller proportion of persons were working less than 50 hours, namely, only 12 per cent in the association and 15 per cent in the nonassociation shops in 1913, and a much higher proportion were working 50 hours in the week, namely, 55 per cent in the association shops and 65 per cent in the nonassociation shops.

As will be seen from Table 74 there is no marked difference in the percentage of employees working different numbers of hours in the nonassociation and association shops. The difference is more marked as regards cutters, the number of cutters working more than 50 hours in 1913 constituting 32 per cent of the total in the association shops and only 20 per cent in the nonassociation shops.

The reason for the greater extent of overtime among cutters in the association shops as compared with the nonassociation shops lies in the fact that during the "rush" weeks there is much greater activity in the shops making the higher-priced garments than in those manufacturing low-priced garments, the association having a higher percentage of the high-grade garment shops than the nonassociation shops. This is shown very clearly on Chart 18, where the high peak in March rises to 147 per cent for the high-grade garment shops, and only to 125 per cent for the low-grade. The market demand may be just as great for the low-grade garments as for the high-grade at that time, but the manufacturers of the low-grade garments have been able to work during the preceding months making up stock, while the high-grade garment manufacturers are not in a position to do so on account of the frequent changes in styles. The relative position of the curves representing these two branches of the industry during the period from the middle of October to the middle of December shows this state of affairs.

HOURS OF WORK OF PIECEWORKERS.

As already stated, very few shops keep records of the time spent at the factory by pieceworkers.

Records were obtained from 22 shops for 333 pieceworkers in 1913 and 98 in 1912. The figures for these are shown in Table 76, giving separately the hours in association and nonassociation shops, as well as the percentage for the two groups combined.

TABLE 76.—HOURS OF WORK OF PIECEWORKERS IN 22 SHOPS DURING THE BUSIEST WEEK OF THE YEAR, 1912 AND 1913.

Hours worked.	Association shops.		Nonassociation shops.		Total.			
					Number.		Per cent.	
	1912	1913	1912	1913	1912	1913	1912	1913
Under 10 hours	....	2	....	2	....	4		
10 and under 20 hours	....	6	1	4	1	10		
20 and under 30 hours	1	12	1	8	2	20	8.2	19.5
30 and under 40 hours	5	19	....	12	5	31		
40 and under 50 hours	32	123	9	16	41	139	41.8	41.7
50	13	62	8	41	21	103	21.4	30.9
51 and under 53 hours	7	18	....	2	7	20	16.3	7.8
53 and under 55 hours	9	6	....	....	9	6		
55 and under 60 hours	9	....	....	....	9	....	12.2	....
60 and under 65 hours	3	....	....	....	3	....		
Total	79	248	19	85	98	333	100.0	100.0

The extent of overtime seems to have been much less among pieceworkers than among week workers, those working more than 50 hours in 1913 being only 7.8 per cent of all the pieceworkers, as against 33.1 per cent among the week workers. Of those working less than 50 hours during the busiest week of the year, two-thirds worked from 40 to 49 hours; about one-fifth of all the workers worked from less than 10 to 39 hours during the busiest week in the year. No pieceworkers were found working more than 54 hours during 1913 among the 333 employees for whom records were obtained. While the number of workers for which these figures are given is comparatively small, the figures may be accepted as fairly representative of the industry, since they were obtained from 22 factories employing a total of about 900 workers, two-thirds of whom were employed in 11 association shops and one-third in 11 nonassociation shops. The significant fact about these figures is that even during the busiest week of the year more than 60 per cent of the workers were at work less than 50 hours a week. Moreover, the figures show merely the number of hours they spent in the factories and not those they actually worked.

CONCLUSION.

The protocol has provided definite minimum weekly rates of wages for the following occupations: Drapers, joiners, examiners, sample hands, ironers, pressers, finishers. There was also a supplementary understanding as to a minimum rate for cleaners. For cutters, in addition to the rate for competent skilled mechanics, three rates were provided for apprentices, according to the length of service. No provision was made as to the rates of wages to be paid in other occupations, except that a basis was provided for the adjustment of piece rates for operators.

The report shows very clearly the effect of providing a single minimum rate for an occupation. Looking at the charts for cleaners, drapers, examiners, finishers, ironers, joiners, and sample makers on the one hand and at those for cutters on the other, there is found in every case in the first-mentioned group one high peak corresponding to the minimum wage rate provided for in the protocol; in the cutters' wages four peaks are found corresponding to the four rates provided for in the protocol. In other words, there is a tendency for a great many, if not most, of the workers in this trade to concentrate about the minimum protocol rate. This explains the general complaint on the part of the workers that the minimum tends to become the maximum, and on the part of some employers that the protocol has dealt unjustly with them in compelling them to pay the minimum rate to apprentices by failing to provide a special rate for the latter. The investigation has shown the contention of either side to be extreme, though each has its justification in fact. The figures show on the one hand that there are almost as many workers receiving more than the minimum protocol rate as there are of those getting the minimum, and on the other that from one-fourth to one-half of the workers in each of the trades covered by the protocol received less than the minimum rate provided therein.

GRADUATED SCALE OF WEEKLY WAGES.

The example of the cutters seems to point the way to a solution of this difficulty by providing for reasonable rates to apprentices of various degrees of skill. The large number of those who were paid less than the protocol rate in the several trades is an indication of the fact that it probably includes a considerable proportion of apprentices who may not be able to earn the minimum rate provided for. The fact that there is no school to teach these trades and that the only means open to newly recruited workers to learn the trade is by entering the shops at wages commensurate with the value of the services they can render, while acquiring the necessary skill, furnishes a further corroboration of the fact that the nonpayment of the minimum rate to a considerable number of workers was not entirely due to a desire on the part of the manufacturers to violate the provisions of the protocol. The fourfold rate for the cutters points the way out of the difficulty for the other trades. At least one rate, it seems, should be provided for apprentices in each trade. One or more additional rates could probably be added for workers of higher skill, the rate being made conditional either upon the time the worker has spent in the trade or upon the skill to be determined in a certain manner. The effect of providing these additional rates on the one hand would be to do away with the improper payment below the protocol scale and thus meet the demand of the manufacturers for a special rate of wages for apprentices, and on the other it would provide for more than minimum rates to highly skilled workers and thus meet the complaint of the workers as to the tendency of the minimum rate to become the principal rate for skilled workers.

While it is not within the province of this report to suggest a detailed scheme and methods of grading the workers for such a purpose, it will unquestionably be recognized by every experienced manufacturer and worker that the workers in the several trades of this industry can be roughly divided into at least four groups: 1, Apprentices; 2, workers who have graduated from the apprentice stage but are of less than average skill; 3, workers of average skill; 4, workers of more than average skill. The four degrees of skill call for four different rates of wages. As a matter of fact there are several gradations from one group to the next which are recognized in actual practice by as many different rates.

In providing for the rates that it has, the protocol has made a beginning in an attempt at collective regulation of wages in the industry under the joint auspices of the two partners to the industry, the employers and the employees, for the benefit of the industry as a whole. This benefit extends to the workers, inasmuch as it helps to protect the weak members and the recent recruits. It benefits the manufacturers, inasmuch as it tends to put an end to unfair competition between manufacturer and manufacturer through the payment of wages in some shops below the current rates.

It is not to be presumed in what has just been said or in what follows that definite recommendations are here made, beyond suggesting a number of measures for the purpose of discussion by the two parties to the protocol. It is conceded on both sides that the protocol has but made a beginning and that it needs further amplification and modification in a number of vital points.

REGISTRATION OF APPRENTICES.

The adoption of a special rate or rates for apprentices in the different occupations suggests the necessity of some method of controlling the apprentice situation. Such registration of each individual apprentice employed in the shops supervised by the association or by the union as will enable the wage-scale board and other officers of the association and the union who are concerned in this matter to control the situation and prevent possible abuse has been under consideration by the wage-scale board and a registration card has even been worked out for that purpose.

TRADE SCHOOL.

Another measure for dealing with the apprentice problem is the establishment of a school for the training of skilled workers. It is a question whether there is another industry that has so difficult a problem in this respect as the dress and waist industry in New York City. On the one hand, standing at the head of the industry in the country, supplying the constantly growing demand for high-grade ready-made women's garments, it is in great need of workers of the highest skill. The seasonal character of the market results in the demand for such help usually outrunning the supply during certain periods of the year. On the other hand, the fact that about 85 per cent of its skilled operators are women, mostly young, of whom it is calculated about one-fifth leave the industry each year to marry, makes the problem of keeping up the supply of skilled workers a very acute and difficult one. The apprenticing, as it goes on in the shops, does not offer a very encouraging solution. As is pointed out in the report, the new recruits enter the shops manufacturing cheaper garments and are there given a training which does not fit them for the work in the shops manufacturing the higher-grade garments. The necessity of establishing a school for the purpose of training new workers is so apparent that it has been suggested repeatedly by both sides. It is to be hoped that means will soon be found for putting into practice the idea here barely sketched.

Through a complete and intimate cooperation between the association and the union it should be possible to establish the school on a large scale, manned by competent instructors, taken preferably from among the foremen and forewomen in the most successful shops, the pupils or apprentices to be taught the trade by being given work of a practical character, preferably on orders to be assigned to the school by the manufacturers. The school could thus act as a contractor for the manufacturer and in this manner would on one hand avoid competing in the markets with established shops, and on the other would offer a ready means for manufacturers to call for assistance when their shops were worked to capacity. Such an arrangement would have the further advantage of enabling the pupils to earn a living while learning the trade and would make the school practically self-supporting.

The registration of apprentices, already suggested, would serve as the first step in determining the available material for such a school and the extent to which the industry could at once utilize it. Such registration could be used also as a means of controlling the admission of apprentices to the school and their distribution in the industry at proper minimum rates of compensation.

UNIFORM PAY ROLL.

A graduated scale of weekly wages, involving as it does some control by the wage-scale board over the matters of interpretation of the degrees of skill possessed by different workers in cases of dispute between manufacturers and their employees, implies the advisability, if not the necessity, of a uniform pay roll to be designed by the wage-scale board and supplied to all the manufacturers in the trade for the purpose of securing a uniform record of wages paid throughout the industry. The form for a uniform pay roll could easily be designed, printed in large quantities by the wage-scale board, and supplied to every manufacturer at a lower cost than the price now paid by them for books of various descriptions bought at retail from stationery stores. It would likewise facilitate future investigations of wages in the industry when required. An investigation such as the present could be carried out and completed in probably one-third the time that it took if a uniform pay roll of the kind suggested were adopted by the industry.

WHITE PROTOCOL LABEL.

At the time of the signing of the protocol the desirability of adopting a label which would serve as a joint guaranty by the union and by the association, as well as by representatives of the outside public, of the conditions under which the products of the industry are manufactured, was clearly recognized, and found expression in article 2 of the protocol, reading as follows:

> To make more effective the maintenance of sanitary conditions throughout the industry, to insure equality of minimum standards throughout the industry, and to guarantee to the public garments made in the shops certificated by the board of sanitary control, the parties agree that there shall be instituted in the industry a system of certificating garments by a label to be affixed to the garment. Recognizing the difficulties of working out the details of such a plan at this time, but believing that the plan has been sufficiently developed and considered in the cloak industry, they believe that a complete plan can be worked out in the dress and waist industry within a year. To this end each party agrees to cooperate to the full extent of its power in the formulation and effectuation of a system for the certification of garments adequately safeguarding the employers, the workers, and the consuming public.

The difficulties attending the working out of the practical application of the protocol during the first year of its existence have kept both parties so busy that thus far little has been done toward the realization of this promise. A beginning, however, has been made. It has been recognized both by the representatives of the association and of the union that the Consumers' League would be an admirable ally in this undertaking and the proper body to represent the public in this matter.

In turn, the National Consumers' League, at its last annual convention in Buffalo, held in December, 1913, authorized its executive officers to join hands with the association and the union whenever the two parties are prepared to introduce the label, and as soon as the Consumers' League feels that the steps taken warrant the withdrawal of its own label and the substitution of the protocol label instead.

The enforcement of the protocol rates of wages in the shops supervised by the association and the union, side by side with the existence of shops not so supervised (especially outside the city of New York) and paying lower wages, readily offers a condition of unfair competition to the manufacturers of New York City. If any argument be needed for the earliest possible adoption of a label which would insure the cooperation of a large part of the public with the dress and waist industry of New York in a common effort to maintain sanitary conditions and living wages in that industry, it is here furnished. The existence of a new thought among the consumers of the country, the great growth in numbers among such people as a result of the agitation of organizations like the Consumers' League and similar bodies offers great encouragement to the industry. The next step is to provide efficient machinery and channels through which fair-minded consumers can exercise intelligently their preference for goods manufactured under fair and wholesome conditions. The taking of this step would be a measure of justice to the manufacturer now paying wages higher than those paid by his competitors outside of the city, and at the same time would tend to protect and maintain the standard of compensation provided in the protocol. Last, but not least, it would protect the public from the use of garments made under insanitary conditions and by greatly underpaid labor.

The adoption of the label would in its turn offer an additional cause for the effective supervision by the wage-scale board or a similar body over the wages paid in the shops desiring to use the label upon their product, and the adoption of a uniform pay roll would furnish a basis for efficient control.

UNIFORM PIECE RATES.

The question of the working out of a schedule of uniform piece rates for work of similar character throughout the industry has been the subject of serious consideration of the wage-scale board from its inception. A beginning has been made through an intensive study of the processes of the manufacture of waists. This study was carried on in a number of shops during the fall season of 1913. Owing to the brevity of the season and the complexity of the problem, material has been collected to furnish a basis for the adoption of uniform piece rates for the $9-a-dozen waists only. This material forms the contents of

Part II of this report. By way of anticipation, it may be stated here that the experiment has furnished an affirmative answer to the question whether the standardization of piece rates in an industry like the dress and waist industry in which the character of the garments undergoes frequent and rapid changes decreed by fashion, is practicable.

The standardization of rates, however, unavoidably carries with it standardization of conditions. A uniform rate for the same kind of work paid in a shop managed with the highest degree of efficiency, where workers can turn out twice the product that is possible for workers of equal skill in a shop suffering from lack of system and intelligent management, would be obviously unfair to the efficient manufacturer on the one hand and to the employees of the inefficient one on the other.

It, therefore, follows that the adoption of uniform piece rates will necessarily have to be preceded by the carrying out of plans such as suggested above tending to lift the lower end of the industry to a higher level and thus bring about greater uniformity throughout the industry.

Without urging the adoption of the suggestions outlined above, and offering them solely as a basis for discussion by the representatives of the association and the union, it is hoped fervently that, having made so promising a beginning in the adoption of the protocol, and having weathered the storm of strife naturally concomitant with the first attempt to bring into play a controlling power over the relations between employer and employee, the industry will gather strength for further progress. Through mutual cooperation and increased confidence of the two great partners in each other, it should proceed with the work of upbuilding and general improvement and substitute orderly and intelligent planning for the blind chance and groping so conspicuously marking the days of the past.

PART II.—STANDARDIZATION OF PIECE RATES.

ADJUSTMENT OF PIECE RATES UNDER THE PROTOCOL.

The protocol adopted the following basis for the adjustment of piece rates for new garments, which is set forth in the following paragraphs of Article X of the protocol:

c. In settling prices the price per garment shall be based upon the estimated number of solid hours it will take an experienced good worker to make the garment without interruption, multiplied by the standard price per hour.

d. If the piece-price committee and the employer shall be unable to agree after a conference, the work shall then be proceeded with, but the determination of the price to be paid for the work shall be made as follows:

e. One or more workers shall be selected to make the test for the purpose of determining the number of solid hours it will take an experienced good worker to make the garment in question.

f. Both the employer and the piece-price committee shall agree upon the operative who is to make the test, but in case they shall fail to agree the wage-scale board shall make such designation.

This method of adjusting piece rates has been in effect for more than a year since the adoption of the protocol. While it has helped employer and employee to arrive at an agreement as to piece rates in cases of disagreement, it has not proved an unqualified success and has met with objections from both parties to the protocol. Although paragraph "e" states that "one or more workers shall be selected to make the test," paragraph "f" speaks of only one operative who is to make the test, and in actual practice only one has been selected as a rule.

The expression "an experienced good worker" is one that lends itself to varied interpretations and as a result leads to dispute between the employer and his employees or the price committee of his shop.

Even after an employer and the price committee have agreed upon a worker who is to make the test, the result of the test is not always accepted without objections on either side. If the employer's idea as to what would be a proper price for a new garment differs very widely from that of the price committee, and the result of the test comes very close to his original offer, the workers are apt to find fault with the test either on the ground that the operator chosen for the test is an exceptionally fast worker, or they may charge speeding up on the part of the manufacturer by holding out special inducements to the test worker to get through with her test in the shortest possible time. The claim is then made that it is impossible for an operator to keep up such speed working day in and out, and that therefore at the rate settled by the test they will not be able to earn an adequate wage.

On the other hand, if the test results in a confirmation of the workers' original demand, or very nearly so, the employer is apt to find fault with it and to claim that the operator chosen for the test, being one of the workers to be benefited by whatever rate may be adopted, has deliberately "soldiered" on the job and taken more time to complete the garment than was necessary.

In all such cases an appeal may be taken to the wage-scale board and a new test ordered under the supervision of the representatives of the union and of the association. All of this engenders friction between the employer and his help, and interferes with the orderly conduct of the business of the employer, and on the other hand creates a great deal of dissatisfaction among the workers on account of the delay in the adjustment of claims for back pay.

While cases of this kind are by no means the rule, they are of sufficiently frequent occurrence to have caused considerable dissatisfaction with the test system, both among manufacturers and operators, and both sides would welcome a method that would do away with the defects inherent in the present method of adjusting piece rates. Even before the method had been sanctioned by the protocol, the desirability of working out a scientific piece-rate schedule was present in the minds of the framers of the protocol, and found expression in the following provision in Article VII of the protocol which charged the wage-scale board with the duty of preserving "data and statistics with a view to establishing as nearly practicably as possible a scientific basis for the fixing of piece and week work prices throughout the industry that will insure a minimum wage and at the same time permit reward for increased efficiency."

SCOPE OF THE INVESTIGATION.

After the completion of the statistical investigation into wages and hours in the industry, the results of which are set forth in Part I of the present report, the wage-scale board instructed the writer to make a study of the manufacturing processes in the dress and waist industry with a view to discovering, if possible, a basis for the construction of a piece-rate schedule or schedules which could be applied throughout the industry or branches of the industry independently of changes in the styles of garments.

This study was carried out during the fall season of 1913, lasting between two and three months. It covered eight shops in which the processes were studied in detail, in addition to several shops in which a general study of the methods of manufacture and the organization of the work was made without the timing of the separate processes.

Of the eight shops investigated, five are exclusively shops making waists to sell at $9 per dozen, the three remaining shops manufacturing waists selling at $16.50 to $42 per dozen, and in a few instances as high as $60 and $72 a dozen. Occasionally these shops also make a few $9 styles to accommodate a special demand; but the bulk of their production covers a range of $16.50 to $24. All the shops mentioned, with the exception of one manufacturing $9 waists, employ their help on a piece-rate basis. By saying that a shop employs its help on a piece-rate basis it is not meant that all the work is paid for by the piece. Certain processes are invariably paid for by the week. Among these are cutting, examining, draping, and sample making. When a shop is designated as a piecework shop, it is meant that the operating is paid for by the piece, but even in that case many of the operating processes are paid for by the week. Thus, taking the $9 shops with which this part of the present report deals, we find the following division of labor and methods of compensation prevailing:

In shop No. 1232 body making, which is paid on a piece basis, includes the following processes: Closing shoulders, making centers, tacking fronts and backs, setting collars.[1] All the trimming is done by special operators called trimmers who are paid by the week. The sleeve making is done by other operators, who are paid by the week; the hemming is done by the piece; the closing and the sleeve setting are done by a man operator, who is paid by the piece; the buttonhole making is paid for by the week, as is also the button sewing.

In shop No. 1284 the body making is likewise done by the piece, but, unlike the preceding shop, the trimming is done by the body makers on a piece-rate basis. The closing and hemming are done by the piece, all being attended to by one operator having four assistants. The same operator with his assistants attends to the sleeve setting; the sleeve making is done by the body makers on a piece-rate basis; the buttonhole making is paid for on a pïece-rate basis and is attended to by one operator, who employs two assistants on a week basis. The same is true of button sewing. Tucking is done by the week.

In shop No. 1230 body making is done by the piece; the trimming is done by the piece by a man having an assistant; the sleeve setting is done by the piece, while the sleeve making, tucking, lace running, buttonhole making, and button sewing are done by the week.

---

[1] For a description of these processes, see Part I of this report, pages 93, 94.

The method of compensation for the different operating processes is shown in the following comparative statement for four of the principal shops investigated, all making waists selling at $9 a dozen:[1]

Shop No. 1191.	Shop No. 1232.	Shop No. 1230.	Shop No. 1284.
Buttonhole making.			
Week work—$15 per week.	Week work — $18 per week.	Week work—$4.50 per week.	Piecework—1 man with assistants.
Button sewing.			
Week work.	Week work.	Week work.	Piecework—1 man with assistants.
Body making.[2]			
Work done by a set of 3 to 5 persons working by the week; each person does one or more processes according to his or her ability or the requirements of the shop at the time.	Work done by an operator (usually a man) working with an assistant (either man or woman); operator paid by the piece; assistant paid by the operator, usually on a weekly basis.	Work done by an operator working singly or with an assistant. Of the body makers whose work was timed, 6 were men working with 1 assistant each; 2 were women with 1 assistant each; 4 were women working in partnerships of 2 each, and 15 were women working singly. Piecework.	Work done by an operator working singly or with an assistant. Of the body makers under observation, 7 were men working with 1 assistant each, 2 were men working singly, 6 were women working in partnerships of 2 each, and 10 were women working singly. Piecework.
Trimming.			
Done by the body makers paid by the week.	Done by "trimmers" working by the week.	Done by body makers on a piece basis.	Done by body makers on a piece basis.
Closing and hemming.			
This is the only work paid by the piece in this shop.	Closing done by a male operator by the piece; hemming done by another man likewise by the piece.	All the closing and hemming done by 1 man pieceworker with 1 assistant who is paid by the operator by the week.	All the closing and hemming done by 1 man pieceworker with 4 assistants who are paid by the operator by the week.
Sleeve making.			
Week work.	Week work.	Week work.	Done by the body makers; piecework.
Sleeve setting.			
Week work—girl, $16; man, $11.	Piecework—1 man.	Piecework—2 men with 1 assistant each.	Piecework by the operator doing the closing and hemming.

[1] In the fifth shop, designated as shop No. 1110, only a few operations outside of body making proper were timed, as will appear from the following pages.

[2] Work includes closing shoulders, making centers, tacking (shirring) fronts and backs, setting high collars.

Tucking.

Week work—10 women, $9 to $15; 3 men, $14 to $18.	Strip tucking by the week; short tucking by the body makers by the piece.	Week work—3 men, $18 each; 1 man $6; 5 women $7.50 to $14.	Strip tucking by the week; short tucking by the body makers by the piece.

Lace running.

Week work—girls, $10 to $13 a week.	Week work—$10 to $16 a week.	Week work—done by the tuckers, $15 to $18 a week.	Week work—$9 to $15 a week.

In the three shops making medium-priced waists the following conditions were encountered:

In one shop an opportunity was furnished to study only a few processes. In each of the other two factories the investigators spent about three weeks. As a result of the study it was discovered that one of the two shops was undergoing a transformation, owing to a radical change in its system of work, which resulted in considerable disorganization during the time the processes were being studied, and therefore yielded data which can not be taken as typical for an average factory. This leaves more or less complete data for only one shop of the class manufacturing medium-priced waists. Some of the processes in this class do not differ from those employed on $9 waists, and therefore have been combined with the figures obtained from the other shops. A large number of the processes, however, are either different from those employed in the $9 shops or are carried on with materials not used in $9 shops, such as chiffon, nets, and laces, and therefore are not embodied in this report, except in the part relating to buttonhole making.

BASIS FOR PIECE-RATE COMPENSATION.

The chief difficulty with a piece-rate schedule for the making of garments is in finding a satisfactory basis that will meet the varying conditions under which the products of the garment industry are made. Styles of garments change very radically, and the amount of work necessary to produce two garments selling at the same price may differ 100 per cent, and sometimes a great deal more. In one case there will be comparatively little labor and finer material, and more or better trimmings. In the other case there will be relatively more labor with a consequent saving in the cost of material and trimmings. The selling price of the garment can not be used, therefore, as a basis in fixing the piece rates for labor, as is, for instance, the case in the coal industry, and in certain branches of the iron and steel industry producing the cruder products. The price of the garment does affect the character of the labor in a broad way, in so far as labor of a higher skill is required in the higher-priced garments and the work has to be done more carefully and therefore more slowly than in the garments of the cheaper grade. It is, therefore, necessary to time separately the operating processes in the $9 shops and in the shops manufacturing the higher-grade garments. But there is no fixed relation between the price of a garment and the piece rate paid to the operator for making the garment. It would not be practicable, therefore, to fix separate rates of compensation for different garments according to their selling prices. In a shop manufacturing waists selling from $16.50 to $42 per dozen, the same operators are usually employed on all the garments except that if only a small quantity of garments of the higher price is produced it will be natural for the foreman to assign them to the best workers in the shop. The greatest differences in the rates of pay according to the price of the garment will occur in connection with body making, since in addition to the work of mere sewing there is a good deal of labor involved in the handling of the waist, which takes more time in the higher-priced garments. Moreover, the higher-priced garments are made in smaller quantities, and it takes an operator more time to turn out a given garment working on a small quantity of garments than on a large one.

In the case of separate processes, however, outside of body making proper, such as closing, hemming, tucking, lace running, buttonhole making, button sewing, etc., the work does not differ much, if at all, as between waists of different prices in the same shops. As between different shops, it may be stated, as a rule, that a smaller stitch is used on the finer garments and a larger one on the cheaper garments, but even that, as will be shown further on, does not seem to have an appreciable effect on the time it takes to do the work.

The amount of time taken for the same processes will differ a great deal with the material used: Silks, such as Japanese or China silk, crêpe de Chine, and messaline are more difficult to handle than cottons like voiles and lawns. In turn, chiffons, nets, and laces are more difficult to handle than the solid silks just mentioned. Each of these groups of materials would therefore require a different rate of compensation and, as the prices of waists would vary with these materials, it may be said in that sense that the price for labor differs with the price of waists, although the relation between the two is but an indirect one.

From the foregoing it will be clear that the price of a garment could not serve as a basis for a piece-rate schedule. The outlook seemed more promising if attention were turned to the discovery of an irreducible unit of work common to all operating processes and to all garments, irrespective of style or materials of which made. A study of the processes of dress and waist manufacture led to the conclusion that the stitch would furnish such a basis. The operating work on all garments, from the cheapest cotton waist to the most expensive silk gown trimmed with fine lace and embroideries, is reduced to one common denominator—the stitch made by the needle of the sewing machine operated by the dress or waist maker known as operator. The single stitch produced by two successive movements of the machine needle forms the irreducible unit in the operating processes corresponding to the atom in the chemical composition of matter.

A further study of the manufacturing processes, however, showed that the stitch would form too fine a basis on the one hand and not an entirely accurate one on the other. The time it takes to do a certain amount of machine sewing will depend not only on the number of stitches, but also on the number of stops the operator will have to make. With the machine making 3,400 revolutions per minute, an operator on a Wilcox & Gibbs machine for one minute can produce a seam containing 3,400 stitches if allowed to work without a stop. If the sewing of the particular garment is made at the rate of 16 stitches to the inch, which is done on fine work, the operator will stitch a seam equal to 212½ inches or nearly 6 yards long. This theoretical standard is more or less approximated on work in which sewing can be carried on in straight seams extending over yards of cloth, although even in this case the work accomplished will fall short of the theoretical estimate on account of unavoidable causes, such as the gradual working up of the speed of the machine at the start, the slowing down of the machine before each stop, the fixing or replacing of the thread, the feeding of the cloth, etc. The only processes in which such work can be done are strip tucking, strip hemming, and lace running, in which work is done on long runs of cloth and is paid for by the yard or 100 yards. In most of the other work the length of a seam can not exceed the length of a waist or a skirt, and is measured in inches and not yards, which means that the operator is obliged, as a rule, to stop the machine at frequent intervals after operating it for a fraction of a minute. That being the case, the time lost in stopping and starting the machine and shifting the material under the needle exceeds the time spent in the productive work of making a seam of ordinary length. An illustration will make this clear:

Taking, for example, two seams on a waist, one 6 inches (the length of a shoulder seam) and the other 10 inches long (length of a side seam from the armhole to the hem), 12 stitches to the inch, the theoretical time required to do each on a Union Special machine making 3,000 revolutions per minute is 1.4 and 2.4 seconds, respectively. But the time it will take the operator to fix the garment in position under the needle, start the machine, stop the machine after the seam is made, take out the garment so as to change its position for the next process, or to replace it with the next garment, will amount to anywhere from 10 to 25 times that interval, making the time spent in stitching the seam so small a fraction of the total as to render the number of stitches or the length of the seam within certain limits immaterial. The number of stitches contained in a given seam would therefore fail to furnish an accurate basis for estimating the time it would take to do the work, and hence would not be suitable as a basis for a piece-rate schedule.

The seam of a waist, irrespective of its length, within certain limits, which will be considered elsewhere, is therefore more suitable as a unit of measure than a stitch. As a matter of fact, some manufacturers have been in the habit of fixing the rate per garment roughly on a seam basis, calling it "a stitch rate." The term "stitch" when used in connection with piece rates in the dress and waist industry is always meant in the sense of a seam. To bring the terms used in this report in close consonance with the trade terms, while avoiding at the same time the erroneous use of the trade term of "stitch," the expression "row of stitching" has been adopted in this report. This term has the advantage of having the sound of "stitch" when pronounced without conveying any other meaning than the word "seam." At the same time it has the advantage over the term "seam" since it can be applied to any kind of sewing, while "seam" usually conveys the idea of the joining of two pieces of cloth.

The conclusion arrived at as to the adaptability of the row of stitching as a unit of measure of an operator's work has met with the approval of all the manufacturers who have either given a study to the question or have tried it out in their own practice, as well as with the approval of experienced operators.

So far as actual practice goes, the row of stitching has been used only in a crude way, workers being paid at the rate of 6, 7, or 8 "stitches for a cent," as the phrase goes in the dress and waist industry. No distinction is made as to the kinds of stitching or the part of the garment on which they are made.

Here again the study of the processes and the timing of the thousands of operations in various shops have shown the great difference in time it takes to do the different kinds of stitching. As will be shown in connection with the discussion of the different processes, an operator may earn as much money by being paid at the rate of 10 rows of stitching for 1 cent on some processes as he will at the rate of 2 rows for 1 cent on others. In a crude way this has been recognized by manufacturers, who pay the body makers a fixed amount for the "body" and an additional amount for the other parts of the garment at the rate of so many rows for 1 cent. The body making proper consists of the closing (i. e., joining) of the shoulders, the making of the center pieces or facings (the parts of the waist holding the buttonholes and buttons), the shirring of the fronts and backs of the waist at the waistline, and the setting of the collar. It consists of 14 to 16 rows of stitching per waist, and is paid at the rate of 45 to 80 cents per dozen waists, which is equivalent to about 2½ to 4 rows of stitching for a cent. For the remaining work the body maker is paid at the rate of 6 to 8 rows for 1 cent.

In this way some measure of discrimination between the different processes is introduced, though in a very crude manner, since some of the processes paid for at the rate of 7 rows for a cent are more difficult and require more time than those included in the "body" at the rate of only 3 to 4 rows for a cent.

The necessity of timing each process separately and fixing a standard of compensation for each, therefore, appeared very clear. The method adopted for this purpose was as follows: In each shop investigated groups of three to five operators each were placed under the observation of an agent of the wage-scale board. The time of starting and completing each operation was carefully noted on a card. All interruptions in the work and the number of minutes they lasted were noted as well as the causes of such interruptions, the causes being grouped under three heads: (1) Waiting for parts, (2) machine fixing, and (3) personal needs.

The work under each process has been reduced to the number of rows of stitching per hour, which may serve as a basis for fixing the compensation for each process in terms of rows of stitching for 1 cent. The details are given below under each process.

TUCKING.

As explained on page 90, the work of tucking consists of making folds or plaits of varying widths, and stitching them over on a machine. Although the work is comparatively simple, some of it requires great skill, and most of the tucking is done by operators called "tuckers" who specialize in this work. Occasionally tucking is done by body makers, especially when a waist contains but a few short tucks, when it does not pay to interrupt the work and turn it over to a tucker.

Tucking is divided into two broad classes—strip tucking and short tucking. By strip tucking is meant tucking done on long strips of cloth, sometimes hundreds of yards long, paid for at the rate of so many cents per hundred yards, if done by the piece. Short tucking consists of making individual tucks of varying length or width on the waist or parts of waist or skirt. In strip tucking, once the strip of cloth has been started going under the needle and the so-called knife attachment has been adjusted to produce a tuck of a given width, the operator has but little to do besides feeding the cloth under the needle. There is no occasion for stopping the machine except when the needle breaks, or the thread breaks or gives out. In short tucking the operator must be constantly on the lookout and the machine is started and stopped at intervals of a few seconds, as the tucks are short, and there is nothing but the operator's watchfulness and skill to regulate the operation of the machine.

From this it follows that, all things being equal, it requires greater skill to do short tucking than strip tucking. Short tucking is done only by body makers, or experienced tuckers, while strip tucking is frequently done by beginners who are learning to do tucking. Even if there were no difference in the wages paid to those who do strip tucking and the operators who do short tucking, strip tucking would naturally be cheaper. In short tucking more time is consumed in stopping and starting the machine and adjusting the material under the needle for each tuck than in the actual process of making the tuck; in strip tucking this loss of time is largely eliminated. For this reason, on all cheap waists and on a large part of the medium-price waists, the effort is always made to arrange the tucking in such a manner as to make it possible to produce it in the form of strip tucks, which are then cut up into the required lengths and fitted into the waists according to the design. This greatly reduces the cost of tucking.

It is not always possible, however, to do the tucking of a waist in this manner. Where the tucks on a waist or part of a waist, such as a sleeve or a cuff, are arranged so that they run through the entire length of that part, strip tucking is possible; on the other hand, where the tucks are arranged in clusters in which the individual tucks are of varying lengths and cover only a part of the length or the width of a waist, sleeve, or cuff, strip tucking is not possible, and the tucks must be made separately on each waist. In some shops an attempt is made in such cases to save time through the process known as "double tucking," which consists of joining together two parts of a waist having similar tucks, such as two fronts or two backs, and making the tuck on the two in one process; the two parts are then cut apart. In spite of the loss of time which is caused by joining the two pieces together and cutting them apart, the time saved in not having to stop and start the machine for each tuck is more than sufficient to result in a net saving of time. The tables following show the average time required to do tucking of various kinds.

STRIP TUCKING.

Strip tucking was timed in 6 shops. Of these, 4 shops, namely, Nos. 1191, 1230, 1232, and 1284, were shops making exclusively $9-a-dozen waists, while shops Nos. 1090 and 1116 manufactured medium-priced waists, selling from $16.50 up. The total number of persons under observation for strip tucking in these 6 shops was 23. The total number of yards tucked, on which these tables are based, was

69,527½, representing a total expenditure of time equivalent to 373 hours and 21 minutes for one person. It is therefore believed that the figures here presented are based upon a sufficiently broad scale to yield a fair average. While these averages represent quite a wide range, they have the merit of representing conditions as they are. Moreover, all the averages are weighted averages; that is to say, the work of each person and of every shop has been given a weight in proportion to their respective output. An illustration will make this clear: If there were two tuckers in a shop, one turning out 50 yards per hour and the other 500 yards per hour, this would represent an average of 275 yards an hour; but if the shop employs only five workers producing 50 yards per hour and 25 workers producing 500 yards an hour each, the true shop average is a weighted average, which is obtained in the manner shown in the following figures:

Number of workers.	Hourly output per worker.	Total output per hour.
5	50	250
25	500	12, 500
30	550	12, 750

Weighted average hourly output per worker—12,750÷30=425. In other words, while the simple average would be 275 yards, the weighted or true average is 425 yards. This method has been used throughout these calculations, both in getting the average output of each worker from the several jobs for which he was timed, as well as in getting the shop average from the several workers' averages, and, finally, the average for the industry from the several shop averages. In this way extremes, whether in the form of very high or very low output, do not appreciably affect the average, since they are given a weight proportional to the extent to which they occur in the shops or in the industry.[1]

The output per hour on strip tucking varies with—

1. The skill of the individual worker.
2. The machine on which it is done.
3. The number of needles on the machine.
4. The width of the tuck.
5. The width of the material.
6. The fineness of the stitch.
7. The material on which the tucking is done.
8. The size of the job; that is to say, the number of yards the operator can work on without a stop.

1. That the skill of the worker will affect his output needs no explanation. Unfortunately, there is no direct way of tracing the connection between the skill of the worker and his output as shown in the

[1] Figures of exceptionally low output due to the fact that they represented the work of apprentices or beginners were discarded.

tables, except in so far as the wages of the week workers give an indication of this, for in a general way it is true that the more skillful workers command higher wages. However, there is no strict proportion between the skill and the wages of the worker, and it will frequently be found that workers of fairly equal skill will be getting different rates of wages, depending on the length of service of the workers in the shop, their ability to bargain for better compensation, and other more or less incidental causes.

2. The machine used is an important factor in determining the output of the operator. The two machines in general use for tucking are the Wilcox & Gibbs and the Singer, the former being the faster of the two. The Wilcox & Gibbs machine makes about 3,400 revolutions per minute, while the Singer makes all the way from 1,600 to 2,400 revolutions, according to the way in which the shafts and pulleys are arranged in the different shops.

3. Much of the tucking is done in clusters of from 2 to 10 tucks each, and sometimes even more. In order to save time, machines are made with more than one needle. The multiple-needle machine most in use in the dress and waist industry is the 5-needle machine, though 8 and 10 needle machines are also to be found. If a cluster of less than 5 tucks has to be made, one or more needles is taken out for the time being. By the use of a 5-needle machine a cluster of 5 tucks can thus be made in one operation, where five operations would be needed if an ordinary single-needle machine were used. However, owing to the more complicated character of the machine, it can not be operated as fast as the single-needle machine, and the greater the number of needles the slower the operation.

4. On tucks not exceeding half an inch in width, the difference in width does not affect the output. On wider tucks, the greater the width the more difficult for the operator to keep the material from creasing under the "foot," and therefore the smaller the output.

5. The wider the material the more difficult it is to handle it in the machine, and therefore the less will be the output of the operator.

6. All other things being equal, the finer the stitch—that is, the greater the number of stitches to the inch—the less will be the number of yards stitched in a given period of time. This is especially true of work like strip tucking, where the machine can be kept in continuous operation over a great many yards of cloth without stopping.

7. The output on cotton material, like voile or lawn, will be greater, all other things being equal, than on material like chiffon, which easily stretches and therefore must be handled with great care and at a lower speed.

8. Other things being equal, the larger the job given to the worker at a time the greater will be the output, since he will be enabled to work longer without interruption. On strip tucking, whether done by a

single-needle or multiple-needle machine, there may be more than one tuck or more than one cluster on a given strip of cloth. If the work calls for, say, 5 tucks on a single-needle machine, or 5 clusters on a multiple-needle machine, the operator will have to make 5 runs on a strip furnished to him before he is through with the job. As the machine must be stopped at the beginning and end of each run, the question is not so much as to the number of yards to the job as of the number of yards to each run. This is indicated in the last column of Tables 77A and 77B.

The results given in Tables 77A and 77B were obtained on the basis explained above. The figures appearing in the column headed "yards per hour," represent in each case an average of two or more jobs completed by the same person, this average being obtained on the same basis as the shop average and the average for the industry—that is to say, each job being given a weight corresponding to its size.

Taking first the work done on a single-needle Wilcox & Gibbs machine, we find a fairly uniform output if we compare the average output of three shops, of which two make $9-a-dozen waists, while one, No. 1116, manufactures a medium grade of goods. This shop shows the lowest output per hour of the three, namely, 239 yards per hour (line 11), while the highest, in shop No. 1230, is only 258 yards per hour (line 4), and the average for the three shops is 247 yards per hour (line 12). On the other hand, the average for shop No. 1090 is only 176 yards per hour (line 14). This is due chiefly to the fact that the tucking in shop No. 1090 was done on a Singer machine. These figures were therefore not included with the average representing the output of the shops mentioned above on a Wilcox & Gibbs machine.

CHIFFONS VERSUS COTTON.

A small amount, 175½ yards of strip tucking, was done on chiffon in shop No. 1090 on a single-needle Singer machine while the investigation was in progress, showing an output of 92 yards per hour. The operator was under observation for 115 minutes, or nearly 2 hours. As this operator earned practically the same amount of money as the one who showed an output of 176 yards per hour on the same machine on cotton material, the two figures seem to offer a fair basis for adjusting the rate on chiffons, which should be higher than the rate on cotton on the same machine.

TABLE 77A.—STRIP TUCKING: WILCOX & GIBBS SINGLE-NEEDLE MACHINE.

Line No.	Shop No. and operator No.	Sex of operator.	Piecework or week work.	Wages or earnings per week.	Material.	Width of tuck.	Stitches per inch.	Number of yards.	Time worked (minutes).	Yards per hour.	Number of jobs.	Number of yards per run.	Number of runs.
	$9-WAIST SHOPS.												
	Shop No. 1230:												
1	Operator No. 7[1]	M.	Week work	$18.00	Lawn	Pin and ¼ inch.	9	11,000	2,552	259	1	440	25
2	Operator No. 7					Pin	9	396	102	233	1	36	11
3	Operator No. 8	M.	do	18.00	do	do	10	252	57	265	1	36	7
4	Average, 3 persons	M.	Week work.	18.00	Lawn	Pin and ¼ inch.	9 to 10	11,648	2,711	258	3	36 to 440	7 to 25
	Shop No. 1191:												
5	Operator No. 13	F.	Week work.	12.00	Voile	Pin	14	1,500	457	197	1	100	15
6	Operator No. 14	F.	do	12.00	do	do	15	4,098	864	285	2	84 to 234	7 to 15
7	Average, 2 persons	F.	Week work.	12.00	Voile	Pin	14 to 15	5,598	1,321	254	3	84 to 234	7 to 15
	MEDIUM-PRICE WAIST SHOPS.												
	Shop No. 1116:												
8	Operator No. 15	F.	Piecework	(2)	Lawn and voile.	Pin and ¼ inch.	12	4,960	1,198	248	5	12 to 36	6, 10, 11, 12, 14, 22 and 24
9	Operator No. 16	F.	do	(2)	Voile	Pin[3]	11	5,813	1,529	228	4	47 to 268	5, 6, 20
10	Operator No. 17	F.	do	(2)	do	do	11	7,818	1,933	243	5	128 and 159	9, 11, 12, 20, 25 and 30
11	Average, 3 persons	F.	Piecework	(2)	Lawn and voile.	Pin and ¼ inch.[3]	11 to 12	18,591	4,660	239	14	12 to 268	5 to 30
12	Average, 3 shops	F. and M.	Week work and piecework.	12.00 to 18.00	Voile and lawn.	Pin and ¼ inch.	9 to 15	35,837	8,692	247	20	12 to 440	5 to 30
13	Shop No. 1232: Operator No. 22	F.	Week work.	9.50	Embroidered strip.	Pin and ¼ inch.	9	800	313	153	2	[4] 160 to 240	2
	Shop No. 1090:[5]												
14	Operator No. 19	F.	do		Voile	⅛ inch	14	2,200	748	176	1	220	10
15	Operator No. 21	F.	do		Chiffon	do	7	175½	115	92	1	29¼	6

[1] Including 3 partners.
[2] Earnings not reported.
[3] One job of 1,225 yards had 245 yards long (one run), ½-inch tuck.
[4] 10-yard pieces.
[5] Singer single-needle machine was used.

TABLE 77B.—STRIP TUCKING: SINGER MULTIPLE-NEEDLE MACHINE.

Line No.	Shop No. and operator No.	Sex of operator.	Piecework or week work.	Wages or earnings per week.	Material.	Width of tuck.	Stitches per inch.	Number of yards.	Time worked (minutes).	Yards per hour.	Number of jobs.	Number of yards per run.	Number of runs.
	4-NEEDLE MACHINE.												
	$9-waist shops.												
	Shop No. 1230:												
1	Operator No. 4	F.	Week work	$7.50	Voile	Pin	16	1,678	636	158	11	27 to 66	2,3
2	Operator No. 3	F.	do	10.50	do	do	14 to 16	4,712	1,826	155	16	44 to 200	1,2,3,4
3	Operator No. 2	F.	do	12.50	Voile and embroidery.	do	14 to 16	3,773	1,445	157	10	63 to 400	1,2,3,4
4	Operator No. 5	F.	do	14.00	Voile	do	14	1,474	766	115	6	30 to 120	3,4
5	Operator No. 6	M.	do	6.00	Lawn	do	13 to 16	3,428	1,170	176	11	48 to 675	1,2
6	Average, 5 persons	M. and F.	Week work.	6.00 to 14.00	Voile and lawn	Pin	13 to 16	15,065	5,843	155	54	27 to 675	1 to 4
	Shop No. 1284:												
7	Operator No. 9	F.	Week work	7.00	Voile and lawn	Pin	12	1,356	580	140	5	24 to 198	1,2,4
8	Operator No. 10	F.	do	11.00	do	do	12 to 15	2,976	899	199	6	50 to 168	3,4,6
9	Operator No. 11	F.	do	13.00	do	do	12	1,392	648	129	3	68 to 120	3,6
10	Operator No. 12	F.	do	8.00	do	do	12	90	70	77	1	15	6
11	Average, 4 persons	F.	Week work.	7.00 to 13.00	Voile and lawn	Pin	12 to 15	5,814	2,197	159	15	15 to 198	1 to 6
	Medium-price waist shops.												
	Shop No. 1116:												
12	Operator No. 18	M.	Piecework		Voile	Pin	12	850	462	110	3	105 to 213	2
13	Average, 3 shops	M. and F.	Week work and piecework.		Voile	Pin	12 to 16	21,729	8,502	153	72	15 to 675	1 to 6

[1] Earnings not reported.

TABLE 77B.—STRIP TUCKING: SINGER MULTIPLE-NEEDLE MACHINE—Concluded.

Line No.	Shop No. and operator No.	Sex of operator.	Piecework or week work.	Wages or earnings per week.	Material.	Width of tuck.	Stitches per inch.	Number of yards.	Time worked (minutes).	Yards per hour.	Number of jobs.	Number of yards per run.	Number of runs.
	5-NEEDLE MACHINE.												
	$9-waist shops.												
	Shop No. 1230:												
14	Operator No. 1	F.	Week work	$13.50	Voile	Pin	16	2,110	695	182	3	64 to 501	3 to 4
15	Operator No. 2	F.	do	12.50	do	do	16	86	20	258	1	86	1
16	Average	F.	Week work	12.50 to 13.50	Voile	Pin	16	2,196	715	184	4	64 to 501	1, 4
	Shop No. 1284:												
17	Operator No. 12	F.	Week work	8.00	Lawn	Pin	13	1,040	857	73	1	260	4
	Shop No. 1232:												
18	Operator No. 23	F.	do	10.50	Voile	do	9	5,100	2,274	135	4	250 to 1,110	1, 2, 4
19	Average, 3 shops	F.	Week work	8.00 to 13.50	Voile and lawn	Pin	9 to 16	8,336	3,846	130	9	64 to 1,110	1 to 4
	8-NEEDLE MACHINE.												
	Medium-price waist shops.												
	Shop No. 1090:												
20	Operator No. 20	F.	Piecework	(1)	Lawn	$\frac{1}{16}$-inch	14	450	185	146	1	225	2

[1] Earnings not reported.

SINGER 4-NEEDLE MACHINE.

The average output per hour on a 4-needle machine in two $9-a-dozen waist shops was 155 and 159 yards per hour, respectively. The hourly output of the individual workers in these shops on this class of work varied from 77 to 199 yards per hour. This variation was due not only to the differences in the speed of the different operators, which is reflected in their weekly wages shown in the fifth column of Table 77B, but also to the differences in the size of their jobs, and more particularly the number of yards to the run. Thus the lowest output of 77 yards per hour (line 10 of Table 77B) was on a job having the smallest number of yards per run, namely, 15; the highest output of 199 yards per hour was by a worker who had from 50 to 168 yards of tucking per run. It is true that the output per hour is not directly proportional to the length of the run so far as it can be seen from the table, but that is due to the presence of other factors affecting the output, mentioned elsewhere. The average output on a 4-needle Singer machine in shop No. 1116, which is outside of the $9-a-dozen group, was 110 yards per hour. Though lower than the figures for the $9-a-dozen shops, it has been included in the general average—first, because there is no reason why the work on the same machine should be any more difficult in this shop than in $9-a-dozen waist shops, there being no essential difference in the stitches per inch, width of the material, width of the tuck, or length of the run; second, because the total quantity timed in this shop (850 yards) is so small, as compared with the total of the other two shops (20,879 yards), as to have no appreciable effect upon the general average.

SINGER 5-NEEDLE MACHINE.

The average output per hour on the 5-needle Singer machine was found to be 130 yards. This average was based on timing the tucking of 8,336 yards in three $9-a-dozen waist shops, and represents a range in individual production of from 73 to 258 yards per hour, the lowest output being that of a girl receiving $8 a week (line 17) and the highest of one receiving $12.50 a week (line 15). It should be noted, however, that the same girl had an output of only 157 yards on a 4-needle machine. The output of 258 yards must therefore be regarded as exceptional and may be partly explained by the fact that it was achieved on a very small job of 86 yards, which lasted only 20 minutes. The output on small jobs of this kind can never be taken as reliable, and is apt to be either too large or too small, as will be seen from the tables in this report. The operator may be fortunate in making a short run under very favorable conditions which could not last if she continued to work for a considerable length of time, and the output will appear very large; or the contrary may be the case, and the output will turn out very small.

SINGER 8-NEEDLE MACHINE.

Only one worker in shop No. 1090 was found to operate an 8-needle machine in the course of the investigation. The job on which she was timed consisted of two runs of 225 yards each, showing an output of 146 yards per hour.

SHORT TUCKING.

Short tucking was timed in the same shops as the strip tucking. The total number of persons under observation for short tucking in these six shops was 54. Of these 22 were men and 32 were women. These people tucked 282$\frac{11}{12}$ dozen waists while under observation, which took the equivalent of 449 hours and 27 minutes for one person. The same method was used in calculating the averages in the case of short tucking as in the case of strip tucking, and in fact this method has been used throughout this part of the report, unless otherwise stated. The output of a worker engaged in making short tucks will depend, apart from the individual speed of the worker and of the machine, (1) on the length of the tuck, (2) the width of the tuck, (3) the fineness of the stitch, (4) the material of which the garment is made, (5) the number of tucks to the waist, (6) the size of the bundle which the worker receives, (7) on whether the tucks are of uniform or various widths, and (8) on whether they are arranged singly or in clusters.

1. All other things being equal, the longer the tuck the more time it will take to make it. That is true, however, only when we speak of tucks differing considerably in length, such as a tuck of 5 or 6 inches as compared with one of 21 to 24 inches. It would not be true of tucks differing by a few inches. Within certain limits the length of the tuck is not material because the time lost in starting and stopping the machine and shifting the material far exceeds the time taken to make the tuck, and as the making of a tuck 4 inches long or 9 inches long is a matter of seconds in either case, the difference in time taken to do the different tucks within those limits is so small as to be negligible for practical purposes. Moreover, as the same worker makes all the tucks on a waist, no matter what their length, the average rate finds its counterpart in the average time it will take to do the average tuck representing different lengths. For purposes of comparison, the data have been tabulated separately in two groups so far as the length of the tucks is concerned, namely, those 9 inches or less and those over 9 and up to 24 inches long, 24 inches being the extreme length of a waist. Occasionally tucks exceed that length when made across the waist, in which case they may reach the length of 36 inches or more.

2. The width of the tuck will affect the output on short tucks in the same manner as on strip tucking as explained above.

3. The number of stitches per inch naturally affects the output, but it is of less practical importance on short tucking than on strip tucking, for reasons already explained.

4. The effect of the material on output has been explained under strip tucking.

5. The number of tucks per waist is of great importance in determining the output. The more tucks a waist contains, the fewer waists an operator must handle to turn out a given number of tucks, and as the handling of the material takes up a considerable part of the total time at work, this is an important factor in affecting the output.

6. The size of the bundle—that is, the number of waists contained in a single job—is of great importance in determining the output of an operator. The larger the job, the longer the operator can carry on his work without interruption. The mere stopping of work to fold the waists and tie up the bundle and take it to the foreman in order to get the next bundle, results in the loss of at least five minutes. If, in addition to that, the operator must wait for his next job because the foreman is too busy to attend to him at once, the time lost between the completion of one job and the commencement of the other may be increased very materially. If the bundle given to the worker is large the time lost in tying up the bundle and getting the next bundle will constitute a much smaller percentage of the time actually spent at work than in case the bundle is small.

7. If the tucks are all of uniform width, the gauge which regulates the width of the tuck has to be set only once. On the contrary, if the tucks are of varying widths, the gauge has to be reset every time that a tuck of a new width has to be made.

8. If tucks are arranged in uniform clusters—that is to say, clusters in which the distance between the tucks is the same, and in which the tucks are of uniform width—it is much easier for the operator to handle them than if the distance between the tucks varies and the width of the tucks varies at the same time.

The only way in which to obtain conclusive data as to the effect of each of these factors on output would have been to test the same worker on jobs of the same character, varying only one of these factors at a time. As the tests had to be conducted in shops without disturbing their routine and merely timing the work of the operators under such conditions as were found to exist at the time, such a procedure was impossible. For this reason it will be difficult to analyze in detail the causes of the difference in output in the different shops given in the tables, though in a general way the connection between the causes mentioned and the output may be seen.

WILCOX & GIBBS MACHINE.

Comparing lines 1 and 2 of Table 77C, we find that both have 34 tucks to a waist, but while the tucks in line 1 are of uniform length and width, 3½ inches long and $\frac{1}{16}$ inch wide, the tucks in line 2 vary in length from 5 to 7½ inches. This makes it more difficult for the operator, who must watch the length of each tuck. The result is a smaller output, 183 tucks per hour, while in the former case it is 219 tucks per hour, in spite of the fact that the smaller output was produced on a Wilcox & Gibbs machine and the larger on the slower machine.

Line 3 shows an output of only 48 tucks per hour. In this case there is only 1 tuck to the waist against 34 tucks to the waist in lines 1 and 2, and the width of the tuck is 1 inch as against $\frac{1}{16}$ inch and ⅛ inch in the jobs given above. As already explained, the fewer tucks to the waist the greater the proportion of time lost on each tuck in handling the work. Likewise the width of the tuck, especially when it reaches 1 inch and over, makes the work more difficult for the operator to handle and reduces the output. Similar causes account for the great difference in output in the other jobs given in the following lines of Table 77C, although it is difficult to point out in each case the particular cause or causes responsible for the result, in view of the fact that frequently two or more causes combine to affect the output. Thus the output in line 5 is 237 tucks per hour, while in line 6 it is 200 tucks. As the number of tucks to the waist in line 5 is 12, and in line 6 it is twice as large, and as there is no essential difference in other respects, the output in line 6 should have been considerably greater than in line 5; instead of that, it is smaller. The reason is that line 5 represents the work of four of the best operators in the shop, receiving $12, $14, $15, and $18 per week, respectively, two of them being men, while the work in line 6 represents the output of two girls receiving $10 and $11 per week who are slower workers than the others.

The same observations can be made with reference to tucks exceeding 9 inches in length. Line 10 shows an output of 123 tucks per hour when there are 18 tucks to the waist.

Line 11 shows an output of 134 tucks per hour with the number of tucks per waist increased to 20.

Line 12 shows an output of 252 tucks per hour with the number of tucks per waist rising to 52.

The number of tucks per waist drops to 42 in line 13, and the output drops to 225 tucks per hour.

TABLE 77C.—SHORT TUCKING: WILCOX & GIBBS SINGLE-NEEDLE MACHINE.

Line No.	Shop No. and operator No.	Number and sex of operators. M.	F.	Piecework or week work.	Wages or earnings per week.	Material.	Number of clusters.	Tucks per cluster.	Number of tucks per waist.	Waists (dozen).	Total tucks.	Time worked (minutes).	Length of tuck (inches).	Width of tuck.	Stitches per inch.	Number of jobs.	Size of job (dozen waists).	Tucks per hour.
	Shop No. 1090:																	
1	Average	....	2	Piecework	$10.61 13.33	Lingerie	......	......	34	$5\frac{7}{12}$	2,278	624	$3\frac{1}{2}$	$\frac{1}{16}$ inch	16	3	$1\frac{7}{12}$ to 2	[1] 219
2	Operator No. 190	....	1	do	12.05	Crêpe	......	......	34	$4\frac{3}{4}$	1,938	635	5 to $7\frac{1}{2}$	$\frac{1}{8}$ inch	16	1	$4\frac{3}{4}$	183
3	Operator No. 191	....	1	do	13.33	Lingerie	......	......	1	10	120	150	5	1 inch	16	1	10	48
	Shop No. 1116:																	
4	Operator No. 196	....	1	do	7.78	Voile	2	6	12	$3\frac{5}{8}$	552	169	7	Pin	11	1	$3\frac{5}{8}$	196
	Shop No. 1191:																	
5	Average	2	2	Week work	12.00, 14.00, 15.00, 18.00	Voile and crêpe	6	2	12	$23\frac{7}{12}$	3,396	860	$6\frac{1}{2}$ to 8	Pin $\frac{1}{16}$ inch	11 to 13	7	$2\frac{1}{4}$ to 5	237
6	Average	....	2	do	10.00, 11.00	Voile	6	4	24	$8\frac{1}{12}$	2,328	700	4	Pin	13 to 15	3	$1\frac{7}{12}$ to 4	200
7	Operator No. 185	1	....	do	14.00	do	2	10	20	$3\frac{3}{4}$	900	141	7	$\frac{1}{16}$ inch	13	1	$3\frac{3}{4}$	383
8	Operator No. 186	1	....	do	16.00	do	......	......	2	25	600	245	7	$\frac{1}{2}$ inch	14	1	25	147
	Shop No. 1090:																	
9	Operator No. 192	....	1	Piecework	9.71	Net	2 2	3 3	12	6	864	470	24 21 } $22\frac{1}{2}$	$\frac{1}{4}$ inch $\frac{3}{8}$ inch	12	1	6	110
10						Linen	[2] 2 4	4	18	8	1,728	845	5 21 } 19	$\frac{3}{8}$ inch	16	1	8	123
11	Average	....	2	do	8.06 9.71	do	[2] 2 6	3	20	12	2,880	1,290	5 23 } 19	$\frac{3}{8}$ inch $\frac{1}{16}$ inch	16	2	$2\frac{1}{2}$ and $9\frac{1}{2}$	134
	Shop No. 1116:																	
12	Average	2	4	do	7.78 to 13.62	Voile	6 2 2 2	3 12 3 2	52	$43\frac{1}{3}$	27,040	6,429	18 23 5 5 } 18	Pin do do $\frac{1}{4}$ inch	11 to 12	9	$2\frac{1}{12}$ to $6\frac{2}{3}$	252
13	Do	1	2	do	7.78 to 10.29	do	4 8	3 3	12 24 4 2 } 42	$8\frac{5}{12}$	4,242	1,129	24 17 17 24 } 21	Pin do $\frac{1}{4}$ inch $\frac{3}{4}$ inch	11	3	$1\frac{11}{12}$ to $4\frac{1}{2}$	225
14	Do	....	4	do	7.78 to 13.62	do	8	2	16 4 2 } 22	$7\frac{1}{3}$	1,936	700	21	Pin $\frac{3}{4}$ inch $\frac{1}{4}$ inch	11 to 12	4	$1\frac{5}{12}$ to $2\frac{1}{12}$	166
15	Do	1	1	do	10.58 11.92	Net	......	......	12 10 } 22	11	2,904	678	24 21 } $22\frac{1}{2}$	$\frac{1}{4}$ inch	11	3	3 to 4	257

[1] This work was done on a Singer machine.

[2] Single tucks.

TABLE 77C.—SHORT TUCKING: WILCOX & GIBBS SINGLE-NEEDLE MACHINE—Concluded.

Line No.	Shop No. and operator No.	Number and sex of operators. M.	Number and sex of operators. F.	Piecework or week work.	Wages or earnings per week.	Material.	Number of clusters.	Tucks per cluster.	Number of tucks per waist.	Waists (dozen).	Total tucks.	Time worked (minutes).	Length of tuck (inches).	Width of tuck.	Stitches per inch.	Number of jobs.	Size of job (dozen waists).	Tucks per hour.
	Shop No. 1116—Con.																	
16	Average		3	Piecework	9.08 13.62	Voile	4 4 6 8	3 3 8 3	66	$5\frac{1}{12}$	4,026	651	25 7 26 6 } 15	Pin	11 to 12	3	1 to $2\frac{1}{4}$	371
17	Do		2	do	7.78 9.08	do	8 2 2 2	3 3 3 3	42	$4\frac{3}{4}$	2,394	577	23 23 13 17 } 20	Pin $\frac{3}{8}$ inch Pin $\frac{3}{8}$ inch	11	2	$2\frac{1}{4}$ to $2\frac{1}{2}$	249
18	Operator No. 197		1	do	11.92	do	2	6	12	$5\frac{5}{8}$	840	205	21	$\frac{3}{8}$ inch	11	1	$5\frac{5}{8}$	246
19	Operator No. 200	1		do	10.58	do	2	5	10	16	1,920	265	21			1	16	435
	Shop No. 1191:																	
20	Average	1	4	Week work	9.00 to 18.00	Voile and crêpe.	4	4	16	$14\frac{1}{3}$	2,752	819	21 to 22	Pin	11 to 15	5	$2\frac{5}{12}$ to $4\frac{5}{12}$	202
21	Do		3	do	9.00 to 12.00	Voile	4	3	12	$9\frac{1}{2}$	1,368	623	19 to 21	$\frac{1}{16}$ inch	12 to 14	3	$1\frac{7}{12}$ to 5	132
22	Do		2	do	10.00, 12.00	Voile and crêpe.	2	7	14	8	1,344	395	21	Pin	9 to 12	2	$3\frac{5}{12}$ to $4\frac{7}{12}$	204
23	Operator No. 182		1	do	12.00	Voile	[1] 4 6	4 4	40	$1\frac{5}{8}$	880	165	21 5 } $11\frac{1}{2}$	Pin	9	1	$1\frac{5}{8}$	320
24	Operator No. 186	1		do	16.00	do	[1] 2 2	10 3	26	$\frac{5}{8}$	260	59	7 22 } $10\frac{1}{2}$	Pin	11	1	$\frac{5}{8}$	264

[1] This work was done on a Singer machine.

In line 14 the number of tucks per waist drops further to 22 with the result that the output per hour goes down to 166. But in line 15, with the same number of tucks per waist, the output rises to 257 tucks per hour, which is accounted for by the fact that in this case the tucks are all of uniform width, namely, ¼ inch, whereas in the preceding cases there were tucks of three different widths: Pin ($\frac{1}{32}$ inch), ¼ inch, and ¾ inch.

In line 16 the number of tucks per waist rises to 66 and all of them are of uniform width, namely, pin-tuck size, and as should be expected, the output per hour increases very materially, namely, to 371 tucks.

Enough has been said in explanation of the figures to show the effect of the different causes on the output per hour.

DOUBLE TUCKS.

As already explained (p. 198), it is customary in many shops to join together two parts of a waist having similar tucks, such as two fronts or two backs, and thus make the tucks on the two waists in one process. In spite of the loss of time in joining the two pieces together and cutting them apart, there is a considerable saving of time, because it does not take much more time to do a tuck of double length than it does to do a single tuck. Table 77D shows the output on double tucks. It will be seen that the output on these double tucks does not differ much from that on single tucks. Thus the output on double tucks of the total length of 10 inches (that is, 2 tucks of 5 inches each), 12 tucks to the waist, is 214 tucks per hour.

Line 2 shows the output to be only 111 tucks per hour when the length of the tucks on the waist is 14 inches and 54 inches.

Line 3 shows an output of 100 tucks per hour when the length of the double tuck is 36 inches and there are only 7 tucks to the waist.

Line 4 shows the output of 154 tucks per hour with the length of the double tuck only 13 inches and the number of tucks to the waist being 9.

In line 5 the output per hour drops to 62 because the length of the double tuck increases to 42 inches, the number of tucks to the waist drops to 6, and the total number of tucks to the job drops to only 144.

Finally, line 6 shows an output of 91 tucks per hour on the same length of tuck with the number of tucks per waist increased to 8.

Lines 8 to 10 show the time it takes to join the two similar parts of a waist in order to make a double tuck. This work was timed only in shop No. 1230, which is a typical $9-a-dozen waist shop. The output of one operator, receiving $18 per week, was 189 rows of stitching per hour; that is to say, 189 pairs of parts. The output of the other operator, also receiving $18 per week, was 206 rows of stitching per hour, the average of the two being 202. Both operators were men.

TABLE 77D.—DOUBLE TUCKS: WILCOX & GIBBS SINGLE-NEEDLE MACHINE.

Line No.	Shop No. and operator No.	Number and sex of operators.		Week work or piecework.	Wages or earnings per week.	Material.	Number of clusters.	Tucks per cluster.	Number of tucks per waist.	Waists (dozen).	Total tucks.	Time worked (minutes).	Length of tuck (inches).	Width of tuck.	Stitches per inch.	Number of jobs.	Size of job (dozen waists).	Tucks per hour.
		Male.	Female.															
	Shop No. 1191:																	
1	Operator No. 186	1		Week work	$16	Voile	3	4	12	$8\frac{3}{4}$	1,260	353	10	Pin	13 to 14	2	$3\frac{3}{4}$ to 5	214
2	Average	2	1		12 to 18	do	3	7	21	$6\frac{1}{3}$	1,596	865	{54, 14} 40	do	11 to 15	3	$1\frac{1}{2}$ to $2\frac{3}{4}$	111
	Operator No. 183		1	Week work	12	do			7	$1\frac{5}{8}$	154	92	36	do	12	1	$1\frac{5}{8}$	100
4	Do		1	do	12	Lawn	3	3	9	$3\frac{1}{3}$	360	140	13	do	14	1	$3\frac{1}{3}$	154
5	Operator No. 13		1	do	12	Voile	2	3	6	2	144	140	42	do	12	1	2	62
6	Operator No. 178		1	do	10	Crêpe	2	4	8	$1\frac{7}{12}$	152	100	42	do	15	1	$1\frac{7}{12}$	91
	Shop No. 1230:																	
7	Average	3		do	18	Voile and lawn.			8	50	4,800	1,424	14	Pin $\frac{1}{8}$ inch.	9 to 10	7	$1\frac{1}{2}$ to 13	202

Joining parts of waist for making double tucks.

Line No.	Shop No. and operator No.	Number and sex of operators.		Week work or piecework.	Weekly rate of pay.	Material.	Number of clusters.	Tucks per cluster.	Rows of stitching per waist.	Waists (dozen).	Total rows of stitching.	Time worked (minutes).	Length of seams (inches).	Stitches per inch.	Number of jobs.	Size of job (dozen waists).	Rows of stitching per hour.
		Male.	Female.														
	Shop No. 1230:																
8	Operator No. 7	1		Week work	$18	Voile			1	5	60	19	11	9	1	5	189
9	Operator No. 189	1		do	18	do			1	20	240	70	11	9 to 10	3	5 to 8	206
10	Average	2		Week work	18	Voile			1	25	300	89	11	9 to 10	4	5 to 8	202

SINGLE-NEEDLE SINGER MACHINE.

Table 77E shows the output on a Singer single-needle machine. The same causes which affect the output on a Wilcox & Gibbs machine will also affect work done on a Singer machine. Thus the output in line 1 on a job in which there are 84 tucks per waist (⅛ inch wide) is 125 tucks per hour, and in line 2, representing similar work by another operator, the output is practically the same, namely, 122 tucks per hour. In line 3 the production drops to 104 tucks per hour on the same class of work, but with only 2 dozen waists to the job instead of 3 dozen as in the preceding case. It should be noted that in each of the above cases the tucks exceeding 23 inches in length were "cross-tucks," i. e., tucks running across the waist, which had to be stitched over the tucks covering the waist lengthwise. This makes the work somewhat more difficult, and therefore takes more time than ordinary tucking. As the cross tucks could not be timed separately from the other tucks, the output is given for the entire job. The average for the three jobs was 118 tucks per hour.

The same operator shows an output of 110 tucks per hour in line 4, although the number of tucks per waist is only 18 instead of 84 as in the preceding case, and although the width of the tuck is ⅜ inch, but in this case the operator had the advantage of having tucks of only two different lengths, whereas in the preceding case she had six different lengths of tucks to look out for; also there were no cross tucks to be made in this case.

The output in line 5 drops to 76 tucks per hour on exactly the same kind of work as that shown in line 4. This work was done by an operator who, on the average, earned more money than the operator in line 4, and who, in line 1, shows a bigger output than the other operator. The only reason which may account for it, so far as it appears from the table, is that the job in line 5 consists of 1 dozen waists whereas in the preceding case it consists of 2 dozen.

Finally, the output in line 6 is only 55 tucks per hour on exactly similar work as in line 5 except that the tucks, instead of being of one width of ⅜ inch, are of two widths, namely, ½ inch and 1 inch, respectively, which makes the job more difficult on account of the necessity of adjusting the gauge twice and of the greater difficulty of handling tucks of greater width.

SHORT TUCKING ON A MULTIPLE-NEEDLE SINGER MACHINE.

The work on a multiple-needle machine is necessarily slower than on a single-needle machine: First, because it requires more careful handling on the part of the operator in looking after more needles and threads at the same time; second, because the multiple-needle

TABLE 77E.—SHORT TUCKING: SINGER SINGLE-NEEDLE MACHINE.

Line No.	Shop No. and operator No.	Sex of operator.	Week work or piecework.	Weekly earnings of pieceworkers.	Material.	Number of clusters.	Tucks per cluster.	Number of tucks per waist.	Waists (dozen).	Total tucks.	Time worked (minutes).	Length of tuck (inches).	Width of tuck (inches).	Stitches per inch.	Number of jobs.	Size of job (dozen waists).	Tucks per hour.
	Shop No. 1090:																
1	Operator No. 191	F.	Piecework	$13.33	Lawn	4, 4, 3, 2, 4, 4	4, 4, 4, 4, 4, 4	84	3	3,024	1,448	27½, 18, 21, 27, 16½, 19 — 21	$\frac{1}{8}$	16	1	3	125
2	Operator No. 190	F.	do	12.05	do	4, 4, 3, 2, 4, 4	4, 4, 4, 4, 4, 4	84	3	3,024	1,485	21½, 23, 21, 27, 17, 20½ — 21	$\frac{1}{8}$	16	1	3	122
3	Operator No. 193	F.	do	10.61	do	4, 4, 3, 2, 4, 4	4, 4, 4, 4, 4, 4	84	2	2,016	1,160	23, 21, 21½, 27, 17, 20½ — 21	$\frac{1}{8}$	16	1	2	104
	Average, lines 1 to 3.	F.	Piecework	12.00	Lawn	4, 4, 4, 3, 2, 4	4, 4, 4, 4, 4, 4	84	8	8,064	4,093	27½, 18, 21, 27, 16½, 19 — 21	$\frac{1}{8}$	16	3	2 to 3	118
	Shop No. 1090:																
4	Operator No. 193	F.	Piecework	10.61	Linen	4	4	{2, 16} 18	2	432	235	{5, 21} 19	$\frac{3}{8}$	16	1	2	110
5	Operator No. 191	F.	do	13.33	do	4	4	{2, 16} 18	1	216	170	{5, 21} 19	$\frac{3}{8}$	16	1	1	76
6	Operator No. 194	F.	do	5.71	do	4	4	{2, 16} 18	1	216	235	{5, 23} 21	{1, $\frac{1}{2}$}	16	1	1	55

machine works more slowly than a single-needle machine; third, because the adjusting of the material under the foot takes longer than on a single-needle machine. Table 77F shows in detail the output on such a machine.

Taking first shop No. 1090, we find the output to vary from 78 to 88 clusters per hour, making an average of 84 clusters (line 4).

As will be seen from the figures in lines 1 to 3, it does not make much difference as to whether the machine contains 5 or 6 needles.

Lines 5 to 10 show the output per hour in shop No. 1116. In this case the output varies more owing to the greater variation in the character of the work, although it is all done by one operator.

Lines 5 and 6 show practically the same output, namely, 101 and 103 clusters per hour, under similar conditions of work, such as the number of tucks per cluster, and the length and width of the tucks.

Line 7 shows an output of only 83 clusters per hour under practically similar conditions, except that the tucks are slightly longer.

Line 8 shows an output of 192 clusters per hour by the same operator when all the clusters are of the same length.

Line 9 shows the output to be only 110 clusters on the same kind of clusters of uniform length when the number of clusters per waist is reduced from 8 to 4.

As the output in lines 5 to 9 represents the work of the same operator, and the work is of a fairly uniform character, an average of the above may be of practical value. Line 10 shows the average output on the above work to be 109 clusters per hour.

Lines 11 to 13 show the output on double clusters in shop No. 1230. In this case similar clusters on similar parts of different waists are made in one operation. That is to say, 2 backs or 2 fronts are joined together, the clusters in both are made in one operation, and the two parts are later cut apart. The work of making a double cluster is, however, a much more difficult operation than making a double tuck. As the cluster does not extend through the entire length of the waist (the length in this case being 11 inches for the double tuck, or 5½ inches for each cluster) the operator must pull the material through the foot until she reaches the point where the cluster is to start. As she has nothing to guide her but her eye, she frequently discovers, after the cluster is completed, that it has not ended at the proper point, with the result that it has to be ripped and the work started over again. At best, the work has to be done slowly in order to make sure that the tuck will be started and finished at the right point. The result is a very low output as compared with the preceding figures, namely, 43 clusters per hour in the case of one operator, and 28 in the case of another, the average being 37 clusters per hour with 3 clusters to the waist.

TABLE 77F.—SHORT TUCKING: SINGER MULTIPLE-NEEDLE MACHINE.

Line No.	Shop No. and operator No.	Sex of operator.	Week work or piecework.	Wages or earnings per week.	Material.	Tucks per cluster.	Number of clusters per waist.	Waists (dozen).	Total clusters.	Time worked (minutes).	Length of tuck (inches).	Width of tuck.	Stitches per inch.	Number of jobs.	Size of job (dozen waists).	Clusters per hour.
	Shop No. 1090:															
1	Operator No. 195	F.	Piecework	$14.47	Lawn	(1)	8	12	1,152	885	5 to 8	$\frac{1}{16}$ inch	16	1	12	78
2	Operator No. 195	F.	Piecework	$14.47	Lawn	6	16	10	1,920	1,311	7 to 11	$\frac{1}{16}$ inch	14	3	2 to 4	88
3	Operator No. 195	F.	Piecework	$14.47	Lawn	5	4	12	576	405	5 to 7	$\frac{1}{16}$ inch	16	1	12	85
4	Average, 1 person.	F.	Piecework	14.47	Lawn		4 to 16	34	3,648	2,601	5 to 11	$\frac{1}{16}$ inch	14 to 16	5	2 to 12	84
	Shop No. 1116:															
5	Operator No. 18	M.	Piecework	(1)	Voile	5	4 4	$\frac{2}{3}$	64	38	21 17 } 19	Pin	12	1	$\frac{2}{3}$	101
6	Operator No. 18	M.	Piecework	(1)	Voile	5	2 2	$1\frac{1}{2}$	72	42	21 17 } 19	do	12	1	$1\frac{1}{2}$	103
7	Operator No. 18	M.	Piecework	(1)	Voile	5	2 4	1	72	52	21 23 } 22	do	12	1	1	83
8	Operator No. 18	M.	Piecework	(1)	Voile	5	8	$\frac{2}{3}$	64	20	21	do	12	1	$\frac{2}{3}$	192
9	Operator No. 18	M.	Piecework	(1)	Voile	4 5	2 2 } 4	$16\frac{1}{6}$	776	425	21	do	12	3	$3\frac{11}{12}$ to $7\frac{3}{4}$	110
10	Average, 1 person.	M.	Piecework		Voile	5	4 to 8	20	1,048	577	19 to 22	Pin	12	7	1 to $7\frac{3}{4}$	109
	Shop No. 1230:															
11	Operator No. 187	F.	Week work.	13.50	Voile	4	3	$27\frac{1}{2}$	990	1,380	11	Pin	16 to 17	4	5 to $9\frac{1}{2}$	43
12	Operator No. 2	F.	do	12.50	do	4	3	$11\frac{1}{2}$	414	885	11	do	16 to 17	4	$2\frac{1}{2}$ to 4	28
13	Average, 2 persons	F.	Week work.	12.50 to 13.50	Voile	4	3	39	1,404	2,265	11	Pin	16 to 17	8	$2\frac{1}{2}$ to $9\frac{1}{2}$	37

[1] Not reported.

LACE RUNNING.

The work of lace running consists of joining strips of lace to strips of cloth, or to other strips of lace of various widths. Most lace running is done in long strips which may run into hundreds of yards, but there is also considerable work done on short pieces which go into individual waists. The skill of the lace runner consists of handling the lace carefully and running the material and the lace in such a manner that the machine is operated steadily without a break and so that the unwinding of the lace and of the cloth which are in rolls takes place almost automatically and without requiring the stopping of the machine on the part of the operator.

Although it takes only a few days to learn lace running, the operator acquires greater skill in the course of time, which accounts for the fact that the wages of lace runners in the dress and waist industry vary all the way from $5 to $16 a week and more. The difference between the $16 and $5 lace runners is accounted for by the great difference in output of the two classes of workers, determined by the skill with which they can fill the requirements described above.

There are two methods of joining lace to cloth. In one the lace is put on top of the cloth; in the other the cloth is put on top of the lace. In either case the operator holds the lace in one hand and the cloth in the other, running the two simultaneously under the needle, taking care that the lace is stitched onto the cloth at a uniform distance from the edge of the cloth. In either case the cloth is run through an attachment which turns in the edge of the cloth so that it will not be seen under the lace.

The "cloth on top" method is the more difficult because when the cloth is put on top of the lace the operator can not see readily the position of the lace, and must stop frequently to make sure that the lace is being stitched to the cloth at a uniform distance from the edge. When the lace is put on top, the entire work is in plain view of the operator who can therefore handle it with greater ease.

The work of lace running was timed in five shops with 9 persons, involving a total expenditure of time equivalent to 103 hours and 39 minutes for one person, and covering 14,680 yards of lace. The output per hour, apart from the individual skill of the worker, will differ with the machine, the character of the material, the width of the material, the number of stitches per inch, and according to whether the lace or the cloth is stitched on top. In the work which was timed the stitches per inch differed so little, running mostly from 9 to 11 to the inch, that no distinction can be made on that score. The same is likewise true of the material, which consisted, in all cases, of cotton goods such as voile, lawn, and crêpe, which do not differ materially from each other so far as their effect on output is concerned. All the work timed was done on Wilcox & Gibbs machines. There are, therefore, only two factors to be considered in determining the output of the work that was timed, namely, the width of the material and the relative positions of the cloth and the lace.

LACE ON TOP.

Taking first the work with the lace on top, we find the average output per hour, with the width of the material from 2½ to 6 inches, to have been 157 yards in shop No. 1284, 151 yards in shop No. 1235, 143 yards in shop No. 1232, and 206 yards in shop No. 1116. Shop No. 1116 thus shows the highest output, although it makes a higher grade of waists than the others; at the same time it is the only shop in which the work was done on a piece-rate basis, lace running being done by week workers in all the other shops reported in the table. The average output for the above shops on the above widths was 162 yards per hour.

On material running in width from 16 to 26 inches the output was naturally less, since the wider the material the more difficult the handling of it. The output for the different shops was 100 yards per hour for shop No. 1284 and 118 for shop No. 1191, the average being 111 yards per hour.

The output of the individual worker in each of these shops is likewise given in Table 78 and shows the variation in output due to difference in individual skill.

CLOTH ON TOP.

In this class of work three different widths of material were used: (1) Material ranging in width from 1½ to 4 inches, the average output on this in shop No. 1284, representing the work of two operators working on 856 yards, being 146 yards per hour; (2) material ranging in width from 9½ to 12 inches, representing the work of one operator working on 425 yards for a period of 3½ hours, the output per hour being 121 yards; (3) with the width of the material running from 16 to 30 inches, the average output for the same shop for the same two operators as above on a total of 655 yards being 81 yards per hour.

JOINING LACE TO LACE.

This work was timed in two shops. In shop No. 1191 (a $9-a-dozen waist shop) a girl receiving $13 a week and timed for a period of 1 hour and 35 minutes showed an output of 126 yards per hour. In shop No. 1116 (manufacturing medium-price waists), a girl working by the piece and timed for a period of 4 hours and 50 minutes, showed an output of 184 yards per hour, the average for the two shops being 170 yards per hour. Either the average or the output of the individual workers can be taken as a basis in determining the rate by taking a corresponding rate per hour in connection therewith.

TABLE 78.—LACE RUNNING.

Line No.	Shop No. and operator No.	Sex of operator.	Week work or piecework.	Wages or earnings per week.	Material.	Kind of work.	Width of material (inches).	Stitches per inch.	Total yards.	Time worked (minutes).	Yards per hour.	Number of jobs.
	Shop No. 1284:											
1	Operator No. 81	F.	Week work	$9.00	Embroidered crêpe	Lace on top	4½	9	180	101	107	1
2	Operator No. 82	F.	do	15.00	Embroidered voile	do	2¼	11	400	154	156	1
3					Voile	do	[1] 2½ to 3½	9 to 11	302	90	201	4
4	Operator No. 81	F.	do	9.00	do	do	4	9	163	114	86	1
5					Lawn	do	4	9	156	72	130	1
6	Operator No. 82	F.	do	15.00	do	do	4	9	960	295	195	1
7	Average, 2 persons.	F.	Week work	9 to 15.00		Lace on top	2½ to 4½	9 to 11	2,161	826	157	9
	Shop No. 1235:											
8	Operator No. 83	F.	Week work	15.50	Voile and lawn	Lace on top	(2)	11	552	219	151	2
	Shop No. 1232:											
9	Operator No. 84	F.	do	10.00	Embroidery	do.[3]	4 to 6	9	1,772	797	133	7
10	Operator No. 85	F.	do	12.00	do	do.[3]	4 to 6	8	1,073	480	134	8
11	Operator No. 86	F.	do	13.50	do	do.[3]	4 to 6	9	720	221	195	3
12	Average, 3 persons.	F.	Week work	10.00 to 13.50		Lace on top	4 to 6	8 to 9	3,565	1,498	143	18
	Shop No. 1116:											
13	Operator No. 87	F.	Piecework	(2)	Voile and lawn	Lace on top	5	(2)	2,763	806	206	7
14	Average, 4 shops.	F.	6 week workers, 1 pieceworker.			Lace on top	2½ to 6	8 to 11	9,041	3,349	162	36
	Shop No. 1284:											
15	Operator No. 81	F.	Week work	9.00	Lawn and embroidered voile.	Lace on top	16	9	740	444	100	2
16	Operator No. 88	F.	do	15.00	Lace on piping	do	(2)	9	12	5	144	1
17	Operator No. 81	F.	do	9.00	Crêpe	do	16	9	100	80	75	1
18	Operator No. 88	F.	do	15.00	do	do	16	9	30	24	75	1
19	Operator No. 82	F.	do	15.00	Lawn	do	26	9	240	118	122	1
20	Average, 3 persons.	F.	Week work	9.00 to 15.00		Lace on top	16 to 26	9	1,122	671	100	6

[1] Two jobs, width unknown.

[2] Not reported.

[3] Beading was used.

TABLE 78.—LACE RUNNING—Concluded.

Line No.	Shop No. and operator No.	Sex of operator.	Week work or piecework.	Wages or earnings per week.	Material.	Kind of work.	Width of material (inches).	Stitches per inch.	Total yards.	Time worked (minutes).	Yards per hour.	Number of jobs.
	Shop No. 1191:											
21	Operator No. 79	F.	Week work.	$11.00	Voile	Lace on top	(1)	11	280	200	84	1
22	Operator No. 89	F.	do	13.00	do	do	(1)	11	1,638	778	126	5
23	Average, 2 persons.	F.	Week work.	11.00 to 13.00	Voile	Lace on top	(1)	11	1,918	978	118	6
24	Average, 2 shops	F.	Week work.	9.00 to 15.00	Voile	Lace on top	16 to 26	9 to 11	3,040	1,649	111	12
	Shop No. 1284:											
25	Operator No. 88	F.	Week work.	15.00	Voile	Cloth on top	1½ to 4	9 to 11	700	281	149	5
26	Operator No. 82	F.	do	15.00	do	do	1½	11	156	70	134	2
27	Average, 2 persons.	F.	Week work.	15.00	Voile	Cloth on top	1½ to 4	9 to 11	856	351	146	7
	Shop No. 1284:											
28	Operator No. 88	F.	Week work.	15.00	Voile and lawn	Cloth on top	9½ to 12	9 to 11	425	210	121	5
29	Operator No. 82	F.	do	15.00	do	do	16 to 25	9 to 11	281	223	76	4
30	Operator No. 88	F.	do	15.00	do	do	19 to 30	10 to 11	374	262	86	4
31	Average, 2 persons.	F.	Week work.	15.00	Voile and lawn	Cloth on top	16 to 30	9 to 11	655	485	81	8
	Shop No. 1191:											
32	Operator No. 89	F.	Week work.	13.00	Lace	Cloth on top	(1)	11	200	95	126	1
	Shop No. 1116:											
33	Operator No. 87	F.	Piecework	(1)	(1)	do	(1)	(1)	888	290	184	1
34	Average, 2 shops	F.	Week work and piecework.			Cloth on top	(1)		1,088	385	170	2
	Shop No. 1116:											
35	Operator No. 87	F.	Piecework	35 cents per hour.	Voile and net	Joining voile and net, plain seams without attachment.	Strips.	(1)	448	190	141	1

	RUFFLING EDGING TO INSERTION.											
36	Shop No. 1232: Operator No. 84	F.	Week work	10.00	[1]	Lace and lace	[1]	9	144	114	76	1
	SHORT RUNS.											
37	Shop No. 1232: Operator No. 90	F.	do	12.00	Voile	Sleeves	16-inch lengths.	8	[2] 1,440	393	[2] 220	12

[1] Not reported.

[2] Sleeves.

In addition to the three kinds of lace running described, a number of special jobs were timed, as follows:

JOINING VOILE AND NET STRIPS.

Work of one operator in one shop, working for 3 hours and 10 minutes, earning 35 cents an hour; output per hour, 141 yards.

JOINING RUFFLED LACE EDGING TO LACE INSERTION.

This represents the work of one operator receiving $10 a week in shop No. 1232, working for 1 hour and 54 minutes; output per hour, 76 yards.

JOINING LACE TO SLEEVES.

This work consists of short runs, each 16 inches long, representing the full width of an open sleeve. Ordinarily, work of this kind is done by body makers, and is given in another table representing short runs of lace joining in which no attachment is used. In the particular case given in this table the work was done by a lace runner with the aid of an attachment. The operator, a girl receiving $12 a week, was timed for 6 hours and 33 minutes, producing an output of 220 sleeves per hour.

HEMMING.

The operation of hemming consists of turning in the raw edge of any material and stitching it over to give it a finished appearance. As a rule a special attachment is used known as the "hemmer," which automatically turns in the cloth so that the turning in of the hem and the stitching over are all done in one operation. There are two kinds of hemming—strip hemming and waist hemming. Strip hemming is done on long strips of cloth—similar to strip tucking and lace running on a Wilcox & Gibbs machine—and is paid for by the 100 yards, while waist hemming consists of hemming the bottom or other parts of a waist.

Strip hemming was timed in three shops, covering the work of 8 persons who hemmed a total of more than 19,000 yards of cotton goods in what is equivalent to 58 hours and 45 minutes for one person. (Table 79A.) In addition to that, 260 yards of chiffon hemming was also timed. The materials hemmed were voile, lawn, net, and chiffon. The average output per hour is given for each person timed, as well as for each material. There being but little difference between voile and lawn, a combined average is given for the two materials, and separate averages are given for net and chiffon. The output per hour on voile and lawn varied from 286 to 451 yards per hour, the average output for the four persons working on the two materials being 358 yards per hour. The output on net for four workers in shop No. 1230 varied from 256 to 350 yards per hour, the average for the shop being 311 yards per hour. In shop No. 1191 the output on net for the two workers timed was 198 and 236 yards per hour, respectively, the average for the shop being 211 yards per hour as against 311 in shop No. 1230. The work in both shops was done on a weekly basis. The difference in output between the two shops is probably due to the fact that all the hemmers in shop No. 1230 are men (tuckers, receiving from $15 to $18 per week), while in shop No. 1191 they are women (lace runners, receiving $11 and $12 per week). In work of this kind (given out by the hundreds and thousands of yards), which can be kept up for hours without a break, physical strength and endurance are the chief factors, and men have a natural advantage over women. The rate for strip hemming could be established on the basis of either shop by making a corresponding hourly rate allowance. The output on chiffon (on which only one worker was timed on 260 yards) in shop No. 1116, manufacturing medium-priced waists, was 153 yards per hour. All the strip hemming was done on the Wilcox & Gibbs machine.

Waist hemming was timed in four shops on about 365 dozen waists, hemmed by four persons. (Table 79B). The hemming in shop No. 1110 was done on a Metropolitan machine, while in the other shops a Singer machine was used. Both on account of the higher speed of the Metropolitan, as well as of the elimination of the loss of time in handling the bundles in that shop, as explained elsewhere, shop No. 1110 shows the highest output, namely, 156 rows of stitching per hour. It has not been included in the general average because a different machine was used. Shop No. 1191 shows the lowest average, namely, 86 rows of stitching per hour, which is due to the great loss of time caused in that shop by the handling of but few waists at a time. For this reason this output was likewise omitted from the general average. The output in shops Nos. 1230 and 1284 is remarkably uniform—137 and 141 rows of stitching per hour—the average for the two shops being 140 rows of stitching per hour.

In using this average as a basis in determining the rate for hemming, the fact should be borne in mind that it represents the output of two exceptionally fast workers, both of them men. The operator employed in shop No. 1230 had one assistant, but the hemming was done exclusively by the principal. The operator in shop No. 1284 employed several assistants on different operations, but the hemming was likewise done exclusively by himself. These men, when fully employed, earn from 50 to 75 cents an hour at current piece rates.

TABLE 79A.—STRIP HEMMING: WILCOX & GIBBS MACHINE.

Line No.	Shop No. and operator No.	Sex of operator.	Piecework or week work.	Wages or earnings per week.	Material.	Width of material (inches).	Stitches per inch.	Total yards.	Time worked (minutes).	Number of jobs.	Yards per hour.
	Shop No. 1230:										
1	Operator No. 76	M.	Week work	$15	Voile	2	12	5,814	1,036	6	337
2	Operator No. 7	M.	do	18	do	2	10	400	84	1	286
3	Operator No. 77	M.	do	15	do	2	8	1,600	232	2	414
4	Operator No. 8	M.	do	18	do	2	9	1,000	152	1	395
5	Operator No. 77	M.	do	15	Lawn	2	8	1,070	154	1	451
6	Average, 4 persons	M.	Week work	15 to 18	Voile and lawn	2	8 to 12	9,884	1,658	11	358
7	Operator No. 7	M.	Week work	18	Net	2	10	1,410	331	1	256
8	Operator No. 77	M.	do	15	do	2	10	2,950	505	3	350
9	Operator No. 78	M.	do	18	do	2	9	1,770	322	2	330
10	Operator No. 8	M.	do	18	do	2	8 to 9	1,970	404	3	293
11	Average, 4 persons	M.	Week work	15 to 18	Net	2	8 to 10	8,100	1,562	9	311
	Shop No. 1191:										
12	Operator No. 79	F.	Week work	11	Net		11	642	195	1	198
13	Operator No. 80	F.	do	12	do		11	432	110	1	236
14	Average, 2 persons	F.	Week work	11 to 12	Net		11	1,074	305	2	211
	Shop No. 1116:										
15	Operator No. 87	F.	Piecework	(1)	Chiffon	Strips		260	102	1	153

[1] 31 cents per hour.

TABLE 79B.—WAIST-HEMMING: SHOP NO. 1110, METROPOLITAN MACHINE; ALL OTHER SHOPS, SINGER MACHINE.

Line No.	Shop No. and operator No.	Sex of operator.	Piecework or week work.	Wages or earnings per week.	Material.	Length of seam. (inches).	Waists (dozen).	Stitching.					Bundles.	
								Rows per waists.	Total rows.	Stitches per inch.	Time worked (minutes).	Rows per hour.	Number.	Dozen per bundle.
1	Shop No. 1110: Operator No. 72	F.	Week work	$6.50	Crêpe and lace	36 to 40	73¾	1	885	(1)	341	156	4	12 7/12 to 34
2	Shop No. 1191: Operator No. 73	M.	Piecework	(1)	Voile	64	106⅙	1	1,274	(1)	894	86	21	1 7/12 to 10
3	Shop No. 1230: Operator No. 74	M.	Piecework	(1)	Voile	30 to 65	64⅓	1	772	9	337	137	23	1/12 to 6¾
4	Shop No. 1284: Operator No. 75	M.	do	(1)	Voile and crêpe	32 to 62	120⅔	1	1,448	9 to 11	615	141	36	¾ to 13½
5	Average, 2 persons	M.	Piecework	(1)	Voile and crêpe	30 to 65	185	1	2,220	9 to 11	952	140	59	¾ to 13½

[1] Not reported.

CLOSING.

The operation of closing consists of joining the front and back parts of the waist, forming a seam on each side of the waist running from the armhole to the hem. On cheap waists this work is usually done on the Union Special machine. This machine works very fast, making about 3,000 revolutions per minute. The machine is equipped with a knife which automatically cuts off the raw edge, and the seam is finished off (felled) on the wrong side in one operation. For this reason the Union Special offers the least expensive way of doing this work. Another machine used on $9-a-dozen waists is the Metropolitan, which likewise cuts off the raw edge automatically, and in addition puts a binding on the wrong side of the seam, all in one operation. This makes the machine more complicated and more difficult for the operator to handle, so that it can not be operated as rapidly as the Union Special.

The medium and high price waists are closed with a French seam, usually on a Singer machine, which involves three separate operations: (1) The sewing together of the two parts of the waist on the right side; (2) cutting off the raw edge with a pair of scissors; (3) turning over the waist and putting in the second row of stitching on the wrong side. Some of the Singer machines are equipped with a knife which automatically cuts off the raw edge, but most of the factories still do without the automatic knife, and scissors are employed instead.

In the old-style waists, in which the sleeves were closed before being joined to the armhole of the waist, the closing of the waist consisted only of joining the sides from armhole to hem, as already explained. In the new-style waists, with the so-called kimono sleeves, as well as in the tailor-made shirt waists, the sleeves are attached to the shoulders of the waist before being closed, and the closer sews up (closes) the sleeves and sides of the waist in one operation.

Table 80 gives the figures for closing both sides and sleeves, closing sides only, and sleeves only. The figures relate to shops making exclusively $9-a-dozen waists. On these the Union Special and Metropolitan machines were used.

TABLE 80.—CLOSING: SIDES AND SLEEVES.

Line No.	Shop No. and operator No.	Sex of operator.	Piecework or week work.	Wages or earnings per week.	Material.	Name of machine used.	Length of seam (inches).	Waists (dozen).	Stitching.				Bundles.	
									Rows per waist.	Total rows.	Time worked (minutes).	Rows per hour.	Number.	Dozen waists in each.
	Shop No. 1110:													
1	Operator No. 61	M.	Piecework	(1)	Lace and voile	Union Special	27 to 32	17⅚	2	428	178	144	6	1 to 8⅓
2	Operator No. 60	F.	do	(1)	Voile, lace, and crêpe	do	27 to 34	48⅔	2	1,168	588	119	11	1¼ to 9
3	Average, 2 persons.	M. and F.	Piecework	(1)	Voile, lace, and crêpe	Union Special	27 to 34	66½	2	1,596	766	125	17	1 to 9
	Shop No. 1191:													
4	Operator No. 62	M.	Week work	(1)	Voile	Metropolitan	35	64 5/12	2	1,546	1,167	79	12	2 to 9½
5	Operator No. 63	M.	do	(1)	do	Union Special	35	31 1/12	2	746	526	85	10	¾ to 5
6	Average, 2 persons.	M.	Week work	(1)	Voile	Metropolitan and Union Special.	35	95½	2	2,292	1,693	81	22	¾ to 9½
	Shop No. 1284:													
7	Operator No. 65	F.	Piecework	(1)	Voile	Union Special	27 to 34	46½	2	1,116	650	103	13	1½ to 6½
8	Operator No. 67	F.	Week work	$7.00	do	do	27 to 34	53¼	2	1,278	711	108	22	1 to 5⅓
9	Operator No. 66	F.	Piecework	(1)	Voile and crêpe	do	30 to 33	20¼	2	486	322	91	9	½ to 4
10	Average, 3 persons.	F.	Piecework and week work.		Voile and crêpe	Union Special	27 to 34	120	2	2,880	1,68	103	44	½ to 6½
	Shop No. 1230:													
11	Operator No. 71	F.	Week work	13.00	Voile	Union Special	25 to 32	23⅚	2	572	298	115	16	⅓ to 3
12	Operator No. 68	M.	Piecework	(1)	do	do	25 to 33	16½	2	396	195	122	15	¼ to 1½
13	Operator No. 69	M.	do	(1)	do	do	25 to 33	18 7/12	2	446	253	106	13	¾ to 2½
14	Operator No. 70	M.	Week work	6.50	do	do	29 to 31	21½	2	516	416	74	12	½ to 4
15	Average, 4 persons.	M. and F.	Piecework and week work.		Voile	Union Special	25 to 33	80 5/12	2	1,930	1,162	100	56	⅓ to 4
16	Average, 11 persons.	M. and F.	Piecework and week work.		Voile, lace, and crêpe	Union Special	25 to 35	362 5/12	2	8,698	5,304	98	139	⅓ to 9½

1 Earnings not reported.

TABLE 80.—CLOSING: SIDES AND SLEEVES—Concluded.

Line No.	Shop No. and operator No.	Sex of operator.	Piecework or week work.	Wages or earnings per week.	Material.	Name of machine used.	Length of seam (inches).	Waists (dozen).	Stitching.				Bundles.	
									Rows per waist.	Total rows.	Time worked (minutes).	Rows per hour.	Number.	Dozen waists in each.
	SIDES ONLY.													
	Shop No. 1191:													
17	Operator No. 62	M.	Week work	15.00	Voile	Metropolitan	14	83⅔	2	2,008	754	160	21	¼ to 6⅓
	Shop No. 1284:													
18	Operator No. 65	M.	Piecework	(1)	Voile	Union Special	13	17½	2	420	138	183	6	2 to 6
19	Operator No. 66	F.	do	(1)	do	do	13½	3½	2	84	27	187	2	½ to 3
20	Average, 2 persons.	M. and F.	Piecework	(1)	Voile	Union Special	13 to 13½	21	2	504	165	183	8	½ to 6
	SLEEVES ONLY.													
	Shop No. 1191:													
21	Operator No. 63	M.	Week work	15.00	Voile	Union Special	14 to 22	117 5/12	2	2,818	925	183	26	1½ to 15
	Shop No. 1230:													
22	Operator No. 70	M.	do	6.50	do	do	19½	7	2	168	57	177	8	½ to 1½
	Shop No. 1284:													
23	Operator No. 66	F.	Piecework	(1)	do	do	16 to 22	69	2	1,656	486	204	32	½ to 3
24	Average, 3 persons.	M. and F.	Week work and piecework.		Voile	Union Special	14 to 22	193 5/12	2	4,642	1,468	190	66	½ to 15
	CLOSING SLEEVES AND SHIRRING TOPS OF SLEEVES.													
	Shop No. 1191:													
25	Operator No. 63	M.	Week work	15.00	Voile	Union Special	12 to 24	20 7/12	2	494	253	117	7	1½ to 5¼

[1] Earnings not reported.

CLOSING SIDES AND SLEEVES.

The operation of closing sides and sleeves was timed in 4 shops and represents the work of 11 persons, closing $362\frac{5}{12}$ dozen waists with a total time expenditure equivalent to 88 hours and 24 minutes for one person.

An examination of the average output of each shop shows the following results: Shop No. 1191, the only shop in which this work is done on a weekly basis, shows the lowest output, 81 rows of stitching per hour. The highest output, 125 rows of stitching per hour, was recorded in shop No. 1110. This figure is exceptionally high and due to conditions which do not prevail in other shops. Shop No. 1110 is a smaller establishment than the other factories for which figures are presented here. It employs from 60 to 70 operators when working to capacity. There is but one person responsible for the closing of all the waists in this shop. This work is done by a man who employs four assistants by the week, who work on closing and hemming. This obviates the necessity of counting the work, the closer being paid each week for as many dozen waists as have been cut up for manufacturing. No time is lost in waiting in line for a "bundle," bringing it to the machine, untying it, counting the waists, folding the waists, making them up into a bundle after the work is finished, and taking it back to the foreman; instead of that, waists are piled up in large heaps as they are finished by other operators, and are turned in in similar heaps without counting after the closing has been finished.

On the other hand, the low figure of 81 rows of stitching per hour in shop No. 1191 can be explained by the fact that the closers in this shop are required to work on very small bundles, getting only a few waists at a time, frequently as few as three or four waists, being obliged to leave the machine at frequent intervals to get a new supply and to go through all the stages preceding and following the work of closing proper, mentioned above. Moreover, most of the closing in this shop was done on a Metropolitan machine, which, for reasons explained above, is a slower machine than the Union Special used in the other three shops.

The average for each of the other two shops is remarkably uniform, being 103 rows of stitching for shop No. 1284 and 100 for shop No. 1230, giving an average for the two shops of 101 rows of stitching per hour. Combining these two normal shops with the high and low output shops mentioned above, a general average is obtained of 98 rows of stitching per hour, which is practically the same as the average for the two normal shops.

CLOSING SIDES.

This operation takes considerably less time, as the seam is only about half the length made in the operation in which the sides and sleeves are closed together. The work was timed in two shops on a total of nearly 105 dozen waists, with a total expenditure of time equivalent to 15 hours and 19 minutes for one person.

In shop No. 1191 the closing was done on a Metropolitan machine by a male operator, who turned out 160 rows of stitching per hour. In shop No. 1284 the work was done by a man working with a woman assistant on a Union Special machine, with an output of 183 rows of stitching per hour.

CLOSING SLEEVES.

As in the case of closing sides, the closing of sleeves takes less time than the combined closing of sides and sleeves. This work was timed in three shops on a total of 193 dozen waists, which took the equivalent of 24 hours and 28 minutes for one person, all the shops using a Union Special machine. The output per hour in the different shops is fairly uniform, being 177 rows of stitching per hour in shop No. 1230, 183 in shop No. 1191, and 204 in shop No. 1284, the highest output being in the shop in which the work is done by the piece. It is interesting to note that the outputs in shops Nos. 1191 and 1230 are practically the same, although in the former the operator receives $15 per week and in the latter only $6.50 per week, both operators being men. The average output for the three shops is 190 rows of stitching per hour.

In addition to the work referred to above, sleeves were closed on 20½ dozen waists in shop No. 1191, while the operator at the same time shirred the top of the sleeves. The output per hour was 117 rows of stitching as compared with 183 rows by the same operator when no shirring was done.

SLEEVE SETTING BY SLEEVE SETTERS.

The work of the sleeve setter consists of sewing the sleeves to the waist. There are two ways of doing this work. In the waists which were mostly in style prior to 1913, the sleeves were closed by the sleeve maker and set into the armhole of the waist by the sleeve setter. The setting of the closed sleeve requires great skill. As a rule the sleeve is larger than the armhole and while it is being set into the waist it has to be gathered into folds (shirred), the sleeve setter knowing practically by instinct just how much to gather in so that the sleeve will fit perfectly into the armhole and will "hang right" from the body of the waist. The work is usually done on a Union Special machine, which has a knife attachment, trimming off the raw edge on the wrong side as fast as the sleeve is sewed onto the waist, and felling the seam. It is also done on a Metropolitan machine, which automatically binds the seam on the wrong side instead of felling it.

In the styles that have been in vogue since 1913 the sleeves are usually sewed onto the body of the waist before being closed. The closer then closes the sleeves and the sides of the waist in one operation. The change in the style and the introduction of the so-called "yoke sleeve" has deprived the sleeve setters of the work of sleeve setting, the open yoke sleeve being usually attached to the waist by the body makers. The sleeve setters are now employed mostly on other work requiring the use of the Union Special or Metropolitan machines. The work of the sleeve setters is given in Table 81, that of the body makers on yoke sleeves in Table 88, and on straight sleeves in Table 99.

The work of sleeve setting proper was timed in three $9-a-dozen waist shops, involving the work of 2 men and 3 women, with a total output of over 252 dozen waists at an expenditure of time equivalent to 77 hours and 53 minutes for 1 person.

In shop No. 1232 the work was done by a week worker on a Union Special machine on open sleeves and shows an output of 123 sleeves per hour.

In shop No. 1284 the work was done on closed sleeves, likewise on a Union Special machine, by 1 male and 1 female working by the piece, and the output was 89 sleeves per hour for 1 worker and 116 sleeves for the other, the average for the shop being 110 sleeves per hour. It is natural that the output on closed sleeves should be less than on open sleeves.

In shop No. 1191 sleeves were also closed before being set, but the sleeve setter was given shirred sleeves instead of plain sleeves, as in shop No. 1284. The work was done by a girl receiving $16 per week and a man receiving $11 per week, the girl being the more skillful of the two. Taking the work of the girl, we find her output to be 101 sleeves per hour when working on a Union Special machine, and 90 sleeves per hour when working on a Metropolitan machine.

Work was also timed in shop No. 1191, in which sleeves were set and shirred at the same time. This naturally slowed down the work still more, the output of the girl dropping to 71 sleeves per hour on a Metropolitan machine, and 72 sleeves per hour on a Union Special. That is to say, while on the preceding work there was a difference of about 10 per cent in output in favor of the Union Special machine as compared with the Metropolitan; there was practically no difference in the output of the two machines when shirring had to be done simultaneously with the sleeve setting. That was probably due to the fact that the difference in speed between the two machines was offset by the delay resulting from the necessity of shirring the sleeves while they were being set. The work of the $11-a-week man likewise showed a larger output when setting sleeves already shirred as compared with the output obtained when the shirring had to be done together with the sleeve setting, his output being 58 and 44 sleeves per hour, respectively.

TABLE 81.—SLEEVE SETTING (BY SLEEVE SETTERS).

Line No.	Shop No. and operator No.	Sex of operator.	Piecework or week work.	Wages or earnings per week.	Kind of material.	Kind of seam.	Name of machines used.	Kind of sleeves.	Length of seam (inches).	Waists made (dozen).	Sleeves. Total number.	Sleeves. Time worked (minutes).	Sleeves. Number per hour.	Sleeves. Number of jobs.	Size of job (dozen waists).
	Shop No. 1232:														
1	Operator No. 52	F.	Week work.	$11	Voile	Union Special.	Union Special.	Open	18 to 22	$52\frac{1}{2}$	1,260	616	123	18	$2\frac{1}{2}$ to 5
	Shop No. 1284:														
2	Operator No. 54	F.	Piecework	(1)	Voile	Union Special.	Union Special.	Closed	18	$11\frac{1}{2}$	276	186	89	5	2 to 3
3	Operator No. 53	M.	do	(1)	do	do	do	do	17 to 18	$54\frac{1}{8}$	1,300	675	116	22	$\frac{7}{12}$ to $4\frac{1}{2}$
4	Average, 2 persons.	M. and F.	Piecework	(1)	Voile	Union Special.	Union Special.	Closed	17 to 18	$65\frac{5}{8}$	1,576	861	110	27	$\frac{7}{12}$ to $4\frac{1}{2}$
	Shop No. 1191:														
5	Operator No. 51	F.	Week work.	16	Voile	Union Special [2]	Union Special.	Closed	16 to 19	$11\frac{1}{4}$	270	160	101	5	$\frac{2}{3}$ to $3\frac{3}{4}$
6	Do	F.	Week work.	16	Voile	Metropolitan, binding.[2]	Metropolitan	Closed	16 to 19	$3\frac{11}{12}$	94	63	90	2	$1\frac{1}{3}$ to $2\frac{7}{12}$
7	Operator No. 50	M.	do	11	do	do	do	do	16 to 19	$13\frac{1}{2}$	324	335	58	4	$\frac{1}{4}$ to $5\frac{11}{12}$
8	Average, 2 persons.	M. and F.	Week work.	11 to 16	Voile	Metropolitan, binding.	Metropolitan	Closed	16 to 19	$17\frac{5}{12}$	418	398	63	6	$\frac{1}{4}$ to $5\frac{11}{12}$
	SLEEVE SETTING AND SHIRRING AT THE SAME TIME.														
	Shop No. 1191:														
9	Operator No. 50	M.	Week work.	11	Voile	Binding and shirring.	Metropolitan	Closed	16 to 19	$39\frac{1}{6}$	940	1,295	44	12	$\frac{1}{3}$ to $8\frac{5}{12}$
10	Operator No. 51	F.	do	16	do	do	do	do	16 to 19	$46\frac{3}{4}$	1,122	949	71	11	$\frac{1}{2}$ to 10
11	Do	F.	do	16	do	Union Special, shirring.	Union Special.	do	16 to 19	$19\frac{5}{6}$	476	394	72	7	$\frac{1}{2}$ to $10\frac{1}{2}$
12	Average, 2 persons.	M. and F.	Week work.	11 to 16	Voile	Metropolitan; Union Special.	Metropolitan; Union Special.	Closed	16 to 19	$105\frac{3}{4}$	2,538	2,638	58	30	$\frac{1}{3}$ to $10\frac{1}{2}$

[1] Earnings not reported.

[2] Shirring on the sleeves was done previously.

The average output on the two kinds of work for shop No. 1191 was 63 and 58 sleeves per hour, respectively. Either the average for the entire shop or the output of either worker could be used as a basis in determining the rate by taking a different rate per hour as a basis in each case.

BUTTONHOLE MAKING.

There are two types of buttonhole-making machines, one made by the Singer Co. and the other known as the Reece machine. The Reece machine is very rapid, but on account of the inferior appearance of its work is used only on cheap garments. The skill of the buttonhole maker consists not only in operating the machine and in being able to properly space the buttonholes on the garment, but in his ability to do the necessary repairing of the machine, which is subject to frequent breakdowns. Where girls are employed they are not expected to attend to this part of the work, which falls on the machinist employed in the factory. In several shops the buttonhole maker acts also as machinist, attending to the ordinary repairing of all the sewing machines on the premises.

Buttonhole making was timed in six shops. Three of these shops used Singer machines exclusively, two used Reece machines exclusively, and one used both. Only one of the shops making cheap waists used a Singer machine.

The output of a buttonhole maker will vary with (1) the machine, (2) the number of buttonholes to the waist, (3) the size of the buttonhole, (4) the material, and (5) last but not least, with the size of the "bundle," that is, the number of waists the operator gets at a time.

Let us consider briefly how each of these factors will affect the output:

1. As already stated, the Reece machine works more rapidly than the Singer, being, on the average, about twice as fast as its rival. On this point, the figures presented in the tables following can not be regarded as conclusive in view of the fact that the two machines were not tested under exactly similar conditions and with the same operators, so that other factors apart from the relative merits of the two machines affected their respective outputs.

SINGER MACHINE.

The new Singer machines are equipped with an automatic thread clipper which saves the time of cutting off the thread between the buttonholes with scissors. It is claimed, however, by some manufacturers that the clipper effects no saving of time, because the machine equipped with the clipper finishes off the buttonhole with a "bar" on either side of the buttonhole, which, while increasing the durability of the buttonhole, takes up enough more time to do the work to offset whatever saving of time the clipper may cause. Moreover, in the shops investigated, with one exception, the cutting off of the thread is done by the cleaners so that it does not take the time of the buttonhole maker. In the shop in which the cutting off is attended to by the buttonhole maker herself it is done while the machine is making the buttonhole on the next waist, which adds to her labor without taking more of her time. The question of the presence or absence of an automatic clipper on the machine is therefore of no importance in considering its output.

NUMBER OF BUTTONHOLES TO A WAIST.

2. The larger the number of buttonholes to a waist the greater will be the output per hour, all other things being equal. This is due to the fact that the greater the number of buttonholes to a waist the less will be the proportion of time lost by the operator in handling the waists. An illustration will make this clear. If a waist has only one buttonhole, the operator must pick up the waist from the bundle, unfold it, find the place where the buttonhole is to be made, place it under the needle, and as soon as the buttonhole is made he must remove the waist from the machine and put it aside, and then go through the same series of motions to make the next buttonhole. Added to this will be the time lost in bringing and taking away the bundle, untying the bundle before starting the work, and putting the waists together and tying up the bundle when the work is finished. When the waist has 8 buttonholes, the time taken by all the motions described above, outside of the actual making of the buttonhole, is no greater per waist than in the case of the waist having but one buttonhole. Therefore the time lost per buttonhole will be only one-eighth of what it was in the former case.

The figures of output, both on the Singer and the Reece machines, have been arranged in Tables 82A and 82B according to the number of buttonholes to a waist, and the output noted in each case.

TABLE 82A.—BUTTONHOLE MAKING: SINGER MACHINE.

Line No.	Shop number.	Material.	Buttonholes to a waist and size of buttonhole (inch).						Dozen waists.	Total holes.	Time worked (minutes).	Number of holes per hour.	Bundles.	
			Back.		Front.		Cuffs.						Number.	Dozen waists in each.
			No.	Size.	No.	Size.	No.	Size.						
1	No. 1235	Cotton			1	$\frac{1}{2}$			$19\frac{11}{12}$	239	78	184	4 3 5	$\frac{1}{2}$ to $\frac{3}{4}$ $1\frac{1}{4}$ to 2 2 to 3
2	No. 1116	do			1	$\frac{7}{16}$	2	$\frac{7}{16}$	11	396	99	240	1	11
3	No. 1116	Net			1	$\frac{7}{16}$			6	72	25	173	1	6
4	Do	do			1	$\frac{7}{16}$	2	$\frac{7}{16}$	$5\frac{3}{4}$	207	88	141	2	4 and $1\frac{3}{4}$
5	Average, lines 3 and 4	Net			1	$\frac{7}{16}$	2	$\frac{7}{16}$	$11\frac{3}{4}$	279	113	148	3	$1\frac{3}{4}$ to 6
6	No. 1235	Cotton			2	$\frac{1}{2}$			$\frac{3}{4}$	18	11	98	1	$\frac{3}{4}$
7	No. 1116	do			4	$\frac{7}{16}$			$26\frac{1}{3}$	1,264	130	583	2	$12\frac{2}{3}$ and $13\frac{2}{3}$
8	No. 1090	do			4	$\frac{3}{8}$ and $\frac{5}{8}$			$40\frac{7}{12}$	1,948	565	207	11 3 2	$\frac{7}{12}$ to 2 $2\frac{7}{12}$ to $3\frac{5}{6}$ $6\frac{1}{2}$
9	Do	do			4	$\frac{3}{8}$ and $\frac{1}{2}$, $\frac{5}{8}$			$4\frac{11}{12}$	236	90	157	3	1 to $2\frac{7}{12}$
10	Do	do			4	$\frac{1}{2}$	[1] 3	$\frac{1}{2}$	14	1,176	255	277	3 2	2 to $2\frac{1}{3}$ 3 and $4\frac{2}{3}$
11	Do	Crêpe de Chine			4	$\frac{3}{8}$ and $\frac{3}{4}$	12	$\frac{3}{4}$	1	192	98	118	1	1
12	Do	Net			4	$\frac{5}{8}$ and $\frac{3}{4}$			6	288	118	146	3	1, 2, and 3
13	No. 1110	Cotton			5	$\frac{3}{8}$ and $\frac{9}{16}$			$45\frac{1}{4}$	2,715	351	464		Bulk.
14	Do	Heavy lace			5	$\frac{3}{8}$ and $\frac{9}{16}$			$102\frac{1}{6}$	6,130	703	523		Bulk.
15	No. 1116	Cotton	3	$\frac{7}{16}$	5	$\frac{7}{16}$	4	$\frac{7}{16}$	7	1,008	129	469	1	7
16	Do	do	3	$\frac{7}{16}$	5	$\frac{7}{16}$	8	$\frac{7}{16}$	$13\frac{2}{3}$	2,624	227	694	1	$13\frac{2}{3}$
17	Do	do			6	$\frac{7}{16}$			7	504	64	473	2	3 and 4
18	Do	do	3	$\frac{7}{16}$	6	$\frac{7}{16}$	2	$\frac{7}{16}$	$7\frac{7}{12}$	1,001	120	501	1	$7\frac{7}{12}$
19	Do	do			6	$\frac{7}{16}$	4	$\frac{7}{16}$	10	1,200	200	360	1	10
20	Do	do			6	$\frac{7}{16}$	8	$\frac{7}{16}$	10	1,680	160	630	1	10
21	Average, lines 13 to 20							$\frac{7}{16}$	$202\frac{2}{3}$	16,862	1,954	518		
22	No. 1090	Cotton			5	$\frac{3}{8}$ and $\frac{9}{16}$			$2\frac{1}{2}$	150	60	150	2	1 and $1\frac{1}{2}$
23	Do	do			5	$\frac{3}{8}$	2	$\frac{1}{2}$	$29\frac{11}{12}$	2,513	864	175	6 2 2	$\frac{1}{2}$ to 2 3 and $3\frac{2}{3}$ $5\frac{1}{4}$ and 7

[1] Buttonholes were made on neckbands.

TABLE 82A.—BUTTONHOLE MAKING: SINGER MACHINE—Continued.

Line No.	Shop number.	Material.	Buttonholes to a waist and size of buttonhole (inch).						Dozen waists.	Total holes.	Time worked (minutes).	Number of holes per hour.	Bundles.	
			Back.		Front.		Cuffs.							
			No.	Size.	No.	Size.	No.	Size.					Number.	Dozen waists in each.
24	No. 1090	Cotton			6	$\frac{3}{8}$			$2\frac{7}{12}$	186	60	186	2	1 and $1\frac{7}{12}$
25	Do	do			6	$\frac{3}{8}$ and $\frac{3}{4}$	2	$\frac{3}{8}$ and $\frac{3}{4}$	$4\frac{1}{4}$	408	141	174	3	$\frac{11}{12}$ to 2
26	Do	do			6	$\frac{3}{8}$ and $\frac{1}{2}$	2	$\frac{3}{8}$ and $\frac{1}{2}$	18	1,728	466	223	2 2 2	$\frac{2}{3}$ to $1\frac{1}{3}$ 2 6
27	Average, lines 22 to 26	Cotton							$57\frac{1}{4}$	4,985	1,591	188	23	$\frac{1}{2}$ to 7
28	No. 1235	Cotton			5	$\frac{5}{8}$ and $\frac{3}{4}$			$15\frac{1}{6}$	910	181	302	4	$2\frac{1}{2}$, the rest 1 to $1\frac{1}{2}$
29	Do	do			6	$\frac{3}{8}$ and $\frac{5}{8}$			$8\frac{11}{12}$	642	117	329	2 3	$2\frac{1}{2}$ and 3 $\frac{11}{12}$ to $1\frac{1}{2}$
30	Do	Cotton, silk, and crêpe.			6	$\frac{1}{2}$			$43\frac{1}{3}$	3,120	692	270	12 5 2	2 to $3\frac{1}{2}$ Less than $\frac{1}{2}$ $1\frac{1}{2}$
31	Average, lines 28 to 30								$67\frac{5}{12}$	4,672	990	283	28	$\frac{5}{12}$ to $3\frac{1}{2}$
32	No. 1090	Net on chiffon.			5	$\frac{1}{2}$	4	$\frac{1}{2}$	$2\frac{1}{2}$	270	60	270	1	$2\frac{1}{2}$
33	Do	Net			6	$\frac{1}{2}$			$7\frac{1}{6}$	516	134	231	1 3	$\frac{1}{2}$ 2 to $2\frac{3}{4}$
34	Do	do			6	$\frac{3}{8}$ and $\frac{1}{2}$	2	$\frac{3}{8}$ and $\frac{1}{2}$	$4\frac{7}{12}$	440	135	196	2	$1\frac{1}{12}$ and $3\frac{1}{2}$
35	Average, lines 32 to 34								$14\frac{1}{4}$	1,226	329	224	7	$\frac{1}{2}$ to $3\frac{1}{2}$
36	No. 1235	Cotton			7	$\frac{3}{8}$ and $\frac{1}{2}$			$14\frac{1}{4}$	1,197	221	325	3 4	$\frac{3}{4}$ to 2 $2\frac{1}{2}$
37	No. 1090	do			7	$\frac{3}{8}$ and $\frac{3}{4}$			$6\frac{1}{12}$	511	108	284	5	1 to 2
38	No. 1235	Crêpe de Chine and taffeta.			7	$\frac{1}{2}$			$1\frac{5}{12}$	119	36	198	2	$\frac{5}{12}$ and 1
39	Do	Net			7	$\frac{1}{2}$			6	504	107	283	4	$1\frac{1}{2}$
40	No. 1090	Cotton			7	$\frac{3}{8}$ and $\frac{1}{2}$			1	84	25	202	1	1
41	Do	do	7	$\frac{5}{8}$			2	$\frac{5}{8}$	$4\frac{1}{6}$	450	128	211	1	$4\frac{1}{6}$
42	Do	do			7	$\frac{3}{8}$ and $\frac{1}{2}$	4	$\frac{3}{8}$ and $\frac{1}{2}$	$20\frac{5}{6}$	2,750	609	271	7 2	$1\frac{1}{4}$ to $2\frac{1}{2}$ 4
43	No. 1235	Cotton, silk, and crêpe.			8	$\frac{1}{2}$			$\frac{3}{4}$	72	15	288	1	$\frac{3}{4}$
44	No. 1090	Cotton			8	$\frac{3}{8}$ and $\frac{1}{2}$			$9\frac{1}{12}$	872	220	238	4 2	1 to $1\frac{1}{12}$ 2 and 3

45	Do	do	8	3/8 and 1/2			2	3/8 and 1/2	43 2/3	5,240	1,082	291	12 6	2 to 4 1/4 1/2 to 1
46	Do	do			8	3/8	4	3/8	1/2	72	18	240	2	1 5/12 to 1 5/8
47	Do	do			8	5/8	4	1/2	3 1/12	564	105	322	1	1/2
48	Do	do			8	3/4 and 3/8	4	3/4	1	144	45	192	2 1	1 1/12 to 2 5/8 1
49	Average, lines 36 to 48								112 2/3	12,579	2,719	278	60	5/12 to 4 1/4
50	No. 1116	Cotton	7	7/16					33 5/12	2,807	275	612	1 2	1 5/12 10 and 11
51	Do	do			7	7/16	2	7/16	15	1,620	178	546	2	3 and 8
52	Do	do	8	7/16			4	7/16	7 1/8	1,032	105	590	1 1	15 7 1/8
53	Do	do			9	7/16			7 1/8	774	78	595	3	3 1/2
54	Average, lines 50 to 53	Cotton	8	7/16	7 and 9	7/16	2 and 4	7/16	62 3/4	6,233	636	588	10	1 5/12 to 15
55	No. 1090	Net, interlined			7	1/2	4	3/8	6	792	135	352	2	2 and 4
56	Do	Silk	1	1/2	7	5/8	8	5/8	4 1/8	800	146	329	2	1 2/3 and 2 1/2
57	Average, lines 55 and 56.								10 1/8	1,592	281	340	4	1 2/3 to 4
58	No. 1116	Net			7	7/16			15	1,260	169	447	3 1	2 6
59	Do	Silk			7	7/16	4	5/8	10 1/3	1,364	157	521	1 2	3 3 and 7 1/3
60	Average, lines 58 and 59.								25 1/3	2,624	326	483	7	2 to 7 1/3
61	No. 1090	Cotton			9	3/4 and 3/8			5 2/3	612	163	225	4	1/2 to 2 1/8
62	Do	do			11	3/8			4	528	145	218	1	4
63	Do	do			13	3/8			1 1/12	169	38	267	1	1 1/12
64	Do	do			28	3/8			7/12	196	49	240	1	7/12
65	No. 1235	do			9	3/8			5 1/6	558	103	325	4	1 to 1 1/2
66	Average, lines 61 to 65								16 1/2	2,063	498	249	11	1/2 to 4
67	No. 1116	Cotton	9	7/16			2	7/16	6	792	69	689	2	3
68	Do	do	9	7/16			4	7/16	19 3/4	3,081	235	787	2 1	4 and 6 9/12 9
69	Do	do			9	7/16	4	7/16	4 5/12	689	84	492	1	4 5/12
70	Average, lines 67 to 69	Cotton	9	7/16	9	7/16	2	7/16	30 1/6	4,562	388	705	6	3 to 9
71	No. 1116	Net			9	7/16			3 1/2	378	33	687	1	3 1/2
72	No. 1090	Silk			9	3/8			2 1/12	225	70	193	2	1 and 1 1/4
73	Do	do			12	3/8			1 1/2	216	82	158	1	1 1/2
74	Do	do	2	3/8	12	3/8			1 1/12	182	39	280	1	1 1/12
75	No. 1235	Voile and net			10	1/2			4	480	99	291	3	2/3, 1 1/2, and 1 5/6
76	No. 1090	Chiffon on net			10	3/8			6 1/6	740	146	304	2 1	1 4 1/6

TABLE 82A.—BUTTONHOLE MAKING: SINGER MACHINE—Concluded.

Line No.	Shop number.	Material.	Buttonholes to a waist and size of buttonhole (inch).						Dozen waists.	Total holes.	Time worked (minutes).	Number of holes per hour.	Bundles.	
			Back.		Front.		Cuffs.						Number.	Dozen waists in each.
			No.	Size.	No.	Size.	No.	Size.						
77	No. 1990	Net			10	$\frac{3}{8}$	4	$\frac{3}{8}$	$1\frac{3}{4}$	294	72	245	1	$1\frac{3}{4}$
78	Do	do			11	$\frac{3}{8}$	4	$\frac{3}{8}$	$1\frac{2}{3}$	300	65	277	1	$1\frac{2}{3}$
79	No. 1235	do			11	$\frac{3}{8}$ and $\frac{1}{2}$			$3\frac{1}{4}$	429	57	452	7	$\frac{1}{4}$ to 1
80	No. 1090	do			13	$\frac{1}{2}$			5	780	102	459	2	$2\frac{1}{2}$
81	Do	do			11	$\frac{3}{8}$	4	$\frac{3}{8}$	$1\frac{2}{3}$	300	65	277	1	$1\frac{2}{3}$
82	Average, lines 71 to 81								$31\frac{2}{3}$	4,324	830	313	23	$\frac{1}{4}$ to $4\frac{1}{8}$

TABLE 82B.—BUTTONHOLE MAKING: REECE MACHINE.

Line No.	Shop number.	Material.	Buttonholes to a waist and size of buttonhole (inch).						Dozen waists.	Total holes.	Time worked (minutes).	Number of holes per hour.	Bundles.	
			Back.		Front.		Cuffs.						Number.	Dozen waists in each.
			No.	Size.	No.	Size.	No.	Size.						
1	No. 1235	Cotton			1	1/2			5 1/4	63	16	236	3 1	1/2 to 1 1/2 2 1/2
2	Do.	do.			2	1/2			1 1/2	36	9	240	2	1 1/2 and 1
3	Average, lines 1 and 2.	Cotton			1 and 2	1/2			6 3/4	99	25	238	6	1/2 to 2 1/2
4	No. 1235	Cotton			4	1			18	864	160	324	4 6	1/2 to 1 1/2 2 to 2 1/2
5	No. 1230	do.			4	3/4			3 5/8	184	20	552	3	2/3 to 1 11/12
6	Do.	do.			[1] 5	1/2 and 3/4			89 1/2	5,370	493	654	15 9 1	1 to 2 11/12 3 1/4 to 6 3/4 11 2/3
7	No. 1284	do.			5	1/2			4	240	17	847	2	1 1/2 and 2 1/2
8	No. 1235	do.			6	1/2			2 2/3	192	23	501	2	1/2 and 2 1/6
9	No. 1230	do.			6	1/2			12 5/12	894	67	801	4	1 5/8 to 8 7/12
10	No. 1284	do.			6	1/2 and 3/4			61 1/2	4,428	283	939	5 3 2 2	1 to 1 1/2 2 to 4 1/2 6 1/2 to 9 1/2 11 to 20
11	No. 1235	do.			7	1/2 and 5/8			13	1,092	91	720	1 4 1	1/2 2 to 2 1/2 3
12	No. 1230	do.			7	1/2			35 5/12	2,975	227	786	3 4 2	1 1/6 to 2 11/12 3 to 4 1/3 6 1/2 to 7
13	No. 1284	do.			7	1/2			59 1/3	4,984	271	1,103	6 4 2	1 to 3 1/2 5 to 7 1/2 10
14	Do.	do.			8	1/2			7	672	40	1,008	2	5 and 2

[1] A few were backs.

The number of buttonholes is indicated in the table separately for the back, front, and cuffs, but the figures of output have been arranged in the table according to the largest number of buttonholes on any one part of the waist; that is to say, if a waist, as in line 15, table 82A, has 3 buttonholes in the back, 5 in the front, and 4 on the cuffs, making a total of 12 buttonholes, it is not classed with the waists having 12 buttonholes, but with those having 5. The reason for this is that the proportion of time lost in the various motions described above to total time at work will be nearer to the 5-buttonhole waist than to the 12-buttonhole waist. While a little time is saved by having the additional buttonholes on the same waist, the time it takes to turn over the waist when the operator is through with the front, then to find the back and place it in position in the machine, and then when he is through with the back, to find the cuff of one sleeve and place that in position in the machine, then remove the cuff and replace it with the other cuff, is almost, and in some cases just as great as in putting one waist aside and taking up another. The advantage of having a large number of buttonholes accrues only when the buttonholes are all arranged in a row, as is the case when they are all in the front or all on the back of the waist, or on the neckband, etc. In that case the skilled operator works with great speed. As fast as a buttonhole is made he moves the waist by a quick jerk a distance of about 3 or 4 inches, according to the waist, which he automatically determines by the movement of his hand, which becomes accustomed to this manipulation when the operator is working continually on the same kind of work. In a shop where there is a great variety of styles, and the number of buttonholes varies a great deal from style to style the operator is less accustomed to measure the distance mechanically and his speed is affected thereby.

SIZE OF BUTTONHOLES.

3. Other things being equal, the larger the buttonhole the longer it takes to make it and the less, therefore, is the number of buttonholes made in a given time. This is true, however, only when there is a considerable difference in size. For buttonholes of less than 1 inch the difference in the time it takes to make a buttonhole forms so small a proportion of the total time, in which is included the loss in handling the waist, as to make no appreciable difference in the output. It is possible that, if a series of tests had been made on buttonholes of different sizes by the same operator under exactly similar conditions, in so far as they affect the output, that a graded scale of output for buttonholes of various sizes, even less than 1 inch, could be constructed. This was impossible, however, under the conditions surrounding the present investigation, when workers had to be timed on such work as they were found to be doing in each shop.

MATERIAL.

4. The material of which a waist or dress is made is the factor of least importance in the matter of output. A waist made of fine net or lace may prove more difficult to handle, owing to the greater delicacy of the material, and therefore show a smaller output.

SIZE OF THE BUNDLE.

5. The size of the bundle has been found to be by far the most important factor in determining the output of an operator in the shops under investigation. As will be seen from Table 82A, shops Nos. 1116 and 1110 show the largest output. A reference to the last column of the table showing the size of the bundles will disclose the fact almost invariably that these two shops furnish work to their employees in large quantities at a time. In shop No. 1110 there is no such thing as a bundle so far as the buttonhole maker is concerned; there being but one buttonhole maker in the shop, there is no attempt to count the waists, and he is paid each week according to the cutter's slip showing the number of waists cut for the shop. When the waists are ready for the buttonhole maker they are either brought to him or taken by himself in as large heaps as he can carry in his arms. They are all dumped in a basket at his side, and when completed are dumped just as indiscriminately in another basket, which is taken to the examiner's table without being counted or put up in bundles. In this way much of the loss of time caused by the handling of the waists in other shops is eliminated here.

In shop No. 1116, where such a system is impossible, owing to the variety of styles and materials and where waists are put up in bundles on the average of about 2½ dozen each, the individual bundles, as they come from the body makers, are combined into larger bundles, so that the buttonhole maker gets large bundles containing as many as 10 or 12 dozen waists or more; moreover, the buttonhole maker never has to go for his work and is not expected to tie and untie the bundles; all that is attended to by a girl assistant who is employed in the shop by the week to serve the buttonhole maker and button sewer in this way. On the other hand, shop No. 1090, which shows as a rule the smallest output, although equipped with as modern machinery as shop No. 1116, furnishes the work to the buttonhole maker in bundles containing frequently less than a dozen waists, and seldom exceeding 2½ dozen, and the buttonhole maker must untie and tie up each bundle, which necessitates the spreading out of each waist so that it will lie flat in the bundle. The results will be seen from the following figures:

Taking up first waists having 4 buttonholes in the front or back, we find the output on cotton waists in shop No. 1116 to be 583 buttonholes per hour (line 7, Table 82A), while in shop No. 1090 the output is 207 buttonholes per hour (line 8, Table 82A), or considerably less than half. When to the 4 buttonholes on the front are added 3 buttonholes on the neckband, the output in shop No. 1090 is increased to 277 buttonholes (line 10). On the other hand, with buttonholes of more than one size requiring a change of knife, which cuts the hole in the material to the required size, the output in this shop is reduced to 157 buttonholes per hour (line 9). On crêpe de Chine and net, the output is further reduced to 118 and 146 buttonholes per hour, respectively.

The same is true of waists having 5 or 6 buttonholes on the front. The output on 5 and 6 buttonhole waists being about the same, the two have been combined into one average. The average output in shops Nos. 1110 and 1116 is 518 buttonholes per hour (line 21), while in shop No. 1090 it is 188 (line 27), or over one-third the output in the other shop. Of the two former shops the work in one is given out in bulk, as already explained, and in the other the bundles vary from 7 to 14 dozen each, while in shop No. 1090 the bulk of the work was in bundles from ½ dozen to 2 dozen each, and only a few bundles were of a larger size. In shop No. 1235 the output is 283 buttonholes per hour (line 31), this shop showing a greater efficiency in production than in shop No. 1090. It should also be observed that shops Nos. 1090 and 1235 employ women buttonhole makers, while shops Nos. 1116 and 1110 employ men, whose earning capacity is much greater than that of the women. Line 35 shows an average output of 224 buttonholes per hour in shop No. 1090 on waists made of net or net and chiffon. This shows that the output of the buttonholes on cotton waists in the same shop is too low and may have been caused by trouble with the machine, the extremely small size of the bundles, or some other cause, although it should be noted that the average of 188 buttonholes was based on a test lasting a total of 1,591 minutes, or more than 26 hours, while the test on the net and chiffon waists lasted only 329 minutes, or 5½ hours.

The same relation between the respective outputs of the above shops is seen in connection with waists having 7, 8, and more buttonholes to the front. Thus shop No. 1116 shows an output on this class of cotton waists of 588 buttonholes per hour (line 54), while the average output for shops Nos. 1090 and 1235 was 278 buttonholes per hour (line 49), or only about one-half. The output on net and silk waists in shop No. 1090 was 340 buttonholes per hour (line 57), which is again higher than the output on cotton waists for the same shop. On the other hand, the average output on silk waists in shop No. 1116 was 483 buttonholes per hour (line 60), which is nearly one-fifth lower than the output on cotton waists in the same shop.

The output on waists having 9 buttonholes or more to the front does not seem to vary much with the number of buttonholes, and the figures are, therefore, combined without regard to the number of buttonholes. The average output on cotton waists having 9 buttonholes or more in shop No. 1116 is found to be 705 per hour (line 70), while in shops Nos. 1090 and 1235 the average was 249 buttonholes per hour (line 66), or only a little over a third. As usual, the chief point of difference between the two seems to be in the size of the bundles and the sex of the operators. The same relation holds good of waists other than cotton. The output on net waists in shop No. 1116 was 687 buttonholes per hour (line 71), while the average for shops Nos. 1090 and 1235 was 404 buttonholes per hour. It is possible, however, that the figure 687 is too high, having been obtained as the result of a test consisting of only one bundle of 3½ dozen, which was done in 33 minutes. Experience has shown that a test is not conclusive unless it is made on several bundles. On the other hand the average of 404 holes for the two shops, Nos. 1090 and 1235, is more reliable, although consisting of figures some of which are not consistent with each other. Thus the output on silk waists in shop No. 1090 varies from 158 to 280 buttonholes per hour (lines 72 to 74), which is less than half the output on net shown in line 80 in the same shop. It is also less than the output on chiffon and net waists, viz, 304 buttonholes per hour, shown in line 76. Both net and chiffon on net are more difficult to handle on the machine than silk, as they stretch and tear more easily. The difference may have been due to accidental causes, such as the condition of the operator as well as the condition of the machine, but being based as it is on a large number of waists with the work extending over 102 minutes, or over an hour and a half, it is nearer to actual average conditions as they prevail in a shop than the figure for shop No. 1116 in line 71.

REECE MACHINE.

As already explained on page 68, the Reece machine is much faster than the Singer, but the appearance of the buttonholes made on this machine is such that it is used only on cheap garments.

The output on cotton waists having one or two buttonholes was found to differ but little, the average output being 238 buttonholes per hour.

On waists having four buttonholes the output in shop No. 1235 was found to be 324 buttonholes per hour, while in shop No. 1230 it was 552. The larger output in shop No. 1230 is due to a number of reasons: The smaller size of the buttonhole, being only ¾ inch in shop No. 1230 and 1 inch in shop No. 1235; the fact that in shop No. 1235 the operators are required to untie and tie the bundles, which carries with it the necessity of spreading out each waist and putting the waists on top of each other in making up the bundle, while in shop No. 1230 the buttonhole maker is not required to untie or make up bundles, with the consequent saving of time.

The output on waists containing five buttonholes was found to vary from 654 buttonholes per hour in shop No. 1230 to 847 in shop No. 1284. As the work is done in both shops under fairly similar conditions, the difference in output is probably due chiefly to the fact that the buttonhole makers in shop No. 1230 are women, while in shop No. 1284 they are men. Either figure could therefore be taken as a basis for a piece rate by making a proper allowance for an hourly rate for men and women operators.

On six-buttonhole waists the output per hour was 501 buttonholes in shop No. 1235, 801 buttonholes in shop No. 1230, and 939 in shop No. 1284. As usual, shop No. 1284 shows the highest output and shop No. 1235 the lowest. The reasons for the low output in shop No. 1235 have already been explained. The high output of shop No. 1284 is due both to the fact that the buttonhole maker is not required to tie and untie bundles, and the further fact that in shop No. 1284 the work is done by men, while in the other two shops it is done by women.

The same relation between the respective outputs of the three shops holds true with regard to seven-buttonhole waists. Again shop No. 1284 leads the rest with 1,103 buttonholes per hour (line 13), and No. 1235 lags behind with 720 buttonholes (line 11).

The output on eight-buttonhole waists does not seem to differ from that on seven-buttonhole waists, being 1,008 buttonholes per hour in shop No. 1284. This shows that when the number of buttonholes on a waist gets fairly large, a difference of one buttonhole has no appreciable effect on the output.

BUTTON SEWING.

FLAT PEARL BUTTONS.

The button sewing timed in the shops was done on machines exclusively. Button sewing by hand is the work of finishers. As explained in Part I of this report (see page 70), most of the button sewers are women, of whom less than one-fifth work by the piece. In the $9-a-dozen waist shops in which button sewing was timed, the work was done by the week with the exception of shop No. 1110, in which it was done by the piece. Piecework also prevailed in shops Nos. 1235 and 1116, the only medium-priced waist shops reported in Table 83A.

The work of the machine button sewer consists of picking up the waist, inserting in the machine the spot marked with a pencil or otherwise, opposite the buttonhole, placing a button in a special holder, and setting the machine in motion, which automatically sews the button to the waist. The operator then removes the waist, moves it to the point where the next button has to be sewed on, inserts a new button, and repeats the same operations.

As in the case of buttonhole making, the output on button sewing will vary (1) with the skill of the operator; (2) with the number of buttons to the waist; (3) with the kind of button; (4) with the size of the bundle which the operator gets at a time; (5) with the conditions governing the handling of the work; that is to say, whether or not the bundle has to be tied and untied by the operator.

1. As a rule, there is only one button sewer in a shop. This was the case in all the shops in which work was timed with the exception of shop No. 1230, in which two button sewers were found. All the button sewers, except one in shop No. 1110, were women. Although this shop shows a slightly higher output per hour than the other two shops on the same kind of waists, the difference is probably due not so much to the difference in ways as to the fact that in this shop there is no tying and untying of bundles, the material being handled in large bulk, as explained under buttonhole making.

2. The number of buttons to the waist is an important factor for the same reason that the number of buttonholes is. (See page 234.)

3. The kind of button may affect the output materially. A pearl button having two bored holes in it is somewhat more difficult to handle than a crochet button, for the reason that the operator need not pay any attention to the way the crochet button is inserted in the holder of the machine, since, no matter what the position of the button is, the needle will go through it, the button consisting of uniform material, with the exception of the outward metal ring around which the crochet thread is wound. Not so with a pearl button: Unless the button is inserted in the holder of the machine so as to place the hole directly under the needle, the needle will strike the hard surface of the button and break, causing stoppage of work and the necessity of replacing the needle. The operator can not, therefore, insert a pearl button as rapidly as she does a crochet button.

4–5. The size of the bundle and the manner of handling it are of great importance for the same reasons which were explained in connection with buttonhole making.

Table 83A shows the output on pearl buttons and 83B on crochet buttons. The work was timed in 5 shops, of which 3 are $9-a-dozen waist shops and 2 making medium-priced waists. The figures have been arranged according to the number of buttons to a front or back of a waist, similarly to the arrangement of the buttonhole data. Taking first the pearl buttons, we find that for 4-button waists the output in shop No. 1230 is 553 buttons per hour (line 1). This average is based upon the work of 1 button sewer on 792 buttons.

TABLE 83A.—BUTTON SEWING: FLAT PEARL BUTTONS.

Line No.	Shop number.	Number and sex of operators.		Week work or piecework.	Wages or earnings per week.	Buttons per waist.			Waists (dozen).	Total buttons.	Time worked (minutes).	Number of buttons per hour.	Bundles.	
		Male.	Female.			Cuff.	Front.	Back.					Number.	Dozen waists in each.
1	Shop No. 1230		1	Week work	$11.50		4		$16\frac{1}{2}$	792	86	553	2	$7\frac{1}{2}$ to 9
2	Shop No. 1230		2	Week work	10.50 to 12.00		5		$102\frac{5}{12}$	6,145	508	726	26	1 to $10\frac{1}{2}$
3	Shop No. 1284		1	do	9.00		5		$6\frac{2}{3}$	400	32	750	1	$6\frac{2}{3}$
4	Shop No. 1110	1		Piecework	(1)		5		$87\frac{5}{6}$	5,270	410	771	7	$2\frac{11}{12}$ to 37
5	Average, 3 shops, lines 2 to 4.	1	3	Week work and piecework.			5		$196\frac{11}{12}$	11,815	950	746	34	1 to 37
6	Shop No. 1230		2	Week work	10.50 to 12.00		6		$61\frac{1}{4}$	4,410	348	760	13	$\frac{11}{12}$ to $10\frac{1}{2}$
7	Shop No. 1284		1	do	9.00		6		$41\frac{11}{12}$	3,018	207	875	5	3 to 14
8	Average, 2 shops, lines 6 and 7.		3	Week work	9.00 to 12.00		6		$103\frac{1}{6}$	7,428	555	803	18	$\frac{11}{12}$ to 14
9	Shop No. 1235		1	Piecework	(1)		6		$2\frac{1}{2}$	180	21	514	1	$2\frac{1}{2}$
10	Shop No. 1116		1	do	(1)		6		$24\frac{1}{2}$	1,764	178	595	3	7 to 10
11	Average, 2 shops, lines 9 and 10.		2	Piecework	(1)		6		27	1,944	199	586	4	$2\frac{1}{2}$ to 10
12	Shop No. 1235		1	Piecework	(1)		7		10	840	121	417	5	$1\frac{1}{2}$ to $2\frac{1}{2}$
13	Shop No. 1230		2	Week work	10.50 to 12.00		7		$33\frac{11}{12}$	2,849	197	868	12	1 to 6
14	Shop No. 1284		1	do	9.00		7		$58\frac{7}{12}$	4,921	358	825	14	1 to 11
15	Shop No. 1116		1	Piecework	(1)	2 and 4	7		$28\frac{1}{2}$	3,642	325	672	4	1 to 21
16	Shop No. 1284		1	Week work	9.00		8		$46\frac{5}{12}$	4,456	320	836	9	1 to 10
17	Shop No. 1116		1	Piecework	(1)	4		8	[2] 14	1,632	159	616	2	6 to 8
18	Do		1	do	(1)	4		9	[3] $45\frac{5}{8}$	6,438	502	769	5	$1\frac{5}{8}$ to 17
19	Average, shops 1230, 1284 and 1116, lines 13 to 18.		7	Week work and piecework.		2 and 4	7 and 8	8 and 9	$218\frac{1}{4}$	23,938	1,861	772	46	1 to 21

[1] Earnings not reported.

[2] 1 dozen had no buttons on the cuffs.

[3] $14\frac{5}{8}$ dozen had no buttons on the cuffs.

TABLE 83B.—BUTTON SEWING: CROCHET BUTTONS.

Line No.	Shop number.	Number and sex of operators.		Week work or piecework.	Wages or earnings per week.	Buttons per waist.			Waists (dozen).	Total buttons.	Time worked (minutes).	Number of buttons per hour.	Bundles.	
		Male.	Female.			Cuff.	Front.	Back.					Number.	Dozen waists in each.
1	Shop No. 1230		1	Week work	$11.50		3		36 5/6	1,326	101	788	6	3 to 9 2/3
2	Do		1	do	10.50		5		22 7/12	1,355	120	677	5	4 to 5
3	Do		2	do	10.50 to 11.50		6		49 1/2	3,564	278	769	6	2 2/3 to 12
4	Shop No. 1235		1	Piecework	(1)		6		7 1/2	540	55	589	3	2 1/2
5	Do		1	do	(1)			7	10 1/4	861	60	861	6	1/4 to 2 1/2
6	Shop No. 1116		1	do	(1)			9	3 2/3	396	19	1,251	1	3 2/3

[1] Earnings not reported.

On the five-button waists we have the record of work done by 4 operators in 3 shops, 3 of them women and 1 man, who were timed on 11,815 buttons. The output is fairly uniform in the 3 shops, ranging from 726 in shop No. 1230 (line 2) to 771 in shop No. 1110, the average for the 3 shops being 746 buttons per hour. The highest output in shop No. 1110 may be due to two causes: (1) That the operator is a man; (2) that the work is handled in bulk instead of in bundles, as explained in connection with buttonhole making.

For six-button waists we have the record of 4 shops, 2 of them $9-waist shops, and 2 medium-priced waist shops. The output seems to vary according to the character of the shops. Thus, in the two $9-a-dozen waist shops (lines 6 and 7) the output is 760 and 875 buttons per hour, respectively, the average being 803 buttons per hour, while in the two medium-priced waist shops (lines 9 and 10) the output is 514 and 595 buttons per hour, respectively, the average being 586 buttons per hour.

In the case of seven-button waists, we have the record of 4 shops, 3 of them with a fairly uniform output per hour, while the fourth shop, No. 1235, has a low output of 417 buttons per hour (line 12). This low output is explained by the fact that the waist had a loose facing which had to be turned over by the button sewer and creased. The respective outputs per hour in the 3 other shops, ranging from 672 buttons per hour in shop No. 1116 (medium-priced waist shop) to 868 in shop No. 1230 ($9-a-dozen waist shop), have been combined with the data for the 8 and 9 button waists into one average for the reason that the output in those shops does not vary much for the three classes of waists. The average for the three, as will be seen from line 19, is equal to 772 buttons per hour based on a total of 23,938 buttons in the 3 shops.

CROCHET BUTTONS.

The work on crochet buttons was timed in three shops. Of these one, No. 1230, was a $9-a-dozen waist shop, and two, Nos. 1235 and 1116, were medium-priced shops.

The three-button waists were timed in shop No. 1230, showing an output of 788 buttons per hour. Another operator in the same shop showed an output of only 678 buttons per hour on five-button waists. As the size of the jobs was practically the same in each case, as will be seen from the table, the only explanation for the lower output on the waist containing the larger number of buttons lies in the difference in skill of the two operators.

The output on six-button waists was 769 buttons per hour in shop No. 1230 and 589 in shop No. 1235. The higher output was turned out by two operators in a $9-a-dozen waist shop on 3,564 buttons. The lower output was produced by an operator in a medium-priced waist shop on 540 buttons which were sewed on 7½ dozen waists furnished to the operator in three bundles of 2½ dozen each, whereas the size of the bundles in the $9-shop varied from 2⅔ to 12 dozen. The chief reason, however, for the lower output was that the buttons had to be sewed on in two rows of three each for ornamental purposes, for which no marking is done. The operator had to see, therefore, that the buttons were spaced equally and each placed in a straight line with the corresponding buttons in the other row. That this was the chief cause of the smaller output may be seen from the fact that the output on seven-button waists by the same operator (line 5), for which the spacing was marked in the usual manner, was 861 buttons per hour on bundles no larger than in the preceding case.

On nine-button waists the output in another medium-priced waist shop (line 6) was 1,251 buttons per hour. This figure was obtained, however, by timing an operator on a small lot of waists (3⅔ dozen) containing a total of 396 buttons.

BODY MAKING.

The operations included in body making have been described in Part I of this report under "Waist operators" (pp. 93, 94) and also on previous pages of Part II. It will therefore be sufficient for the present to state briefly that body making includes all the operations which are required to make the body of the waist and which are described in greater detail in the following sections. The body makers are among the most skillful operators in the trade, since they make practically the entire garment outside of the few special operations described in the preceding sections.

Most of the headings of the columns in the tables which follow speak for themselves. The column marked "Kind of seam" is subdivided into two columns, marked "First" and "Second," which require an explanation. While most operations are done with one seam, there are some operations which it takes two seams to complete. This is true of the French seam (described under "Closing," p. 226) and of most of the work of joining lace to other material. As each seam is made under different conditions, the second seam usually requiring a great deal less time than the first, the work on each seam was timed separately whenever possible and the data tabulated accordingly.

In timing work in which a seam consisted of two rows of stitching, it was not always possible to time the first and second rows of stitching on the identical waists. An operator might be timed on the first row on an entire bundle and before she took up the work of the second row of stitching she might be started on a new bundle and not have an opportunity to return to the old bundle until the investigator had left the shop, or had been assigned to time a new set of operators. In such case it would be necessary to time the second row of stitching upon a different bundle of waists, consisting perhaps of a larger or a smaller number. For this reason the total number of waists, as well as the total number of rows of stitching timed on the first seam, as shown in Tables 84 to 89, 91, 92B, 93 to 96, 98, and 99, is seldom the same as that on the second row. But in figuring out the time it will take to do the entire operation consisting of the two rows of stitching, it was necessary to take an equal number of waists for each row of stitching, since this is the way the work is actually done, and because otherwise either the first or the second row of stitching would be given an undue weight. The following illustration will show the method of calculation followed:

Kind of seam.		Dozen waists.	Rows of stitching.		Minutes work took.	Rows per hour.
First.	Second.		Per waist.	Total.		
Plain		$4\frac{1}{6}$	2	100	20	300
	Plain	$2\frac{1}{12}$	2	50	5	600

To find the average output per hour on the combined process, reduce the number of rows of stitching in the first seam from 100 to 50, so as to have the same number of rows in the first and second seam. The number of minutes will have to be reduced in the same proportion, so that we will have the following computation:

	Rows.	Minutes.
First seam	50	10
Second seam	50	5
Total	100	15

If it takes 15 minutes, or one-quarter of an hour, to do 100 rows of stitching in the combined operation, the number of rows per hour will be four times as large, or 400.

The following symbols are used in the tables to indicate the different kinds of seams used:

P stands for a plain (ordinary) seam.

F is a French seam. (For explanation of French seam, see p. 226.)

S signifies shirring. (For a description of shirring, see pp. 278, 279.)

PS signifies a shirred seam. It is used in the tables of this report to indicate that the operator had to join a shirred part of a waist to another part.

P+S indicates that the operator had to join two or more parts of a waist while shirring one of them at the same time.

PB means that the seam is made on a bias.

JOINING PARTS OF SHOULDERS WITH LACE BEADING BETWEEN THEM.

This work was timed on two distinct styles of waists, the old-style waist, which was common before 1913, in which the fronts and backs were joined at the shoulder, the seam extending from the neck to the armhole over a length of 5 to 7 inches, and the new-style waist in which the shoulder seam joins the front and back parts of the waist, or of the yoke, extending some distance over the arm, forming the so-called "drop shoulder," the seam being from 11 to 15 inches long.

The work consists of sewing on a narrow strip of lace, known as "lace beading," to the front and back shoulder pieces and then turning back the edge of the material, visible under the lace, on the wrong side and stitching it over so that the raw edge will not protrude under the lace. The work of stitching over the raw edge forms the second seam or "stitch," as it is called in the trade. The work on the first seam naturally takes a longer time to do than on the second, for the reason that on the first seam the operator must handle two pieces of material, the lace beading and the shoulder piece, and must take care that the seam forms a straight line at a uniform distance from the edge of the material. On the second seam she has only the raw edge to stitch over but no joining of separate pieces, and the work can therefore be done much more quickly. In all the three shops both on the short and the long seams, as well as on the French seam, it will be found that the output on the second seam is uniformly higher than on the first. Thus in the first item in Table 84 we find the output on the first seam to be 194 rows of stitching per hour (line 1), while on the second it is 291 or 50 per cent higher than on the first. Similar differences between the output on the first and second seams will be found on comparing line 4 with line 5, lines 7 and 8, 10 and 11, 13 and 14.

Another interesting comparison which Table 84 furnishes is as to the respective productivity of men and women operators. Lines 1 to 3 of the table show the output of 10 men, lines 4 to 6 that of 10 women on the same kind of work in the same shop. The average output of the 10 men on both seams is 233 rows of stitching per hour and of the 10 women 171 rows per hour. That is to say, the men show an output over 36 per cent greater than the women.

The work was timed in two shops: No. 1232, the most efficient of the shops investigated, and No. 1284, which has been found to fall below the average shop on several operations. The short seam was timed in shop No. 1284, while the long seams were found in shop No. 1232. As will be seen from Table 84, the average output per hour was 210 rows of stitching in shop No. 1284 (line 9), and 207 in shop No. 1232 (line 12), the somewhat higher figure in the less efficient shop being due in this case to the much shorter seams which were made in that shop. In determining the stitch rate for these operations on the basis of the figures given here, it would be necessary to take into account the differences in the earning capacities of the operators in the respective shops.

The French seam work was found in shop No. 1230, although this shop manufactures only cheap waists. The work was done by four men and three women, and showed an average output of 162 rows of stitching per hour on the first seam, 243 on the second, and 194 on the complete operation.

TABLE 84.—JOINING PARTS OF SHOULDERS WITH LACE BEADING BETWEEN THEM.

[For explanation of method of computing averages in this table see p. 250.]

Line No.	Shop number.	Number and sex of operators.		Kind of seam.		Length of seam (inches).	Waists (dozen).	Stitching.			
		Male.	Female.	First.	Second.			Rows per waist.	Total rows.	Time worked (minutes).	Rows per hour.
1	Shop No. 1284	10		P.		5 to 7	$91\frac{1}{4}$	2	2,190	676	194
2	Do	10			P.	5 to 7	$92\frac{1}{2}$	2	2,220	458	291
3	Average										233
4	Shop No. 1284		10	P.		5 to 7	$40\frac{5}{6}$	2	980	433	136
5	Do		10		P.	5 to 7	$41\frac{1}{2}$	2	996	258	232
6	Average										171
	Average, shop No. 1284:										
7	First seam	10	10	P.		5 to 7	$132\frac{1}{12}$	2	3,170	1,109	172
8	Second seam	10	10		P.	5 to 7	134	2	3,216	716	269
9	Average										210
10	Shop No. 1232	4	7	P.		11 to 15	110	2	2,640	864	183
11	Do	5	6		P.	11 to 15	110	2	2,640	666	238
12	Average										207
13	Shop No. 1230	4	3	F.		$6\frac{1}{2}$ to 8	$23\frac{1}{2}$	2	564	209	162
14	Do	2	3		F.	7 to 8	$13\frac{1}{2}$	2	324	80	243
15	Average										194

JOINING YOKES TO FRONTS OR BACKS WITH INSERTIONS.

Seam 12 to 15 inches long.

This work was observed in three shops making waists to sell for $9 per dozen, involving the work of 19 men and 21 women, who spent the equivalent of 54 hours and 38 minutes for one person in turning out from 160 to 165 dozen waists.

The character of this work involves the same operations as in sewing on lace beading to shoulders, described in the preceding section, and in joining lace to material, described under lace running. That is to say, a distinction must be made in the first place between the process in which the lace is sewed on top of the cloth and that in which the cloth appears on top of the lace; in the second place, the first row of stitching, which involves the sewing on of the lace, must be distinguished from the second row by which the protruding edge of the cloth is stitched back. As will be seen from Table 85, two shops (Nos. 1284 and 1230) follow the method of sewing the cloth on top, while in one shop (No. 1232) the lace is stitched on top. As a result, the first two shops show a smaller output per hour than the last-mentioned shop. Where the cloth appears on top the rows of stitching per hour vary from 96 to 108 on the first seam, and from 139 to 144 on the second, the average for the two seams in both shops being 116 rows of stitching per hour. For the lace on top process the rows of stitching per hour were 168 on the first seam and 207 on the second, the average for the two seams being 186 per hour.

The last item in the table represents the same work as described above, except that cording is inserted instead of lace beading. This work is much more difficult and takes more time; the cording being quite thick, its movement under the "foot" (the name of the attachment which presses down the material, thereby helping the gears under the material to push it along as fast as it is stitched), is slow; care must also be taken that the seam is put in neatly next to the cord so that the needle neither catches the cord nor makes the seam too far from the cord, which would leave it loose in the cloth. All these conditions combine to greatly reduce the output.

Only 7½ dozen waists with cording were made while the investigation was in progress, and this happened in shop No. 1232 which has the highest output of any shop on most of the work on which comparison can be made between the different shops. These 7½ dozen were made by three different operators, all men, each making 2½ dozen. The average output was 87 rows of stitching per hour. For additional figures on cording, see page 281 relating to sleeve setting.

TABLE 85.—JOINING YOKES TO FRONTS OR BACKS WITH INSERTIONS.

Seam 12 to 15 inches long.

[For explanation of method of computing averages in this table, see p. 250.]

Line No.	Shop number.	Number and sex of operators.		Kind of seam.		Waists (dozen).	Stitching.			
		Male.	Female.	First.	Second.		Rows per waist.	Total rows.	Time worked (minutes).	Rows per hour.
	Cloth on top:									
1	Shop No. 1284	2	9	P.		53⅓	2	1,280	798	96
2	Do	4	12		P.	64 7/12	2	1,550	668	139
3	Average									114
4	Shop No. 1230	2	5	P.		22	2	528	294	108
5	Do	2	8		P.	30⅔	2	736	307	144
6	Average									123
	Average, shops Nos. 1230 and 1284:									
7	First seam	4	14	P.		75⅓	2	1,808	1,092	99
8	Second seam	6	20		P.	95¼	2	2,286	975	141
9	Average									116
	Lace on top:									
10	Shop No. 1232	13	1	P.		84½	2	2,028	723	168
11	Do	13	1		P.	70¼	2	1,686	488	207
12	Average									186
	With cording:									
13	Shop No. 1232	3		P.		7½	2	180	124	87

JOINING YOKE BEADING TO BACKS.

Seam 27 to 30 inches long.

This work was timed in three $9-a-dozen waist shops, involving the work of 10 men and 9 women, with a total output of $49\frac{11}{12}$ to $57\frac{1}{2}$ dozen waists at an expenditure of time equivalent to 15 hours and 17 minutes for one person. The work is in every way similar to that described in the preceding section except that it is done on waists having closed backs which are double the length of the open backs given in the preceding section. As will be seen by comparing the figures in Tables 85 and 86, the output for each shop is materially lower on the full backs as compared with the half backs. Thus, taking first the shops where the cloth is stitched on top of the lace, we find that in shop No. 1284 the average output is 79 rows of stitching per hour on the full backs (see table below), as against 114 on the half backs (see preceding table), a difference of 31 per cent. For shop No. 1230, the respective outputs are 75 and 123 rows per hour, or a difference of 39 per cent. The average output for the two shops is 71 rows of stitching per hour on the first seam, 87 rows on the second, and 78 rows per hour for the combined process as compared with 116 rows of stitching for the half backs, or a difference of 33 per cent. That is to say, in the two shops mentioned the output on full backs was on the average about one-third less per hour than the output on half backs.

For shop No. 1232, in which the lace is stitched on top of the cloth, the output on full backs was 98 per hour as compared with 186 on half backs, or a difference of 47 per cent.

TABLE 86.—JOINING YOKE BEADING TO BACKS.

Plain seam 27 to 30 inches long.

[For explanation of method of computing averages in this table, see page 250.]

Line No.	Shop number.	Number and sex of operators.		Kind of seam.		Length of seam (inches).	Waists (dozen).	Stitching.			
		Male.	Female.	First.	Second.			Rows per waist.	Total rows.	Time worked (minutes).	Rows per hour.
	Cloth on top:										
1	Shop No. 1284		6	P.		27	20	1	240	203	71
2	Do		6		P.	27	25	1	300	201	90
	Average										79
3	Shop No. 1230		2	P.		27 to 30	5	1	60	50	72
4	Do	2	2		P.	27 to 30	5	1	60	46	78
	Average										75
	Total, shops Nos. 1230 and 1284:										
5	First seam	2	8	P.		27 to 30	25	1	300	253	71
6	Second seam		8		P.	27 to 30	30	1	360	247	87
	Average										78
	Lace on top:										
7	Shop No. 1232	8		P.		27 to 31	$32\frac{1}{2}$	1	390	318	74
8	Do	6	1		P.	29 to 31	$19\frac{11}{12}$	1	239	99	146
	Average										98

JOINING YOKES WITH LACE BEADING TO OPEN FRONTS OR BACKS, WITH A SHIRRED SEAM.

Seam 11 to 15 inches long.

This work was timed in only one $9-a-dozen waist shop, involving the work of 11 men and 8 women, with a total output of 46 to 53 dozen waists, at an expenditure of time equivalent to 17 hours and 5 minutes for one person. The work differs from that described in the preceding section in that a shirred seam takes the place of a plain seam. This process is naturally more difficult for the operator. Comparison is possible only for one shop, No. 1232, since only in that shop work was found of a similar character with plain and shirred seams, respectively. The average output for this shop on this kind of work was 143 rows of stitching per hour, as compared with 186 rows of the plain seam (see lines 10 and 11 in Table 85). In other words, the additional work of shirring or handling a shirred seam results in a loss of about 23 per cent in the output of the operator, and work of this kind seems to call for a proportionately greater compensation than in the case of a plain seam.

An examination of Table 87 shows that the operators do their work in different ways. In the column headed "Kind of seam" it will be found that the first seam has been made in two different ways, indicated by the symbols "PS" and "P+S," respectively. The former indicates that the shirring was done before the joining in a separate operation; the latter, that the joining and the shirring were done together in the same operation. A comparison of lines 1 and 4 of Table 87 shows an output of 116 rows of stitching per hour by the first method and 111 by the second, or a difference of 4 per cent in favor of the former method. But this does not take account of the time taken to do the shirring as a separate operation, which does not appear in the table. The fact should be noted that when the separate operation of shirring is saved, the handling of the work becomes much more difficult for the operator, so that what is saved by eliminating one operation is largely or entirely offset through the loss of time in handling the combined operation in one process.[1] Moreover, as it is left to the discretion of the operator to do the work either by the one or by the other method, there is no occasion for different rates for the two methods.

[1] It will be noted that there is no difference in the time it takes to do the second seam under either process, since the second seam is identical in both cases, consisting of stitching over a shirred seam. For this reason no attempt was made to separate the work on the second seam under the two processes, and lines 2 and 5 represent the same work.

TABLE 87.—JOINING YOKES WITH LACE BEADING TO OPEN FRONTS OR BACKS WITH SHIRRED SEAM.

Seam 11 to 15 inches long.

[For explanation of method of computing averages in this table see page 250.]

Line No.	Shop number.	Number and sex of operators.		Kind of seam.		Length of seam (inches).	Waists (dozen).	Stitching.			
		Male.	Female.	First.	Second.			Rows per waist.	Total rows.	Time worked (minutes).	Rows per hour.
	Joining yoke to a shirred front or back:										
1	Shop No. 1232	7	8	PS.		11 to 15	$42\frac{5}{12}$	2	1,018	528	116
2	Do	11	8		PS.	11 to 15	$46\frac{1}{12}$	2	1,106	352	189
3	Average										143
	Joining yoke to front or back and shirring at the same time:										
4	Shop No. 1232	6		P+S.		11 to 15	$11\frac{1}{8}$	2	268	145	111
5	Do	11	8		P+S.	11 to 15	$46\frac{1}{12}$	2	1,106	352	189
6	Average										140
7	Average for both operations										143

JOINING YOKE SLEEVES TO FRONTS OR BACKS WITH BEADING BETWEEN.

This work was timed in three $9-a-dozen waist shops, involving the work of 17 men and 40 women, with a total output of 508 dozen waists at an expenditure of time equivalent to 163 hours for one person. As in the case of the operations described above, the average output per hour in the shops using the "cloth on top" method of sewing on the lace beading is below that in the shop using the "lace on top" method, the two being 143 and 184 rows of stitching, respectively.

Lines 9 to 12 of Table 88 represent the same work as described above, except that the operator has to shirr the front or back in the same operation. This makes the work more difficult and consequently slower. As will be seen from lines 9 and 10 of Table 88, the output for shop No. 1230 in this case is 104 rows of stitching per hour as compared with 144 rows of stitching without the shirring, or a reduction of output equal to about 28 per cent. The average for shop No. 1232 (lines 11 and 12 of the table) is 138 rows of stitching per hour as compared with 184 without the shirring, or a reduction of output equal to 25 per cent.

TABLE 88.—JOINING YOKE SLEEVES TO FRONTS OR BACKS WITH LACE BEADING BETWEEN.

Plain seam 11 to 16 inches long.

[For explanation of method of computing averages in this table see page 250.]

Line No.	Shop number.	Number and sex of operators.		Kind of seam.		Stitches per inch.	Waists (dozen).	Stitching.			
		Male.	Female.	First.	Second.			Rows per waist.	Total rows.	Time worked (minutes).	Rows per hour.
	Cloth on top:										
1	Shop No. 1284	6	13	P.			113½	2	2,724	1,305	125
2	Do	6	10		P.		97½	2	2,340	861	163
	Average										142
3	Shop No. 1230	8	23	P.		8 to 10	345⅙	2	8,284	3,953	126
4	Do	8	23		P.	8 to 10	337 5/12	2	8,098	2,883	169
	Average										144
	Average, shops Nos. 1284 and 1230:										
5	First seam	14	36	P.			458⅔	2	11,008	5,258	126
6	Second seam	14	33		P.		434 11/12	2	10,438	3,744	167
	Average										143
	Lace on top:										
7	Shop No. 1232	3	4	P.			50	2	1,200	471	153
8	Do	3	4		P.		51¼	2	1,230	319	231
	Average										184
	Shirring fronts or backs at the same time.										
	Cloth on top:										
9	Shop No. 1230	4	12	P+S.			37 1/12	2	890	636	84
10	Do	4	9		P+S.		32¾	2	786	347	136
	Average										104
	Lace on top:										
11	Shop No. 1232	2		P+S.			7½	2	180	105	103
12	Do	2			P+S.		7½	2	180	52	208
	Average										138

JOINING PARTS OF BACK WITH FRENCH SEAM, FORMING TUCK AT THE SAME TIME.

This work does not frequently occur and was found in only one shop, No. 1230, in which 6 men and 9 women operators were timed on nearly 57 dozen waists, working for a period equivalent to 1,126 minutes, or more than 18 hours for one person. In this style of waist, buttoning in the front, the back was cut in three parts, the central part consisting of a strip 3 inches wide which was joined to each of the other two parts with a French seam, in which the second seam was finished on the right side instead of the wrong side, as is usually done, and thus formed a tuck. The output on this work on the first seam, in which 6 men and 9 women were engaged, was 100 rows of stitching per hour. On the second seam the output of 3 men was 148 rows of stitching per hour, and of 5 women, 114 rows, the average for the men and women on the second seam being 127 rows of stitching per hour. The output for the two seams was 112 rows of stitching per hour.

TABLE 89.—JOINING PARTS OF BACK WITH A FRENCH SEAM, FORMING A TUCK AT THE SAME TIME.

Line No.	Shop number.	Number and sex of operators.		Kind of seam.		Length of seam (inches).	Waists (dozen).	Stitching.			
		Male.	Female.	First.	Second.			Rows per waist.	Total rows.	Time worked (minutes).	Rows per hour.
1	Shop No. 1230	6	9	P.		16 to 17	[1]56 11/12	2	1,366	816	100
2	Do	3			P.	16 to 17	12 5/12	2	298	121	148
3	Do		5		P.	16 to 17	15	2	360	189	114
4	Average, lines 2 and 3										127
5	Average, lines 1 and 4, 1st and 2d seams										112

[1] 29½ dozen did not have the second stitch.

JOINING SIDE PIECES TO FRONTS.

This work consists of sewing side pieces or gores to fronts below the waist line. The pieces are short, ranging from 3 to 9 inches in length, most of them being between 3 and 5 inches. The work was done by 26 men and 26 women in three shops on nearly 236 dozen waists at an expenditure of time equivalent to over 22 hours for one person. The output ranged from 191 rows of stitching per hour in shop No. 1284 to 310 in shop No. 1232, the average being 250 rows of stitching per hour.

TABLE 90.—JOINING SIDE PIECES (GORES) TO FRONTS.

[No hemming attachment used.]

Line No.	Shop number.	Number and sex of operators.		Kind of seam.		Length of seam (inches).	Waists (dozen).	Stitching.			
		Male.	Female.	First.	Second.			Rows per waist.	Total rows.	Time worked (minutes).	Rows per hour.
1	Shop No. 1284		4	P.		3 to 4	12½	2	300	94	191
2	Do	3		P.		3 to 5	6½	2	156	41	228
3	Shop No. 1232	15	8	P.		5 to 9	117 11/12	2	2,830	547	310
4	Shop No. 1230	8		P.		5 to 8	48½	2	1,164	318	220
5	Do		14	P.		5 to 8	50⅓	2	1,208	358	202
6	Average, 3 shops										250

JOINING LACE TO STANDING COLLARS.

This work was timed in three shops, taking in the work of 13 men and 8 women on 118 dozen waists in a period of time equivalent to 1,065 minutes, or more than 17 hours for one person. The work consists of joining the lace to a collar of voile or lawn, or lace, the lace in each case appearing on top of the other material, and stitching back the raw edge of the material on the second seam. The results are found to be fairly uniform in all shops, ranging from 132 rows of stitching in shop No. 1284 to 182 in shop No. 1232, the average for the three shops on both seams being 161 rows of stitching per hour. On collars made of lace, which were found only in shop No. 1284, the output was 119 rows of stitching per hour for 5 men and 101 rows of stitching for 4 women. It being more difficult to join lace and lace than to join lace and cotton material, it is natural that the output on the former should be less than on the latter.

Line 19 shows the output when the lace is joined to the collar in one seam instead of by the two-seam process described above, the raw edge of the material being turned in while the lace is stitched to it. The output of one man and two women, working on 25 dozen waists for a period equivalent to 139 minutes, or practically 2⅓ hours for one person, was 129 rows of stitching and 129 "bendings"[1] per hour. Figuring 2 bendings as equivalent to 1 row of stitching, as is the custom among some manufacturers, this would be equivalent to 194 rows of stitching per hour, or 11 rows of stitching more than the output in the same shop by the two-seam process.

Lines 20 and 21 show the output on facing collars with a finished binding. The binding is attached only at the two extreme ends of the collar, being 3 to 4 inches long. The work is done in two operations, the binding being first stitched to the edge of the collar on the right side and then turned over and stitched to the collar on the wrong side, which makes it look like a facing on the collar corresponding to the facing on the back. Five men and three women were timed in shop No. 1232 on 57½ dozen waists, working for a period equivalent to 218 minutes, or more than 3½ hours for one person. The average output of the 8 operators was 613 rows of stitching on the first seam, 867 rows on the second, and 720 rows of stitching per hour on the combined operation.

---

[1] Whenever the material is turned in as described above, a fold is formed which is known in the trade as a "bending."

TABLE 91.—JOINING LACE TO STANDING COLLARS.

[For explanation of method of computing averages in this table see p. 250.]

Line No.	Shop number.	Number and sex of operators.		Kind of seam.		Length of seam (inches).	Waists (dozen).	Stitching.				Bendings.		
		M.	F.	1st.	2d.			Rows per waist.	Total rows.	Time worked (minutes).	Rows per hour.	Per waist.	Total.	Per hour.
	Collars made of cotton material:													
1	Shop No. 1232	6	...	P.	....	14 to 18	65	1	780	277	169	......	....	......
2	Do	6	...	....	P.	14 to 18	32½	1	390	118	198	......	....	......
3	Average	...	...	....	....	....	....	......	......	......	182	......	....	......
4	Shop No. 1230	...	1	P.	....	17	4	1	48	18	160	......	....	......
5	Do	1	2	....	P.	15 to 17	3$\frac{11}{12}$	1	47	20	141	......	....	......
6	Average	...	...	....	....	....	....	......	......	......	148	......	....	......
7	Shop No. 1284	2	...	P.	....	14 to 15½	13½	1	162	61	159	......	....	......
8	Do	...	2	....	P.	14 to 15½	17½	1	210	111	114	......	....	......
9	Average	...	...	....	....	....	....	......	......	......	132	......	....	......
	Average, 3 shops:													
10	First seam	8	1	P.	....	14 to 18	82½	1	990	356	167	......	....	......
11	Second seam	7	4	....	P.	14 to 18	53$\frac{11}{12}$	1	647	249	156	......	....	......
12	Average	...	...	....	....	....	....	......	......	......	161	......	....	......
	Collars made of lace:													
13	Shop No. 1284	5	...	P.	....	15 to 16½	26	1	312	182	103	......	....	......
14	Do	5	...	....	P.	15 to 16½	26	1	312	132	142	......	....	......
15	Average	...	...	....	....	....	....	......	......	......	119	......	....	......
16	Shop No. 1284	...	4	P.	....	15 to 16½	9½	1	114	73	94	......	....	......
17	Do	...	4	....	P.	15 to 16½	11	1	132	73	108	......	....	......
18	Average	...	...	....	....	....	....	......	......	......	101	......	....	......
19	Shop No. 1232	1	2	P.	....	14 to 15	25	1	300	139	[1] 129	1	300	129
	Facing collars with a finished binding:													
20	Shop No. 1232	5	3	P.	....	3 to 4	57½	2	1,380	135	613	......	....	......
21	Do	5	3	....	P.	3 to 4	50	2	1,200	83	867	......	....	......
22	Average	...	...	....	....	....	....	......	......	......	720	......	....	......

[1] Collars made of voile.

JOINING "LITTLE SKIRTS" TO WAISTS.

Practically all medium and high priced waists are cut in such a manner as to end at the waist line, an additional piece called "skirt" or "little skirt" being joined to the waist so as to form its continuation below the waist line. Most of the $9-a-dozen waists are cut full length, so as to save the labor of joining the little skirt to the waist. Sometimes little skirts are used in these waists. This happens either when embroidered fronts are used and it is desired to save the embroidery below the waist line, where it is not seen at all or where the nature of the pattern makes it advisable to cut the waist in this manner so as to utilize the material to better advantage.

Table 92A gives the record of various operations in connection with the joining of little skirts to waists.

JOINING LITTLE SKIRTS TO OPEN FRONTS AND SHIRRING AT THE SAME TIME.

Lines 1 to 5 show the output on the operation of joining little skirts to open fronts and shirring at the same time. The work consists of two operations: In the first, the little skirt and the front are put right side to one another and joined along the raw edge. In the second operation the raw edge is stitched back. This work was timed in two $9-a-dozen waist shops covering the work of 9 men and 4 women on nearly 48 dozen waists, involving an expenditure of time equivalent to 544 minutes, or over 9 hours, for one person.

Lines 1 and 2 show the output on the first seam in two different shops, the figures being 132 and 108 rows of stitching per hour, respectively, the average for the two shops being 126 (line 3).

Line 4 shows the output on the second seam, which is always much greater than on the first, to be 319 rows of stitching per hour. This makes the output on the combined operation, taking the first and second seams, 187 rows of stitching per hour, as shown in line 5.

JOINING TO OPEN FRONTS WITHOUT SHIRRING.

In this case the shirring or tacking of the waist was done after the little skirts were joined to the fronts. This accounts for the length of the seam of the open front at the waist line being as much as 14 inches. The work was timed in shop No. 1232, which has the record of the highest output of all the shops investigated, and represents the work of 3 men and 3 women on 15 dozen waists for a period of time equivalent to 99 minutes for 1 person. The operation consisted of sewing the front and skirt together, as explained above, except that there was no shirring, and the output was 218 rows of stitching per hour as compared with 132 in the same shop on the same kind of fronts when shirring had to be done at the same time. In other words, the addition of shirring resulted in this case in nearly 40 per cent reduction of output.

JOINING TO CLOSED FRONTS WITHOUT SHIRRING.

Four men and three women were timed on this work in the same shop on nearly 50 dozen waists, which took the equivalent of 344 minutes, or nearly 6 hours, for 1 person. The work was exactly the same as that recorded in the preceding operation, and the output is nearly half, namely, 104 rows of stitching per hour, which is explained by the fact that the length of the seam was more than double that in the preceding case, since the work was done on a closed front.

JOINING TO CLOSED BACKS AND SHIRRING AT THE SAME TIME.

The shirring on a closed back is very slight and therefore does not reduce the output of the operator very much. The work was timed in shop No. 1232 only, but was done in two different ways. On the 7½ dozen reported in line 8 of Table 92A the raw edge of the little skirt was turned in before it was joined to the waist, and the output was 90 rows of stitching and 90 bendings per hour. On the 27½ dozen waists recorded in line 9, the raw edge was not turned in, and the output was 137 rows of stitching per hour. If a bending be considered equivalent to half a row of stitching, as is customary with some manufacturers, the output in the two cases will be practically the same.

JOINING TO VESTS, NO SHIRRING.

This work, given in line 10, is similar to the joining of the skirts to fronts, given in line 6, the only difference being the length of the seam which was only from 1½ to 4 inches in this case as compared with 12 to 14 inches in the former case. The output was 200 rows of stitching per hour as against 218 rows of stitching on the 14-inch seam. The reason for the smaller output is the fact that the side edge of the little skirt was hemmed before being joined to the vests, and in joining the two the operator had to be careful to have the facing of the vest and the turned-in edge of the little skirt form one straight line. To what extent this reduced the output of the operator will be seen from the operation recorded in lines 11 to 13, the description of which follows:

JOINING TO EMBROIDERED CENTERS.

In this case the part of the little skirt attached to the embroidered center, forming a seam of practically the same length as in the preceding case, has no turned-in edge, and therefore it does not matter whether the raw edge of the center and of the little skirt coincide exactly, since both of them will be faced later. The result is a much larger output, namely, 294 rows of stitching per hour in shop No. 1232 and 269 in shop No. 1230, making an average of 282 rows of stitching per hour for the two shops.

Line 14 represents the same work except that the upper edge of the little skirt, before being attached to the center, is turned in, there being thus one bending to each row of stitching. The total output is 182 rows of stitching and 182 bendings per hour.

JOINING TO OPEN FRONTS WITH TWO SEAMS AND TWO BENDINGS TO EACH FRONT.

In this case the fronts are cut in such a manner as to leave a corner into which the little skirts fit, so that instead of being joined to the front along the waist line only, as is usually the case, they are joined along two sides: First along part of the waist line, a distance of 6 inches, and then along a line forming an angle with the waist line and running below it a distance of 4 inches. In this manner two seams and two bendings are formed on each front, making a total of 4 seams and 4 bendings to the waist. This work was done in shop No. 1230 by 1 man and 4 women on 15 dozen waists, working for a period equivalent to 231 minutes, or nearly 4 hours for one person, and showed an output of 187 rows of stitching and 187 bendings per hour.

JOINING LITTLE SKIRTS TO BACKS OR FRONTS OF WAIST, SHIRRING AT THE SAME TIME AND SEWING ON TAPE.

In the operations described in Table 92A no tape is used to cover up the raw edges of the little skirt and the waist on the wrong side. On higher-grade waists it is customary to cover up the raw edges with tape. This was also found to be the case with some of the cheaper waists in the shops investigated. The output per hour on this class of work is given in Table 92B.

Lines 1 to 3 show the output when little skirts are joined to closed fronts, the front being shirred at the same time, and the tape being sewed on to the little skirt, all in one operation. That is to say, the operator must handle at the same time the following parts: The front, the little skirt, and the tape; and while she joins the three together she must shirr the front at the same time. In the second operation the tape is stitched over the shirred front so as to cover up the raw edge. The second operation being much simpler than the first, the output is greater, as will be seen from lines 1 and 2, namely, 84 rows of stitching as compared with 50 on the first seam, the average for the two being 63 rows of stitching per hour.

Lines 4 to 6 relate to the same class of work, except that the work is done in 3 operations instead of 2, as follows:

First operation, shirring the front and joining the little skirt to the front at the same time.

Second operation, sewing on tape to the little skirt.

Third operation, stitching tape over the raw edge of the shirred front.

The second and third operations were timed together, and show an output of 130 rows of stitching as against 60 on the first operation, or an average of 82 for the combined output as compared with only 63 when the whole work was done in two operations.

Lines 7 to 9 relate to similar work except that the little skirt is joined to closed backs instead of closed fronts. As the backs are not shirred as much as the fronts, the work does not take so much time. As will be seen from lines 7 to 9, the output on the first seam was 83 rows of stitching per hour, on the second 207, the average being 119 rows of stitching per hour.

Lines 10 to 12 relate to similar work, except that instead of one closed front we have two open fronts, with the result that the seam measures only from 9½ to 11 inches as against 18 to 21 inches on a closed front, and the output was 90 rows of stitching per hour on the first seam, 193 on the second, the combined output being 122 rows of stitching per hour.

All of this work was timed in only one shop, No. 1284.

TABLE 92A.—JOINING LITTLE SKIRTS TO WAIST.

[For explanation of method of computing averages in this table see p. 250.]

Line No.	Shop number.	Number and sex of operators.		Kind of seam.		Length of seam (inches).	Waists (dozen).	Stitching.				Bendings.		
		M.	F.	1st.	2d.			Rows per waist.	Total rows.	Time worked (minutes).	Rows per hour.	Per waist.	Total.	Per hour.
	Joining little skirts to open fronts, shirring at the same time:													
1	Shop No. 1232	7	2	P+S		8 to $13\frac{1}{2}$	$37\frac{1}{2}$	2	900	409	132			
2	Shop No. 1230	2	2	P+S		10 to 15	$10\frac{1}{12}$	2	242	135	108			
3	Average										126			
4	Shop No. 1232	6	2		PS	8 to $13\frac{1}{2}$	25	2	600	113	319			
5	Average, lines 1 and 4										187			
	Joining to open fronts, no shirring:													
6	Shop No. 1232	3	3	P		12 to 14	15	2	360	99	218			
	Joining to closed fronts, no shirring:													
7	Shop No. 1232	4	3	P		26 to 30	$49\frac{5}{8}$	1	598	344	104			
	Joining closed backs, shirring at the same time:													
8	Shop No. 1232	2	1	P+S		15 to 16	$7\frac{1}{2}$	1	90	60	90	1	90	90
9	Do	4	1	P+S		15 to 18	$27\frac{1}{2}$	1	330	145	137			
	Joining to vests, no shirring:													
10	Shop No. 1232	4	2	P		$1\frac{1}{2}$ to 4	15	2	360	108	200			
	Joining to embroidered centers:													
11	Shop No. 1232		4	P		4	20	2	480	98	294			
12	Shop No. 1230	2	4	P		3 to 6	$15\frac{1}{2}$	2	372	83	269			
13	Average										282			
14	Shop No. 1230	5	2	P		3 to 6	$19\frac{1}{4}$	2	462	152	182	2	462	182
	Joining to open fronts, with two seams and two bendings to each front:													
15	Shop No. 1230	1	4	P		6	15	4	720	231	187	4	720	187

TABLE 92B.—JOINING LITTLE SKIRTS TO BACKS OR FRONTS OF WAIST, SHIRRING AND SEWING ON TAPE AT THE SAME TIME.

[For explanation of method of computing averages in this table, see p. 250.]

Line No.	Shop number.	Number and sex of operators.		Kind of seam.		Length of seam (inches).	Waists (dozen).	Stitching.			
		Male.	Female.	First.	Second.			Rows per waist.	Total rows.	Time worked (minutes).	Rows per hour.
	Joining to closed fronts, shirring, and sewing on tape:										
1	Shop No. 1284	3	5	P+S		18 to 21	$36\frac{1}{2}$	1	438	526	50
2	Do	3	5		PS	18 to 21	$36\frac{1}{2}$	1	438	313	84
3	Average										63
4	Shop No. 1284	2		P+S		19	17	1	204	205	60
5	Do	1	1		{PS P}	19	$16\frac{7}{12}$	2	398	183	130
6	Average										82

TABLE 92B.—JOINING LITTLE SKIRTS TO BACKS OR FRONTS OF WAIST, SHIRRING AND SEWING ON TAPE AT THE SAME TIME—Concluded.

Line No.	Shop number.	Number and sex of operators.		Kind of seam.		Length of seam (inches).	Waists (dozen).	Stitching.			
		Male.	Female.	First.	Second.			Rows per waist.	Total rows.	Time worked (minutes).	Rows per hour.
	Joining to closed backs, shirring, and sewing on tape:										
7	Shop No. 1284	3	7	P+S	......	[1]13 to 15½	36½	1	438	316	83
8	Do	3	9	......	PS	13 to 15½	42½	1	510	148	207
9	Average										119
	Joining to open fronts, shirring, and sewing on tape:										
10	Shop No. 1284	3	7	P+S	......	9½ to 11	44¾	2	1,074	720	90
11	Do	4	7	......	PS	....	48¼	2	1,158	360	193
12	Average										122

[1] One case of 17 inches.

HEMMING EDGES OF LITTLE SKIRTS AND JOINING PARTS OF LITTLE SKIRTS.

The work of joining two parts of a little skirt together is very simple, the two being put right side to one another and joined, either leaving the edges raw, or turning in the raw edges like a hem.

Lines 1 to 3 (Table 92C) show the output on the simpler process, that is, when the edges are left raw. This work was done in shop No. 1232, known for its high output, which in this case was 450 rows of stitching per hour, the work being done by 5 men and 3 women on 50 dozen waists.

Lines 4 to 6 show the output when the raw edges are turned in before being stitched together. This work was done in shop No. 1284, and shows an average output of 212 rows of stitching per hour and an equal number of bendings per hour. Assuming 2 bendings to be equal to 1 row of stitching, the output does not vary much from that of shop No. 1232, given in line 30.

Line 7 shows the output when a French seam is used in joining the two pieces together. This method is used very seldom on cheap waists, and was timed in shop No. 1230 on about 6½ dozen waists, representing the work of 1 man and 2 women, and showed an output of 220 rows of stitching per hour, which, as should be expected, is much below that shown by the other operations.

Lines 8 to 11 show the output when the edges of little skirts are turned in so as to form a hem, the work being done on a Singer machine without any hemming attachment. The output of the three shops will be seen to vary from 213 rows of stitching per hour in shop No. 1230 to 320 in shop No. 1232, the average for the three shops being 252 rows of stitching per hour.

JOINING LITTLE SKIRTS TO WAISTS BY A CLOSER.

Although the work of joining little skirts to waists is usually done by body makers, as has been shown in this section, occasionally it can be done by a closer, as was the case in shop No. 1230, shown in line 12 of the table. The work of joining in this case is somewhat similar to closing sides, being done on a Union Special machine, but the seam is much longer, being 24 to 34 inches long, and the work takes more time than ordinary closing, because the waist has to be shirred while the work of joining takes place. This requires greater care in adjusting the folds so as to make the length of the skirt and the shirred waist exactly alike.

As will be seen from line 12 of Table 92C, the output was 48 rows of stitching per hour in shop No. 1230, the work being done by a male operator of average speed. This figure could not be taken, however, as a basis for a rate to body makers doing the same work on a Singer machine.

TABLE 92C.—HEMMING EDGES OF LITTLE SKIRTS AND JOINING PARTS OF LITTLE SKIRTS TOGETHER.

Line No.	Shop number.	Number and sex of operators.		Kind of seam.		Length of seam (inches).	Waists (dozen).	Stitching.				Bendings.		
		M.	F.	1st.	2d.			Rows per waist.	Total rows.	Time worked (minutes).	Rows per hour.	Per waist.	Total.	Per hour.
	Joining little skirts together in front of waist:													
1	Shop No. 1232	5	...	P.	...	[1] 4 to 5	32½	1	390	57	411	......	...	......
2	Do	...	3	P.	...	....	17½	1	210	23	548	......	...	......
3	Average	...	...	.....	...	....	......	......	......	......	450	......	...	......
4	Shop No. 1284	5	...	P.	...	4	39½	1	474	111	256	1	474	256
5	Do	...	7	P.	...	3½ to 4	36½	1	438	147	179	1	438	179
6	Average	...	...	.....	...	....	......	......	......	......	212	......	...	212
7	Shop No. 1230	1	2	F.	F.	5	6 5/12	2	154	42	220	......	...	......
	Hemming edges of little skirt, two skirts to the waist:													
8	Shop No. 1232	5	8	P.	...	5	50	2	1,200	225	320	......	...	......
9	Shop No. 1230	3	12	P.	...	4½ to 6	54⅛	2	1,300	366	213	......	...	......
10	Shop No. 1284	2	1	P.	...	4 to 5	19	2	456	114	240	......	...	......
11	Average	...	...	.....	...	....	......	......	......	......	252	......	...	......
	Joining little skirts to waists by a closer, shirring at the same time.[2]													
12	Shop No. 1230	1	...	P+S	...	24 to 34	27	1	324	409	48	......	...	......

[1] One case of 4.

[2] Union Special machine used.

CENTERS.

The extreme ends of the backs or fronts of waists are lined with material to give them extra strength to hold the buttonholes and buttons, and are therefore known as buttonhole pieces and button pieces, respectively.

As a rule, the lining consists of a separate piece of material. Sometimes it is formed by turning in the end of the back or front about three-quarters of an inch, so as to give it double thickness. On light materials, such as lawn, chiffon, etc., the strip is made usually of triple thickness by adding a separate strip to the above. The piece of double or triple thickness thus formed is known as a facing, in addition to being also called a buttonhole piece or button piece, according to the use to which it is put. When the separate strip is stitched over the front on the outside instead of being stitched on the inside as a lining, the piece of double or triple thickness thus formed is called a "center." A center may, therefore, be defined as a narrow strip of cloth running longitudinally in the center of the front. Facings are made both in the front and back of waists. Centers are made only in front. The line is not always clearly drawn between facings and centers in the trade, and frequently all kinds of button and buttonhole pieces are referred to as centers. In some cases by centers are also meant embroidered or lace-trimmed strips of cloth attached to or inserted in the front of the waist to secure an ornamental effect, as well as to save material in laying out the patterns on the cloth; such centers may consist of one or more thicknesses of material.

A great variety of work is connected with centers, some of which was timed in the various shops as recorded in the tables following.

JOINING CENTERS TO LACE OR LACE BEADING ATTACHED TO FRONTS.

This work was timed in three shops on 60 dozen waists made by 7 men and 11 women working what would be equivalent to 1,762 minutes, or more than 29 hours for one person.

The work consists of sewing on the lace to the centers or fronts by means of two seams, as explained in sections 8 and 9.

As will be seen from lines 1 to 9 of Table 93, the output on the work of joining centers to lace beading was fairly uniform in the two shops in which the work was timed. The output on the first seam was 101 rows of stitching per hour in shop No. 1232, and 94 in shop No. 1230. The output on the second seam was 189 rows of stitching per hour in the former shop, and 153 in the latter. The combined output on the two seams was 132 rows of stitching per hour in shop No. 1232, and 116 in shop No. 1230, the average for the two shops being 122 rows of stitching per hour. In the work just described, the center was joined to the lace beading after the beading had been joined to the front, the beading being stitched on top of the cloth.

Lines 10 to 12 relate to similar work, except that instead of being joined to a lace beading, the center is joined to lace. This work is more difficult for the reason that a lace beading has a fairly heavy selvage which makes it easy to sew it on to the cloth, requiring no particular care on the part of the operator, as the seam remains practically invisible on the selvage. This is not the case with lace, in which the selvage frequently consists of only 1, 2, or 3 threads. In stitching the lace to the cloth the operator must be careful to have the seam run along this narrow selvage, which results in slowing down the work considerably. The output, as will be seen from lines 10 to 12, was only 79 rows of stitching per hour as compared with 122 with lace beading, mentioned before. In determining the relative merits of the two kinds of work, it should be borne in mind that the tests were not made in the same shops, the work on lace beading having been done in shops Nos. 1232 and 1230, while that with lace was done in shop No. 1284 in which some of the operators who were timed on this work were neither so skilled nor so fast as the operators in the other two shops.

FACING BACKS.

Line 13 shows the output in forming a facing on one back by turning it in and interlining, while on the other back, instead of a lining, a label is inserted, making a total of 2 rows of stitching and 4 bendings per waist. The output on this work was 133 rows of stitching and 266 bendings per hour.

FACING FRONTS WITH MATERIAL OF DOUBLE THICKNESS.

This work is done by taking a strip of material 2½ inches wide and folding it over lengthwise to the required width of the facing and joining it to the edge of the front on the right side in two operations, as follows: First, stitching on the facing to the edge of the front on the right side; second, the facing is turned over on the wrong side of the front, the raw edge of the facing is turned in and stitched to the front. As will be seen from lines 14 to 22 of Table 93 the output on this work on the first seam was 82 rows of stitching per hour in shop No. 1230 and 84 in shop No. 1284; on the second seam it was 120 rows of stitching in shop No. 1230 and 106 in shop No. 1284. The combined output on the two seams was 97 rows of stitching in shop No. 1230, 94 in shop No. 1284, the average for the two shops being 94 rows of stitching and 94 bendings per hour.

FACING BACKS WITH MATERIAL OF DOUBLE THICKNESS.

This work is done in the same manner as facing fronts, described above, except that the facing is extended along the collar and in addition to the two operations just mentioned, there is a third operation consisting of turning in the top of the facing and stitching it to the collar, making a seam three-fourths inch long. The second and third operations being done one after the other, they had to be timed together, and are therefore given in the form of a combined product per hour. The output on the first operation, as will be seen from line 23, was 86 rows of stitching and 86 bendings per hour. On the second and third operations, the output was 57 rows of stitching 23 to 24 inches long and 57 rows three-fourths inch long with an equal number of bendings in each case.

FACING FRONTS AND INSERTING LACE ON ONE SIDE OF WAIST AT THE SAME TIME.

This work includes the following operations: One front ends with an embroidered center having a scalloped edge. A strip of lace was used as a facing and in turn was lined by a strip of material folded in two, lengthwise, with each of its raw edges bent in. The three parts, that is to say, the embroidered front, the lace and the facing were placed on top of each other in the order named, and all joined in one seam, thus making three bendings and one row of stitching for one front. The other front had an ordinary facing. Only one row of stitching in that operation was timed in connection with the work recorded in line 25, the stitching over and the bendings being timed in connection with another operation. We thus have a total of 2 rows of stitching and 3 bendings per waist, the output per hour being 36 rows of stitching and 55 bendings.

JOINING CENTERS TO FRONTS WITH BENDINGS IN FORM OF A TUCK.

In this work the raw edge of the center is turned in and stitched on top of the front. The stitching is done at some distance from the edge so as to form a tuck. This work is necessarily slower than the ordinary way of finishing the strip, because the operator must be careful to see that the width of the tuck is the same as that of the other tucks on the front. The output of 2 men and 1 woman, working on 8½ dozen, was 57 rows of stitching and 57 bendings per hour.

TABLE 93.—CENTERS.

[For explanation of method of computing averages in this table see page 250.]

Line No.	Shop number.	Number and sex of operators.		Kind of seam.		Length of seam (inches).	Waists (dozen).	Stitching.				Bendings.		
		M.	F.	1st.	2d.			Rows per waist.	Total rows.	Time worked (minutes).	Rows per hour.	Per waist.	Total.	Per hour.
	Joining fronts with lace beading to centers:													
1	Shop No. 1232	1	2	P.	....	19	7½	2	180	107	101	.....	.....	.....
2	Do	1	2	....	P.	19	5	2	120	38	189	.....	.....	.....
3	Average	...	...	....	....	....	....	.....	.....	.....	132	.....	.....	.....
4	Shop No. 1230	2	3	P.	....	16 to 18	14½	2	348	223	94	.....	.....	.....
5	Do	2	3	....	P.	16 to 17	6½	2	156	61	153	.....	.....	.....
6	Average	...	...	....	....	....	....	.....	.....	.....	116	.....	.....	.....
	Average, shops Nos. 1230 and 1232:													
7	First seam	3	5	P.	....	16 to 19	22	2	528	330	96	.....	.....	.....
8	Second seam	3	5	....	P.	16 to 19	11½	2	276	99	167	.....	.....	.....
9	Average	...	...	....	....	....	....	.....	.....	.....	122	.....	.....	.....
	Joining front with lace to embroidered center:													
10	Shop No. 1284	4	5	P.	....	19 to 23	38	2	912	796	69	.....	.....	.....
11	Do	2	6	....	P.	18 to 23	34½	2	828	537	93	.....	.....	.....
12	Average	...	...	....	....	....	....	.....	.....	.....	79	.....	.....	.....
	One back turned in and interlined; other back turned in and label inserted:													
13	Shop No. 1232	4	2	P.	....	21	42½	2	1,020	461	133	4	2,040	266
	Facing fronts with material of double thickness:													
14	Shop No. 1230	1	1	P.	....	21	4	2	96	70	82	2	96	82
15	Do	...	2	....	P.	21	3	2	72	36	120	2	72	120
16	Average	...	...	....	....	....	....	.....	.....	.....	97	.....	.....	97
17	Shop No. 1284	6	3	P.	....	19 to 23	22½	2	540	385	84	2	540	84
18	Do	6	1	....	P.	19 to 23	20	2	480	272	106	2	480	106
19	Average	...	...	....	....	....	....	.....	.....	.....	94	.....	.....	94
	Average, shops Nos. 1230 and 1284:													
20	First seam	7	4	P.	....	21	26½	2	636	455	84	2	636	84
21	Second seam	6	3	....	P.	21	23	2	552	308	108	2	552	108
22	Average	...	...	....	....	....	....	.....	.....	.....	94	.....	.....	94
	Facing backs with material of double thickness:													
23	Shop No. 1284	2	1	P.	....	23 to 24	27	2	648	450	86	2	648	86
24	Do	3	...	....	P.	23 to 24 ¾	27 27	2 2	648 648	680	57 57	2 2	648 648	57 57
	Facing fronts and inserting lace on one side of waist at the same time:													
25	Shop No. 1284	2	...	P.	....	18	4	2	96	158	36	3	144	55
	Joining centers to fronts with bendings in form of tuck:													
26	Shop No. 1230	2	1	P.	....	19	8½	2	204	215	57	2	204	57

RUFFLES AND CENTERS.

JOINING PLAITED RUFFLES TO FRONTS AND CENTERS.

Line 1 of Table 94 relates to work in which the center is folded in two, the ruffle is put on top of the open edge of the center, and the free edge of the lace beading which is attached to the front is put on top of the ruffle, and all of this is joined in one seam. In addition to being obliged to handle all these parts at the same time, the operator must shirr the ruffle while the stitching is being done. The complicated character of the work makes it necessarily slow. The output on this work in shop No. 1230 was found to be 58 rows of stitching per hour in addition to 58 bendings.

Line 2 represents the same class of work except that instead of a folded center we have a vest and the front has a raw edge instead of a lace beading. In this case the ruffle is inserted in the same manner as in the preceding case, except that instead of the lace beading the turned-in raw edge of the front is put on top of the ruffle and the whole stitched together, there being thus 2 bendings to each row of stitching. The output on this operation is slightly greater than in the preceding case, namely, 63 rows of stitching per hour and 126 bendings. This is due to two reasons: First, that the ruffles had been shirred and stitched before they were given to the operator, whereas in the preceding case they had to be shirred by the operator while the rest of the work was being done; second, the work was done in shop No. 1232, which has generally a record for a higher output than shop No. 1230, in which the preceding job was done.

Line 3 relates to somewhat more difficult work. An embroidered center is stitched to the front on the wrong side.[1] It is then turned over on the right side of the front and the ruffle inserted between the free edge of the center and the front, and the three stitched together. The reason this work is more difficult than the preceding two is that the center and front having been stitched together in the first place, it is necessary to take care that the center lies flat on the front, and that the three pieces are perfectly aligned, as the material on top (in this case the center) has a tendency to get out of line with the material underneath (i. e., the front) on account of the pressure of the "foot," which is greater on the top layer of the material than on the lower one. If this is not corrected by the operator before it is stitched, the center will wrinkle all over and spoil the appearance of the waist. This accounts for the smaller output on this kind of work which was only 51 rows of stitching and 102 bendings per hour in the same shop in which the work described in the preceding paragraph was done.

[1] This part of the work is not included in the figures given in line 3 of the table.

JOINING SHIRRED LACE TO LACE CENTERS.

Line 4 shows the output when shirred lace is stitched to a lace center 1 inch wide and 20 inches long, the lace being stitched on along the upper and side edge of the center. The difficult part of this work is in turning the corner as the operator turns from the upper to the side edge. At this corner the shirred lace must be bent in and extra shirring and stitching must be done to prevent the turned-in part of the lace from protruding at the corner, so as to give it a neat and flat appearance. The operation requires only one seam and resulted in an output of 31 rows of stitching per hour.

Line 5 represents a similar process except that the lace was shirred at the same time as it was joined to the center instead of having been shirred previously, as in the preceding case. This made the work still slower, resulting in an output of 26 rows of stitching per hour in the same shop, No. 1284.

JOINING LACE TO PLAITED RUFFLES.

Line 6 shows the output when lace is stitched to a plaited ruffle, the shirring being done while the stitching goes on. As this work was done on a straight line, there being no corners to turn, the output was larger than in the two preceding cases, namely, 36 rows of stitching per hour on the first seam. On the second seam, consisting of the stitching back of the raw edge of the ruffle, the output was 97 rows of stitching per hour, the average for the two being 53.

JOINING LACE BEADING TO PLAITED RUFFLES.

Lines 9 to 11 represent practically the same operations, except that lace beading is used in place of lace and that the work is done by the yard instead of on individual waists. This work was likewise done in shop No. 1284. The output on the first seam was 27 yards per hour. On the second seam, consisting of stitching back the raw edge of the ruffle, the output was 80½ yards per hour, the average of the two being 40 yards.

TABLE 94.—RUFFLES AND CENTERS.

[For explanation of method of computing averages in this table see p. 250.]

Line No.	Shop number.	Number and sex of operators.		Kind of seam.		Length of seam (inches.)	Waists (dozen).	Stitching.				Bendings.		
		M.	F.	1st.	2d.			Rows per waist.	Total rows.	Time worked (minutes).	Rows per hour.	Per waist.	Total.	Per hour.
	Joining plaited ruffles to fronts and centers:													
1	Shop No. 1230...	2	2	P+S	....	17½ to 19	14⅛	1 and 2	190	196	58	1 and 2	190	58
2	Shop No. 1232...	1	3	PS	....	24	10	2	240	228	63	4	480	126
3	Do..........	3	4	PS	....	23	17½	2	420	493	51	4	840	102
	Joining shirred lace to lace centers:													
4	Shop No. 1284...	...	1	PS	....	20	1	2	24	46	31	......	...	.....
5	Do..........	...	1	P+S	....	18	2	2	48	109	26	......	...	.....
	Joining lace to plaited ruffles:													
6	Shop No. 1284...	...	3	P+S	....	19 to 20	7	1	84	139	36	......	...	.....
7	Do..........	...	3	.....	PS	19 to 20	7	1	84	52	97	......	...	.....
8	Average.......	...	...	.....	....	....	......	......	......	......	53	......	...	.....
	Joining lace beading to plaited ruffle:													
9	Shop No. 1284...	2	1	P+S	....	....	......	1	[1] 3,048	188	[2] 27	......	...	.....
10	Do..........	2	...	.....	PS	....	......	1	[1] 2,076	43	[2] 80½	......	...	.....
11	Average.......	...	...	.....	....	....	......	......	......	......	[2] 40	......	...	.....

[1] Inches. [2] Yards.

VESTS AND FLIES.

A vest is made by folding a piece of material about 24 inches long lengthwise and stitching over the upper end of it diagonally across. Some vests are made of a piece of material of single thickness lined with a layer of other material. This is true especially of vests made of heavy material, such as madras, heavy linen, or any embroidered material, the lining being made of much lighter material. The next step is to turn the vest inside out; the two open ends are then turned in slightly to conceal the raw edges, and the raw edge of the front of the waist is inserted and the whole is stitched together, thus forming a vest.

JOINING LINED VESTS TO FRONTS.

Line 1 of Table 95 shows the output on work of this kind in which only the operation of joining the vest to the front was timed. Instead of inserting the raw edge of the front into the open vest, the work was simplified, since it was done on very cheap waists, by turning in the raw edge of the front, placing it on top of the open end of the vest, and stitching the whole together. This work was done by 6 men and 4 women in shop No. 1232, and showed an output of 63 rows of stitching and 63 bendings per hour.

TURNING OUT AND JOINING LINED VESTS TO FRONTS.

Line 2 shows the output on the same kind of work, to which is added the turning out of the vest which precedes its joining to the waist. The output is therefore less than in the preceding case—namely, 53 rows of stitching and 53 bendings per hour.

TURNING OUT VESTS.

Finally, line 3 shows the operation of turning out lined vests, the output being 147 vests per hour in addition to 147 bendings. The turning out of the lined vests takes more time than that of vests made of one piece of material folded over, because in the case of the lined vest the operator must see to it that the seam joining the vest with the lining lies exactly on the edge of the turned-out vest.

MAKING FLIES.

The making of a fly is similar to the making of a vest. A strip of material is folded over lengthwise, but instead of being stitched at the top on a bias line, it is stitched straight across—that is, along the top edge—and then, as in the case of the vest, it is turned inside out. The raw edges of the strip are then turned in and the open ends of the fly are closed by stitching the two together. In some cases the fly is left open, and the stitching is done simultaneously with the joining of the fly to the waist.

JOINING FLIES TO FRONTS.

Line 4 shows the output on the work of joining flies to fronts, the work having been done by 3 women in shop No. 1284 on 7½ dozen waists. The output was 39 rows of stitching and 39 bendings per hour. The turning-in in this case is that of the raw edge of the front to which the fly is attached. It should be taken into account that while joining the flies the operator had to carefully measure the front so that the collars, laces, etc., on the two fronts would "match," that is, come exactly opposite each other when the waist is buttoned, and this necessarily slows down the work. Also, that instead of one row of stitching on each front, there were really two rows of stitching, one from 18 to 20 inches long, and the other 3 inches long, made as a continuation of the long seam connecting the upper end of the fly with the collar on a bias line.

Line 5 shows the second part of the operation of making flies, consisting of turning out the fly, turning in the two raw edges, and closing up the fly by stitching them together. The output was 61 rows of stitching in addition to 123 bendings, shown in the table, and the further addition of the turning out of 61 flies, which is not shown in the table.

BINDING TOP OF A V-SHAPED CENTER.

Lines 6 to 8 refer to the binding of the upper V-shaped edge of a center. As in all work of this kind, the binding is first stitched along the upper edge of the center and then turned over on the wrong side of the center and the raw edge of the binding is turned in and stitched over the center. As will be seen from lines 6 and 7, the output per hour on the first seam is 132 rows of stitching, while on the second it is only 64. In addition to the 64 rows of stitching, the second operation also includes 64 bendings. Moreover, the binding had to be turned in at each of the 3 parts of the V-shaped center so as to keep the ends from protruding and give the whole a neat appearance.

FACING CENTERS ON TOP.

This is done by folding the center in two along a vertical line and stitching it over along the upper edge. Line 9 shows the output on a center with a V-shaped top edge, so that when folded over lengthwise, it forms a vest whose upper edge runs on a bias, the output being 253 rows of stitching per hour in addition to 253 bendings. Line 10 shows the output on similar work on a center whose upper edge consists of a straight horizontal line. In this case the stitching is done on a straight instead of a bias line, and the output is greater, namely, 313 rows of stitching per hour in addition to 313 bendings.

TABLE 95.—VESTS AND FLIES.

[For explanation of method of computing averages in this table see p. 250.]

Line No.	Shop number.	Number and sex of operators.		Kind of seam.		Length of seam (inches).	Waists (dozen).	Stitching.				Bendings.		
		M.	F.	1st.	2d.			Rows per waist.	Total rows.	Time worked (minutes).	Rows per hour.	Per waist.	Total.	Per hour.
	Joining lined vests to fronts:													
1	Shop No. 1232...	6	4	P	....	20 to 24	49 11/12	2	1,198	1,145	63	2	1,198	63
	Turning out and joining lined vests to fronts:													
2	Shop No. 1232...	...	1	P	....	19½	5	2	120	136	53	2	120	53
	Turning out vests:													
3	Shop No. 1232...	2	4	....	....	23	12 1/12	......	......	123	......	2	302	147
	Joining flies to fronts:													
4	Shop No. 1284...	...	3	P	....	{18 to 20; 3}	7½	2	180	278	39	2	180	39
	MAKING FLIES.													
	Turning out and stitching side:													
5	Shop No. 1284...	...	2	P	....	20½ to 23	5½	2	132	129	61	4	264	123
	Binding top of a V-shaped center:													
6	Shop No. 1230...	1	4	P	....	6	11	1	132	60	132	......	......	......
7	Do.........	1	4	....	P	6	11	1	132	124	64	1	132	64
8	Average.......	...	...	....	....	......	......	......	......	......	86	......	......	......
	Facing centers on top:													
9	Shop No. 1232...	2	...	FB	....	5	4 11/12	2	118	28	253	2	118	253
10	Do.........	3	...	P	....	2	10	2	240	46	313	2	240	313

TACKING FRONTS AND BACKS.

This work was timed on more than 175 dozen waists in three $9-a-dozen waist shops, representing the work of 9 men and 16 women, at a total expenditure of time equivalent to 32 hours and 6 minutes for 1 person.

The process of tacking consists of gathering in (or shirring) the material at the waistline in folds, and stitching them over so as to retain them permanently. The work is divided into two operations: First, the waist is gathered in, either by hand or with the aid of a shirring attachment,[1] and as fast as the folds are formed they are pushed under the needle and stitched over. The second operation consists of putting in an additional row of stitching a short distance from and parallel to the first row so as to secure them more firmly.

The first lot of waists, represented by lines 1 and 2 of Table 96, consisting of 65 dozen waists, operated by 6 men and 2 women operators, was made up of waists buttoning in the back, and therefore having closed or full fronts and open or half backs. As the waist is always more full in the front than it is in the back, a great deal more shirring must be done in the front than in the back; since, in addition, the front in a back-buttoned waist is more than twice as wide as either of the backs, it will take a great deal more time to tack the front than either back. The result of the timing of the lot mentioned, which consumed 573 minutes, or nearly 10 hours, shows that the output per hour in tacking the closed fronts was 297 rows of stitching, while on the open backs it was 614, or more than twice the above number. As the operators are not paid for tacking fronts or backs, but for tacking the whole waist, and as there were two backs to each front, the average was found by adding the output on one front to that on two backs and dividing the total by 3, the average output thus obtained being 454 rows of stitching per hour (line 3). It should be observed, however, that this output was obtained in shop No. 1232, which shows on all work a higher output than any other shop, and that on this work the men predominated, numbering 6, to 2 women, and that the average earnings of these men are 50 cents an hour and more.

Lines 4 to 10 of the same table show the output on front-buttoned waists; that is, waists having closed backs and open fronts. While in this style of waist the front is likewise shirred more fully than the back, there being two fronts, the amount of tacking in the back exceeds that in either front, though it is less than the tacks of the combined fronts. Lines 4 to 6 show the output on the above work in shop No. 1232. The work was done by the same 6 men assisted by 4 women on 76¾ dozen waists, which consumed the equivalent of 837 minutes for one person, and shows an output of 375 rows of stitching

[1] No shirring attachment was used in the work covered by Table 96.

per hour on the closed backs and 408 rows of stitching on the open fronts. The average output for both operations is 396 rows of stitching per hour. In shop No. 1230, in which there were 3 men operators as against 12 women, the average output on the same kind of work was 286 rows of stitching per hour. Lines 9 and 10 represent the average of the two shops, which is 354 rows of stitching per hour. In determining a standard rate, either the output of shop No. 1232, No. 1230, or the average may be taken, provided the proper allowance per hour be made corresponding to the figure chosen.

TACKING FRONTS OR BACKS WITH TAPE.

Lines 11 and 12 show the output for tacking fronts or backs with tape. This work differs from that described above in that the operator sews on a piece of narrow tape over the "little skirt" (the part of the waist below the waistline) and the shirred front or back on the wrong side of the waist to keep the folds in place more firmly. The operations of shirring the front or back of the waist, sewing on the little skirt to the waist, and sewing on the tape to the two, are all done at the same time, which makes the work more difficult for the operator than ordinary tacking and reduces the output. The figures obtained are for shop No. 1284, which, on work of this kind, shows an output similar to that of shop No. 1230. The output shown here for open backs on seams from 4½ to 7 inches long is 256 rows of stitching per hour, and on fronts open and closed (mostly closed) on seams from 7 to 8 inches, 151 rows per hour.

TABLE 96.—TACKING FRONTS AND BACKS.

[For explanation of method of computing averages in this table see p. 250.]

Line No.	Shop number.	Number and sex of operators.		Kind of seam.		Length of seam after it is tacked (inches).	Waists (dozen).	Stitching.			
		Male.	Female.	First.	Second.			Rows per waist.	Total rows.	Time worked (minutes).	Rows per hour.
	Tacking closed fronts:										
1	Shop No. 1232	6	2	P+S	PS	[1] 7 to 10	65	2	1,560	315	297
	Tacking open backs:										
2	Shop No. 1232	6	2	P+S	PS	3½ to 5	55	4	2,640	258	614
3	Average	.....	.....	.....	.....	.....	.....	.....	.....	.....	454
	Tacking closed backs:										
4	Shop No. 1232	6	4	P+S	PS	4½ to 8	76¾	2	1,842	295	375
	Tacking open fronts:										
5	Shop No. 1232	6	4	P+S	PS	[2] 3½ to 6	76¾	4	3,684	542	408
6	Average	.....	.....	.....	.....	.....	.....	.....	.....	.....	396
	Tacking closed backs:										
7	Shop No. 1230	2	10	P+S	PS	[3] 4 to 6	34⅙	2	820	516	286
	Tacking open fronts:										
8	Shop No. 1230	3	12	P+S	PS	3½ to 7	34⅙	4	1,640		
	Average, shops 1232 and 1230:										
9	Tacking closed backs.	8	14	.....	.....	[3] 4½ to 8	110 11/12	2	2,662	1,353	354
10	Tacking open fronts	9	16	P+S	PS	3½ to 7	110 11/12	4	5,324		
	Tacking fronts or backs with tape:										
11	Backs—Shop No. 1284.	1	2	P+S	PS	4½ to 7	17½	4	840	197	256
12	Fronts—Shop No. 1284	3	1	P+S	PS	7 to 8	15⅔	2 to 4	552	219	151

[1] One case of 12. [2] Two cases of 8. [3] One case of 2.

SHIRRING.

This work differs from the tacking described in the preceding section in that it is done with only one row of stitching, the folds being left quite loose, while in tacking two rows of stitching are made which keep the folds in a fixed position. The shirring with one row of stitching is done merely in preparation for the next operation. Lines 1 to 3 in Table 97 relate to the shirring of backs and fronts at the top where they are to be attached to the yoke. Some operators do this work by placing the finger behind the "foot" (the attachment which helps to push the material forward as fast as it is stitched). This prevents the material from passing forward after it is stitched over, and it automatically piles up in folds, that is to say, it is being shirred. Although this method offers the quickest way of doing this work, there is danger of the material being caught in the gear under the foot, and many operators prefer to shirr the material by hand as described under tacking.

When the shirring is done at the bottom (i. e., near the waist line), it can not be done in the manner first described, for the reason that the folds are too many and too full to form automatically under the "foot" and the material is gathered into folds (shirred) by hand and pushed under the needle. An examination of Table 97 will show that the output on fronts and backs varied in the same shop from 285 to 367 rows of stitching per hour (lines 1 and 2). This was due to the difference in the length of the seam, which is practically double in one case as compared with the other. While ordinarily a difference of a few inches in the length of a seam does not perceptibly affect the output, the case is different in this instance, since the time of the operator is taken up chiefly by the handwork of shirring rather than by the machine work of stitching.

Line 4 shows the output on shirring an entire waist at the waist line, the length of the seam being from 28 to 30 inches as compared with from 3 to 12 inches on the work described above. This work is more difficult and takes a longer time. First, because a row of stitching in this case represents a back and 2 fronts, or 1 front and 2 backs, according to whether the waist is buttoned in the front or in the back; second, because the operator must be very careful, in shirring the waist, to see that the fronts, backs, and sides retain a proper proportion; third, because the shirring at the waist line is much more elaborate than at the top and therefore takes more time. The output in line 4 is seen to be 56 rows of stitching per hour, which is equivalent to 168 fronts and backs, and is considerably below the output in shops Nos. 1232 and 1230 on separate fronts or backs.

Lines 5 to 7 show the output per hour in shirring lace. This lace comes in narrow strips, about 12 yards long, and the work of shirring these strips is much simpler than shirring parts of waists. The average output per hour in shop No. 1230 was 52 yards, in shop No. 1284 71 yards, the average for the two being 65¼ yards.

TABLE 97.—SHIRRING DIFFERENT PARTS OF WAIST: SHOPS NOS. 1232 AND 1230, SINGER MACHINE; SHOP NO. 1284, STANDARD MACHINE.

Line No.	Shop number.	Number and sex of operators.		Kind of shirring.	Length of seam after shirring (inches).	Waists (dozen).	Shirring.			
		Male.	Female.				Rows per waist.	Total rows.	Time worked (minutes).	Rows per hour.
1	Shop No. 1232	9	7	Fronts and backs.	7 to 12	63⅛	1 to 2	997	210	285
2	Do	8	5	Fronts	5 to 6	65	2	1,560	255	367
3	Shop No. 1230	2	3	Backs	3 to 5	22½	1	270	62	261
4	Shop No. 1284		3	Whole waist	28 to 30	5¼	1	63	67	56
5	Shop No. 1230		3	Lace			1	[1] 1,854	59	[2] 52
6	Shop No. 1284	1	3	do			1	[1] 5,623	132	[2] 71
7	Average									[2] 65¼

[1] Inches. [2] Yards.

SETTING HIGH COLLARS.

This work is done in two operations. In the first operation the collar and waist are joined together. In the second operation the raw edge is turned in and stitched over. The work on the first seam, however, is not as simple as sewing on an ordinary piece of lace. The neck of the waist forms a more or less circular curve, while the collar is cut in almost a straight line. In joining the collar to the waist, the least deviation of the seam from the edge of the neck sends the collar along a more or less concentric line of a larger circumference since it is farther from the center of the circle formed by the neck line. As a result of this, after the collar has been stitched down to the waist, it will be found not to reach all the way around, and the operator must rip it off and do the work all over again. As an aid to the operator, and to save ripping, the collar is folded so as to indicate the middle, and a notch is made in the neckband of the waist at the corresponding point. But even with these guides it takes considerable skill and experience to set a collar that will be smooth and even, and whose ends will meet without wrinkling the waist at the neck.

TABLE 98.—SETTING HIGH COLLARS.

[For explanation of method of computing averages in this table see p. 250.]

Line No.	Shop number.	Number and sex of operators.		Kind of seam.		Length of seam (inches).	Waists (dozen).	Stitching.			
		Male.	Female.	First.	Second.			Rows per waist.	Total rows.	Time worked (minutes).	Rows per hour.
1	Shop No. 1232	7	......	P	......	14 to 15½	60	1	720	517	84
2	Do	7	......	......	P	14 to 15½	60	1	720	350	123
3	Average	......	......	......	......	......	......	......	......	......	100
4	Shop No. 1284	4	......	P	......	14 to 15½	37	1	444	286	93
5	Do	1	3	......	P	14 to 15½	34½	1	414	264	94
6	Average	......	......	......	......	......	......	......	......	......	94
	Average, shops Nos. 1232 and 1284:										
7	First seam	11	......	P	......	14 to 15½	78½	1	1,164	803	87
8	Second seam	8	3	......	P	14 to 15½	77¼	1	1,134	614	111
9	Average, lines 7 and 8	......	......	......	......	......	......	......	......	......	97

SLEEVE SETTING BY BODY MAKERS.

In the new style of waists, in which the sleeves are not set in at the armhole of the waist, but are attached a few inches below the shoulder, the sleeves are attached in a straight line to the edge of the drop shoulder, and the work is done by body makers, as it does not differ from the stitching that has to be done by body makers on other parts of the waist. The work is, therefore, done on a Singer machine, although this machine is not as fast as the Union Special or Metropolitan, which are used by the sleeve setters, and although the sleeve setters have the further advantage of specializing exclusively in the work of sleeve setting, it will be seen by comparing the figures in Tables 81 and 99 that the output of the body makers exceeds that of the sleeve setters, which is due to the fact that the sleeves on which sleeve setters are employed are set in at the armhole on a curve and therefore are more difficult to handle than the sleeves attached by the body makers in a straight line.

Table 99 shows the output on work of this kind done under different conditions. Lines 1 and 2 show the output when sleeves are joined with a plain seam, without lace or other insertion. The work was timed only in one shop, No. 1232, which has the record of having the highest output of all the shops investigated, and shows an average output of 159 sleeves per hour, as against only 123 sleeves in the same shop by sleeve setters. (See line 1, Table 81.) The output on similar sleeves in the same shop in which a tuck ⅜-inch wide was made in stitching over the sleeve where it is attached to the drop shoulder was 139 (lines 3 and 4, Table 99), or a reduction of nearly 13 per cent in the output as compared with the preceding case.

Lines 5 and 6 show an output of 149 sleeves per hour when the sleeve is joined first to lace beading and the latter joined in turn to the drop shoulder. Line 7 shows the output in shop No. 1230 in joining sleeves to a beading in one operation instead of two operations, as indicated in lines 5 and 6. As explained elsewhere, the necessity of turning in the edge of the cloth and stitching it down at the same time as the joining of the two pieces of material takes place results in the slowing down of the operation, which offsets to a large extent the saving of time due to the elimination of one seam. The output in this case was 79 rows of stitching per hour in addition to 79 bendings, which, if figured at the rate of two bendings to one row of stitching, would be equivalent to nearly 120 rows of stitching per hour, as compared with 149 rows of stitching per hour in shop No. 1232 (lines 5 and 6), done by the two-seam process. However, the 79 rows of stitching and 79 bendings take the place of 158 rows of stitching under the double-seam process, resulting in a saving of 9 rows of stitching per hour. This saving is insignificant; as a rule, it is much greater; but true comparison in the present instance is impossible because the two processes were timed in two different shops with different sets of workers who differ in skill and speed.

Lines 8 and 9, shop 1230, show the output to be 127 rows of stitching per hour when instead of a lace beading the insertion consists of a hemstitched beading. As already explained, the work of inserting a hemstitched beading always takes more time than that of a lace beading, because in the former case the cloth is sewed on top of the beading, while in the latter the lace is sewed on top of the cloth, which does not require the same care in stitching.

Line 10 shows the output on the same kind of work with a cording to be only 108 rows of stitching per hour, or about one-third less than without a cording in the same shop (lines 1 and 2). The reasons for the smaller output on work with cording are explained on page 253 in connection with the work of joining yokes to fronts or backs (Table 85). It should be noted that this output does not include the sewing on of the cord, and that a special attachment known as the "cording foot" was used in joining the sleeve to the drop shoulder.

TABLE 99.—SLEEVE SETTING BY BODY MAKERS: SINGER MACHINE.

[For explanation of method of computing averages in this table see p. 250.]

Line No.	Shop number.	Number and sex of operators.		Kind of seams.		Length of seam (inches).	Waist (dozen).	Stitching.				Bendings.		
		M.	F.	1st.	2d.			Rows per waist.	Total rows.	Time worked (minutes).	Rows per hour.	Per waist.	Total.	Per hour.
	Sleeve setting:													
1	Shop No. 1232	4	4	P		17 to 18	$17\frac{1}{2}$	2	420	181	139			
2	Do	4	4		P	17 to 18	$17\frac{1}{2}$	2	420	135	187			
	Average										159			
	Setting sleeves and forming $\frac{3}{8}$-inch tuck at the seam:													
3	Shop No. 1232	2	4	P		17 to 18	15	2	360	154	140			
4	Do	2	4		P	17 to 18	15	2	360	156	138			
	Average										139			
	Joining lace beading to sleeve and then to drop shoulder:													
5	Shop No. 1232	6	6	P		15 to 16	$82\frac{11}{12}$	2	1,990	919	130			
6	Do	6	6		P	15 to 16	$82\frac{11}{12}$	2	1,990	685	174			
	Average										149			
7	Shop No. 1230	1	8	P		13 to 17	$21\frac{2}{3}$	2	520	397	79	2	520	79
	Joining hemstitched beading to sleeve and then to edge of drop shoulder:													
8	Shop No. 1230	4	10	P		13 to 17	$61\frac{1}{6}$	2	1,468	784	112			
9	Do	2	9		P	13 to 17	$42\frac{7}{12}$	2	1,022	417	147			
	Average										127			
	Setting sleeves with cording:[1]													
10	Shop No. 1232	2		P			$7\frac{1}{2}$	2	180	100	108			

[1] Sewing on of cord not included.

JOINING BELTS TO WAISTS.

By a belt in the waist industry is meant a piece of material about 3 to 4 inches wide and from 26 to 34 inches long, which is joined to the waist at the waistline. The work requires several operations, which are described below in the order in which they were timed in the shops.

FOLDING OVER EDGE OF BELT AND STITCHING.

The belt is folded over about $1\frac{1}{2}$ inches. The turned-in raw edge is then stitched to the belt so that the belt now consists of two parts, one part of double thickness, about $1\frac{1}{2}$ inches wide, the other of single thickness also about $1\frac{1}{2}$ inches wide.

This work was timed in shop No. 1284 on $18\frac{3}{4}$ dozen waists, done by 1 man and 3 women, with an average output of 102 rows of stitching and 102 bendings per hour (line 1, Table 100).

JOINING BELT TO SHIRRED WAIST.

The belt is now ready to be joined to the waist, which is either shirred previously or at the same time as the joining is done. The belt is joined to the waist by stitching the remaining raw edge to the waist on the wrong side.

Line 2 of Table 100 shows the output when a belt is joined to a waist previously shirred, while lines 3 to 5 show the output when a belt is attached to a waist while the waist is being shirred. The output in the first case is 46 rows of stitching per hour in shop No. 1284. In the second case it is 40 rows of stitching per hour, or 15 per cent less in the same shop but with different operators, and 51 rows of stitching per hour in shop No. 1232, making an average output for the two shops of 44 rows of stitching per hour. It is natural that the output should be considerably less when the shirring has to be done while the belt is joined to the waist than in the case when the shirring has been done previously. The difference in output would probably be greater than shown in the table if both operations were timed with the same operators. Unfortunately, this could not be done because different methods were used by different operators. The operators who did the shirring at the same time as the joining were more skilled and faster workers than the 3 women who did the work of shirring and joining in separate operations.

STITCHING BELT OVER SHIRRED WAIST.

After the belt has been joined to the waist on the wrong side, it is turned over on the right side of the waist and stitched to the waist along its (the belt's) upper edge. At each side of the belt, which is now about 1 inch wide, the raw edge is turned in as in a facing and stitched over. The belt is then stitched over the waist along its lower edge. In this way it forms, together with the part of the waist over which it is stitched, a belt of triple thickness. The operations involve a total of 4 rows of stitching (2 long and 2 short) and 3 bendings (1 long and 2 short). As it was impossible to time the long and short seams separately, the output must be given for the two combined. The output in this case was 58 long and 58 short rows of stitching per hour, in addition to 29 long and 58 short bendings.

JOINING BELT TO WAIST AND SHIRRING AT THE SAME TIME.

The operation for which the figures are given in line 7 of the table is similar to that given in line 4, except that in this case after the raw edge of the belt has been turned in it is stitched right side to the wrong side of the waist, while in the operation given in line 4 it was stitched wrong side to the wrong side of the waist (the raw edge of the belt to the raw edge of the waist), and therefore required no bendings. The output in the case of line 7 is 39 rows of stitching and

39 bendings as compared with 51 rows of stitching with no bendings in line 4. The belt is now turned over on the right side of the waist; the raw edge of the belt is turned in and stitched over the waist; the side ends, 1 inch each, are likewise turned in and stitched to the belt as in the operation given in line 6. That is to say, on the second operation there is one long seam and two short seams, and two long and two short bendings to each waist, figuring the turning of the belt over the right side of the waist as a bending. The output on this operation (line 8) was 39 long and 79 short rows of stitching and 79 long and 79 short bendings per hour.

TABLE 100.—JOINING BELTS TO WAISTS.

Line No.	Shop number.	Number and sex of operators.		Kind of seam.		Length of seam (inches).	Waist (dozen).	Stitching.				Bendings.		
		M.	F.	1st.	2d.			Rows per waist.	Total rows.	Time worked (minutes).	Rows per hour.	Per waist.	Total.	Per hour.
	Folding over edge of belt and stitching:													
1	Shop No. 1284.	1	3	P	......	26 to 35	18¾	1	225	133	102	1	225	102
	Joining belt to shirred waist:													
2	Shop No. 1284.	...	3	PS	......	27 to 34	14¼	1	171	222	46	......	......	......
3	Do.	2	1	P+S	......	26 to 32	4	1	48	72	40	......	......	......
4	Shop No. 1232.	1	...	P+S	......	26	2½	1	30	35	51	......	......	......
5	Average, lines 3 and 4.	3	1	P+S	......	26 to 32	6½	1	78	107	44	......	......	......
	Stitching belt over shirred waist:													
6	Shop No. 1284.	...	4	......	PS. P[1]	26 to 34 1	[1] 16½	2 2	396 396	407	58 58	1 2	198 396	29 58
	Joining belt to waist and shirring at the same time:													
7	Shop No. 1232.	2	...	P+S	......	26	5	1	60	93	39	1	60	39
8	Do.	2	1	......	PS[2] P[2]	26 1	7½	1 2	90 180	137	39 79	2 2	180 180	79 79

[1] One-half dozen waists were stitched over the shirring only, and not over flat material.
[2] Only one (upper) row of stitching was done over shirred material; the other was done over flat material (lower edge of the belt).

LOSS OF TIME.

While the work was being timed in the different shops, loss of time on the part of the operators was carefully noted. Broadly speaking, loss of time in the factories can be divided into two classes: (1) Loss of time which is beyond the control of the operator; (2) loss of time which can either be prevented by the operator or is caused by his or her personal needs. For the sake of brevity the former may be called "involuntary loss of time" and the latter, "voluntary loss of time."

In the first category may be included the loss of time caused by (1) waiting for work; (2) waiting for parts; (3) waiting for repairs on the machine, or cleaning or repairing the machine by the operator himself; (4) time taken to receive instructions from the foreman or instructor as to the way the work is to be done.

In the second category may be included: (1) The loss of time due to tardiness in arriving in the morning or after lunch and leaving earlier than the regular time for the noon recess and the closing hour of the evening; (2) leaving the machine to attend to various personal needs; (3) time spent in repairing work which has been returned by the examiners on account of some defect.

All such losses were noted at the shops and the results are tabulated in Table 101.

Body Making.—The most complete information as to loss of time is available in the case of body makers, the data covering 112 operators in three shops, all of them making $9-a-dozen waists. The data in these tables are in keeping with those relating to output; that is to say, the shops which showed the highest output showed likewise the least loss of time, and vice versa. Most of the headings of the columns of Table 101 are self-explanatory. "Total time under observation" is equal to the sum of the "Total time worked" and of all the losses of time given in the preceding columns. The column preceding the last shows what per cent the "involuntary loss of time" is of the time the operator actually spends at work. The last column shows what per cent the time lost on account of breakdown of machinery constitutes of the time the operator actually spends at work. The percentages in the last two columns have been computed for each operator as well as for each shop as a whole. The percentages that the other losses of time bear to the time at work are so small that it has not seemed necessary to compute them for each operator separately, but they are given for each shop as a whole.

As regards the involuntary loss of time—that is to say, the total loss which the operator suffers through no fault of her own—we find it to vary in shop No. 1230 from 0.2 per cent for operator No. 106 to as much as 28.2 per cent for operator No. 110. The average involuntary loss for the entire shop on the basis of 39 body makers who were timed in this shop was 3.9 per cent. In shop No. 1232 the involuntary loss of time varied from 0.4 per cent to 5.9 per cent, the average for 30 operators in the shop being 3.1 per cent; while in shop No. 1284, in which the system of distribution of work and of parts is very poor, and operators are frequently obliged to wait for the necessary parts, the involuntary loss of time varied from 1.3 per cent to as high as 45.8 per cent for individual operators, the average for 38 operators in the shop being 7.7 per cent. We thus have three different percentages for the three shops, two of them being between 3 and 4 per cent and the third nearly 8 per cent. Each of these figures is believed to be accurate for the respective shops, being based on the timing of 39, 30, and 38 operators, respectively, whose combined time at work under observation was equivalent to 729 hours in shop No. 1230, 503 hours in shop No. 1232, and 743 hours in shop No. 1284, yet these data are inadequate as a basis for an average for the industry as a whole. The significance of these figures lies chiefly in showing how great the variation actually is and how much loss of time can be eliminated in shops under proper management in the light of what is being done in other shops.

It should be noted that all of this loss of time was found to take place during the busiest part of the season. This is a time when it is to the mutual interest of the employers and employees to reduce such losses to a minimum. There is no doubt that such loss is much greater at other times of the year when the foreman knows that he has not enough work to keep the operators busy throughout the day, so that the incentive is lacking to try to utilize every minute of the operator who is paid by the piece. It should also be noted that the figures of loss of time for body making are given here only for shops making exclusively $9-a-dozen waists. In these shops the loss of time caused by waiting for work and waiting for parts is usually less than in shops manufacturing the higher-priced waists, owing to the great variety of waists and parts which have to be handled in the latter and the smaller bundles which are generally the rule there.

If we analyze the involuntary loss of time in detail we will find that waiting for work constitutes more than half of the total involuntary loss in shops Nos. 1230 and 1284, and more than a third in shop No. 1232, which holds the highest record for efficiency among the shops investigated.

In noting loss of time caused by waiting for work only those cases were considered where operators were required to remain at the machines in expectation of work. Whenever work was so scarce that operators were allowed to leave the factory such loss of time was not included. Nor was it included if the enforced idleness was of long duration, even if the operators remained at the factory. This was due to the fact that on the average each operator was timed for only about three days, and whenever an operator remained idle for any length of time he was dropped by the investigator, who transferred his attention to some other operator. Such a procedure would not be justified if an exhaustive investigation of idleness during work hours were undertaken. Such an investigation would have to be based on at least one month's continuous timing of the operators and repeated at different seasons of the year. As the present investigation, however, was primarily conducted for other purposes and operators were timed for only a few days, idleness lasting several hours at a time would have formed an abnormally high percentage of the total time in many cases and was therefore not included in the tables presented here.

Waiting for parts was the next largest item of loss of time, being more than a third of the total involuntary loss in shop No. 1230 and more than 40 per cent in shops Nos. 1232 and 1284. Under this head was included all the time an operator was obliged to remain idle while waiting for any material or parts needed in his work, such as lace, embroideries, and parts of waists, thread, tape, etc. In some shops not included in the three for which body-making data are presented the practice prevails of starting operators on new jobs whenever they are short of any parts which can not be readily furnished. The result is that operators have as many as three or four unfinished bundles on hand which are alternately taken up and put aside as the missing material or parts for the different bundles turn up. While such a practice may be preferable to total idleness, it is extremely uneconomical and wasteful of the operator's time and makes efficient work impossible. It is one of the principal reasons for the low output in shop No. 1090, as shown in several tables in this report. In such a shop the loss of time caused by waiting for parts might appear very small, and yet the real loss of time caused by constant interruptions and changing back and forth from one job to another be very large.

The loss of time due to breakdowns and repairs of machinery is small, being from 0.2 per cent to 0.5 per cent of the time at work and from 2 per cent to 15 per cent of the total involuntary loss. It should be added that the three shops for which the data are given are all well equipped with new machinery.

The loss of time on account of instruction given to operators on new work is still less than that caused by machine breakdowns. This is an item that is naturally present to a much smaller extent in shops making $9-a-dozen waists than in those manufacturing garments of higher grade. Moreover, it is a practice that manufacturers could well afford to extend, for the more thorough and frequent the instruction received by the operators the more efficient will be their work. At present too little is being done in this regard in most shops, and every additional dollar spent on instructors would prove a most profitable investment to the manufacturers as well as result in increased earnings by the operators at the same piece rates.

As to the loss of time caused by the operator himself or incurred for the operator's own needs, it seems to be much less than that beyond his control. Thus the loss of time caused by tardiness and leaving early was 1.5 per cent of the time worked in shop No. 1230, 1.2 per cent in shop No. 1232, and 1.2 per cent in shop No. 1284. The loss of time due to personal needs was 1 per cent in shop No. 1230, 0.9 per cent in shop No. 1232, and 0.5 per cent in shop No. 1284. The time spent in repairing defective work was 0.4 per cent in shop No.

1230, 0.6 per cent in shop No. 1232, and 0.7 per cent in shop No. 1284. These figures may also be below the average for the year, for just as the foreman is more anxious to save unnecessary loss of time at the height of the season than at other times, so are the operators more punctual in coming and going when work is plentiful than when the season is slack.

CLOSING.—The data were obtained for five shops, all of them making $9-a-dozen waists. The involuntary loss of time constituted 8.8 per cent of the time spent at work in shop No. 1110, 7 per cent in shop No. 1191, 6.9 per cent in shop No. 1232, 5.6 per cent in shop No. 1284, and 18.5 per cent in shop No. 1230. The other details appear in the table.

SLEEVE SETTING.—Information on this was obtained in two shops. The involuntary loss of time constituted 26.7 per cent of the time worked in shop No. 1284 and 6.2 per cent in shop No. 1191. The voluntary loss of time (on account of tardiness, early leaving, and personal needs) varied from 1.4 per cent to 2.2 per cent of the time worked.

WAIST HEMMING.—Information on waist hemming was obtained in three shops. The involuntary loss of time was, as usual, the lowest in shop No. 1110, being only 2.9 per cent of the time worked. The highest loss was in shop No. 1284, being 14.7 per cent. The voluntary loss of time in these three shops varied from nothing to 2.1 per cent of the time at work.

STRIP HEMMING.—On strip hemming information was obtained for only one shop, No. 1230, showing the involuntary loss of time to be 4.2 per cent of the total time at work.

STRIP TUCKING.—Information is presented in the table for three shops in which the involuntary loss of time varied from 3.6 per cent to 4.8 per cent of the total time at work. The voluntary loss in these three shops varied from 0.6 per cent to 2.3 per cent of the time at work.

SHORT TUCKING.—Information is presented for four shops, covering a total of 31 persons. The total involuntary loss varied from 1.5 per cent in shop No. 1090 to 36.8 per cent of the total time at work in shop No. 1191. The time lost involuntarily varied in these four shops from nothing to 3.7 per cent of the time worked.

BUTTONHOLE MAKING.—These data are available for four shops using the Singer machine and three shops using the Reece machine.

Taking first the Singer machine, we find that the involuntary loss constituted 34.8 per cent of the time worked in shop No. 1090, 9.4 per cent in shop No. 1110, 2.2 per cent in shop No. 1116, and 6.4 per cent in shop No. 1235, the average for the four being 21.3 per cent. The chief item in this involuntary loss was waiting for work, which was especially large, namely, 31.4 per cent of the time spent at work, in shop No. 1090. As may be seen from section 6 relating to buttonhole making, there is a greater variety of styles of waists in this shop than in any other of those under investigation, and the work is given in smaller bundles than in any of the other shops, the bundles frequently consisting of only a few waists. This accounts for the great loss incurred in waiting for work, which is additional to the loss, to both the firm and the employees, shown in the low output per hour, the output being less than in any of the other shops investigated.

The involuntary loss of time on the Reece machine varied from 11.7 per cent in shop No. 1284 to 20.4 per cent in shop No. 1230, the average being 13.8 per cent, or less than on the Singer machine. This is due not to the relative merits of the two machines, but to the fact that the Reece machine is used in shops making $9-a-dozen garments. In these shops the work is made in larger quantities than in the shops making medium-priced waists, and there is, therefore, less loss of time. On the other hand, the average loss of time on account of breakdown of machinery was 4.4 per cent of the total time at work on the Reece machine, while on the Singer machine it was only 1½ per cent. This is due to the more complicated character of the Reece machine, which, therefore, gets more easily out of order.

BUTTON SEWING.—These data were secured in three shops, of which one, No. 1116, makes medium-priced waists. The total involuntary loss of time was 7.6 per cent of the time spent at work in shop No. 1284, 12.3 per cent in shop No. 1230, and only 1.1 per cent in the medium-priced shop. The time lost in waiting for work was likewise the lowest in shop No. 1116.

TABLE 101.—LOSS OF TIME.

A. Body making: Singer machine.

Shop No. and operator No.	Sex of operator.	Loss of time for which the employee is not responsible (minutes).					Loss of time for which the employer is not responsible (minutes).			Total time—		Per cent involuntary loss of time was of time worked.	Per cent time lost on account of breakdown of machine was of time worked.
		Waiting for work.	Waiting for parts.	Breakdown of machine.	Receiving instruction.	Total.	Tardiness and early leaving.	Personal needs.	Repairing work.	Worked (minutes).	Under observation (minutes).		
Shop No. 1230.													
Operator 117[1]	F.	35	41	......	9	85	23	14	......	1,881	2,003	4.5	......
Operator 118	F.	30	25	......	......	55	43	10	......	1,160	1,268	4.7	......
Operator 119	F.	12	5	......	......	17	50	6	......	1,284	1,357	1.3	......
Operator 120	F.	6	6	......	......	12	......	6	......	1,189	1,207	1.0	......
Operator 122[1]	F.	10	45	......	......	55	26	4	......	1,717	1,802	3.2	......
Operator 123	F.	85	29	25	......	139	......	6	14	1,215	1,374	11.4	2.1
Operator 124[1]	F.	47	48	......	10	105	125	41	3	2,478	2,752	4.2	......
Operator 126	F.	......	19	......	......	19	4	......	......	599	622	3.2	......
Operator 127	F.	4	......	......	......	4	30	......	......	586	620	.7	......

[1] And 1 female partner.

TABLE 101.—LOSS OF TIME—Continued.

A. Body making; Singer machine—Concluded.

Shop No. and operator No.	Sex of operator.	Loss of time for which the employee is not responsible (minutes).					Loss of time for which the employer is not responsible (minutes).			Total time—		Per cent involuntary loss of time was of time worked.	Per cent time lost on account of breakdown of machine was of time worked.
		Waiting for work.	Waiting for parts.	Breakdown of machine.	Receiving instruction.	Total.	Tardiness and early leaving.	Personal needs.	Repairing work.	Worked (minutes).	Under observation (minutes).		
Shop No. 1230—Concluded.													
Operator 129	F.	......	......	......	......	......	......	......	......	768	768	......	......
Operator 109	F.	......	34	8	......	42	10	7	......	1,537	1,596	2.7	0.5
Operator 110	F.	193	33	......	......	226	27	......	......	802	1,055	28.2	......
Operator 111	F.	31	......	......	11	42	10	10	......	1,388	1,450	3.0	......
Operator 104	F.	13	......	......	......	13	5	9	......	1,223	1,250	1.1	......
Operator 105	F.	38	40	......	......	78	10	9	......	1,366	1,463	5.7	......
Operator 106[1]	F.	3	......	......	......	3	25	15	......	1,446	1,489	.2	......
Operator 102	F.	7	2	......	......	9	140	28	7	1,061	1,245	.8	......
Operator 103	F.	29	25	......	......	54	10	6	......	970	1,040	5.6	......
Operator 114	F.	28	......	8	......	36	59	3	......	1,712	1,810	2.1	.5
Operator 100	F.	23	55	......	......	78	......	......	13	1,113	1,204	7.0	......
Operator 115	M.	......	55	......	......	55	10	8	......	1,163	1,236	4.7	......
Operator 116[2]	M.	57	......	......	22	79	......	24	59	1,689	1,851	4.7	......
Operator 121[2]	M.	74	20	......	21	115	......	39	17	2,422	2,593	4.7	......
Operator 125	M.	......	......	......	......	......	......	10	43	997	1,050	......	......
Operator 128[2]	M.	66	46	30	19	161	42	20	......	2,751	2,974	5.8	1.1
Operator 112[1]	M.	19	5	7	......	31	......	16	23	2,514	2,584	1.2	.3
Operator 101	M.	15	15	3	......	33	......	17	......	1,320	1,370	2.5	.2
Operator 113[1]	M.	32	9	......	......	41	5	61	......	2,488	2,595	1.6	......
Operator 108[1]	M.	47	74	......	......	121	......	73	......	2,882	3,076	4.2	......
Total	......	904	631	81	92	1,708	654	442	179	43,721	46,704	......	......
Per cent of time worked	......	2.1	1.4	0.2	0.2	3.9	1.5	1.0	0.4	......	......	3.9	.2
Shop No. 1232.													
Operator 141	F.	14	34	6	......	54	......	......	15	1,426	1,495	3.8	.4
Operator 142	F.	28	41	3	......	72	40	5	39	1,712	1,868	4.2	.2
Operator 144	F.	21	20	8	......	49	10	......	7	996	1,062	4.9	.8
Operator 145	F.	41	23	......	......	64	11	4	......	1,642	1,721	3.9	......
Operator 147[3]	F.	28	13	......	3	44	4	......	3	2,625	2,676	1.7	......
Operator 148	F.	10	17	3	......	30	10	......	......	1,570	1,610	1.9	.2
Operator 130[2]	M.	33	33	29	5	100	28	26	60	2,765	2,979	3.6	1.0
Operator 131[2]	M.	40	42	7	27	116	48	31	6	1,954	2,155	5.9	.4
Operator 132[1]	M.	10	62	2	17	91	5	57	......	3,073	3,226	3.0	.1
Operator 133[2]	M.	3	27	4	......	34	30	29	5	1,314	1,412	2.6	.3
Operator 134[2]	M.	6	7	......	2	15	......	20	......	932	967	1.6	......
Operator 135[2]	M.	12	13	1	......	26	......	7	......	1,080	1,113	2.4	.1
Operator 136[1]	M.	......	......	......	7	7	......	......	2	243	252	2.9	......
Operator 137	M.	26	23	......	......	49	52	59	14	1,791	1,965	2.7	......
Operator 138	M.	14	16	5	......	35	56	24	......	1,451	1,566	2.4	.3
Operator 139	M.	11	3	2	......	16	20	9	5	1,179	1,229	1.4	.2
Operator 140	M.	3	......	......	......	3	4	5	14	746	772	.4	......
Operator 143[1]	M.	6	2	......	......	8	......	6	4	712	730	1.1	......
Operator 146[1]	M.	26	4	26	......	56	......	......	4	1,966	2,026	2.8	1.3
Operator 149	M.	14	2	43	......	59	39	......	13	1,004	1,115	5.9	4.3
Total	......	346	382	139	61	928	357	282	191	30,181	31,939	......	......
Per cent of time worked	......	1.1	1.3	0.5	0.2	3.1	1.2	0.9	0.6	......	......	3.1	.5

[1] And 1 female assistant. [2] And 1 male assistant. [3] And 1 female partner.

TABLE 101.—LOSS OF TIME—Continued.

Standard machine.

Shop No. and operator No.	Sex of operator.	Loss of time for which the employee is not responsible (minutes).					Loss of time for which the employer is not responsible (minutes).			Total time—		Per cent involuntary loss of time was of time worked.	Per cent time lost on account of breakdown of machine was of time worked.
		Waiting for work.	Waiting for parts.	Breakdown of machine.	Receiving instruction.	Total.	Tardiness and early leaving.	Personal needs.	Repairing work.	Worked (minutes).	Under observation (minutes).		
Shop No. 1284.													
Operator 150	F.	218	......	......	......	218	......	73	......	2,214	2,505	9.8	......
Operator 153 [1]	F.	138	60	......	......	198	42	2	43	3,162	3,447	6.3	......
Operator 154	F.	79	13	......	......	92	20	......	30	1,311	1,453	7.0	......
Operator 156 [1]	F.	50	39	......	......	89	112	2	28	4,166	4,397	2.1	......
Operator 157	F.	4	17	......	......	21	......	......	......	924	945	2.3	......
Operator 158	F.	8	96	......	......	104	......	5	......	1,120	1,229	9.3	......
Operator 160	F.	318	59	......	15	392	37	......	......	1,413	1,842	27.7	......
Operator 161	F.	16	34	......	4	54	7	3	......	1,631	1,695	3.3	......
Operator 162	F.	3	55	......	......	58	38	7	......	593	696	9.8	......
Operator 163	F.	12	27	3	......	42	......	......	6	753	801	5.6	0.4
Operator 164	F.	121	106	......	7	234	......	10	......	1,768	2,012	13.2	......
Operator 165 [2]	F.	9	226	......	......	235	......	......	58	2,193	2,486	10.7	......
Operator 172	F.	74	14	12	......	100	40	10	......	297	447	33.7	4.0
Operator 173	F.	24	55	......	......	79	50	7	......	512	648	15.4	......
Operator 174 [1]	F.	81	48	......	5	134	32	23	67	1,163	1,419	11.5	......
Operator 151 [1]	M.	......	50	......	......	50	......	......	......	2,110	2,160	2.4	......
Operator 152 [3]	M.	21	43	......	......	64	36	11	......	1,642	1,753	3.9	......
Operator 155 [3]	M.	35	27	......	......	62	10	......	32	2,515	2,619	2.5	......
Operator 159	M.	3	174	12	......	189	......	4	......	413	606	45.8	2.9
Operator 166 [2]	M.	181	40	......	......	221	......	5	......	1,700	1,926	13.0	......
Operator 167 [1]	M.	30	29	8	......	67	8	10	......	2,019	2,104	3.3	.4
Operator 168 [1]	M.	98	126	9	......	233	37	23	16	2,747	3,056	8.5	.3
Operator 169 [3]	M.	7	76	29	......	112	10	15	......	2,935	3,072	3.8	1.0
Operator 170 [1]	M.	......	191	......	......	191	15	13	7	2,528	2,754	7.6	......
Operator 171	M.	70	82	......	25	177	50	2	......	1,241	1,470	14.3	......
Operator 175	M.	3	16	......	......	19	......	2	5	1,487	1,513	1.3	......
Total	......	1,603	1,703	73	56	3,435	544	227	292	44,557	49,055	......	......
Per cent of time worked	......	3.6	3.8	0.2	0.1	7.7	1.2	0.5	0.7	......	......	7.7	.2

[1] And 1 female assistant. [2] And 1 female partner. [3] And 1 male assistant.

B. Closing: Union Special machine.

Shop No.	Number and sex of operator.		Loss of time for which the employee is not responsible.								Loss of time for which the employer is not responsible.				Total time.	
			Waiting for—				Breakdown of machine.		Total.		Tardiness and early leaving.		Personal needs.		Worked.	Under observation.
			Work.		Parts.											
	M.	F.	Minutes.	Per cent of time worked.	Minutes.	Per cent of time worked.	Minutes.	Per cent of time worked.	Minutes.	Per cent of time worked.	Minutes.	Per cent of time worked.	Minutes.	Per cent of time worked.	Minutes.	Minutes.
1110	...	1	41	7.0	....	......	11	1.9	52	8.8	....	......	5	0.9	588	645
1191	2	...	240	7.0	....	......	....	......	240	7.0	....	......	....	......	3,434	3,674
1232	...	1	86	6.9	....	......	....	......	86	6.9	12	1.0	20	1.6	1,255	1,373
1284	1	2	30	1.3	9	0.4	91	3.9	130	5.6	15	.6	12	.5	2,334	2,491
1230	1	...	163	18.5	....	......	....	......	163	18.5	....	......	....	......	882	1,045

TABLE 101.—LOSS OF TIME—Concluded.

Shop No.	Number and sex of operators.		Loss of time for which the employee is not responsible.								Loss of time for which the employer is not responsible.				Total time.	
			Waiting for—				Breakdown of machine.		Total.		Tardiness and early leaving.		Personal needs.		Worked.	Under observation.
			Work.		Parts.											
	M.	F.	Minutes.	Per cent of time worked.	Minutes.	Per cent of time worked.	Minutes.	Per cent of time worked.	Minutes.	Per cent of time worked.	Minutes.	Per cent of time worked.	Minutes.	Per cent of time worked.	Minutes.	Minutes.
C. Sleeve setting: Union Special machine.																
1284	1	1	157	18.2	25	2.9	48	5.6	230	26.7	5	0.6	14	1.6	861	1,110
1191	1	1	182	5.6	.....	......	20	.6	202	6.2	45	1.4	.....	......	3,279	3,526
D. Waist hemming: Shop No. 1110, Union Special machine; other shops, Singer machine.																
1110	...	1	5	1.5	.....	......	5	1.5	10	2.9	.....	......	2	0.6	341	353
1191	1	...	42	4.7	.....	......	.....	......	42	4.7	.....	......	.....	......	894	936
1284	1	...	89	13.3	.....	......	9	1.3	98	14.7	14	2.1	5	.7	668	785
E. Strip hemming: Singer machine.																
1230	1	...	44	4.2	.....	......	.....	......	44	4.2	.....	......	.....	......	1,036	1,080
F. Strip tucking: Singer and Wilcox & Gibbs machines.																
1230	3	4	323	2.8	.....	......	120	1.1	443	3.9	32	0.3	65	0.6	11,416	11,956
1284	...	4	60	1.8	.....	......	99	3.0	159	4.8	.....	......	19	.6	3,280	3,458
1090	...	3	140	3.6	.....	......	.....	......	140	3.6	88	2.3	.....	......	3,867	4,095
G. Short tucking: Singer and Wilcox & Gibbs machines.																
1191	3	10	3,443	36.8	.....	......	.....	......	3,443	36.8	.....	......	.....	......	9,357	12,800
1230	3	2	173	2.0	.....	......	126	1.5	299	3.5	87	1.0	46	0.5	8,616	9,048
1090	...	7	180	1.4	.....	......	.....	......	[1] 184	1.5	363	2.9	105	.8	12,667	13,319
1116	3	3	3,882	29.5	.....	......	.....	......	3,882	29.5	210	1.6	.....	......	13,163	17,255
H. Buttonhole making: Singer machine.																
1090	...	4	2,269	31.4	37	0.5	124	1.7	[2] 2,508	34.8	206	2.8	15	0.2	7,237	9,976
1110	2	...	70	7.2	.....	......	22	2.3	92	9.4	.....	......	7	.7	974	1,073
1116	1	...	64	2.2	.....	......	.....	......	64	2.2	.....	......	.....	......	2,964	3,028
1235	...	2	44	2.2	31	1.6	47	2.4	[3] 127	6.4	.....	......	.....	......	2,000	[4] 2,139
Total	3	6	2,447	18.6	68	.5	193	1.5	[5] 2,791	21.3	206	1.6	22	.2	13,175	[4] 16,216
I. Buttonhole making: Reece machine.																
1230	...	1	62	13.6	.....	......	21	4.6	83	20.4	.....	......	.....	......	456	549
1235	...	1	10	6.3	.....	......	9	5.6	19	11.9	5	3.1	.....	......	160	184
1284	2	...	93	7.4	.....	......	53	4.2	146	11.7	27	2.2	17	1.4	1,250	1,440
Total	2	2	165	8.9	.....	......	83	4.4	248	13.8	32	1.7	17	.9	1,866	2,173
K. Button sewing: Union Special machine.																
1284	...	1	57	6.1	.....	......	14	1.5	71	7.6	.....	......	20	2.1	931	1,022
1116	...	1	24	1.1	.....	......	.....	......	24	1.1	.....	......	.....	......	2,216	2,240
1230	...	1	90	9.5	.....	......	27	2.8	117	12.3	.....	......	.....	......	951	1,068

[1] 4 minutes getting instruction.
[2] 78 minutes getting instruction.
[3] 5 minutes getting instruction.
[4] 12 minutes repairing work.
[5] 83 minutes getting instruction.

CONCLUSION.

The figures presented in Part II of this report show that in spite of the great variation in the productive capacity of the individual workers in different shops and even in the same shops, the differences between the shops as a whole are sufficiently small on a large number of operations to allow of the establishment of standard rates for all the shops of a certain class. With the exception of a few operations, outside of body making, the figures presented here relate exclusively to shops manufacturing cheap waists selling at $9 per dozen to retail stores. In so far as the figures for the same operations differ radically for various shops, they can be traced to distinct causes, due chiefly to differences in systems of management and organization of the work. While the variation is not sufficiently great in the $9 shops to prevent standardization of piece rates in that branch of the industry, the wide differences in the systems of factory management and in the conditions under which the operators are obliged to work in different shops, make it exceedingly difficult to devise a scheme of uniform piece rates to be paid in all shops manufacturing garments of a higher grade. A scale of rates paid in shops in which efficiency is the keynote, in which the operator is able to work steadily through the day without waste of time, with up-to-date machinery and appliances, and amid sanitary surroundings, may be fully adequate to enable the workers to earn good wages in that shop. The same schedule of piece rates may prove totally inadequate for operators of equal skill working in a shop where lack of system on the part of the management results in frequent interruptions and stoppages of work; because the operator constantly misses necessary parts of garments which should be supplied to him at the time he gets his "bundle"; because the cutting is done poorly, causing the operator to stop in his work to make the different parts fit or to take the parts to the cutter to have them trimmed down; because the force in different departments is not properly balanced, thereby causing partial or total stoppage of work in one department, while another department is behind with its work and unable to furnish the parts needed in the first department; because work is furnished to the operators in small bundles, which results in more handling of the garments and more frequent interruptions in passing from one operation to another than is the case in the first shop where larger bundles are the rule; because it is the practice in the shop to start the operator on a new bundle before he is through with the one he has on hand and to follow this up with a third and a fourth bundle before any of these is completed, so that the work on each of these has to be interrupted as the missing parts for the different bundles turn up or as the demands of the customers call for the earlier completion of one or the other of the bundles; because the machinery is old or in poor condition and breaks down frequently, causing stoppage of work, as well as producing less while working; because little or no instruction is given to operators to secure uniformity in methods of work, resulting in great waste of time on the part of the less experienced workers, to the detriment of the firm and employees alike. These are a few of the conditions which determine the relative efficiency of different shops. This explains why in many cases the output per hour in different factories (as e. g., in buttonhole making) has been found to differ 100 per cent and even more. It is therefore clear that no successful attempt can be made to bring about uniform rates throughout the industry without first establishing greater uniformity in factory management and the system under which operators are required to work.

It would be an utterly hopeless task, however, to undertake to bring about absolutely uniform methods of factory management. The great difference in the size of the factories, employing, as has been shown in the first part of this report, anywhere from less than 25 to more than 500 workers each, calls necessarily for different systems of work distribution and, to some extent, of division of labor; the difference in their financial resources will enable the larger manufacturers, making the same kind of goods, to use superior machinery, cut larger bundles, employ instructors, and do a great many other things to cheapen production which would be beyond the means of the smaller manufacturer working with insufficient capital. A great many things, however, can be standardized and adopted throughout the industry irrespective of the size of the resources of the individual firms. But to accomplish this in an industry having more than 700 firms working in keen competition with one another and therefore each jealous of its own real or fancied secrets of business or of factory management and extremely reluctant to throw their shops open to investigation by representatives of an organization of which they are a part, would take years of patient and persistent effort.

But while it is impracticable to undertake the introduction of uniform methods of factory management, it does not follow necessarily that the standardization of piece rates is impossible. What may be done, is to standardize conditions under which certain piece rates are to apply. The piece rates may be the result of a series of tests made in a number of shops with several workers of more or less average speed under conditions to be carefully noted, and as nearly as possible like those which can reasonably be expected to prevail in an ordinary well-managed shop. The tests could be of two kinds: (1) For the purpose of standardizing separate operations; (2) for establishing piece rates on standard garments.

As to the first, the proposed investigation for standardization of operations would not differ in its aims and its ultimate form from the results presented in this report, so far as positive results have been obtained. The difference would be in the methods to be pursued. Instead of timing hundreds of workers on thousands of dozens of garments under conditions as they happen to be found in the shops, the method would consist in selecting a comparatively limited number of skilled operators, say a dozen, of a fairly average speed, and timing each of these operators on hundreds if not thousands of operations under various conditions, but never varying more than one condition at a time, so as to be able clearly to trace cause and effect. An illustration will make the meaning clear: In discussing the figures for tucking, it has been shown in this report that the output per hour will vary with (1) the width of the tuck; (2) the length of the tuck; (3) the number of stitches per inch; (4) the presence or absence of tucks of more than one width; (5) whether the tucks are arranged in clusters or not; (6) whether the distances between the tucks and the clusters are uniform or not; (7) whether all the tucks run the full length of the waist; (8) and if they do not, whether they are of uniform or varying length; (9) and if of varying length, how many different lengths there are; (10) on the number of tucks to the waist; (11) the number of waists to the bundle; (12) the material of which the garment is made; (13) the make of the machine on which the work is done; (14) whether the tucks are made free-hand or with a gauge, etc.

On account of the conditions under which the present investigation was carried on we were forced to time the operator while working in the regular performance of his or her duties on such work as happened to be done at the time at the particular factory. The result was that when the same operator was found to vary anywhere from 10 to 100 per cent in his output on the same operation, it has rarely, if ever, been possible to place the finger on any one cause. The second job might differ from the first not only in the size of the bundle, but also in the number of tucks to the waist, in their arrangement, width, and in three or four other points. For this reason it has proved impossible to submit, with the present report, a basis for a scale of rates except on a more or less average basis taking in a wide variety of conditions for each of which there ought to be a separate rate. The proposed method would require putting each operator selected for the test to work on a certain style of tucks and then varying one condition at a time to ascertain how the output would differ with each change. Such a method would require the testing of each operator for at least a week on tucking alone.

In view of the great number of operations and especially the almost endless variation in the combination of different conditions affecting the output for each operation, as illustrated above in the case of tucking, it would probably take not less than two years to work out a scale of piece rates which would cover the most common requirements of shops manufacturing staple lines of garments.

A schedule of this kind in prescribing a rate for any operation would specify the conditions under which it was to be applied. If the standard size of bundle were, say, 2½ dozen waists, and a shop furnished work to its operators in bundles of 1 dozen or 5 dozen, the rate would have to be adjusted by the wage-scale board in each case unless the schedule provided a sliding scale for the automatic adjustment of the rate under specified conditions. In this manner without attempting to tell each manufacturer how he is to run his factory, an inducement would be created for each manufacturer in the trade to bring the conditions of work in his shop as nearly as possible in accord with the standards laid down in the schedule so that he could get the benefit of rates allowed in shops in which standard conditions prevailed.

As stated, the complete working out of such a scale of piece rates would be a matter of years. Much as it may seem desirable to undertake the task for an industry like this, which is here to stay, it is confronted with the necessity of meeting immediately the pressing problems of piece-rate adjustment which claim the attention of the wage-scale board from day to day as disputes arise between individual manufacturers and their employees as to what is a proper rate for a given garment. It is with this in mind that the second series of tests has been suggested above, viz, the establishment of piece rates on standard garments.

Apart from the short-comings of the present test system, pointed out in the introductory chapter to this part of the report, the chief objection to it, raised both by the employers and the union, is that it fails to bring about uniformity of piece rates for the same class of work in different shops. Manufacturers who believe that they are paying, or that they are called upon to pay, higher rates than some of their competitors refuse to accede to the demands of their employees, while the union on its part claims that certain manufacturers are taking advantage of the presence of a large proportion of non-union workers in their shops, or of the ignorance of their employees to pay lower rates than their competitors. To overcome this difficulty a committee of the wage-scale board has had under consideration a proposed modification of the present test system which promises to bring about greater uniformity in rates paid in different shops for similar garments. The chief features of the proposed scheme are (1) the creation of a set of standard garments; (2) the selection of a number of typical shops for the purpose of testing the standard garments; (3) the determination of the hourly rate of the test workers by means of standard rates adopted for the standard garments.

1. It is proposed to make up a set of standard garments embodying all the operations which are required in making garments currently in style.

2. The wage-scale board is to select a number of leading shops, typical of the industry, in each of which two or more experienced workers of about average speed are to be selected as test operators by both sides in the same manner as it is done at present. These workers are to make up the standard garments from the samples furnished them, and the average time taken by all the test operators in all of the shops selected, multiplied by a rate agreed upon for these workers, is to constitute the standard piece rate for each of the standard garments, and is to be used as a common basis in all the other shops in the industry in determining rates on new garments.

3. Whenever a new garment is to be tested in a shop, it is to be done under practically the same conditions as at present, except that the hourly rate of the test worker is to be determined in a different way. Under the present system the hourly rate of the test worker is ascertained by averaging up the weekly earnings of that worker for a number of weeks as shown on the pay roll, and dividing the amount by 50, which constitutes the normal working hours for a week. This is open to two objections: The first, on the part of the workers, that the pay roll does not show the number of hours actually put in by the worker. It is well known that at times some workers may be idle for a great many hours during the week on account of lack of work or other causes, and the 10 per cent allowance for loss of time which is usually made in these cases is not considered by the union as meeting this objection. It is, therefore, claimed by the union that the hourly rate, as thus determined, is below the actual earning capacity of the worker, which could be demonstrated if she were given an opportunity to work in the same manner as she is during the test on a new garment, when only the time she is actually at work is considered in determining the time it takes her to make the new garment.

The second objection to which this method is open is raised both by the manufacturers and the union, and is to the effect that it does not secure a uniform hourly rate for workers of the same skill in different shops, since it tends to perpetuate the differences in the methods of compensation prevailing in these shops.

The proposed method aims to do away with these shortcomings and to reduce the determination of the hourly rate of the test workers to a uniform basis in the following manner:

To determine the hourly rate of the test worker, she is to be given one or more samples of standard garments suitable to the production of the shop in which she is working, and on which she is to be tested, in the same manner as she is tested on the new garment. That is to say, if it is decided that in testing a new garment she is to make half a dozen for a test, then in determining her hourly rate she is likewise to make half a dozen of the standard garment; if she is given only one or two garments to make in testing the new garment, then this should be the number in testing the standard garment for determining her hourly rate. The time taken to make these garments would determine the hourly rate of each test worker. To illustrate: If the rate for a certain standard garment were $1, and it took the test worker three hours to make it, the hourly rate of that operator would be 33 cents per hour. If an operator selected for a test in another shop makes the same garment in two hours, her rate would be 50 cents per hour. In this way, the rates of the different test operators would continue to differ, as they do at present, according to their individual skill and speed, as well as according to the methods of manufacturing prevailing in the different shops; but they will all be based on uniform rates for standard garments which would apply to all shops. The method holds out the promise of a fair degree of uniformity of rates for similar garments in different shops while leaving each shop free to follow its own way of making the garments. While it would not secure absolute uniformity on account of many technical difficulties which would beset the carrying out of this plan, yet it would mean the taking of a long stride toward such uniformity and would put the industry in a position to wait for a more detailed adjustment of piece rates for separate operations as outlined above.

APPENDIX A.

PROTOCOL OF PEACE IN THE DRESS AND WAIST INDUSTRY.

Protocol of Peace in the dress and waist industry entered into this 18th day of January, 1913, between the International Ladies' Garment Workers' Union (hereinafter called the union) and the Dress and Waist Manufacturers' Association (hereinafter called the association).

Both parties to this protocol are desirous of raising conditions in the industry, and obtaining the equalization of standards of labor throughout the industry by peaceful and honorable methods. They recognize the value, to accomplish this end, of an organization representing the workers in the industry, and of an organization representing the employers. They recognize also the value of an understanding or agreement between them capable of revision from time to time, with adequate machinery and institutions to enforce and carry out the principles of the understanding.

I. SANITARY CONDITIONS.

Both parties agree to create a joint board of sanitary control in all jurisdictional respects similar to the joint board of sanitary control now existing in the cloak industry, two members thereof to be chosen by the manufacturers, two by the union, and three to represent the public—the three representatives of the public now upon the board in the cloak industry. Said board is empowered to establish standards of sanitary conditions to which the manufacturers' association and the union shall be committed, and the manufacturers and the union obligate themselves to maintain such standards to the best of their ability and to the full extent of their power. The standards of such board, to begin with, shall be at least as high as the standards now existing in the cloak industry.

II. THE WHITE PROTOCOL LABEL.

To make more effective the maintenance of sanitary conditions throughout the industry, to insure equality of minimum standards throughout the industry, and to guarantee to the public garments made in the shops certificated by the board of sanitary control, the parties agree that there shall be instituted in the industry a system of certificating garments by a label to be affixed to the garment. Recognizing the difficulties of working out the details of such a plan at this time, but believing that the plan has been sufficiently developed and considered in the cloak industry, they believe that a complete plan can be worked out in the dress and waist industry within a year: To this end each party agrees to cooperate to the full extent of its power in the formulation and effectuation of a system for the certification of garments adequately safeguarding the employers, the workers, and the consuming public.

An additional increase of 10 per cent (approximately) shall be granted in all wages as soon as the system of certificating garments to the consumer herein referred to shall have been in operation for one year.

III. ADJUSTMENT OF GRIEVANCES.

Both parties recognize the necessity for providing modern and peaceful methods for adjusting disputes and grievances that arise. The system and method for adjusting disputes and determining controversies in the cloak industry having proved successful, they agree that there shall be created in the dress and waist industry a board of grievances to consist of 10 members—5 chosen by the manufacturers and 5 by the union—with the rules, regulations, and precedents now governing the board of grievances in the cloak industry so far as they are practically applicable in the dress and waist industry.

IV. CONFERENCES.

The board of grievances shall also be the continuous conference body to which shall be brought all problems and all plans for improvement in the industry, which both parties are to consider.

V. PERMANENT PEACE.

The parties to this protocol agree that there shall be no strike or lockout concerning any matters in controversy or any disagreement until full opportunity shall have been given for the submission of such matters to the board of grievances and to the board of arbitration created hereunder, and in the event of a determination of such controversy or difference by said board of arbitration only in case of failure to accede to the determination of said board of arbitration.

The parties hereby establish a board of arbitration to consist of three members, composed of one nominee for the manufacturers, one nominee for the union, and one representative of the public, the latter to be agreed upon by both parties to this protocol, or in the event of their disagreement, by the two arbitrators selected by them.

Until otherwise determined, the gentlemen constituting the board of arbitration in the cloak industry shall constitute the board of arbitration in this industry.

VI. TENTATIVE SCHEDULES.

The parties agree that the industry is very large, and the conditions complicated; that there are many types of shops and that the earnings of the employees in the shops vary widely in scale; and further frankly admit that they are not now in full possession of the facts as to present conditions in the industry. The provisions in this agreement or protocol relating to schedules of wages or other standards of labor are therefore tentative, and no final determination of these matters shall be made until after a complete investigation of conditions as hereinafter provided for and the board of grievances shall have had opportunity to pass thereon, and in the event of the failure of the members of such board to agree then until the final determination by the board of arbitration in the manner herein provided.

VII. WAGE-SCALE BOARD.

The parties hereby establish a wage-scale board to consist of eight members—four to be nominated by the manufacturers and four by the union. Such board shall standardize the prices to be paid for piece and week work throughout the industry; it shall preserve data and statistics with a view to establishing, as nearly practicable as possible, a scientific basis for the fixing of piece and week work prices throughout the industry that will insure a minimum wage, and at the same time permit reward for increased efficiency. It shall have full power and authority to appoint clerks or representatives expert in the art of fixing prices, and its procedure, so far as practicable, shall be the same as now followed by the board of grievances in the cloak industry. It shall have full power and authority to settle all disputes over prices, make special exemptions for week work where special exigencies arise, or a special scale is required.

VIII. IMMEDIATE INVESTIGATION.

Immediately after the signing of this protocol the wage-scale board shall, at the expense of both parties, make a complete and exhaustive examination into the existing rates paid for labor, the earnings of the operatives, and the classification of garments in the industry, and shall report in writing within six months from the date hereof the result of its labors. It shall be the duty of the board of grievances thereafter immediately to convene and to act upon said report, and, based upon such report, said board of grievances shall establish a rate or rates per hour for the adjustment of piece prices and to readjust any of the schedules tentatively agreed upon in the schedule hereto annexed.

IX. TENTATIVE STANDARDS OF LABOR.

The parties agree upon the standards of labor and wages set forth in schedule A, subject to revision by the grievance board in the light of experience, and after full investigation of the facts as provided in Article VI.

Where higher standards now exist they shall in no case be lowered.

X. ADJUSTMENT OF PIECE PRICES.

The following method for determining piece prices for operators is adopted:

(*a*) There shall be in each shop a piece-price committee selected by the workers.

(*b*) In the first instance, piece prices shall be settled by the employer and the piece-price committee.

(*c*) In settling prices the price per garment shall be based upon the estimated number of solid hours it will take an experienced good worker to make the garment without interruption, multiplied by the standard price per hour.

(*d*) If the piece-price committee and the employer shall be unable to agree after a conference, the work shall then be proceeded with, but the determination of the price to be paid for the work shall be made as follows:

(*e*) One or more workers shall be selected to make the test for the purpose of determining the number of solid hours it will take an experienced good worker to make the garment in question.

(*f*) Both the employer and the piece-price committee shall agree upon the operative who is to make the test, but in case they shall fail to agree, the wage-scale board shall make such designation.

Pending the determination of standard prices per hour by the wage-scale board, operators shall receive the following temporary increases:

In all shops where the standard per hour is now less than 28 cents, there shall be an increase of at least 15 per cent.

In all shops where the standard per hour is less than 30 cents and more than 28 cents, there shall be an increase of at least 10 per cent.

In all shops where the standard per hour is now 31 cents or 32 cents, the standard shall be advanced to 33 cents. In no shop shall the standard rate per hour be less than 30 cents, and where the rate is now 33 cents or more, the present standard rate shall in no case be reduced.

In case of any dispute or controversy in any shop as to what is the standard per hour now paid, such dispute or controversy shall be settled by the wage-scale board, and its decision shall be final.

There shall be no stoppage of work because of any dispute over piece prices, but the matter shall be adjusted in the manner herein provided, and when the prices are fixed they shall relate back to the time of the beginning of the work.

XI. INDIVIDUAL CONTRACTS WITH EMPLOYERS.

The union recognizes the moral obligation of every employer in the industry to belong to the manufacturers' association and to contribute to the expense of the institutions created by the two parties for the uplift of the industry. It acknowledges the value of such an association in the maintenance of standards throughout the industry. Accordingly, all employers desiring to settle with the union in the pending strike will be referred first to the association and requested to apply for membership. If for any reason the association rejects their application, the grounds for such rejection shall be stated to a committee on review, consisting of six members—three nominated by the union and three by the manufacturers. If any employer in the industry shall fail to join the association and shall enter into an individual contract with the union, there shall be no difference in maximum standards of hours, or minimum standards of wages, or sanitary conditions (except that the period within which changes to conform to sanitary standards shall be made shall be fixed by the joint board of sanitary control).

The union agrees to lay before said committee on review every original contract entered into between it and individual employers, together with a true statement of the nature and amount of any security taken for the faithful performance of such contract.

During the general strike the association will remain in executive session to pass upon applications for membership.

XII. EQUALIZATION OF STANDARDS.

Whether or not specifically referred to in any of the provisions of this protocol, the parties agree that it is essential that competition in the industry, so far as labor is concerned, shall be placed upon a plane of equality (making due allowance for difference in skill), and that both parties to the full extent of their power shall establish such equality.

XIII. THE PREFERENTIAL UNION SHOP.

The parties hereby accept the principles and the obligations of the "preferential union shop" as defined and understood in the cloak industry, and more fully described under that heading at pages 215–217 of Bulletin No. 98 of the United States Bureau of Labor.

XIV. IMMEDIATE PROBLEMS FOR ARBITRATION.

The question of which legal holidays shall be observed in the industry shall be submitted to the board of arbitration created under this protocol, and, without prejudice to the merits of the question, Lincoln's Birthday and Washington's Birthday, 1913, shall be observed, unless the decision of the board is rendered prior thereto.

XV. SUBCONTRACTING.

All inside subcontracting shall be abolished.

XVI. MISCELLANEOUS.

The provisions of Paragraph XIX of the protocol in the cloak industry, with reference to filling vacancies in boards or committees, shall apply hereto, and, so far as applicable to the dress and waist industry, the precedents, usages, and rules of procedure already established and existing in the cloak industry shall be followed.

The minutes of the proceedings of the conferences resulting in the acceptance of this protocol shall govern all matters not specifically referred to herein.

In witness whereof, the parties have hereto set their hands and seals, and authorized their respective officers to affix the signature of the respective organizations hereto.

For the Dress and Waist Manufacturers' Association:

SAM'L FLOERSHEIMER, *President.*
WALTER H. BARTHOLOMEW, *General Manager.*

For the International Ladies' Garment Workers' Union:

ABRAHAM ROSENBERG, *President.*
JOHN A. DYCHE, *Secretary.*

The American Federation of Labor will stand back of the International Ladies' Garment Workers' Union in the faithful performance of the foregoing protocol.

SAMUEL GOMPERS,
President American Federation of Labor.
HUGH FRAYNE,
General Organizer American Federation of Labor.

In the presence of—
JULIUS HENRY COHEN.

SCHEDULE "A."

(Tentative; pending final decision by the grievance board or board of arbitration.)

HOURS OF LABOR.

Fifty hours shall constitute a week's work. After there shall have been in operation for one year the system of certificating garments referred to in the annexed protocol the hours of labor shall be reduced to 49 hours per week, provided the other branches in the women's wear industry then under union agreement shall also have agreed to a standard of 49 hours per week.

WEEK WORKERS.

CUTTERS:

Full-fledged cutters shall receive not less than $25 per week.

Apprentices shall be divided into three grades—

Grade A: Apprentices of less than one year's standing.

Grade B: Apprentices of more than one year's and less than two years' standing.

Grade C: Apprentices of more than two years' and less than three years' standing.

Apprentices shall receive:

Grade A: $6 per week.

Grade B: $12 per week.

Grade C: $18 per week.

On or about the 15th days of June and November in each year Local No. 10 shall hold an examination for the purpose of admitting apprentices of grade C to the class of full-fledged cutters.

After January 1, 1914, the following rule shall be adopted: In each shop there shall be not more than one apprentice for each five cutters employed, but in case there shall be less than five cutters employed one apprentice may be employed.

At least one cutter shall be employed in each shop of members of the association.

DRAPERS: Not less than $14 per week.

JOINERS: Not less than $12 per week.

EXAMINERS: Not less than $10 per week.

SAMPLE HANDS:

Not less than $14 per week;

Not more than one assistant to each four sample hands.

IRONERS:

Women not less than $12 per week;

Men not less than $15 per week.

An increase of a dollar per week in the minimum scale after the agreement shall have been in force for one year.

PRESSERS:

Not less than $20 per week.

An increase of $2 per week in the minimum scale after the agreement shall have been in force for one year.

DRESSMAKER FINISHERS: Not less than $8 per week.

PLAIN FINISHERS:

Sewing hooks and eyes, four for 1 cent.

Sewing patent hooks and eyes, four for 1 cent.

Sewing ordinary buttons, six for 1 cent.

Sewing self-shank buttons, three for 1 cent.

Sewing belts, two for 1 cent.

Basting bottom of skirts, 2 cents each.

Sewing in belts, 2 cents each.

But in no case less than $8 per week for 50 hours' work, after one week's trial.

LACE RUNNERS—TUCKERS—BUTTONHOLE MAKERS—BUTTON SEWING—SLEEVE SETTING—CLOSING AND HEMMING:

Pending investigation by the wage-scale board for the purpose of establishing standards for lace running, buttonhole making, button sewing, sleeve setting, closing and hemming, and tucking, shall be settled as to prices in each shop by the piece-price committee and the employer, and in the event of controversy, the matter shall be settled by the wage-scale board in the manner provided for in the protocol for operators.

OPERATORS:

Operators shall be paid by the piece the standard price per hour to be fixed after the investigation by the wage-scale board within six months, and in the meantime there shall be the percentages of increase referred to in Paragraph X.

OVERTIME.

Not more than four (4) hours in any one week, nor two (2) hours in any one day, except for cutters, who are allowed to work overtime not more than two and one-half (2½) hours in any one day. No overtime between Saturday at 1 p. m. and Monday at 8 a. m., except on specials requiring completion by finishers or pressers for immediate delivery, and then for not more than two (2) hours. Double pay for overtime (week workers).

ADDITIONAL INCREASES.

An additional increase of 10 per cent, approximately, shall be granted by the manufacturers as soon as a system of certificating garments to the consumer, referred to in Paragraph II of the annexed protocol, shall have been in operation for one year.

APPENDIX B.

LIST OF FIRMS IN THE DRESS AND WAIST INDUSTRY OF GREATER NEW YORK COVERED BY THIS REPORT.

1. ASSOCIATION SHOPS.

Abraham, Roman & Co.
A. Adler & Co.
Adler & Ast.
Louis Adler.
Advance Waist Co.
Aero Waist Co.
Alco Waist & Dress House.
Adolph Alper.
Alpern & Co.
American Suit & Dress Co.
American Lady Waist Co.
American Shirt Waist Co.
Arkin & Guild.
M. Arluck.
Sam'l Aronson.
Artistic Waist Co.
Artistic Waist & Dress Co.
J. Atkin.
D. Basin.
Bass & Silverman.
Bedford Waist & Dress Co.
Beerman & Frank.
M. B. Behrman.
Besthoff Sonn Co.
Robert Bernhard.
Bijou Waist Co.
M. Block & Co.
Bloom & Millman.
Emil Blumenthal.
Blumenthal & Co.
M. Brambir.
Brill-Abrams Co.
Brill & Kaplan Co.
S. Brookstone & Sons.
Lane Bryant.
Buchwald & Polak.
E. Cashman Costume Co. (Inc.).
Cederbaum & Wassow.
Century Dress Co.
Citron Bros.
Daniel Cohen.
Henry Cohen & Co.
H. Cohen & Co.
J. & M. Cohn.
Costuma & Zimetbaum.
Crans, Shane & Scherr.
Crescent Costume Co.
Dallet & Weyl.
Danziger & Sanville.
Davis & Ginsberg.
Casper Davis & Son.
Ben. S. Deutsch.
Dicker & Ginsberg.
A. W. Drubin & Kantrowitz Co.
The Drubin Co.
Eclipse Silk Waist Co.
Max Edison.
J. & S. Elisberg.
Embroidered Garment Co.
Empire Waist Co.
Ess Kay Waist Co.
A. & H. Evalenko.
Excel Mfg. Co.
Famous Waist Co.
Fashion Garment Co.
Leo Feinberg.
Feldman Bros.
Wm. Fels (Inc.).
Felsenthal Bros.
Fernbach & Schulman.
Feinman Bros.
Leo Finkenberg.
Flan & Rosner.
Sam'l Floersheimer & Bros.
The Floersheimer Co.
B. Frank.
B. N. Frank.
Frank Bros. & Barsha.
Frank & Bauer.
Frankenthal Bros.
Frechtel Bros.
J. L. Friedman.
Freitag & Keim.
John Fried.
Friedman & Mally.
Jonas Fuld.
Gaiety Waist Co.
B. Geist & Co.
Henry George & Rosenbaum Co.
Ginsberg Bros.
J. Glockner & Co.
J. W. Goetz.
J. Goldberg.
Goldman Costume Co.
Goldschmidt & Co.
Henry Goldstein & Co.
Nathan Goldstein & Co.
M. & E. Goodman.
I. Goodstein.
Gotham Waist Co.
Grauer & Avedon.
Max Greenberg & Co.
Greenberg, Weiner & Co.
Greenwald, Friedman & Co.
Sol. Gross & Co.
Gross & Weiss.
Sam'l Grossman.
Albert Harris.
Benjamin Height.
Geo. C. Heimerdinger Co.
Max Held (Inc.).
I. Heller & Co.
H. Himmelstein.
Hirsch & Cohen.
Hirsch-Cohen-Wise Co.
Hirschberg & Kohn.

Hollow & Perlow.
Holtzman & Weinstein.
Hommel Manufacturing Co.
Hopf & Daxon.
Horwitz & Horwitz.
Howard & Dennis (Inc.).
Howard Ladies' Apparel Manufacturing Co.
I. B. Hyman Co. (Inc.).
Ideal Rose Waist Co.
Chas. Iger & Bros.
Immergut & Drucker.
Imperial Dress Co.
Integrity Garment Manufacturing Co.
International Manufacturing Co.
Iris Waist Co.
Joel Isaacs & Sons.
I. X. L. Waist Co.
E. A. Jackson.
Nathan H. Jacobson & Co.
H. Jacoby & Co.
Jaffy & Barnett.
Kabat Bros.
Kohn, Weiss & Feig.
J. Kaplon.
Max Kass.
Kastner & Lewison.
Kaufman Costume Co.
Kaufman, Gladstone & Co.
Kayanee Waist & Dress Co.
King, Davidson & Co.
Klein Bros.
Klubock & Silverberg.
Regina Kobler.
Kondell Bros.
Krugman & Peltz
Kupfer Bros. Co.
Kurzrok Bros.
Lahm & Deutz.
La Rose Waist Co.
Lask Manufacturing Co.
Lowell Dress Co.
Lefcourt & Brenner.
I. Lefkowitz.
Leibowitz Bros.
Louis Leiserson.
Lenox Dress Manufacturing Co.
Nathan Lepow & Son.
Lesser-Kalb Manufacturing Co.
Levine & Marcus Co.
M. Levy.
Graber, Lipshitz & Adelson.
I. Lipshitz.
Litwin & Diamond.
Maisner & Co.
Majestic Dress Co.
Larry J. Margulies.
Markowitz Waist Co.
Mayer & Ikelheimer.
Mayfair Waist Co.
Melman Bros.
A. B. Mergentheim & Co.
Meyer Bros.
Mitchell, Bloch & Kronenberg.
Mikola & Bro.
Mitchell & Weber.
Mitnick & Canaan.
Model Waist & Dress Co.
Monarch Waist & Dress Co.
Geo. H. Montrose & Co.
Jos. A. Morris & Co.
Murphy Waist House.
Mutual Waist & Dress Co.
M. I. Nathan (Inc.).
National Dress Co.
National Shirt Waist Co.
Newport Waist Co.
J. Opoznauer & Co.
Oriental Shirt Waist & Dress Co.
Paramount Manufacturing Co.
Parisian Dress Co.
Parisian Manufacturing Co.
H. J. Pasternak.
Perlman Bros.
M. Perlman.
Phoenix Waist Co.
G. M. Piermont & Co.
Pioneer Ladies' Garment Co.
Princess Shirt Waist Co.
Princess Waist Co.
Propp & Gerrick.
Queen Manufacturing Co.
Rabinowitz Bros.
M. Rabinowitz.
S. Rakusin & Co.
Rapp-Jelenko Co.
Regent Waist Co.
Reliance Waist Co.
M. & H. Rentner.
Rosen Bros.
Joseph Rosenberg.
Rosenmeyer & Diamond.
Rosenthal Bros. Co.
Sig. Rosenthal.
B. Rosenwasser & Co.
Ph. Rosenwasser.
Milius Rothfeld & Co.
Rothstein & Rothstein.
Royal Dress Co.
Sachs & Freed.
Sansome & Gotlieb.
Shlang & Co.
Schleif & Greenberg.
Schmidt, Raymond & Co.
B. Schenfeld.
Schulman & Isaacs.
David Schustack & Co.
Seeligman & Stern.
G. & B. Seid & Co.
Sachs & Kessler.
Senner & Kaplan.
Shanley Dress Co.
M. Sobel.
Sherr Bros.
Shulsky Bros.
Siegel-Foster-Adair Co.
A. Schwartz & Co.
M. Schwartz.
Siegel-Foster Co.
Siegel & Solomon.
Chas. F. Siemons.
Silverman & Becker.
S. Simon & Co.
Siren Manufacturing Co.
I. B. Skudowitz.
Smith & Meyer.

Solomon, Benedikt & Co.
Solomon & Meltzer.
Son & Ash.
Arthur H. Spiro.
Spiegelman & Gottlieb.
Star Dress Manufacturing Co.
David Stein.
Stein & Perlman.
Alfred Stern Co.
Sterngold & Brill.
M. Stern & Co.
Stern & Frances.
H. Sternberg.
Superior Waist Co.
Tiptop Waist & Dress Co.
Triangle Waist Co.
Tutelman Bros.
David Ullman.
Universal Waist Co.
Venus Costume Co.
Waldorf Waist Co.
Wallach Bros.
Aaron Webster.
Martin H. Weil & Co.
Weil & Hoey.
Weiler Bros.
Arthur M. Weiner.
Sam'l Weintraub.
Jos. Weisman.
M. Weisman & Sons.
Jos. Wien.
Wiesen & Goldstein.
Windsor Manufacturing Co.
E. D. Winter & Co.
H. Wolpert & Co.
Jesse Woolf & Otto B. Shulhof.
Yankee Waist Co.
Yorkville Dress Co.

2. NONASSOCIATION UNION SHOPS.

A. D. Abrahams Co.
Alsfrom Bros. & Gottfried.
Alton Dress House.
American Beauty Waist Co.
American Waist & Garment Co.
Arlington Dress Co.
Chas. Ashendorf.
B. B. Manufacturing Co.
A. Bandersky.
The Bell Dress House.
Beverman & Freidman.
Berger & Koeppel.
Black & Silverman.
Bomzer & Freedman.
Belmont Waist Co.
D. Bendersky.
Benwit Costume Co.
Berkly Dress Co.
J. Berman.
L. Berman & Co.
Boston Dress Co.
Brenner Bros.
Brown & Ginsburg.
Bull Moose Dress Co.
Bull Moose Tucking Co.
Mezer Canter.
R. R. Casale.
Clever Waist Co.
H. Cohen.
Cohen Bros.
L. Cohen.
Cohen & Ginsburg.
Cohen & Levinson.
Claremont Waist Co.
Columbia Waist Co.
Cosmopolitan Dress Co.
Countess Dress Co.
Crescent Waist Co.
L. Corin.
Jos. Damoras.
Diamond-Hammer.
I. Dicker.
Dolowitz Tea Gown.
Drachlis & Spivack.
Ehronson & Deutch.
Electra Dress Co.
Ellis, Solomon & Co.
H. Ensler.
A. Epstein.
Eureka Waist Co.
Everight Waist & Dress Co.
Excellent Manufacturing Co.
Fair Waist Co.
Favorite Waist & Dress Co.
H. Feldstein.
Field & Samuel.
L. Finkelstein.
Chas. J. Fishel.
Frances Manufacturing Co.
Frankel Coat & Dress Co.
French Dress Co.
Woolfe Futeransky & Sons.
Giant Waist Co.
M. Ginsberg.
Ginsberg & Rosen.
Glassburg & Milnick.
Globe Dress & Suit Co.
Gabbe, Block & Co.
Gold Bros.
L. Goldberg.
Goldberg & Sonim.
J. Goldstein.
Jacob Goldwine.
Good Wear Dress Co.
L. Goodman.
Gottfried & Schwartz.
Greenberg & Ugilow.
Greenwald & Fegelman.
Gross Bros.
Groshberg & Felstein.
Guaranty Dress Co.
Halper & Freidman.
Max S. Halpern.
M. Halpern.
Halpern Bros.
Heimler Bros.
Abraham Hammar.
Adolph Hays & Co.
Hecht, Lerner & Rosenbaum.
Herald Dress & Waist Co.
Herzenstein Bros.
Hilf Costume Co.
Hirst & Miller.
Hirshkowitz & Rubenstein.
Hirshner & Schwartz.

Harry Hodas.
L. Hoffer.
Hornick & Weiss.
Ideal Tucking Co.
Independent Garment Co.
M. Ingerman & Co.
Ipp & Kwint.
J. R. Waist & Dress Co.
Geo. Jacobson.
Juffet & Co.
Justright Waist Co.
Eastern Waist Co.
D. Kaplan.
S. Karp.
Kean, Jones & Co.
Kaslin & Co.
A. Kitzer.
Klein & Schlecher Waist Co.
Klein & Ungar.
Harry Kottler.
Kram & Match.
S. Keehn & Co.
Ladin Bros.
Landau & Solan.
Lang & Lang.
Laxer Bros.
Laxer & Sandberg.
Lehman & Spector.
Leighter Bros.
Lemchick & Co.
M. Leonard.
H. Lepow.
E. Lerner.
Levine Bros.
Levine & Harris.
Levine & Katz.
Levine & Keller.
Lichtman Waist Co.
Levy Bros.
Long Island Waist Co.
Lucerne Waist Co.
Manhattan Tucking Co.
Harry Manson.
Mermaid Waist Co.
Metropolis Waist Co.
Metropolitan Dress Co.
Henry J. Meyers.
Miller Shirt Waist Co.
Jos. Mirsky.
Modern Dress Co.
Mitnick.
Chessen & Zeitlin.
Moskowitz & Priest.
Mutual Waist Co.
McLane, Karll & Levy Co.
Nathans & Nathans.
Nelson, Burstein & Gussow.
Niagara Waist & Dress Co.
Morris Nikola.
M. Nomas.
N. Y. Middy Blouse Co.
Olympic Waist & Dress Co.
Onica Dress Co.
Original Waist & Dress Co.
Pacific Waist Co.
Sam'l Pacs.
Peerless Dress & Costume Co.
Peral Waist & Dress Co.
Phreno Dress & Waist Co.
Paragon Dress Co.
Louis Pasachow.
Paskin.
Piccadilly Waist Co.
Piller Bros.
Plaza Waist & Dress Co.
Benj. Pollick.
Popular Manufacturing Co.
S. Posner.
Queensboro Waist Co.
Regal Waist Co.
A. Rappaport & Co.
Ray Waist & Dress House.
Rhinrock.
Rosenberg Tucking Co.
Robins Dress Co.
Roman & Bloom.
Rosebud Mfg. Co.
Roth & Brodsky.
Rothrosen Bros.
Royal Dress Co.
L. Salesky.
Selsky Bros.
Savoy Waist Co.
Schlessel & Wilner.
J. Schlesinger & Co.
Phillip Schwartz.
Schwartz Bros.
Schwartz & Jiengman.
J. Schapiro.
Schapiro & Co.
Louis Schapiro.
Shapiro, Rothman & Co.
Silverman & Slavitz.
I. Simpson.
Solomon & Steiner.
Sorin & Rappaport.
W. Simon.
Solomon & Silverstein.
Speigelman & Michelson.
Stanley Dress Co.
I. Stegman.
Standard Dress Co.
H. Steinberg.
Stelson & Co.
I. Steinberg & Co.
J. Stein.
Stern & Cohen.
Stone Bros.
Samuel Striefer.
Sun Dress Co.
Supreme Waist Co.
Surprise Dress Co.
M. Sussman.
M. Treuhold.
Victoria Waist Co.
Wechsler Bros.
Weinberg Bros.
Nathan Weinberg.
Weinberg & Weinman.
Welfare Waist Co.
Well Designed Waist Co.
Weisenthal Tucking Co.
H. Wolf.
M. Zeffer & Cross.
Zigler Bros.

INDEX.

○

www.ingramcontent.com/pod-product-compliance
Lightning Source LLC
LaVergne TN
LVHW020220110826
845151LV00003B/771

* 9 7 8 1 4 2 5 5 3 2 8 6 4 *